ADVANCED

Physical Education & Sport

JOHN HONEYBOURNE,
MICHAEL HILL AND HELEN MOORS

Stanley Thornes (Publishers) Ltd

First published in 1996 by:
Stanley Thornes (Publishers) Ltd
Ellenborough House
Wellington Street
CHELTENHAM
GL50 1YW
United Kingdom

98 99 00 / 10 9 8 7 6 5

A catalogue record for this book is available from The British Library.
ISBN 0 7487 2386 2

Cover photograph: Zefa Pictures Ltd

Typeset by Florencetype Ltd, Stoodleigh, Devon

Printed and bound in Great Britain by Scotprint, Musselburgh

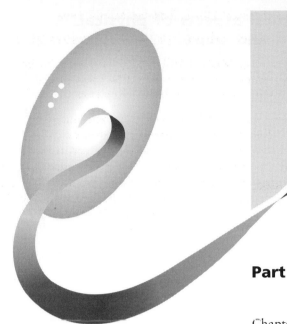

Contents

Part 1: Anatomy, biomechanics and physiology   **1**

Chapter 1: Introduction to the skeletal system   2
Chapter 2: Joints and muscles   9
Chapter 3: Skeletal muscle: structure, function and control   21
Chapter 4: The mechanics of movement   30
Chapter 5: Structure and function of the heart   38
Chapter 6: Structure and function of the vascular system   48
Chapter 7: The respiratory system   56
Further reading   67

Part 2: Exercise physiology   **69**

Chapter 8: Energy   70
Chapter 9: Energy and exercise   78
Chapter 10: The recovery process   84
Chapter 11: Physical fitness   90
Chapter 12: Training: theory and practice   100
Chapter 13: Response to exercise   112
Further reading   121

Part 3: Motor learning   **123**

Chapter 14: Skill and its characteristics   124
Chapter 15: Theories related to the learning of skills   131
Chapter 16: Theories related to the teaching of skills   146
Further reading   160

Part 4: Psychology of physical education and sport   **161**

Chapter 17: Individual differences   162
Chapter 18: Social influences   184
Chapter 19: Stress and its management   198
Further reading   207

Part 5: Sociocultural aspects of physical education and sport 209

Chapter 20: The history of sport 210
Chapter 21: The organisation of sport in the United Kingdom 231
Chapter 22: Sport in society 244
Further reading 269

Glossary 270

Index 279

Introduction

There is little doubt that physical education has been one of the largest 'growth' subjects at 'A' level and that the units related to this subject in GNVQ Leisure and Tourism and Health and Social Care have also been well received. Until now, no one book has covered the material to be found in all 'A' level syllabuses and GNVQ specifications related to this subject area.

Sir Ron Dearing's 16–19 Education report has identified the opportunity to develop common source elements between 'A' level physical education and GNVQ units. This book is likely to cover most of the material in any combined course or in any new sport-related 'applied' 'A' level or 'A–S' level.

We have written this book for students to use as a direct, no-nonsense resource. We have all had considerable experience in teaching 'A'-level physical education, sports studies, GCSE physical education and sport, GNVQ leisure and tourism and GNVQ health and social care. We are all senior examiners at 'A' level and have set questions and marked answer scripts for the syllabuses currently available.

Students and teachers who use this book will realise that the aim is to give only information which is relevant and clearly expressed. This book will give students enough information to pass an 'A'-level examination in this area or to build a portfolio for GNVQ work. It will also push those at a higher level who wish to take the subject into higher education and gives useful reference for further reading.

This book is clearly set out in sections and chapters. Each section covers the main areas of the subject and represents the content of all syllabuses in this area at the time of writing. There are five Parts to the book. Part 1 deals with anatomy, biomechanics and physiology. Part 2 includes a much more in-depth treatment of exercise physiology. Part 3 is concerned with the area of motor learning and, more specifically, skill acquisition. Part 4 is concerned with the psychological aspects of physical education and sport. Part 5 is a wide-ranging section, dealing with the sociocultural aspects of physical education and sport, including historical and contemporary issues and comparative studies.

At the beginning of each chapter *learning objectives* clearly state what the reader can expect to learn in the chapter. *Activity boxes* include ideas to reinforce learning and *In practice boxes* look at the application of theory to practical situations. All the 'A'-level examinations and the work required for GNVQ demand that the student applies theory to practice. To help understanding *Definition boxes* expand on some key words and phrases. At the end of each chapter there is a list of *Key terms* which the student should learn and understand and the *Key revision boxes* throughout the text will help to focus students' attention on key concepts. A list of questions at the end of each chapter will also help students to rehearse what they have learned in the chapter. The *Glossary* of the main key terms can also be used for revision purposes.

This is a fascinating and rewarding subject area and should be studied with a view to applying theoretical principles to practical situations. We hope that students and teachers will get maximum benefit from this textbook and will share our enjoyment of studying and teaching physical education and sport at advanced level.

The information in this book will not go out of date, and will give students the background they need for examination success.

About
the authors

About the authors

John Honeybourne is the Head of the Sixth Form College at Baverstock GM School, Chief Examiner with the AEB and Principal Examiner for the University of Cambridge Local Examinations Syndicate.

Michael Hill is Director of Physical Education at the City of Stoke on Trent Sixth Form College, and Reviser and Senior Examiner for the AEB.

Helen Moors teaches 'A'-level physical education at the City of Stoke on Trent Sixth Form College, is a Senior Examiner for the AEB and Principal Examiner for the University of Cambridge Local Examinations Syndicate.

Acknowledgements

The authors and the publishers are grateful to the following for permission to reproduce photographs:

- Supersport Photographs: 72, 91, 103, 125, 127 (top), 129 (top), 133, 135, 138, 139, 142, 143, 144, 147, 148, 153, 155, 156 (top), 158, 163, 165, 168 (top and bottom), 170 (top and bottom), 174, 179 (top and bottom), 180, 182, 186 (top), 193, 195 (top and bottom), 201, 202, 203 (top and bottom), 205 (top), 210, 222 (bottom).
- Associated Sports Photography: 131, 173, 260, 261
- The Broadgate Club: 243
- Mike Brett Photography: 28, 32 (top and bottom), 137, 154, 156 (bottom), 171, 177 (top and bottom), 190, 198, 199, 216 (bottom), 222 (top), 229, 252, 254 (top), 263
- Pictor International: 150
- Mary Evans Picture Library: 213, 214 (bottom)
- Hulton Deutsch Collection: 212, 214 (top)
- Karine Hoskyns: 256
- Scottish Sports Council: 167, 169, 254 (bottom)
- Associated Press Photo: 257
- Sport Presse Fotos: 124
- Allsport: 127 (bottom), 166, 178, 185, 186 (bottom), 187, 189, 194, 205 (bottom), 216 (top), 245, 248
- Sporting Pictures (UK) Ltd: 196
- Graham Bool: 129 (bottom), 259

Anatomy, biomechanics and physiology

This part of the book contains:

Chapter 1   Introduction to the skeletal system

Chapter 2   Joints and muscles

Chapter 3   Skeletal muscle: structure, function and control

Chapter 4   The mechanics of movement

Chapter 5   Structure and function of the heart

Chapter 6   Structure and function of the vascular system

Chapter 7   The respiratory system

The following chapters provide an introduction to anatomy, physiology and, in particular, to the systems that play a significant role in the production of skilled human movement – the skeletal, muscular, cardiovascular and respiratory systems. It is important to know both the structure of these systems and how they function, including basic biomechanics, in order to develop a better understanding of how the body works and to appreciate the body's capabilities and limitations in performance of sport.

Introduction to the skeletal system

Learning objectives:

- To have a general understanding of the structure of the skeletal system.
- To be aware of the main functions of the skeletal system.
- To know the structure and type of the major joints of the body.
- To know the types of movement that can be produced around each joint.

1.1 The skeletal system

The skeletal system is made up of two kinds of tissue: *bone* and *cartilage*.

1.1.1 Bone

There are five different types of bone, which are classified by their shape rather than their size.

Long bones, such as the femur
Short bones, for example the metatarsals
Irregular bones: the vertebrae are examples of these
Flat bones, for example the scapula
Sesamoid bones, such as the patella

Examples of each type of bone are shown in *Figure 1.1.*

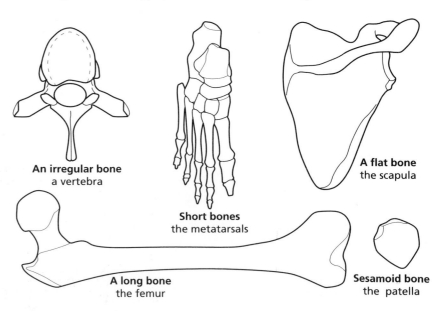

An irregular bone
a vertebra

Short bones
the metatarsals

A flat bone
the scapula

A long bone
the femur

Sesamoid bone
the patella

Figure 1.1 Classification of bones

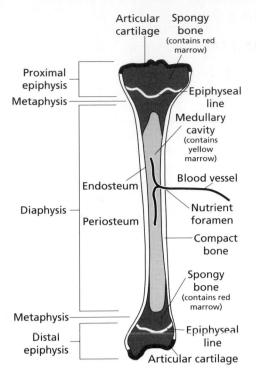

Figure 1.2 Structure of a typical long bone – the tibia

Bone is the hardest connective tissue in the body. *Hard*, or *compact*, bone makes up the outer layer of all bones, giving them strength. *Cancellous*, or *spongy*, bone is typically found at the ends of the long bones. Cancellous bone is not as dense as hard bone because it contains cavities filled with bone marrow. An outline of the structure of a typical long bone can be seen in *Figure 1.2*.

1.1.2 Cartilage

There are three types of cartilage:

Yellow elastic cartilage, which is soft and slightly elastic. Examples may be found in the ear lobe and epiglottis.

White fibrocartilage, which is tough and slightly flexible. This cartilage acts as a shock absorber, helping to prevent damage to the bone. The cartilage between the vertebrae is white fibrocartilage.

Hyaline or *articular cartilage*, which is solid and smooth. Hyaline cartilage protects the bone from the constant wear and tear of moving and can be found on the articulating surface of bones.

ACTIVITY

Examine the bones of a skeleton and see if you can classify the following bones: the parietal bone (part of the skull), the ilium (part of the pelvis), phalanges, the sternum, the ulna and the metatarsals.

1.2 The skeleton

The skeleton is made up of 206 bones (*Figure 1.3*). It comprises the *axial* skeleton and the *appendicular* skeleton.

Definition

ARTICULATION

The place where two or more bones meet to form a joint. The articulating surface is the point of contact between the bones.

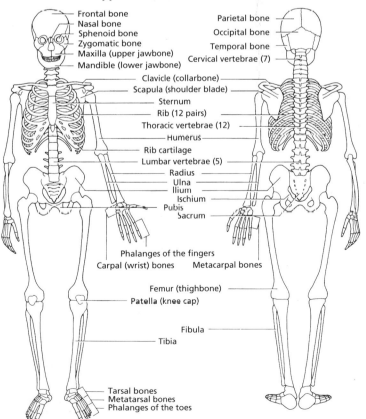

Figure 1.3 The bones making up the human skeleton

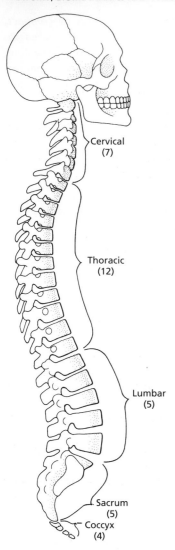

Figure 1.4 *Lateral view of the spinal column*

1.2.1 The axial skeleton

This is made up of the skull, the vertebral column, the sternum and the ribs.

1.2.2 The appendicular skeleton

The appendicular skeleton is composed of the shoulder girdle, the hip girdle, the bones of the arms and hands and the bones of the legs and feet.

Although you do not need to know about the individual bones which make up the head and face or the hands and feet for your courses, a more detailed knowledge of the spine is useful. This is outlined in *Figure 1.4.*

1.2.3 Function of the skeletal system

The skeletal system has four main functions:

● to provide support for the body;
● to provide protection for vital organs;
● to produce blood corpuscles (cells);
● to provide attachment for muscles.

For sport enthusiasts it is the last of these functions which is the most interesting. In order for us to perform the sophisticated movements demanded by many sports, we need a sophisticated system of joints and levers capable of producing a wide range of movements. As you will see, we have been very well designed to do this.

1.3 Joints

Joints can be classified in two ways: by considering their structure, or by considering how much movement they allow.

1.3.1 Classification by structure

The following classification of joint by structure should be used.

Fibrous

These joints have no joint cavity and the bones are held together by fibrous connective tissue. Examples are the sutures of the skull bones.

Cartilaginous

Cartilaginous joints also have no joint cavity. There is cartilage between the bones of the joint. Cartilaginous joints may be found between the vertebrae of the spine.

Synovial

A synovial joint has a fluid-filled cavity surrounded by an articular capsule. The articulating surfaces of the bones are covered in hyaline cartilage. The hinge joint of the knee is a synovial joint.

1.3.2 Classification by movement allowed

When it comes to classifying joints by the movement they allow the following terms are applied.

Fibrous joint or synarthrosis

This type of joint does not allow any movement. When you consider where these joints occur this makes sense as some parts of the body, such as the brain, need protection. A moveable joint could not provide this protection.

Cartilaginous joint or amphiarthrosis

This joint allows limited movement.

Synovial joint or diarthrosis

A synovial joint allows free movement, or certainly as much movement as the shape of the articulating surfaces permits.

As you may have gathered by now, there always seem to be several types of everything you come across in anatomy and physiology. Joints are no exception. There are six different types of synovial joint – and as these are the joints that allow movement, we need to know more about them.

1.4 Synovial joints

The synovial joints allow movement to take place. How much movement is permitted depends on the shape of the articulating surfaces. Six different joint constructions have been identified. *Figure 1.5* illustrates each joint type.

Ball and socket: a ball-like head fits into a cup-shaped depression – an example of this is the shoulder joint.

Hinge: a convex surface articulates with a concave surface the elbow is a typical hinge joint.

Pivot: part of a bone fits into a ring-like structure the most well known pivot joint is the atlas and axis.

Saddle: a bone fits into a saddle-shaped surface on another bone - the thumb is a good example.

Gliding: two relatively flat surfaces slide over one another – this may be seen at the articular processes of the vertebrae.

Condyloid: a convex surface fits into an elliptical cavity – the wrist joint is a condyloid joint.

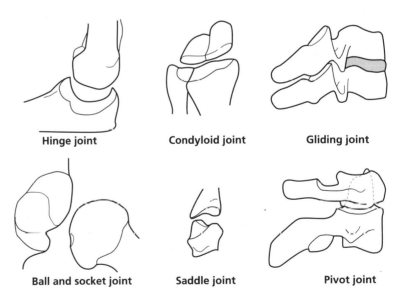

Hinge joint   **Condyloid joint**   **Gliding joint**

Ball and socket joint   **Saddle joint**   **Pivot joint**

Figure 1.5   The six types of synovial joint

The six types of synovial joint differ in the amount of movement that they allow, but are very similar in structure and share common features. *Figure 1.6* highlights the common features of a synovial joint using the hinge joint of the knee as an illustration.

The *articular/joint capsule* is a fibrous tissue encasing the joint, forming a capsule.

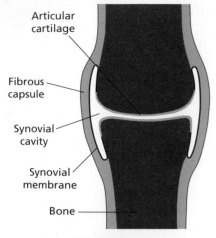

Synovial joint
(generalised)

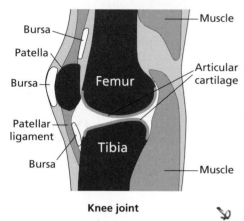

Knee joint

Figure 1.6 A typical synovial joint – the knee

The *synovial membrane* acts as a lining to the joint capsule and secretes synovial fluid.

Articular/hyaline cartilage covers the ends of the articulating bones.

Synovial fluid fills the joint capsule and nourishes and lubricates the articular cartilage.

Ligaments are white fibrous connective tissues joining bone to bone, making the joint more stable.

Bursa is found where tendons are in contact with bone. The bursa forms a fluid-filled sac between the tendon and the bone and helps to reduce friction.

Articular discs of cartilage act as shock absorbers.

Pads of fat act as buffers to protect the bones from wear and tear.

ACTIVITY

Try to construct a joint by taking the appropriate bones and fastening them together. For example, you could use tape to represent the ligaments and felt or moulding clay for the articular cartilage. If you don't have any bones, improvise!

1.5 Movement terminology

Later in Part 1 we will look at the structure of some joints in more detail, but here we will consider the range of movement that the body can perform. There are a lot of terms that you need to be familiar with, and you will remember the terms much more easily if you put them into practice.

The terms that you are most likely to use are given below, and are illustrated in *Figure 1.7*.

Flexion: a decrease in the angle around the joint.

Extension: an increase in the angle around the joint.

Abduction: movement away from the midline of the body.

Adduction: movement towards the midline of the body.

Rotation: movement of a bone around its longitudinal axis. Rotation can be inward (medial) or outward (lateral).

Circumduction: the lower end of the bone moves in a circle. It is a combination of flexion, extension, adduction and abduction.

Lateral flexion: bending the head or trunk sideways.

Elevation: moving the shoulders upwards.

Depression: moving the shoulders downwards.

Plantar flexion: bending the foot downwards, away from the tibia.

Dorsiflexion: bending the foot upwards, towards the tibia.

Pronation: facing the palm of the hand downwards.

Supination: facing the palm of the hand upwards.

More simply, *flexion* occurs when you bend a limb and *extension* occurs when you straighten it, for example the movement at the elbow joint when you do press-ups involves both flexion and extension. When performing star jumps, as you move your arms outwards you are *abducting* the shoulder joint and as you bring your arms back to the side of your body you are *adducting* the shoulder joint. As a ballet dancer moves into first position he or she must *rotate* their hip joints laterally. When bowling, a cricketer moves the arm in a full circle – this is *circumduction* of the shoulder joint. Remember: movement occurs around a joint and not a body part, so it is incorrect to say (for example) 'flexion of the leg'. You must refer to the actual joint involved, as in flexion of the hip, knee or ankle joint. Remember to be precise.

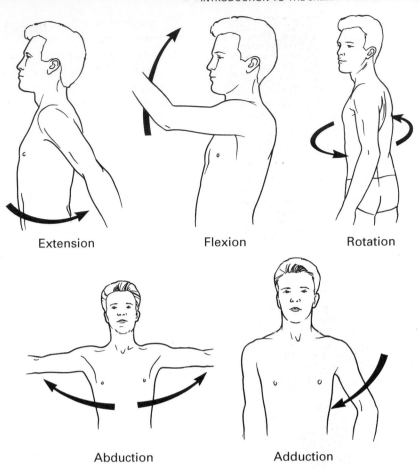

Figure 1.7 Movement terminology

When you take part in your next practical session, break down the skills you attempt into simple phases and try to identify the specific movements. It is quite difficult to begin with, but with practice becomes very straightforward.

ACTIVITY

Look back to the list of synovial joints. Working with a partner, locate each of the joints given as examples and determine the types of movement that can take place at each. For example, the elbow joint can flex and extend.

Key revision box

There are six types of synovial joint: ball and socket, hinge, pivot, gliding, condyloid and saddle. All synovial joints allow some degree of movement and share common features, such as a synovial membrane, synovial fluid, articular cartilage and ligaments.

KEY TERMS

You should now understand the following terms. If you do not, go back through the chapter and find out.

Axial skeleton
Appendicular skeleton
Fibrous joint
Cartilaginous joint
Synovial joint
Flexion
Extension
Rotation
Abduction
Adduction
Circumduction

PROGRESS CHECK

1 List the bones that form the axial skeleton.
2 List the bones that form the appendicular skeleton.
3 What are the functions of the skeleton?
4 Where would you find hyaline cartilage?
5 How may joints be classified?
6 Which category of joint allows free movement?
7 Give an example of a gliding joint.
8 List the common features of a synovial joint.
9 Which features of a synovial joint help increase joint stability?
10 List the movements possible at a ball and socket joint and give a brief description of each movement.
11 What movements can take place at the ankle joint?
12 Name two joints which allow circumduction. Give an example in sport of when this movement occurs.
13 The first two cervical vertebrae form a joint. What type of joint is it, and what type of movement does it allow?
14 The range of movement around a joint can be restricted by a number of factors. List three of these factors.

Joints and muscles

Learning objectives:

- To know the bones that articulate at the major joints of the body.
- To be able to identify the muscles that act as prime movers at each major joint.
- To know the type of movement that the prime movers can produce.
- To be able to analyse sporting actions in terms of the joint and muscle used and the movement produced

A joint cannot move by itself – it needs muscles to manoeuvre the bones into the correct position. Muscles are attached to bones by connective tissue and we refer to the ends of the muscle as the *origin* and the *insertion*. The origin is the more fixed, stable end and the insertion is usually attached to the bone that moves.

When a muscle contracts it shortens and the insertion moves closer to the origin, creating movement around a joint. For example, biceps brachii causes flexion of the elbow. The origin of this muscle is on the scapula and the insertion is on the radius. When the muscle contracts the radius is pulled upwards towards the shoulder, as the insertion moves closer to the origin.

The muscle directly responsible for creating the movement at a joint is called the *prime mover*. There is usually more than one prime mover at a joint, and other muscles can assist the movement. The number of muscles involved depends on the type and amount of work being carried out.

Any sports performer, at whatever level, should have a working knowledge of joint and muscle action. The human body is very complex and is made up of hundreds of muscles acting on numerous joints – see *Figure 2.1*. As an introduction we will look at the joints most involved in the production of gross motor skills in more detail.

In practice

A warm-up is useful only if you are warming up the muscles and joints that you are about to use. When preparing a training schedule the exercises you choose should reflect the movement pattern you will be performing in competition.

Definition

PROXIMAL

The proximal end of a bone is the end nearest the centre of the body.

DISTAL

The distal end of the bone is the end furthest away from the centre of the body.

2.1 The elbow joint

The elbow is a hinge joint, with the distal end of the humerus articulating with the proximal end of both the radius and the ulna. The joint is strengthened by four ligaments. Movement is possible in one plane only, allowing flexion and extension to take place.

Also within the elbow joint capsule the radius articulates with the ulna to form a pivot joint. This radioulnar joint allows pronation and supination of the lower arm (medial and lateral rotation).

Figure 2.2 shows the bones that articulate at the elbow joint.

The movements possible at the elbow and radioulnar joints are shown in *Figure 2.3*. The muscles that create these movements are outlined in

In practice

When throwing a ball underarm the radioulnar joint is supinated and when throwing a ball overarm the radioulnar joint is pronated.

Definition

CONDYLE

A large knuckle-shaped articular surface, e.g. lateral condyle of the femur.

HEAD

A ball-shaped articular surface, e.g. the head of the femur.

SPINOUS PROCESS

A long slender projection, e.g. the processes of the vertebrae.

TUBEROSITY

A large rounded surface, for example on the proximal end of the radius.

FORAMEN

A hole – e.g. the vertebral foramen allows the spinal chord to pass through.

FOSSA

A depression, e.g. the olecranon fossa of the humerus.

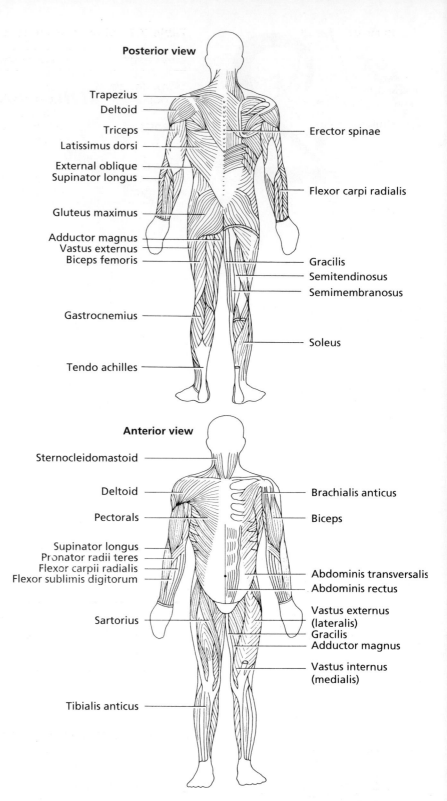

Figure 2.1 Muscles of the human body

Table 2.1 and illustrated in *Figure 2.4*. The specific origins and insertions are not given, but a general location of the muscle is provided to help with future movement analysis.

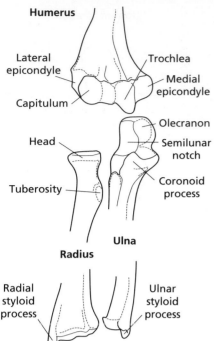

Humerus

Lateral epicondyle

Trochlea

Medial epicondyle

Capitulum

Olecranon

Head

Semilunar notch

Tuberosity

Coronoid process

Ulna

Radius

Radial styloid process

Ulnar styloid process

Figure 2.2 Bony structures of the elbow and radioulnar joints. Surface markings such as bumps and grooves are visible, usually where a tendon inserts or where a joint articulates

Table 2.1 Muscles of the elbow joint

Movement	Prime mover(s)	Origin	Insertion
Elbow (hinge)			
Flexion	Biceps brachii	Scapula	Radius
	Brachialis	Humerus	Ulna
Extension	Triceps brachii	Scapula and humerus	Ulna
	Anconeus	Humerus	Ulna
Radioulnar (pivot)			
Pronation	Pronator teres	Humerus and ulna	Radius
Supination	Supinator	Humerus and ulna	Radius

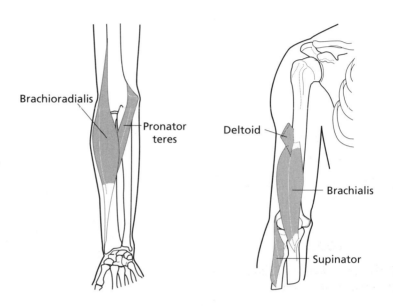

Brachioradialis

Pronator teres

Deltoid

Brachialis

Supinator

Figure 2.4 Prime movers of the elbow and radioulnar joints

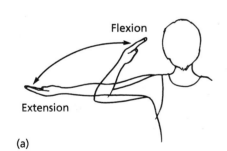

Flexion

Extension

(a)

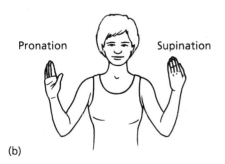

Pronation

Supination

(b)

Figure 2.3 Movements of the elbow and radioulnar joints. (a) Flexion and extension; (b) right radioulnar joint pronated, left radioulnar joint supinated

---

ACTIVITY

Try to think of a sporting example when each prime mover of the elbow would be in action. For example, during the shot putt elbow extension is caused by contraction of triceps brachii.

2.2 The shoulder joint and shoulder girdle

The structure of the shoulder joint and the shoulder girdle are shown in *Figure 2.5*.

2.2.1 The shoulder girdle

The shoulder girdle is a gliding joint (with slight rotation) where the clavicle articulates with the scapula, usually moving as a unit. We are not particularly aware of the involvement of the shoulder girdle in the numerous arm actions we perform (these are illustrated in *Figure 2.6*).

The prime movers of the shoulder girdle are outlined in Table 2.2 and illustrated in *Figure 2.7*.

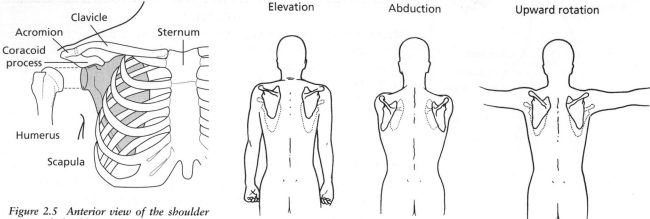

Figure 2.5 Anterior view of the shoulder joint and shoulder girdle

Figure 2.6 Possible movements of the shoulder girdle

Table 2.2 Muscles of the shoulder girdle

Movement	Prime mover(s)	Origin	Insertion
Elevation	Trapezius part one	Skull	Clavicle
Depression	Trapezius part four	Thoracic vertebrae	Base of spine
Upward rotation	Trapezius part two	Ligaments of the neck	Acromion process
Downward rotation	Rhomboids	Cervical and thoracic vertebrae	Scapula
Abduction	Serratus anterior	Side of ribs	Scapula
Adduction	Trapezius part three	Cervical and thoracic vertebrae	Scapula

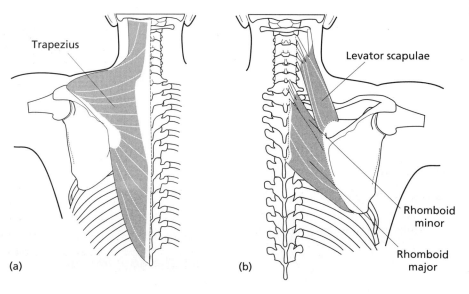

Figure 2.7 Prime movers of the shoulder girdle

2.2.2 The shoulder joint

The shoulder joint is a ball and socket joint, with the head of the humerus fitting into a very shallow cavity on the scapula called the glenoid fossa. The shoulder joint is the most mobile joint in the body but also one of the most unstable because the shallow cavity gives little support to the head of the humerus. Stability has to be provided by ligaments and muscles.

The movements possible at the shoulder joint are shown in *Figure 2.8*. They include flexion, extension, horizontal flexion and extension, abduction, adduction, external and internal rotation and circumduction.

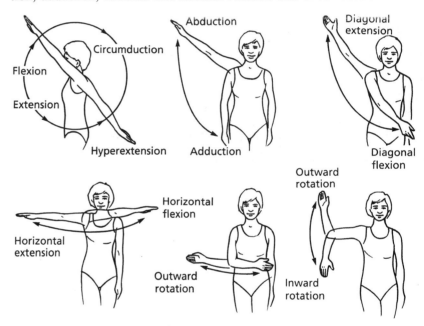

Figure 2.8 Movements possible at the shoulder joint

In practice

Lack of stability of the shoulder means that in contact sports, such as rugby, a dislocated shoulder is a very common injury.

For some skills analysis of the shoulder movement is quite straightforward, for example lifting the arms above the head in preparation for a handstand clearly involves flexion of the shoulder joint and upward rotation of the shoulder girdle. Unfortunately, most of the actions we perform in sport, for example a tennis serve, are a combination of several movements and are therefore quite difficult to analyse. Students at 'A' level are not expected to attempt complex movement analysis – but have a go at the next activity.

Table 2.3 details the muscles and movements of the shoulder joint and the prime movers are illustrated in *Figure 2.9*.

Table 2.3 Muscles of the shoulder joint

Movement	Prime mover(s)	Origin	Insertion
Flexion	Anterior deltoid	Clavicle, scapula and acromion process	Humerus
Extension	Latissimus dorsi	Ilium, lumbar and thoracic vertebrae	Humerus
Abduction	Middle deltoid	Clavicle, scapula and acromion	Humerus
Adduction	Pectoralis major	Clavicle, ribs and sternum	Humerus
Inward rotation	Subscapularis	Scapula	Humerus
Outward rotation	Infraspinatus	Scapula	Humerus

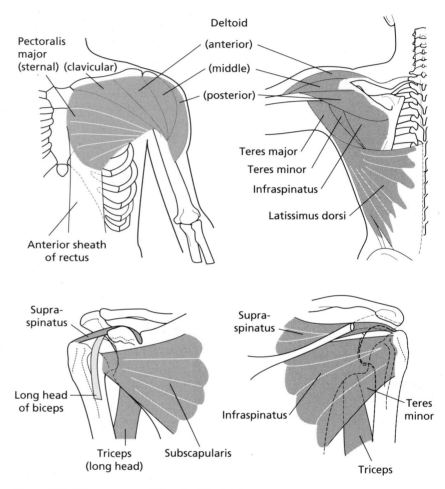

Figure 2.9 Prime movers of the shoulder joint

2.3 The spine

The spinal column has to fulfil many functions. It has to be weight bearing, provide stability and support, act as a shock absorber, protect the spinal cord and allow movement. Although there are five regions of the spine (look back to Figure 1.4 to refresh your memory) we will consider the cervical, thoracic and lumbar regions here, as the sacrum and coccyx are fused together.

The spinal column has three types of joint:

a *cartilaginous* joint between the individual vertebrae;
a *gliding* joint between the vertebral arches; and

a *pivot* joint formed by the first two cervical vertebrae (the atlas and axis). The atlas articulates with the occipital bone of the skull and allows flexion and extension, as in nodding. The atlas and axis articulate and allow rotation, as in shaking your head.

To make the column more stable several ligaments hold the vertebrae together.

2.3.1 Movement at the spine

The movements possible at the spine are shown in *Figure 2.10*. Overall the spine allows flexion, extension, lateral flexion and rotation. The combination of flexion, lateral flexion and hyperextension results in circumduction. Movement is not uniform throughout the three regions and before you read on try to decide which region moves more freely.

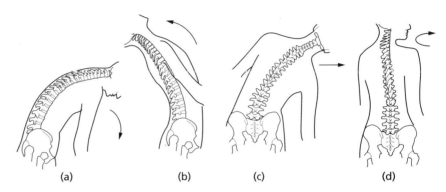

Figure 2.10 Movements of the spinal column. (a) Flexion; (b) hyperextension; (c) lateral flexion to the right; (d) rotation to the right

---

> **Definition**
>
> **HYPEREXTENSION**
>
> *Continuing to extend a limb beyond 180°.*

Flexion

Most flexion occurs in the cervical region, with some occurring in the lumbar region. There is little flexion in the thoracic region.

Extension

This is quite free in the cervical and lumbar regions, but very limited in the thoracic region.

Lateral flexion

This takes place in all regions of the spine but more so in the cervical and lumbar regions.

Rotation

This is good in the cervical and upper thoracic regions, but minimal in the lumbar region.

Table 2.4 outlines the prime movers of the spine. These are illustrated in *Figure 2.11*.

ACTIVITY

In warm-up sessions the muscles of the spine are often neglected. Devise a series of exercises that would involve all possible movements of the spine, and therefore would involve all the prime movers of the spine.

Table 2.4 Muscles of the spine

Movement	Prime mover(s)	Origin	Insertion
Flexion	Rectus abdominis	Pelvis	Base of sternum and ribs
	External oblique	Lower ribs	Pelvis
	Internal oblique	Pelvis	Lower ribs
Extension	Sacrospinalis / erector spinal group	Pelvis, sacrum, lumbar and lower ribs	Ribs, base of skull and all vertebrae
Lateral flexion	External oblique	Lower ribs	Pelvis
	Internal oblique	Pelvis	Lower ribs
	Sacrospinalis	Pelvis, sacrum, lumbar and lower ribs	Ribs, base of skull and all vertebrae
Rotation to the same side	Internal oblique	Pelvis	Lower ribs
Rotation to the opposite side	External oblique	Lower ribs	Pelvis

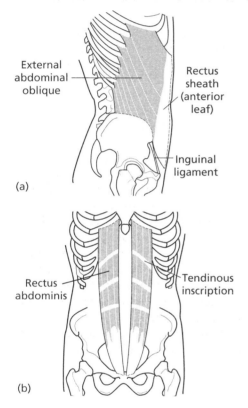

Figure 2.11 Prime movers of the spine

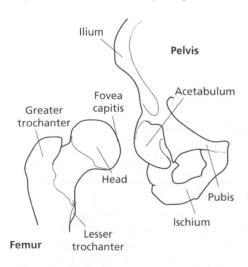

Figure 2.12 The hip joint

2.4 The hip joint

The hip joint is another ball and socket joint, where the head of the femur fits into a deep cavity, called the acetabulum, on the pelvic bone (*Figure 2.12*). Although it is desirable to have a wide range of movement at this joint, it is perhaps more desirable to have stability. The cavity on the pelvis is much deeper than the cavity on the scapula, so the hip joint is much more stable (but less mobile) than the shoulder joint The hip joint is also reinforced by extremely strong ligaments, making it much more difficult to dislocate the hip than the shoulder even though they are similar in structure.

Movements possible at the hip include flexion, extension, abduction, adduction, rotation and circumduction – see *Figure 2.13*.

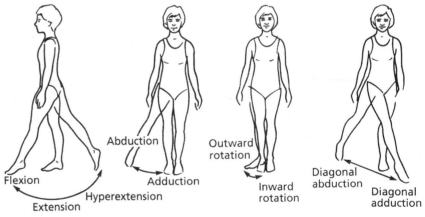

Figure 2.13 Movements possible at the hip joint

ACTIVITY

Using a goniometer or a 360° angle measurer, work with a partner and measure the range of movement possible at both the shoulder and hip joints. Compare your results with other people in your group: is there a significant difference between males and females, or between gymnasts and footballers?

The prime movers of the hip joint are outlined in Table 2.5, and these are illustrated in *Figure 2.14*.

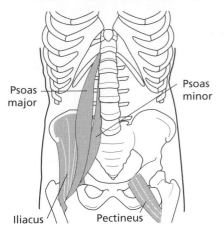

Psoas
major

Psoas
minor

Iliacus

Pectineus

(a)

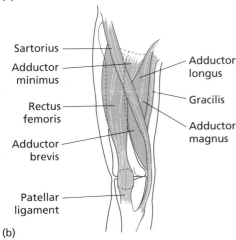

Sartorius

Adductor
minimus

Rectus
femoris

Adductor
brevis

Patellar
ligament

Adductor
longus

Gracilis

Adductor
magnus

(b)

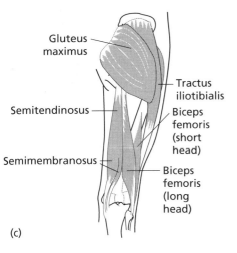

Gluteus
maximus

Semitendinosus

Semimembranosus

Tractus
iliotibialis

Biceps
femoris
(short
head)

Biceps
femoris
(long
head)

(c)

Figure 2.14 Prime movers of the hip.
(a) Anterior view; (b) anterior view;
(c) posterior view

Table 2.5 The muscles of the hip joint

Movement	Prime mover(s)	Origin	Insertion
Flexion	Iliopsoas	Pelvis and lumbar vertebrae	Femur
Extension	Gluteus maximus	Pelvis and sacrum	Femur
Abduction	Gluteus medius	Pelvis	Femur
Adduction	Adductors longus, brevis and magnus	Pelvis	Femur
Inward rotation	Gluteus minimus	Pelvis	Femur
Outward rotation	Gluteus maximus	Pelvis and sacrum	Femur

ACTIVITY

Analyse the movements of a hurdler and compare the actions at the hip of the lead leg with the actions at the hip of the trail leg.

2.5 The knee joint

The knee joint (shown in detail in Figure 1.6) is referred to as a hinge joint but it is not a true hinge joint because, although it allows both flexion and extension, it also allows slight medial and lateral rotation (to facilitate full extension and locking of the knee – see *Figure 2.15*).

The condyles of the femur articulate with the proximal end of the tibia. The patella, attached to the quadriceps tendon, helps provide a better angle of pull, and is a functional part of the knee joint (*Figure 2.16*). The fibula is not part of the knee joint and therefore the tibia bears all the weight. The weight-bearing function of the knee is considerable and it is important that the ankle, knee and hip are aligned properly to allow the line of stress to pass through the centre of the knee joint.

The strong ligaments surrounding the knee and the large muscle groups of the thigh help to maintain the most mechanically efficient position.

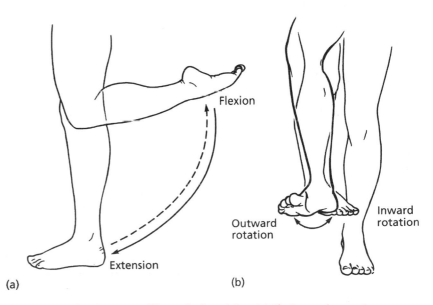

Flexion

Extension

Outward
rotation

Inward
rotation

(a)

(b)

Figure 2.15 Movements possible at the knee joint. (a) Flexion and extension;
(b) inward and outward rotation (in a flexed, no-weight-bearing position)

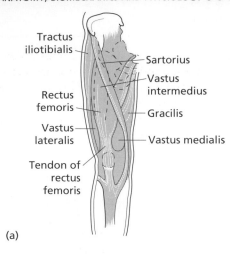

(a)

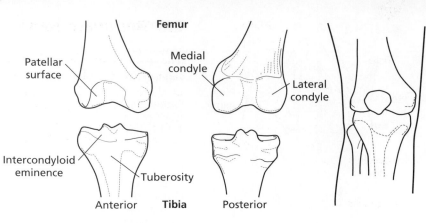

Figure 2.16 The bones of the knee joint

The prime movers of the knee are outlined in Table 2.6, and illustrated in *Figure 2.17*.

Table 2.6 Muscles of the knee joint

Movement	Prime mover(s)	Origin	Insertion
Flexion	Biceps femoris	Pelvis and femur	Tibia and fibula
	Semimembranosus	Pelvis	Tibia
	Semitendinosus	Pelvis	Tibia
Extension	Rectus femoris	Pelvis	Patella
	Vastus lateralis	Femur	Tibia
	Intermedius lateralis	Femur	Tibia
Inward rotation	Popliteus	Femur	Tibia
Outward rotation	Biceps femoris	Pelvis and femur	Tibia and fibula

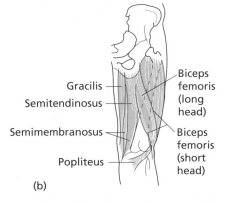

(b)

Figure 2.17 Prime movers of the knee. (a) Anterior view; (b) posterior view

Figure 2.18

ACTIVITY

Analyse the three hurdling positions shown in Figure 2.18. Describe the movements taking place at the hip and knee joints and name the prime mover responsible for each movement.

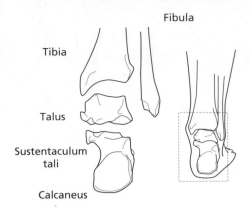

Fibula

Tibia

Talus

Sustentaculum
tali

Calcaneus

Figure 2.19 Bones of the ankle and subtalar joints

2.6 The ankle joint

The ankle joint (shown in *Figure 2.19*) is a hinge joint, the talus articulating with the tibia and fibula. This allows both flexion and extension – at the ankle this is referred to as dorsiflexion and plantarflexion (*Figure 2.20*). As in all synovial joints ligaments provide additional stability. On the medial (inner) side of the ankle there are five ligaments and on the lateral (outer) side of the ankle there are three ligaments.

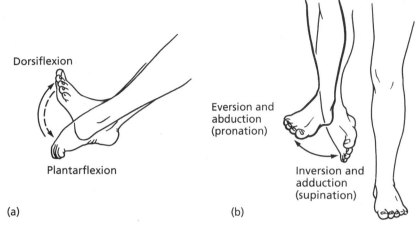

Dorsiflexion

Plantarflexion

Eversion and
abduction
(pronation)

Inversion and
adduction
(supination)

(a)   (b)

Figure 2.20 Movements possible at the ankle and tarsal joints. (a) Dorsiflexion and plantarflexion; (b) supination and pronation (tarsal joint only)

In practice

The apparent imbalance in support at the ankle joint could explain why ankle sprains are such a common sporting injury.

Figure 2.21 illustrates the prime movers of the ankle outlined in Table 2.7.

This section of the book is meant only as an introduction to kinesiology. It therefore takes a very simplified view of the joints, and in particular the muscles, used in sporting activities, as a basis for further study. A reading list is suggested at the end of this part of the book.

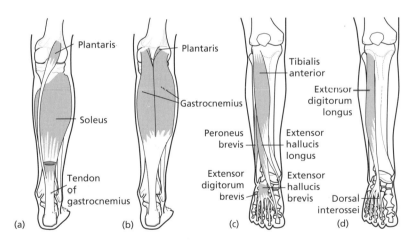

Plantaris

Plantaris

Tibialis
anterior

Gastrocnemius

Soleus

Extensor
digitorum
longus

Peroneus
brevis

Extensor
hallucis
longus

Tendon
of
gastrocnemius

Extensor
digitorum
brevis

Extensor
hallucis
brevis

Dorsal
interossei

(a)   (b)   (c)   (d)

Figure 2.21 Prime movers of the ankle joint

Table 2.7 Muscles of the ankle joint

Movement	Prime mover(s)	Origin	Insertion
Dorsiflexion	Tibialis anterior	Tibia	Tarsal bone
Plantarflexion	Soleus	Tibia and fibula	Tarsal bone
	Gastrocnemius	Femur	Tarsal bone

KEY TERMS

You should now understand the following terms. If you do not, go back through the chapter and find out.

Origin
Insertion
Proximal
Distal
Condyle
Process
Tuberosity
Hyperextension
Foramen
Fossa
Prime mover

Key revision box

Movement takes place around a joint and at least one prime mover is responsible for each type of movement that can be produced at a specific joint. You need to know the name and location of the prime mover for each movement possible around the major joints outlined in this chapter.

PROGRESS CHECK

1 The first two cervical vertebrae form a joint. What type of joint is it and what type of movement does it allow?
2 What regions of the spine allow rotation?
3 Apart from rotation what other movements are possible at the spine?
4 List three functions of the spine.
5 Is body weight transmitted mainly through the tibia or through the fibula?
6 Where would you find the glenoid fossa?
7 Which bones articulate at the following joints:
  a the shoulder
  b the elbow
  c the hip
8 Name three hinge joints.
9 Does the proximal or distal end of the tibia articulate with the femur?
10 Which of the following statements are true, and which false?
  a Biceps femoris flexes the elbow.
  b Iliopsoas flexes the hip.
  c Latissimus dorsi originates on the radius.
  d Rectus femoris extends the knee.
  e The posterior deltoid abducts the shoulder.
  f Pectoralis major adducts the shoulder.
  g Tibialis anterior dorsiflexes the ankle.

Skeletal muscle: structure, function and control

CHAPTER 3

Learning objectives:

- To know the structure of skeletal muscle.
- To know the characteristics of the three muscle fibre types.
- To understand the role of the nervous system in muscular control.
- To be aware of the different functions of muscle.
- To know the different types of muscular contraction.

3.1 Muscle tissue

Muscle tissue has four main characteristics: excitability, contractility, extensibility and elasticity. This means that muscles react to a stimulus, contract and apply force, stretch and return to their original length.

There are three types of muscle tissue found in the body.

Cardiac muscle is a very specialised tissue located in the wall of the heart.
Smooth/visceral muscle is found in tubular structures such as blood vessels.
Skeletal muscle is usually attached to bone, or in some cases to other muscles. Skeletal muscle creates movement around a joint, but can also act to hold a body part in a stable position. Unlike cardiac or smooth muscle skeletal muscle is under voluntary/conscious control – we know what we are going to do and when we are going to do it.

3.2 Structure of skeletal muscle

Skeletal muscle is made up of individual *muscle fibres* (muscle cells) grouped together to form bundles (*fasciculi*), which in turn are grouped together to form the muscle itself (*Figure 3.1*). Each element of the muscle is covered by connective tissue to help provide shape and add strength. The muscle fibre is covered by the *endomysium*, the fasciculi by the *perimysium* and the muscle by the *epimysium*. More connective tissue, in the form of a tendon or an aponeurosis, joins the muscle to bone or another muscle.

3.2.1 Skeletal muscle fibres

In order to understand how a muscle can shorten we need to take a more detailed look at the structure of each individual muscle fibre. There are lots of terms to remember here, so keep going over the text and referring back to the diagrams – don't expect to understand it first time through.

The muscle fibre is surrounded by a membrane called the *sarcolemma* and within the cell are *myofibrils*, long tubular structures running the length of the muscle fibre. The myofibrils are embedded in the cell's *sarcoplasm*

Definition
TENDON

A round cord or band of connective tissue joining muscle to bone.

APONEUROSIS

A fibrous sheet of connective tissue joining muscle to bone or muscle to muscle.

21

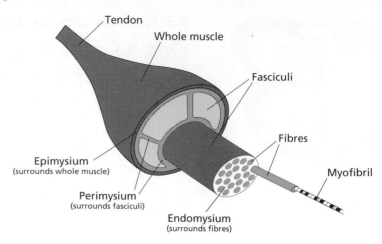

Figure 3.1 Anatomy of skeletal muscle

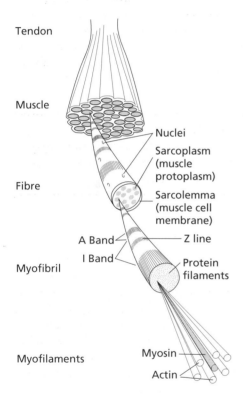

Figure 3.2 Skeletal muscle, showing the microscopic delineation of fibres, myofibrils and myofilaments. Note the striations in the fibre and the myofibril. These are alternating light and dark bands caused by the geometric arrangement of the filaments of actin and myosin

(muscle tissue's equivalent to cytoplasm). Surrounding the myofibrils within the sarcoplasm is the *sarcoplasmic reticulum,* a series of channels that store and secrete calcium (this is essential for muscle contraction). Also in the sarcoplasm are *transverse tubules/T vesicles* that transmit the nerve stimulus from the sarcolemma into the cell, causing the sarcoplasmic reticulum to release calcium. *Figure 3.2* shows the structure of a skeletal muscle fibre.

3.2.2 Myofibrils

Figure 3.3 shows the structure of a myofibril. The myofibrils are an arrangement of separate units connected end on to form long strands. These units are called *sarcomeres* and are the contractile units of the muscle. Within the sarcomeres are two protein filaments called *myosin* and *actin,* the myosin filament being the thicker of the two filaments. The myosin and actin filaments run adjacent to each other but at rest are not attached. The sarcomere is the area between the two *Z lines,* the *I band* contains only the thin filaments of actin, the *H zone* contains only myosin filaments and the *A band* contains both actin and myosin filaments.

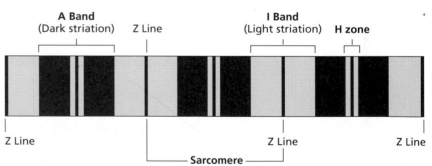

Figure 3.3 Sarcomeres and myofibril bands

When a muscle contracts the actin and myosin filaments slide over each other, rather like a pair of patio doors. As the actin filaments are attached to the Z lines the result is to pull the two Z lines closer together, shortening the sarcomere. This process will be discussed in more detail in Section 3.4.

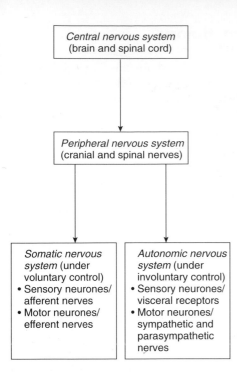

Figure 3.4 The nervous system

3.3 Neuromuscular control

All skeletal muscle reacts to an electrical stimulus, which is conducted from the brain to the muscle via nerves.

The brain and spinal cord are referred to as the *central nervous system* and nerves that carry information from the central nervous system to skeletal muscle are called *motor* or *efferent* nerves. Motor nerves form part of the *somatic nervous system*, which in turn forms part of the *peripheral nervous system*. *Figure 3.4* gives an overall view of the nervous system.

Motor neurones (nerves) are made up of three parts: the *cell body*, the *dendrites* and the *axon*. The structure of a motor neurone is shown in *Figure 3.5*. Stimuli are received from the central nervous system by the dendrites and passed on via the axon. At the end of the axon is the *axon terminal*, which connects with the motor end plate of the muscle to form the *neuromuscular junction*.

As there are so many muscle fibres it would take a lot of internal 'wiring' to connect them all to a separate motor neurone, so instead one motor neurone branches off and stimulates between 15 and 2000 muscle fibres – this is called a *motor unit*. The number of muscle fibres in a motor unit depends on the type of work the muscle performs and the degree of muscular control required. Once the motor unit is stimulated then all the fibres in it will contract. This is known as the 'all or none' law.

ACTIVITY

Name a muscle that you think might have motor units containing a lot of muscle fibres and one muscle that may only have a few muscle fibres per unit. Give reasons for your answer.

3.3.1 The nerve impulse

Information is relayed from the brain to the muscle via a nerve impulse. A nerve impulse is an electrical current running the length of the nerve, starting at the brain and passing down the spinal column to the relevant cell body. The cell bodies of individual motor neurones are located in various regions of the anterior horn of the spinal column. These collections of cell bodies are referred to as *motor neurone pools*. The cell bodies are positioned in relation to the muscle they stimulate, for example the circumflex nerve, which stimulates the deltoid, is found in the fifth cervical vertebra, whereas the sciatic nerve (stimulates the biceps femoris) is found in the fifth lumbar vertebra.

The nerve impulse is passed along the axon of the motor neurone. If you refer back to Figure 3.5 you will notice that the axon is covered in a myelin sheath. This sheath is mostly made up of fat and acts to insulate the nerve; however, it is not continuous. Where there is a gap in the myelin sheath there is a node of Ranvier. The impulse is passed from one node of Ranvier to the next, rather than along the whole length of the axon. This means that the impulse can travel more quickly. This method of nerve impulse propagation is called *saltatory conduction* and the thicker the myelin sheath the faster the nerve impulse that can be conducted.

When the impulse reaches the axon terminal the nerve transmits the information to the muscle by releasing a chemical transmitter, called *acetylcholine*, at the neuromuscular junction.

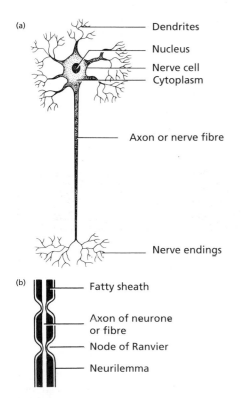

Figure 3.5 (a) A motor neurone;
(b) diagrammatic view of the myelin sheath

23

3.4 The sliding filament theory

The muscle responds to a nerve impulse by shortening. The sliding filament theory was put forward to explain how a muscle alters its length.

When a muscle contracts three things can be observed.

- The width of the I band decreases (the I band is the area in the sarcomere that contains only actin filaments).
- The A band remains the same length (the A band is the area in the sarcomere that is equal to the length of the myosin filaments).
- The H zone disappears (the H zone is the area in the sarcomere that contains only myosin filaments).

These changes to the sarcomere are shown in *Figure 3.6*. These three events can be explained by the myosin pulling the actin across so that the two filaments slide closer together, rather than either of the two filaments physically getting shorter.

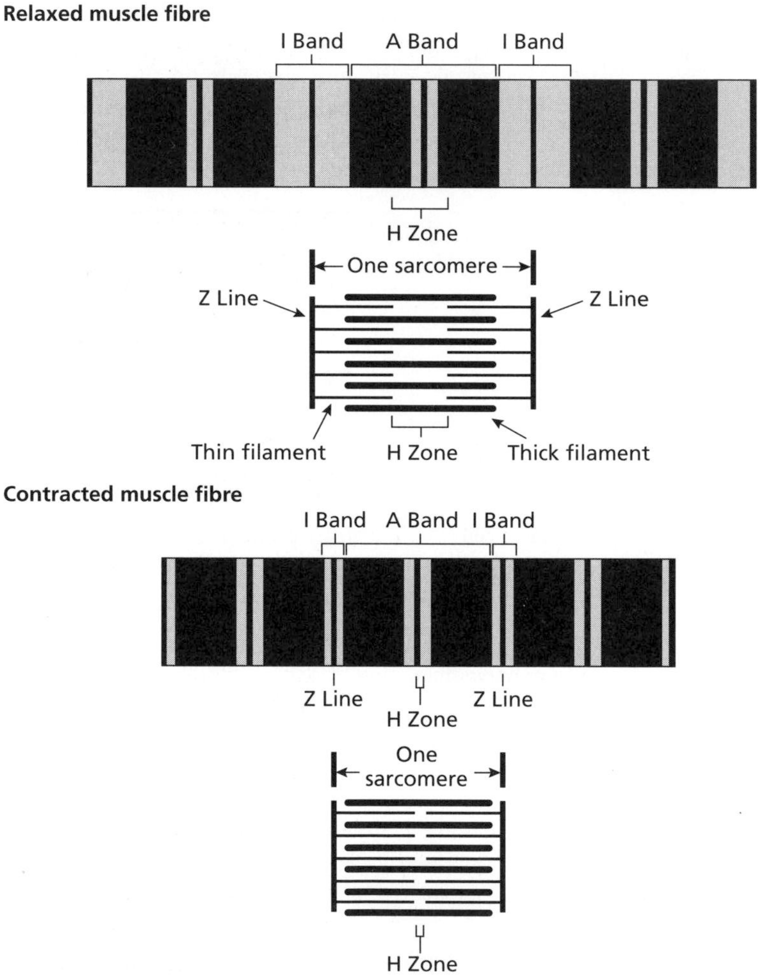

Figure 3.6   Changes that occur in the sarcomere during muscle contraction

3.4.1 Cross-bridges

The myosin filaments have small projections called myosin heads, which extend towards the actin but are not actually attached to it. A protein called tropomyosin bound to the actin filament prevents the myosin heads forming cross-bridges with the thin filament. Another protein bound to actin, troponin, can neutralise the effect of tropomyosin, but only in the presence of calcium. When the nerve impulse is transmitted down the

> **Definition**
> ## ATP
>
> *This stands for adenosine triphosphate. ATP is a form of chemical energy found in all cells. When ATP is broken down to adenosine diphosphate (ADP) and phosphate then energy is released.*

transverse tubules it stimulates the release of calcium from the sarcoplasmic reticulum. The troponin is then able to move the tropomyosin so that cross-bridges form between the myosin and the actin filament to produce actomyosin. Coupling of actomyosin stimulates the breakdown of ATP, releasing energy. The cross-bridges swivel towards the middle of the sarcomere, pulling the actin over the myosin and making the muscle shorter. When the stimulus from the nerve stops the calcium ions diffuse back into the sarcoplasmic reticulum and the muscle returns to its normal resting state.

ACTIVITY
Try to produce a flow chart showing the chain of events from the start of the nerve impulse to the muscle actively shortening.

3.5 Types of muscle fibre

Why are some people able to run so much faster than others, while some people may run slower but can keep going for hours? One reason for this is that there are three different types of muscle fibre and any one individual will have a different mix of these fibre types. As the fibres have distinct characteristics this will affect performance in certain sporting activities. The mix of fibres in your physiological make-up is genetically determined.

The three fibre types are referred to as *type I slow oxidative* (SO), *type IIa fast oxidative glycolytic* (FOG) and *type IIb fast glycolytic* (FG). Each muscle contains all three types but not in equal proportions. The fibres are grouped in motor units – you will find only one fibre type in any given motor unit.

3.5.1 Type I slow oxidative fibres

These fibres are known as *slow twitch fibres* because they contract more slowly than the type II (*fast twitch*) fibres. The myelin sheath of the motor neurone stimulating the muscle fibre is not as thick as that of the fast twitch unit, and this reduces the amount of insulation, slowing down the nerve impulse. Slow twitch fibres do not produce as much force as fast twitch fibres but can easily cope with prolonged bouts of exercise. They are more suited to aerobic work as they contain more mitochondria and myoglobin and have more blood capillaries than fast twitch fibres. Slow twitch fibres have the enzymes necessary for aerobic respiration and are able to break down fat and carbohydrate to carbon dioxide and water. This is a slower process than releasing energy anaerobically but it does not produce any fatiguing byproducts.

3.5.2 Type IIa fast oxidative glycolytic fibres

The motor neurone stimulating the type IIa fibre has a thicker myelin sheath than the slow twitch fibre, so it can contract more quickly and exert more force. This fibre type can produce energy both aerobically and anaerobically by breaking down carbohydrate to pyruvic acid but it is much more suited to anaerobic respiration, which means it can release energy very quickly. The rapid build up of lactic acid (a byproduct of anaerobic respiration) lowers the pH and has a negative affect on enzyme action, causing the muscle fibre to fatigue quickly.

3.5.3 Type IIb fast glycolytic fibres

These muscle fibres are also very quick to contract and can exert a large amount of force. They rely heavily on anaerobic respiration for releasing energy as they have very few mitochondria. This means energy is rapidly released but that the muscle fibre is quick to fatigue.

Table 3.1 summarises the characteristics of the different fibre types.

Table 3.1 Characteristics of muscle fibres

Characteristic	Type I	Type IIa	Type IIb
Contraction speed	Slow	Fast	Fast
Size	Small	Large	Large
Force produced	Small	Large	Large
Fatiguability	Slight	Great	Great
Mitochondria	Many	Many	Few
Glycogen store	Slight	Great	Great
Capillaries	Many	Moderate	Few
Aerobic capacity	High	Moderate	Low
Anaerobic capacity	Low	High	High

Table adapted from *Physiology of Exercise*, by DR Lamb.

ACTIVITY

Study Table 3.1 and decide which fibre type you think would be predominantly recruited for the following activities: a 5000 m run, a diving save from a goalkeeper, a 400 m hurdle race and a fast break in basketball.

In practice

Research has shown that the percentage of slow twitch fibres in the leg muscles of distance runners is high (about 80% of fibres) and that sprinters have a higher percentage of type IIa and type IIb fibres (roughly 50% and 30%, respectively). This research is by no means conclusive as so many other factors contribute to good sporting performance, but certainly some people are more physiologically suited to some activities than others.

3.6 Muscle function

Muscles can only *actively* contract so when, for example, biceps brachii is stimulated it contracts and causes the elbow to flex. In order to straighten the arm we need another muscle to contract to complete the opposite action. When triceps brachii is stimulated it causes extension of the elbow joint. These two muscles are said to be working as an *antagonistic pair*. The muscle initiating the movement (shortening) is the *prime mover* or *agonist* and the muscle that is relaxing and returning to its original length is the *antagonist*. When you flex your elbow the biceps is the prime mover and the triceps is the antagonist. When you extend your elbow the triceps is acting as the prime mover and the biceps as the antagonist. The muscles work as a unit, which requires a high degree of coordination. This coordination is achieved by nervous control. When the prime mover is being stimulated the nerve impulse to the antagonist is inhibited – this is known as *reciprocal innervation*.

ACTIVITY

Identify the muscles that cause flexion and extension of the knee joint and decide which muscles act as the prime mover and which muscles act as the antagonist during both movements.

A muscle may also assist the work of a prime mover at a particular joint, making the movement more efficient. This second muscle is sometimes referred to as a *synergist*. The term can also be used to describe a muscle that acts to counteract an unwanted movement of a prime mover,

In practice

When you perform an arm curl during a weights session you can feel the tension in the deltoid muscle as it helps to stabilise the shoulder joint.

for example a prime mover that acts around two joints where only one movement is required. Either way, synergistic muscle action is difficult to analyse and is beyond the scope of this book.

The third function of a muscle is to act as a *fixator*. A fixator allows the prime mover to work more efficiently, usually by stabilising the bone where the prime mover originates. The fixator muscle increases in tension but does not allow any movement to take place.

ACTIVITY

Identify the muscles that act as prime movers and as antagonists when you perform a squat thrust. Identify any muscles that you think act as fixators.

3.7 Types of muscular contraction

There are four different ways that a muscle can contract, reflecting the function that the muscle is performing.

3.7.1 Isotonic or concentric contraction

This is the most common form of muscular contraction. It occurs when a muscle is acting as a prime mover and shortening under tension, creating movement around a joint.

3.7.2 Eccentric contraction

This is the opposite of concentric action. In eccentric contraction the muscle acting as the antagonist lengthens under tension (usually returning to its normal resting length). A muscle contracting eccentrically is acting as a 'brake' to help control the movement of a body part during *negative work*. Negative work describes a resistance that is greater than the contractile strength of the muscle, for example gravity.

When you perform a press-up, starting from the floor, you push your body upwards by extending your elbow joints. The triceps works as the prime mover and contracts concentrically (it shortens under tension), while the biceps acts as the antagonist, relaxing and returning to its normal length. During the downward phase (lowering the body) you are performing negative work and the triceps, working as the antagonist, contracts eccentrically (lengthens under tension) and helps to control the movement.

In practice

In any activity where you are lowering the body, body part, or an object, muscles will be working eccentrically.

ACTIVITY

Identify the muscles of the spine involved during a sit-up and complete the table.

Phase	Movement	Muscle used	Function	Type of contraction
Upward				
Downward				

A rugby scrum – muscles are working hard but there is no movement (isometric contraction)

3.7.3 Isometric contraction

The muscle increases in tension but there is no change in its length and therefore no movement. This type of contraction occurs when a muscle is acting as a fixator or when it is working against a resistance that it cannot overcome, for example when two equally strong packs collide in a rugby scrum.

3.7.4 Isokinetic contraction

During this type of contraction the muscle shortens and increases in tension while working at a constant speed against a variable resistance. The muscle works throughout the full range of movement but this can only be achieved by using isokinetic weight training equipment.

3.8 Gradation of contraction

There is just one more term to introduce: *gradation of contraction*. Put simply, this refers to the strength of contraction exerted by the muscle. Gradation of contraction depends on:

● The number of motor units stimulated (*recruitment*). If only a few of the motor units within the muscle are stimulated obviously the strength of contraction will be weak. For maximal contraction to occur all motor units must be stimulated.
● The frequency of the stimuli (*wave summation*). For a motor unit to maintain a contraction it must receive a continuous string of impulses. Usually a frequency of 80–100 stimuli per second is required. Slow twitch muscle fibres have a lower threshold for activation than fast twitch fibres and so tend to be recruited first.
● Timing of the stimuli to various motor units (*synchronisation* or *spatial summation*). If all the motor units are stimulated at exactly the same time then maximum force can be applied. If, however, a muscle needs to work over a long period, fatigue can be delayed by rotating the number of motor units being stimulated at any one time.

Key revision box

Skeletal muscle creates movement by actively contracting and shortening. The muscle is stimulated by a motor neurone. This stimulation results in each individual sarcomere decreasing in length as the actin and myosin filaments slide over each other. The nature of the contraction produced is a result of the fibre type recruited, the number of fibres stimulated and the frequency and timing of the stimuli.

KEY TERMS

You should now understand the following terms. If you do not, go back through the chapter and find out.

Fasciculi
Myofibril
Axon
Sarcomere
Transverse tubules
Sarcoplasmic reticulum
Actin
Myosin
Myosin cross-bridges
Antagonist
Fixator
Prime mover

PROGRESS CHECK

1 Name the two types of connective tissue that attach muscle to bone and muscle to muscle.
2 List four common features of muscle tissue.
3 Why do muscles work in antagonistic pairs?
4 What is the difference between a muscle fibre and a myofibril?
5 What is a sarcomere?
6 Name the two protein filaments responsible for muscle contraction.
7 Sketch and label a diagram showing the structure of a sarcomere.
8 Explain the role of the sarcoplasmic reticulum in muscle contraction.
9 What are the three fibre types found in skeletal muscle?
10 Give four characteristics of each fibre type found in skeletal muscle.
11 Give an example in sport to show when each muscle fibre type would be used.
12 What is the relationship between fibre type distribution and athletic performance?
13 What is the role of a fixator?
14 When would a muscle contract eccentrically?
15 What is meant by gradation of contraction?
16 What is the transmitter substance at the neuromuscular junction called?
17 What is meant by reciprocal innervation?
18 What is the 'all or none' law?
19 What effect does the myelin sheath have on propagation of nerve impulses?

CHAPTER 4

The mechanics of movement

Learning objectives:

- To know the three orders of levers.
- To understand the effect of the length of lever and the angle of pull on the movement produced.
- To be familiar with and able to apply Newton's laws of motion.
- To understand the effects of the centre of gravity on balance and rotation.

An ability to analyse movements is extremely helpful to both performer and coach. The ability to identify the joints and muscles involved in a movement and their roles enables development of a suitable training programme. Even though an athlete may work out regularly using weights he or she may not be exercising the correct muscles, or might be working them concentrically when some eccentric work is also needed. A basic understanding of the principles of movement can help to identify and correct problems with technique. This chapter provides a brief introduction to the mechanics of movement and shows how this knowledge can be applied to help improve sporting performance.

4.1 Levers and their functions

When we think of levers crowbars and wheelbarrows spring to mind rather than ulnas and femurs. The skeleton forms a system of levers that allows us to move. A *lever* is a rigid bar that rotates around a fixed point (a *fulcrum*) and is used to apply force (*effort*) against a *resistance*. In the human body the bones are the levers, the joints the fulcrums, the muscles act as the effort and the weight of the body part, plus anything that it holds, is the resistance.

A single body part, such as an arm, can also act as a lever, providing it works as a rigid unit. *Figure 4.1* shows the lever system of the forearm.

A lever has two functions:

- to overcome a larger resistance than the effort applied
- to increase the distance a resistance can be moved by using an effort greater than the resistance.

In other words, a lever provides strength or improves the range of movement. The strength and range of movement of a muscle depend on the position of its insertion (where the effort is applied) relative to the joint it moves (the fulcrum). The greater the distance between the joint and the muscle insertion, the more strength can be generated; the closer the insertion is to the joint the better the range of movement will be.

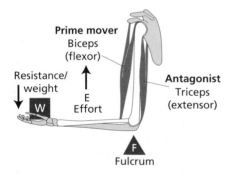

Figure 4.1 The lever system in the forearm

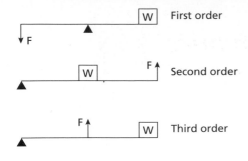

Figure 4.2   Classes of lever

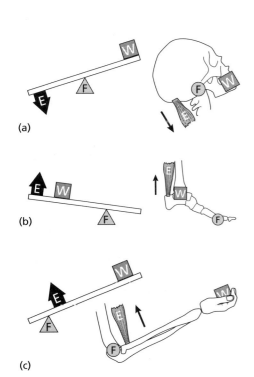

(a)

(b)

(c)

Figure 4.3   First (a), second (b) and third-order levers (c) in the human body

The type of lever formed by the joint and the surrounding musculature affects the movement produced, but two related factors also need to be considered: the angle of pull and the length of the lever. These will be described below.

4.2 Classification of levers

A lever can be defined as first-order, second-order or third-order. The three classes of lever are illustrated in *Figure 4.2*. This classification is based on the relative positions of the fulcrum (joint), effort (muscle insertion) and resistance (body part or external weight).

4.2.1 First-order levers

A first-order lever is organised like a set of scales, with the fulcrum between the effort and the resistance. The head is a good example of the action of a first-order lever in the body when the head and neck are being flexed and extended, as in nodding (see *Figure 4.3*).

4.2.2 Second-order levers

When the resistance lies between the fulcrum and the effort a second-order lever is produced. When you raise up on to your toes (plantar flexion of the ankle) you are using a second-order lever. Where the toes are in contact with the floor is the fulcrum, the resistance is at the ankle joint where the body's weight is transferred to the foot and the effort is produced at the position on the ankle where the Achilles tendon inserts onto the calcaneus (see *Figure 4.3*).

4.2.3 Third-order levers

In a third-order lever the effort lies between the fulcrum and the resistance. This is the most common form of lever in the human body. In terms of applying force this is a very inefficient lever, but it allows speed and range of movement. An example within the body is the forearm during flexion (see *Figure 4.3*).

4.3 Angle of pull

This refers to the position of the insertion of the muscle relative to the position of the joint, measured in degrees. The angle of pull changes continuously as the limb is moved and these changes have a direct effect on the efficiency of the muscle's pulling force. In the resting position the angle of pull for most muscles is quite small and does not exceed 90° throughout the movement. Structures within joints can act as pulleys to increase the angle of pull and therefore the efficiency of the muscle. For example, the patella, attached to the quadriceps tendon and the patellar ligament, acts as a pulley at the knee joint. A muscle works most effectively as it nears an angle of pull of 90° (*Figure 4.4*) and where it is not advantageous the only solution is to increase the strength of the muscle.

ACTIVITY

Choose three hand-held weights that you consider to be light, manageable and heavy. Using *Figure 4.4* as a guide try to lift each weight using a different angle of pull. Discuss your results with others in your group.

A combination of levers is used in batting

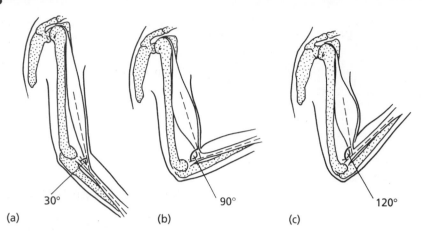

Figure 4.4 Angles of pull: (a) less than 45°; (b) 90°; (c) more than 90°

4.4 Length of lever

The longer the lever the greater the change in momentum, and consequently change in velocity, that can be imparted on an object. This can be an advantage in sports in which you hit objects, for example a squash ball can be hit harder when the elbow joint is fully extended rather than flexed; the use of a racket lengthens the lever arm further. To generate a much greater overall force the effects of several levers can be combined, as in batting in cricket where the trunk, upper arm, forearm and bat all work together as one unit.

ACTIVITY
Contrast the length of club and stroke technique used in golf at the tee shot with that used in the approach to a short putt. Your answer should make reference to the choice of joint, joint action and lever arm length.

The tee shot in golf

4.5 Force

Forces can be used to make something move, stop something that is already moving or to prevent something from moving altogether. A force might be internal or external. In the human body, muscles act as internal forces, whereas the effect of gravity is external.

The effect that a force has on a body is influenced by three factors.

● *The size, or magnitude, of the force* is measured in newtons (N) or in pounds. The magnitude of the force refers to the weight of a body, which is a product of its mass and the external force of gravity. A muscle's force is determined by the size and number of the fibres contained within any one muscle.
● *The direction of the force.* If a single force is applied to a body through its centre of gravity the body will move in the same direction as the force.
● *The position of application of the force.* Applying the force slightly off-centre will produce angular motion – e.g. hitting a snooker ball off-centre will create spin (see *Figure 4.5*).

In sport, a performer must gauge how much force to apply in any given situation. If you are performing a closed skill, for example a free throw

---

Definition
NEWTON
One newton is the force required to produce an acceleration of one metre per second per second on a mass of one kilogram.

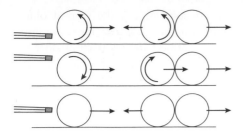

Figure 4.5 Applying a force slightly off-centre will cause spin

in basketball, you are at an advantage in that the amount of force, the direction and the application of the force required are the same each time you perform the throw. Therefore practice can lead to a habitual response. In open skills the situation will vary each time and errors can be made – a footballer not connecting with the ball correctly will cause it to veer off to one side, a hockey player with an enthusiastic backswing applying too much force to the ball will over-hit a pass. Errors can be rectified very quickly if a coach is able to point out the basic mechanical weaknesses in a technique.

4.6 Newton's laws of motion

Motion (movement) will only occur if a force is applied; most movement of the body is caused by the internal force created by the muscles. Motion occurs either in a straight line (linear motion) or around an axis (angular motion). Isaac Newton formulated three laws of motion, which can be applied to sports performance.

4.6.1 Newton's first law of motion (law of inertia)

This law states that:

'a body continues in its state of rest or of uniform motion unless a force acts on it.'

A body or an object is said to be in a *state of inertia* and a force must be applied to it before any change in velocity can occur. The greater the mass of a body the more force is required to overcome its inertia. You can throw a 5 kg weight further than you can throw a 10 kg weight using the same force.

4.6.2 Newton's second law of motion (law of acceleration)

'the acceleration of an object is directly proportional to the force causing it and is inversely proportional to the mass of the object.'

The speed that a person can throw a tennis ball is proportional to the amount of force applied by the muscles. It also depends on the inertia of the ball.

In sport we often refer to the *momentum* of an object. This is a product of velocity × mass. A defender in hockey usually uses a heavier hockey stick than a forward because it allows him or her to transfer more momentum to the ball, and consequently to hit it further. Momentum can also be built up and transferred from one body part to the rest of the body, resulting in more force – for example swinging the arms backwards and forwards before take-off transfers momentum to the rest of the body for a vertical jump.

In practice

Skilled sports performance depends on selecting joint, joint action and lever arm length correctly. To do this requires a combination of good physical preparation and good coaching.

Definition
MASS
Mass is the quantity of matter a body contains.

In practice

A medicine ball has greater inertia than a tennis ball and therefore more force is needed to alter its speed.

ACTIVITY

Perform a vertical jump with no preparatory arm swings. Note the height of the jump and then perform the jump using your arms to build up momentum. Compare the two heights.

4.6.3 Newton's third law of motion (law of reaction)

This law states:

'for every action there is an equal and opposite reaction.'

When an object exerts a force on a second object, the second object exerts an opposite and equal force back on the first. The most common sporting illustration of this law is when an athlete pushes back against the starting blocks at the beginning of a sprint race (exerting a force on the blocks), causing the opposite and equal reaction of being pushed forward out of the blocks. When in mid air it is possible to move one body part to cause another body part to react in opposition; for example in trampolining a half twist is achieved by swinging the arms to the right, rotating the rest of the body to the left.

4.7 Centre of gravity

The centre of gravity, sometimes referred to as the point of balance, is the point in an object where all its mass is concentrated. The centre of gravity of a performer is continually changing as the body position changes. As the centre of gravity is the point of balance of the body we commonly refer to performers being 'balanced' or 'off-balance'. A gymnast plainly displays good balance when performing a handstand (_Figure 4.6_), but balance is a less obvious requirement of most sports and we often refer to a games player as being well balanced. Therefore balance has both a static and dynamic dimension.

Figure 4.6

Figure 4.7 In some body positions the centre of gravity is located outside the body

In a uniformly shaped body (such as a snooker ball) the centre of gravity lies at its geometric centre, but the centre of gravity of a non-uniform body is determined by the distribution of its mass and density. When standing upright the centre of gravity of most people is in the hip region, the centre of gravity for males being slightly higher than that for females. As the body's position changes so does its centre of gravity – in some cases it may even be located outside the body (see _Figure 4.7_).

4.7.1 Maintaining balance

To be in a state of balance the centre of gravity must be over the area of support. For example when you stand upright the area of support is your feet. The larger the area of support, the easier it is to maintain balance. Lowering or raising the centre of gravity will affect stability. By raising your arms above your head you are redistributing your mass, and your centre of gravity will move higher up your body. When you learn to do a headstand you are encouraged to form a triangle with your head and hands because this position forms a large area of support, making it easier to balance. In the early stages of learning to do a headstand, you bring your legs into a tuck position and hold the balance, rather than extend your legs vertically. It is relatively easy to balance in the tuck position as the centre of gravity is lowered, increasing stability. However, as the legs are extended the centre of gravity is raised, making the position less stable and consequently more difficult to perform.

Figure 4.8

ACTIVITY

Rank the gymnastic positions shown in *Figure 4.8* in order of stability and difficulty.

4.7.2 Use of the off-balance position

Occasionally a performer needs to become off-balance. A sprinter in the 'set' position holds their body so that the line of gravity is as close as possible to the edge of the area of support. On the 'go' signal the sprinter moves out of the area of support, causing loss of balance – literally he or she falls forwards. A new area of support now needs to be established.

As mentioned previously, when a force is applied in line with the centre of gravity this will result in linear motion, but when a force is applied out of line with the centre of gravity or the centre of rotation, then rotation will occur. This is known as eccentric force and is used extensively in gymnastics and trampolining. For example, in order to produce a forward somersault in a gymnastic routine the centre of gravity must be displaced in front of the feet.

4.8 Movement analysis

To complete an anatomical and mechanical analysis (kinesiological analysis) of a motor skill you need to be able to

1 describe the skill and its purpose
2 evaluate the performance in terms of
    (a) the joint action, muscle action and function and
    (b) the mechanical principles applied
3 correct faults where applicable.

The following analysis of the take-off phase of the standing broad jump is an example of the detail required at 'A' level and shows how the basic principles of mechanics can be applied to sporting performance.

4.8.1 Description

The standing broad jump is a forward jump to cover as much horizontal distance as possible. The performer takes off from both feet and lands on both feet.

Definition

KINESIOLOGY

The study of the science of movement.

4.8.2 Joint and muscle action during take-off

Joint	Joint type	Movement observed	Main muscle involved	Muscle function	Type of contraction
Elbow	Hinge	Extension	Triceps brachii	Prime mover/agonist	Concentric
Shoulder	Ball and socket	Flexion	Anterior deltoid	Prime mover/agonist	Concentric
Shoulder girdle	Gliding	Upward rotation Abduction	Trapezius part 2 Serratus anterior	Prime mover/agonist Prime mover/agonist	Concentric Concentric
Spine	Gliding and cartilaginous	Extension	Sacrospinalis	Prime mover/agonist	Concentric
Hip	Ball and socket	Extension	Gluteus maximus	Prime mover/agonist	Concentric
Knee	Hinge	Extension	Quadriceps group	Prime mover/agonist	Concentric
Ankle	Hinge	Plantarflexion	Soleus	Prime mover/agonist	Concentric

35

4.8.3 Mechanical principles involved in take-off

- The application of force at take-off needs to be in line with the centre of gravity. If it isn't the performer will jump slightly to one side and the horizontal distance jumped will be less.
- The speed of projection depends on the total impulse (force × time) generated at take-off. This is the combination of the forces exerted at the ankle, knee, hip and shoulder joints. How strongly and quickly the musculature around these joints can contract affects the distance jumped. Careful timing of joint action is essential, because if joints act out of sequence the overall force that can be applied will be reduced. For the standing broad jump the hips should initiate the movement, followed by the shoulders, knees and ankles.
- The amount of force that can be generated at take-off will increase the upward reaction force (Newton's third law).
- Preparatory swings of the arms and flexion of the knees will help to overcome inertia (Newton's first law).
- Momentum can be increased by swinging the arms forwards and upwards at take-off (Newton's second law), adding to the overall force of the movement.

ACTIVITY

Observe the action of an athlete who performs a good standing broad jump, and compare it with a person who performs a relatively poor standing broad jump. List any major differences between the two techniques.

Key revision box

A basic kinesiological analysis needs to include three features: a description of the skill; an evaluation of both the joints and muscles used and the mechanical principles applied; and identification and correction of any faults.

KEY TERMS

You should now understand the following terms. If you do not, go back through the chapter and find out.

Lever
Fulcrum
Resistance
Momentum
Inertia
Application of force
Linear motion
Angular motion
Magnitude of force
Length of lever
Reaction force
Kinesiology
Angle of pull
Centre of gravity

PROGRESS CHECK

1 Give examples within the body of a first-order lever, a second-order lever and a third-order lever.
2 What two functions can a lever perform?
3 Which type of lever allows the greatest range of movement?
4 Give an example from sport, other than batting in cricket, where the effects of several levers are combined to form one unit in order to generate more force.
5 What is the optimum angle of pull for a muscle?
6 What is the advantage of lengthening the lever arm?
7 How can a person raise their centre of gravity?
8 What benefit is gained by lowering your centre of gravity?
9 Give an example from sport where a performer might deliberately lower their centre of gravity.
10 Why is it easier to perform a headstand than a handstand?
11 What benefit does an athlete gain by performing preparatory swings with the arm before throwing the discus?
12 What happens if a force is applied in line with an object's centre of gravity?
13 Describe the three factors that determine the effect that a force will have on a body.
14 Complete a kinesiological analysis of a vertical jump.

CHAPTER **5**

Structure and function of the heart

Learning objectives:

- To know the structure of the heart and be able to describe the flow of blood through the heart.

- To describe and explain the structure and function of the conduction system of the heart.

- To understand the relationship between stroke volume, heart rate and cardiac output.

- To be able to describe how the body regulates heart rate.

- To be aware of the effects of exercise on heart rate.

The heart forms part of the *cardiovascular system*; 'cardio' meaning heart and 'vascular' meaning the circulatory networks of the blood vessels. The cardiovascular system ensures constant distribution of blood to the body. *Figure 5.1* gives an overview of the cardiovascular system.

The heart acts as two completely separate pumps. The pump at the right side of the heart sends deoxygenated blood to the lungs and the pump on the left side sends oxygenated blood round to the body's tissues. The two sides of the heart are separated by a muscular wall called the *septum*.

5.1 Structure of the heart

The heart is about the size of a closed fist and lies within the *pericardial cavity*. The pericardial cavity forms part of the *mediastinum*, which in turn forms part of the thoracic cavity.

The heart is made up of four chambers. The two top chambers are the *atria* and the bottom two are the *ventricles*.

The close proximity of the heart to the lungs means that the right side of the heart has very little work to do compared with the left side. This is reflected in the size and shape of the heart, as the left side is larger.

The heart is surrounded by a closed sac known as the *pericardium* and is bathed in *pericardial fluid* within the pericardium. As the heart is continually moving this fluid is needed to reduce the effects of friction on the heart wall.

The heart wall is made up of three different layers (*Figure 5.2*).

- *The endocardium* is the inner layer. It is made up of very smooth tissue to allow uninterrupted flow of blood through the heart.
- *The myocardium*, the middle layer, is made up of cardiac muscle tissue. Cardiac muscle cells are similar to skeletal muscle cells in that they appear striated but they are highly specialised. Cardiac muscle cells

<table>
<tr><td>*Definition*</td></tr>
<tr><td>**THORACIC CAVITY**</td></tr>
<tr><td>*The thoracic cavity is the area surrounded by the ribs and bordered by the diaphragm. The thoracic cavity is separated into two halves by the mediastinum.*</td></tr>
</table>

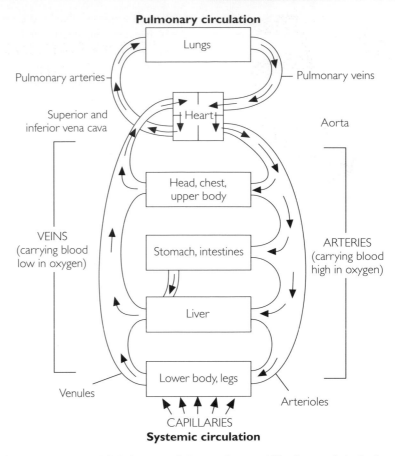

Figure 5.1 Simplified diagram of the circulation of blood around the body

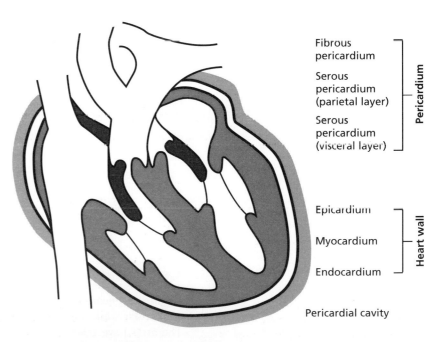

Figure 5.2 The pericardium and the wall of the heart

have a single nucleus and contain many mitochondria (*Figure 5.3*). This is because the heart needs a good supply of ATP to avoid fatigue. Unlike skeletal muscle cells, cardiac muscle cells are connected by intercalated discs. This connection allows a coordinated wave of contraction to occur when the heart muscle is stimulated.

● *The epicardium* is the outer layer of the heart and also forms the inner layer of the pericardium. The outer layer of the pericardium is made of strong fibrous tissue that helps to protect the heart.

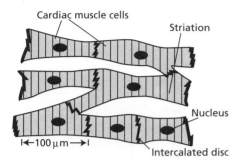

Figure 5.3 Cardiac muscle cells

5.1.1 Arteries and veins of the heart

Numerous blood vessels are attached to the heart, bringing blood to the heart or taking blood away from it (*Figure 5.4*). Blood enters the heart via the atria and exits through the ventricles. To be more precise, the inferior and superior *venae cavae* bring deoxygenated blood from the body to the right atrium and the four *pulmonary veins* bring oxygenated blood from the lungs to the left atrium. The *pulmonary artery* carries deoxygenated blood from the right ventricle to the lungs and the *aorta* carries oxygenated blood from the left ventricle round the body.

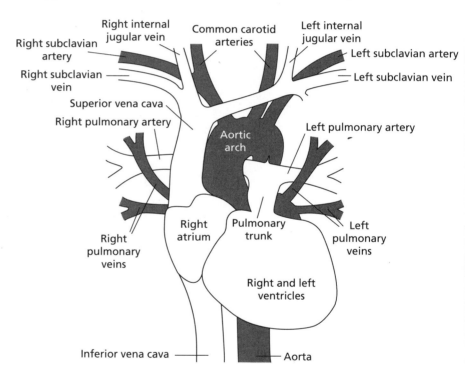

Figure 5.4 External view of the heart, showing the major blood vessels. The vessels shaded carry oxygenated blood

The heart itself requires a good blood supply and the *coronary artery*, which branches from the aorta, distributes oxygenated blood to the heart through an extensive network of capillaries. Deoxygenated blood is returned by the veins of the heart directly into the right atrium through the *coronary sinus*.

5.1.2 Chambers of the heart

As already mentioned, the two pump units of the heart are separated by a muscular wall called the septum; each unit has an atrium and a ventricle. The atria have relatively thin muscular walls as the force needed to push the blood from them into the ventricles is quite small. The ventricles, as the mechanism pumping blood around the whole body, need much thicker, stronger, muscular walls. The wall of the right ventricle usually exerts a pressure of 25 mmHg, whereas the left ventricle exerts a pressure of about 120 mmHg at rest. This difference is because the right ventricle pumps blood only as far as the lungs, but the left ventricle needs to provide sufficient force to carry the blood round the systemic circulation.

5.1.3 Valves of the heart

The flow of blood through the heart needs to be regulated so that blood flows only in one direction. Four valves inside the heart help to control blood flow through the heart – two separating the atria from the ventricles and two in the arteries carrying blood from the ventricles. The valves operate only one way and when properly closed prevent backflow of blood. The valves between the atria and the ventricles are known collectively as the *atrioventricular* valves, the valve between the right atrium and right ventricle is the *tricuspid valve* and that between the left atrium and the left ventricle is the *bicuspid valve*. Blood flowing from the atria into the ventricles pushes the valves open, and they are closed by thin connective tissues called the *chordae tendineae*. The chordae tendineae are attached to the papillary muscles, which are attached to the walls of the ventricle. When the ventricles contract so do the papillary muscles, causing the chordae tendineae to tighten and preventing the valves from collapsing inwards.

The a*ortic valve* is found between the left ventricle and the aorta and the *pulmonary valve* lies between the right ventricle and the pulmonary artery. These two valves are known collectively as the *semilunar valves*. Ejection of blood from the ventricles forces the semilunar valves open. When the ventricles relax backflow of blood is prevented because the semilunar valves, like the atrioventricular valves, operate in only one direction. The internal structure of the heart is shown in *Figure 5.5*.

ACTIVITY

Borrow a stethoscope and working in pairs try to pick up your partner's heart sounds.

In practice

The closing of the valves creates the heart sounds that can be heard through a stethoscope. The sound is described as 'lubb dupp', the 'lubb' corresponding to the closing of the atrioventricular valves and the 'dupp' to the closing of the semilunar valves. A muffled sound usually indicates a malfunction of one of the valves and is known as a heart murmur.

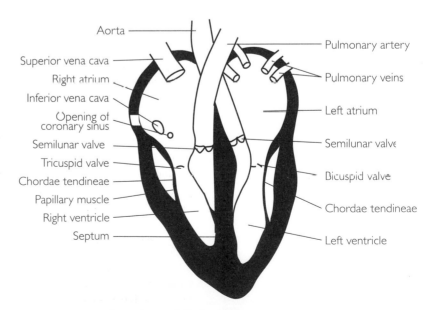

Figure 5.5 Internal structures of the heart

5.2 Flow of blood through the heart and the cardiac cycle

Deoxygenated blood flows into and fills the right atrium from the superior and inferior venae cavae. At the same time, oxygenated blood enters the left atrium via the pulmonary veins from the lungs. As the left and right ventricles relax blood flows from both atria into them. The atria contract to ensure that the ventricles are completely filled. The ventricles then contract (when this happens the atrioventricular valves close to prevent backflow of blood into the atria) and the blood is pushed out of the ventricles through the semilunar valves into the pulmonary artery and the aorta. When the ventricles relax the semilunar valves close, preventing backflow. The atria relax and begin to fill again – and the whole process repeats itself.

This process is known as the *cardiac cycle* and at rest takes approximately 0.8 seconds. The cardiac cycle involves rhythmic contraction and relaxation of the heart muscle. The contraction phase is known as *systole* and takes about 0.3 seconds at rest, the relaxation phase (*diastole*) lasts roughly 0.5 seconds at rest. Note: these terms are usually used to refer to the contraction and relaxation phases of the *ventricles*.

ACTIVITY

On a copy of *Figure 5.5* illustrate the flow of blood through the heart. Then complete the flow chart below to show the journey of a red blood cell through the heart and the circulatory systems.

Inferior and superior venae cavae → ? → Tricuspid valve → ? → ? → Pulmonary artery → Lungs → ? → Left atrium → ? → Left ventricle → ? → ? → Tissues of the body → Inferior and superior venae cavae.

5.3 The conduction system of the heart

The muscular pump of the heart needs a stimulus to make it contract. Unlike skeletal muscle, cardiac muscle needs to create a wave-like contraction so that the atria contract before the ventricles. An added problem

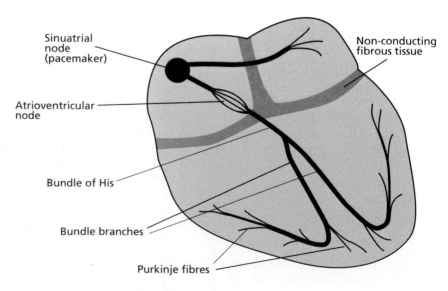

Figure 5.6 Conduction system of the heart

is that blood needs to flow downwards from the atria into the ventricles and then flow upwards out of the aorta and pulmonary artery. The system of nerves that stimulate the heart is shown in *Figure 5.6*.

The wave of contraction is initiated by a specialised node in the wall of the right atrium, called the *sinuatrial* (SA) *node* or *pacemaker*. The SA node is controlled by the autonomic nervous system (the regulation of the heart rate will be discussed later in this chapter). The nerve impulse spreads through the cardiac muscle tissue, rather like a 'Mexican wave', as all the muscle fibres are interconnected. This causes the atria to contract, pushing the blood into the ventricles. The impulse then spreads over the ventricles from the bottom (the *apex*) of the heart. This is achieved by a second node sited in the atrioventricular septum, known as the *atrioventricular* (AV) *node*. The impulse travels across the atria to the AV node and then down a specialised bundle of nerve tissue in the septum (the *bundle of His*). The nerve impulse is carried to the apex of the heart, where the specialised fibres branch out into smaller bundles, called *purkinje fibres*. The purkinje fibres extend upwards and across the ventricles, causing the ventricles to contract and push blood up and out of the heart. Once the ventricles have completely relaxed another impulse is initiated at the SA node and the cycle is repeated.

In practice

The ECG is used extensively in the medical profession as a diagnostic tool as it will highlight any problems with the conduction system of the heart.

5.3.1 The electrocardiogram

The electrical activity of the heart's conduction system can be measured by electrodes on the skin of the chest. The information is recorded in the form of a trace such as that illustrated in *Figure 5.7*. This trace is an electrocardiogram (also known as an ECG). The P wave occurs just before the atria contract, the QRS complex occurs just before the ventricles contract and the T wave corresponds to repolarisation of the ventricles before ventricular diastole.

5.4 Cardiac output

The amount of blood the heart manages to pump out per minute is known as the cardiac output ($\dot{Q}$). The cardiac output is a product of the amount of blood ejected by the ventricle after each contraction (the stroke volume, SV) multiplied by the number of times the heart actually beats per minute (the heart rate, HR):

$$\dot{Q} = SV \times HR$$

The stroke volume is measured in millilitres of blood per beat, the heart rate is measured in beats per minute, giving a cardiac output in litres per minute.

At rest the average stroke volume is 70 ml and the average heart rate 72 beats per minute, giving an overall cardiac output of just over 5 litres/min.

The resting heart rate of an individual can vary greatly, although we all need to produce roughly the same cardiac output. If a person does a lot of aerobic work (prolonged periods of submaximal exercise) their resting pulse rate often drops to 60 beats per minute or lower. In order to produce the same cardiac output, the stroke volume must increase to compensate for this drop in heart rate.

$$\dot{Q} = SV \times HR$$

$$5 \text{ litres} = ? \times 60 \text{ (beats/min)}$$

By rearranging the equation,

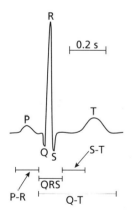

Figure 5.7 Some of the important events on an ECG

Definition
STROKE VOLUME
The volume of blood pumped out of the heart by each ventricle during one contraction.

ANATOMY, BIOMECHANICS AND PHYSIOLOGY ● ● ●

In practice

For the amount of energy required at rest 5 litres of blood ensures an adequate supply of oxygen. If the body becomes more active and uses up more energy more oxygen will be required and the cardiac output will increase.

| Definition |

HYPERTROPHY

Growth of a tissue through an increase in cell size.

END-DIASTOLIC VOLUME

The amount of blood in the ventricles just before the contraction phase (systole).

Table 5.1 Distribution of blood to the vital organs

Organ	Percentage of cardiac output at rest
Bone	5
Brain	15
Heart	5
Kidney	25
Liver	25
Muscle	15
Skin	5
Other	5

$$SV = \dot{Q}/HR$$
$$= 5 \text{ litres}/60$$
$$0.83 \text{ ml}$$

In this case the stroke volume increases to about 83 ml per beat. In effect, it is the increase in SV that produces the drop in heart rate, and not the other way round, because as the heart gets used to regular exercise it gets bigger (undergoes hypertrophy) and stronger.

This means that the *end-diastolic volume* of the ventricle increases (it can physically hold more blood). The ventricle is thus capable of stronger contraction and able to push more blood out per beat.

The heart subjected to regular exercise does not have to beat as often as an untrained heart to produce the same cardiac output at rest. This also means that the maximum cardiac output will increase.

A person's maximum heart rate is estimated as being 220 minus their age, so the maximum heart rate of an athlete aged 20 will be about 200 beats per minute. The maximum SV reached during exercise increases with training – from 110–120 ml per beat for an untrained male to 150–170 ml per beat for an endurance athlete.

In exceptional cases the maximum cardiac output can be as high as 40 litres.

$$HR \times SV = \dot{Q}$$

	HR × SV	= $\dot{Q}$
Untrained:	200 × 120 ml	= 24 litres
Trained:	200 × 170 ml	= 34 litres

This is an obvious benefit because more oxygen can be delivered to the working tissues, enabling them to work harder or for longer periods of time.

The 5 litres of blood pumped out of the heart at rest is circulated around the body. The proportion of the cardiac output distributed to the particular organs is shown in Table 5.1.

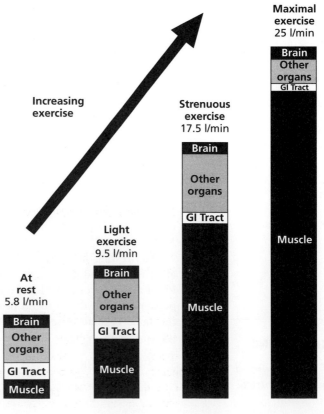

Figure 5.8 Effect of exercise on cardiac output and blood distribution

When the body starts to exercise the distribution of the blood changes. The main change is that about 85% is now channelled to the working muscles. The flow of blood to the brain is maintained, but flow to the kidneys, liver and the gastrointestinal tract decreases. The effect of exercise on the cardiac output and blood distribution may be seen in *Figure 5.8*.

ACTIVITY

Take the resting pulse of all the members of your group and discuss the amount and type of exercise that each person participates in. Is there a relationship between exercise and resting heart rate?

5.5 Control of heart rate

Heart rate is controlled by three factors:

1 neural control
2 hormonal control
3 intrinsic control.

Of these, neural control is the most important control mechanism.

5.5.1 Neural control

Figure 5.6 shows that the SA node (the pacemaker) in the wall of the right atrium is controlled by the autonomic nervous system. Two nerves stimulate this node: the *sympathetic cardiac accelerator nerve*, which speeds up the heart rate, and the *parasympathetic vagus nerve*, which slows it down.

Overall control of the two nerves is coordinated by the cardiac control centre in the medulla of the brain. The cardiac control centre is stimulated by:

● muscle receptors in the muscles and joints that stimulate the cardiac control centre at the onset of exercise
● chemoreceptors in the muscle that respond to changes in muscle chemistry, such as a rise in lactic acid
● emotional excitement
● changes in blood pressure, detected by the baroreceptors in the aorta and carotid arteries – for example a decrease in blood pressure will result in an increase in heart rate and stroke volume
● chemoreceptors in the aorta and carotid arteries that respond to changes in oxygen, carbon dioxide and pH levels.

5.5.2 Hormonal control

Adrenaline is secreted from the adrenal glands into the bloodstream and stimulates the SA node, causing an increase in heart rate. Adrenaline also increases the strength of contraction produced by the myocardium (heart muscle).

5.5.3 Intrinsic control

When any muscle gets warmer the conduction of nerve impulses seems to speed up – this is also true of heart muscle. The heart rate of a warm heart increases, and a drop in temperature reduces the heart rate. In addition, during exercise the amount of blood returning to the heart (the venous return) is increased, stretching the cardiac muscle more than usual. This stimulates the SA node and increases the heart rate – it also increases the

Definition

AUTONOMIC NERVOUS SYSTEM

The autonomic nervous system is made up of sensory nerves and motor nerves. The motor nerves are referred to as the sympathetic and parasympathetic nerves. The autonomic nervous system is under involuntary control.

force of contraction. The relationship between an increase in venous return and an increase in stroke volume is known as *Starling's law*.

5.6 Exercise and control of heart rate

The heart rate needs to increase during exercise in order to increase the supply of oxygen to working muscle and to remove waste products such as carbon dioxide and lactic acid. Before you even begin to exercise your heart rate will start to increase. This *anticipatory rise* in heart rate is caused by the release of adrenaline and the impact of emotional excitement on the medulla. As soon as exercise begins the heart rate rises rapidly, mainly due to a nerve reflex response, initiated by the muscle receptors, that stimulates the cardiac control centre. Also within the muscles chemoreceptors respond to the increase in lactic acid and other chemical changes by sending messages to the cardiac control centre to increase heart rate. As the body continues to exercise the heart muscle begins to get warmer and venous return increases, increasing the heart rate further – see above.

When you stop exercising the muscle receptors stop stimulating the cardiac control centre and the heart rate begins to fall quite rapidly. The activity of the chemoreceptors also reduces and this, combined with the reduced levels of adrenaline, the drop in venous return and the drop in body temperature returns the heart rate to normal within a matter of minutes. *Figure 5.9* shows a typical response of the heart to submaximal exercise.

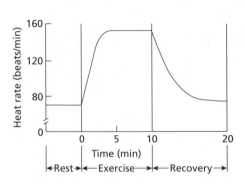

Figure 5.9 Change in heart rate with exercise

ACTIVITY

For this activity work in groups of four. You will need access to a cycle ergometer and a pulse meter. Monitor the heart rate of each subject for two minutes before the activity, for a six minute work period and for a six minute recovery period.

Subject one works at 60 r.p.m., with a constant resistance of 1.0 kg.

Subject two works at 60 r.p.m., with an initial load of 0.5 kg for two minutes, increasing to 1.0 kg after two minutes, and finishing with 1.5 kg for the third two minutes.

Subject three works at 60 r.p.m. with 1–1.5 kg, increasing to 2–3.0 kg after two minutes, and to 3–4.5 kg for the last two minutes. The choice of load will depend on the age, sex, weight and fitness of the subject. If at any time a subject becomes uncomfortable or distressed they should stop the exercise immediately.

Plot the results on to a graph and compare the heart rate response of each subject

---

The heart rate increases with an increase in workload. Initially the cardiac output increases as a result of both the heart rate and the stroke volume increasing, but maximum stroke volume is achieved during submaximal work and any increase in cardiac output during maximal exercise is solely due to an increase in heart rate. As the workload is increased the heart rate steadily rises until a maximum heart rate is reached. By this stage most of the energy is being produced anaerobically and you will soon have to stop exercising because of fatigue. If you are working submaximally your heart rate will usually rise until you reach a point where the oxygen delivered to the working muscles is sufficient to release enough energy aerobically to cope with the demands of the exercise. The heart rate will then reach a plateau. This is known as 'steady state' exercise.

ACTIVITY

Using a pulse meter to monitor your heart rate response go for a jog/run and adjust your pace so that you run at a steady state, first with a heart rate of 100 beats per minute then increasing to 120 and finally to 140. Compare your heart rate response and pace with those of other members of your group. Suggest reasons for any differences.

When you stop exercising your heart rate does not immediately return to normal but takes a number of minutes to recover. This is because you need to maintain an elevated rate of aerobic respiration in order to replenish some of the energy stores you have used during the exercise and also to remove some of the waste products that have accumulated, for example lactic acid and carbon dioxide (Figure 5.9).

Key revision box

The heart acts as two separate pumps, distributing oxygenated blood round the body. Deoxygenated blood returns to the heart via the pulmonary and systemic circulatory systems. The heart responds to the demands made on the body when exercising by increasing the heart rate and stroke volume to increase the overall cardiac output.

KEY TERMS

You should now understand the following terms. If you do not, go back through the chapter and find out.

Pericardial cavity
Myocardium
Atrioventricular node
Cardiac output
Systole
Mediastinum
Semilunar valve
Bundle of His
Stroke volume
Diastole
Atrioventricular valve
Sinuatrial node
Purkinje fibres
End-diastolic volume
Cardiac control centre

PROGRESS CHECK

1 Name the two circulatory systems.
2 Where would you find the pericardium?
3 What centre controls the heart rate and where is it situated in the body?
4 List three factors that directly affect the control centre resulting in a change of heart rate.
5 Which nerve speeds up the heart rate?
6 Describe how the wave of excitation spreads through the heart muscle.
7 Briefly describe the cardiac cycle.
8 Define 'cardiac output' and give typical values at rest and during exercise.
9 How does stroke volume affect cardiac output?
10 Where would you find the papillary muscle? What is its function?
11 List four ways in which cardiac muscle fibre differs from skeletal muscle fibre.
12 What is Starling's law?
13 What name is given to the heart's own blood supply?
14 List three factors that affect cardiac output during the first few moments of exercise and explain what they do.
15 Briefly describe the pathway of a drop of blood through the heart.
16 When someone has trained aerobically for over three months their resting pulse drops. Why?
17 Explain 'steady state' in terms of heart rate and workload.
18 How and when during the cardiac cycle are the heart sounds generated?

6

Structure and function of the vascular system

Learning objectives:

- To know the major constituents of blood.
- To describe the structure and function of the arteries, capillaries and veins.
- To know the major arteries and veins of the body.
- To describe the factors influencing venous return.
- To understand the role of the vasomotor centre in regulation of blood flow and blood pressure.
- To know how blood pressure changes within the circulatory system and what changes occur during exercise.

As mentioned in Chapter 5, the blood vessels are part of the cardiovascular system and form the body's transport network. It is essential that a sports performer has an efficient vascular system, to deliver oxygen and food supplies to the working muscles and to remove waste products such as carbon dioxide. The blood carries all the vital ingredients needed for the muscles to work and the blood vessels form a *closed circulatory network*, allowing distribution of blood to all cells.

6.1 Constituents of the blood

The blood accounts for about 8% of the total body weight. It is made up of *blood cells* and *platelets* floating in the *plasma*.

The plasma makes up 55% of the blood volume. Approximately 90% of the plasma is water. The following substances may be found dissolved in the plasma:

Salts
Glucose and fatty acids
Blood proteins
Waste products
Enzymes
Hormones
Gases such as oxygen and carbon dioxide.

The blood cells make up 45% of total blood volume. There are three types of blood cell.

Red blood cells (*erythrocytes*) are biconcave discs just small enough to pass through a capillary. These form about 95% of the blood cells. The main function of the erythrocytes is to transport oxygen and carbon dioxide round the body. They contain a protein called *haemoglobin*, which has a high affinity for carbon monoxide, carbon dioxide and oxygen. Haemoglobin is capable of carrying up to four oxygen molecules and transports 97% of the oxygen in the body (the remaining 3% is dissolved in the plasma). Oxygen is carried bound to the haemoglobin as *oxyhaemoglobin*. Haemoglobin can also carry carbon dioxide (about 20% of the carbon dioxide is transported this way, the rest is dissolved in the plasma). However, haemoglobin has highest affinity for carbon monoxide and will pick up carbon monoxide in preference to either carbon dioxide or oxygen.

White blood cells (*leukocytes*). There are five different types of leukocytes but they basically all have the same function of protecting the body from bacteria, viruses and foreign bodies.

Platelets are small cell fragments that help clot the blood.

One of the advantages of aerobic training is that the total blood volume increases (by about 8% at rest) because the amount of plasma and the number of erythrocytes increase. More erythrocytes means that more oxygen can be transported to the cells, allowing more aerobic respiration to take place. Another way of increasing the number of erythrocytes is to train at high altitude – at higher altitudes the blood oxygen levels decrease, stimulating the body to produce more erythrocytes.

6.2 Blood vessels

Five different types of blood vessels in the body link together to form the vascular system. The flow of blood around the body through these vessels is shown in *Figure 6.1*.

All blood vessels are basically a muscular wall surrounding a central *lumen*, or opening. The walls of the blood vessels (except those of the capillaries) comprise three layers (*Figure 6.2*).

The *tunica interna* forms the inner lining of the vessel. It contains endothelial cells and collagen.

The *tunica media*, or middle layer, is made up of smooth muscle and elastin fibres. The smooth muscle is stimulated by the sympathetic nerves of the autonomic nervous system.

The *tunica externa* is made up mostly of collagen with some elastin fibres. Vessel walls need to be elastic as they have to cope with large fluctuations in blood volume.

6.2.1 Arteries and arterioles

Arteries always carry blood away from the heart. The major arteries in the human body are shown in *Figure 6.3*. As the arteries branch and become smaller they eventually form arterioles. The largest arteries contain a lot of elastin fibres but as they get smaller the muscular middle layer becomes much thicker and the amount of elastin relatively less. The smaller, more muscular, arteries and the arterioles are used to control blood flow. Contraction of the smooth muscle in these vessels narrows their lumen and restricts blood flow.

6.2.2 Capillaries

The arterioles transport blood to the capillaries. The capillaries are the smallest of the blood vessels and their walls are extremely thin – the exchange of gases and nutrients takes place here. Although capillaries are small they form an extensive network, particularly around skeletal muscle, the heart and the lungs. Capillaries are so small that blood cells can only pass through one at a time. The flow of blood through the capillaries is controlled by *precapillary sphincters*. Capillaries ensure a constant supply of blood to all cells.

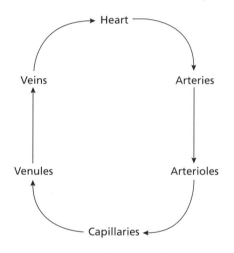

Figure 6.1 Blood flow through the vessels

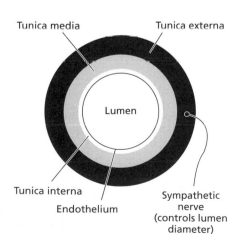

Figure 6.2 Cross-section through a blood vessel

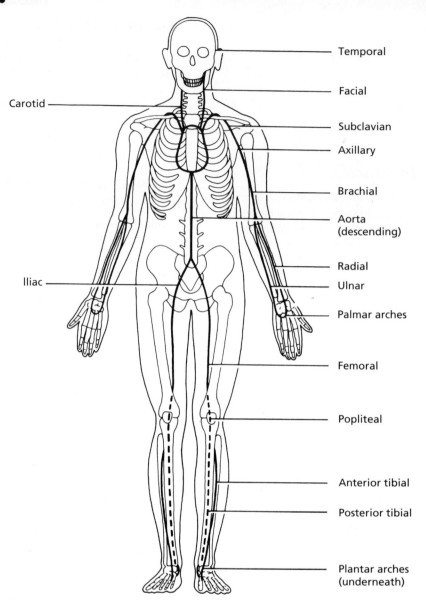

Figure 6.3 The main arteries of the human body

Labels on figure:
- Temporal
- Facial
- Carotid
- Subclavian
- Axillary
- Brachial
- Aorta (descending)
- Radial
- Ulnar
- Palmar arches
- Iliac
- Femoral
- Popliteal
- Anterior tibial
- Posterior tibial
- Plantar arches (underneath)

6.2.3 Veins and venules

Blood flows from the capillaries into the venules. As the venules decrease in number they increase in size and eventually form veins. Veins have much thinner inner and middle layers than arteries and the larger veins contain valves. These valves allow blood to flow only in one direction – back towards the heart – helping venous return.

6.3 Venous return

As we mentioned in Chapter 5, stroke volume depends on venous return. If the venous return decreases the stroke volume will decrease, reducing the overall cardiac output.

A vein has quite a large lumen and offers very little resistance to blood flow. However, by the time blood enters the veins the blood pressure is low, and active mechanisms are needed to ensure venous return.

6.3.1 The skeletal muscle pump

This is the most important mechanism of venous return. When we are moving our muscles contract, squeezing and compressing nearby veins. This

---

Definition

PRECAPILLARY SPHINCTER

A sphincter is a ring of muscle surrounding an opening. A precapillary sphincter is found between an arteriole and a capillary and can effectively open or close the capillary.

VENOUS RETURN

Flow of blood through the veins back to the heart.

action pushes the blood back towards the heart as the vein valves prevent backflow. If you have been exercising to maximum and suddenly stop without an active cool-down you may feel light-headed. This happens because during exercise much of the cardiac output has been redirected to the working muscles and when you stop one of the major ways of returning blood to the heart has also stopped. This results in blood 'pooling' in the muscles, causing a drastic drop in venous return and consequently reducing cardiac output. In extreme cases insufficient blood reaches the brain, making you dizzy and faint.

6.3.2 The respiratory pump

When air is breathed into and out of the lungs the volume of the thoracic cavity changes, creating changes in pressure. During inspiration the pressure around the abdomen increases as the diaphragm lowers to increase the volume of the thoracic cavity. This pressure squeezes the blood in the abdominal veins back towards the heart. During expiration the pressure in the thoracic region increases as the diaphragm and ribs move back to reduce the volume of the thoracic cavity. This has a similar squeezing effect on the veins.

6.3.3 The valves

Obviously the valves play an important role in venous return as they direct the flow of blood towards the heart.

Another consideration in venous return is the effect of *gravity*, especially on veins returning blood from areas above the heart.

6.4 Vasomotor control

The flow and pressure of blood are controlled by the *vasomotor centre* in the medulla of the brain. The vasomotor centre is stimulated by baroreceptors (which respond to changes in blood pressure) in the aorta and carotid arteries. Most blood vessels are stimulated by sympathetic nerves of the autonomic nervous system. Blood vessels receive a continual low-frequency impulse that is known as the *vasomotor tone*. The vasomotor centre controls this stimulus by

- increasing vasomotor tone, causing *vasoconstriction* (the lumen decreases in size, resulting in an increase in blood pressure and a reduction in blood flow) or
- decreasing vasomotor tone, causing *vasodilatation* (the lumen increases in size, resulting in a decrease in blood pressure and an increase in blood flow).

As the arterioles have a relatively thick tunica media they are responsible for most of the changes in blood flow and blood pressure.

6.4.1 The vascular shunt

During exercise the demand for oxygen from the skeletal muscles increases dramatically and more oxygenated blood must flow to them to meet this demand. The increase in stroke volume and heart rate helps to increase the overall cardiac output and therefore increases oxygen supply, but this in itself is not enough. Blood must also be redistributed so that more goes to the skeletal muscles and less to the other organs. This is known as the *vascular shunt*.

The vascular shunt involves two mechanisms:

1 Vasodilatation of the arterioles supplying the skeletal muscles increases the blood flow to them. Vasoconstriction of the arterioles supplying the

---

Definition

VASOCONSTRICTION

A decrease in the size of the lumen of a blood vessel as the smooth muscle in the tunica media contracts.

VASODILATATION

An increase in the size of the lumen of a blood vessel as the smooth muscle in the tunica media relaxes.

other organs, such as the kidneys and liver, reduces blood flow to these organs.

2   Opening of the precapillary sphincters in the capillary network supplying skeletal muscle and closure of the precapillary sphincters in the capillary networks supplying the other organs increases the flow of blood to the skeletal muscles and decreases flow to the other organs.

The net effect is to substantially increase the percentage of the cardiac output going to the muscles. *Figure 6.4* shows the flow of blood through a muscle at rest and during exercise.

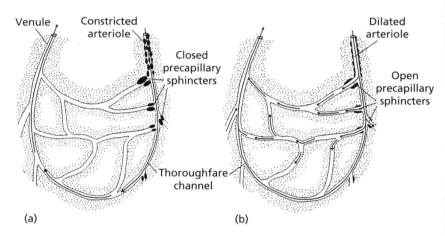

(a)   (b)

Figure 6.4   Local blood flow through skeletal muscle (a) at rest; (b) in exercising muscle

The vascular shunt mechanism doesn't only increase blood flow to working muscles. If you are involved in strenuous or prolonged periods of exercise you begin to get hot. The body's response to overheating is to dilate the blood vessels near the skin, increasing the blood flow to the skin and allowing heat to escape from the body.

6.5 Blood flow and blood pressure

Blood, like any other fluid, flows from areas of high pressure to areas of low pressure. The area of high pressure in the human body is the pressure created by contraction of the ventricles, which forces blood out of the heart into the aorta. Blood pressure is equal to blood flow × resistance. The resistance is caused by the friction between the blood and the vessel walls.

> *Definition*
>
> **BLOOD PRESSURE**
>
> *Blood pressure = blood flow × resistance.*

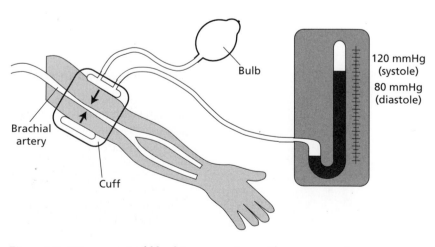

Figure 6.5   Measurement of blood pressure using a sphygmomanometer

Definition

HYPERTENSION

The clinical name given to high blood pressure.

During ventricular contraction (systole) the blood pressure at rest for a young adult is about 120 mmHg and during relaxation of the ventricles (diastole) the pressure drops to about 80 mmHg. A doctor normally uses a sphygmomanometer, shown in *Figure 6.5*, to monitor blood pressure. Blood pressure is usually quoted as systolic pressure 'over' diastolic pressure, for example '120 over 80'. Various factors (such as exercise, stress and pregnancy) can affect blood pressure and the blood pressure varies between individuals. However a resting blood pressure of 150 over 90 mmHg or above would cause concern because it is indicative of *hypertension*.

ACTIVITY

Using a sphygmomanometer and a stethoscope attempt to measure your partner's blood pressure. Place the stethoscope over the brachial artery and inflate the cuff to about 180 mmHg, then slowly decrease the pressure. As soon as you detect the sound of the blood through the stethoscope make a note of the pressure: this is the systolic blood pressure. Continue to decrease the pressure until the sound of the blood disappears: this will be the diastolic blood pressure.

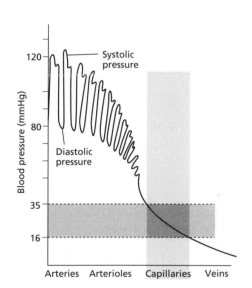

Figure 6.6 Pressure changes in the systemic circulation

As blood flows into the large arteries the blood pressure is quite high because they have relatively large lumens and offer little resistance to blood flow. When the blood reaches the arterioles the pressure drops suddenly because the resistance exerted by the vessel walls is much greater. By the time blood reaches the capillaries the blood pressure has dropped to about 35 mmHg. As the blood passes back through the venous system the pressure continues to fall, and is almost zero by the time the blood enters the right atrium (*Figure 6.6*).

The arterioles play a significant role in regulating blood pressure. By changing the diameter of the lumen (vasoconstriction or vasodilatation) of these vessels their resistance can be increased or decreased, which in turn increases or decreases the blood pressure.

6.6 Velocity of blood flow

At rest a blood cell will take about a minute to be carried round the circulatory system, but the velocity of the blood flow is far from constant as it passes from one vessel to another. The velocity of the blood flow is affected by the cross-sectional area of the blood vessels. Blood travels through the aorta at about 40 cm/s. As it travels through the smaller arteries and arterioles the *total* cross-sectional area of these vessels increases (although the cross-sectional area of the individual vessels decreases, there are a great many of them), decreasing the velocity of the blood. The greatest *total* cross-sectional area is found in the capillary network as there are so many capillaries. In the capillary network the velocity of the blood is only 0.1 cm/s, slow enough to allow exchange of gases, nutrients and waste products. The blood then flows back through the venules and veins, where the *total* cross-sectional area decreases, resulting in an increase in velocity. The relationship between blood velocity and total cross-sectional area of the vessels is shown graphically in *Figure 6.7*.

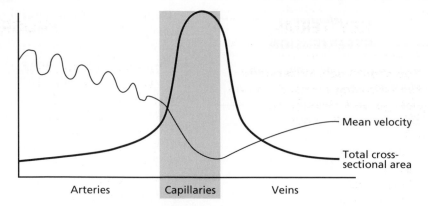

Mean velocity

Total cross-sectional area

Arteries Capillaries Veins

Figure 6.7 The velocity of blood flow varies inversely with the total cross-sectional area of the vessel

6.7 Effects of exercise on blood pressure and blood volume

Overall, systolic blood pressure tends to increase during exercise. The vasodilatation that occurs in skeletal muscle causes a drop in blood pressure because of the decrease in resistance, but the cardiac output increases significantly and negates the effect of this vasodilatation. During exercise there is very little change in diastolic pressure; diastolic pressure only increases during isometric work because of the resistance to blood flow caused by the contracting muscle.

After a period of exercise it is much better to perform a series of cooling-down activities rather than to stop abruptly. If you do stop suddenly the blood 'pools' in the working muscles, causing a dramatic drop in blood pressure.

Blood volume can change during exercise, but whether it increases or decreases depends on the type of activity and the fitness of the individual. A decrease in volume is mostly caused by plasma moving out of the capillaries into the surrounding tissues. This increases the viscosity of the blood and therefore increases the peripheral resistance. After a period of aerobic training the usual trend identified is an increase in blood volume. This is of great benefit to athletes as it increases their capacity to carry oxygen.

Key revision box

Five different types of vessel form the closed circulatory network that distributes blood to all cells. The distribution of the cardiac output is controlled by the vasomotor centre and is achieved by altering the flow and pressure of the blood. This is mainly brought about by opening or closing of the arterioles and the precapillary sphincters.

KEY TERMS

You should now understand the following terms. If you do not, go back through the chapter and find out.

Arteries
Veins
Capillaries
Haemoglobin
Erythrocyte
Leukocyte
Vasodilatation
Sphygmomanometer
Lumen
Vasoconstriction
Venous return
Vasomotor tone
Blood pressure
Precapillary sphincter
Vascular shunt

PROGRESS CHECK

1 Describe how the different blood vessels link together to form the circulatory system.
2 Give one structural and one functional difference between arteries, capillaries and veins.
3 What is the role of haemoglobin?
4 What is meant by venous return?
5 Describe three factors that help maintain venous return.
6 What is the average resting blood pressure?
7 What happens to blood pressure when you start to exercise?
8 If you have a heart problem, or suffer from high blood pressure, what kind of exercise should you avoid?
9 Why does the velocity of the blood change as it passes through the vascular system?
10 Which vessel is mostly responsible for the control of blood flow and blood pressure?
11 What is a precapillary sphincter and what function does it perform?
12 How does smoking affect your capacity for transporting oxygen?
13 Why is it important to perform cooling-down exercises?
14 Name the three layers that form the wall of a blood vessel.
15 What is one of the effects of training at high altitude?
16 What is the function of the vasomotor centre?
17 During exercise a lot more blood is distributed to the working muscles. How is this achieved?

CHAPTER 7

The respiratory system

Learning objectives:

- To be able to describe the structures of the respiratory system.
- To understand the process of respiration.
- To describe and explain the mechanics of breathing, both at rest and during exercise.
- To know the definitions and capacities of the pulmonary volumes and how these volumes change with exercise.
- To be able to describe the control mechanisms of the respiratory system.

In order to stay alive, we need an adequate supply of oxygen. We use oxygen to break down food to release energy and produce carbon dioxide as a waste product. We need to continually take in oxygen from the air and expel carbon dioxide into the air. This process of exchanging gases is known as *respiration*.

External respiration is the exchange of respiratory gases (oxygen and carbon dioxide) between the lungs and the blood.

Internal respiration is the exchange of respiratory gases between the blood and the tissues.

'Respiration' is also used to describe the process occurring in the mitochondria that uses oxygen to produce ATP. This is usually referred to as *cellular respiration*.

7.1 Structure of the respiratory system

Air taken from the atmosphere passes through several structures before it reaches the bloodstream (*Figure 7.1*).

7.1.1 The nose

Air enters the body through the nose where hairs and mucus help to filter it. The air is also warmed.

7.1.2 The pharynx

Air passes from the nose into the pharynx. Both food and air pass through the pharynx. At the bottom of the pharynx air is directed through the larynx and food is directed down the oesophagus.

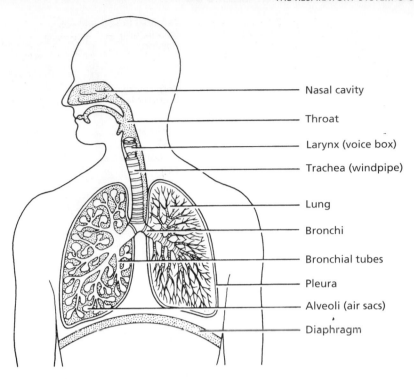

Figure 7.1 Respiratory structures

7.1.3 The larynx

The larynx is commonly known as the 'voice box' as it contains the vocal folds. A flap of elastic cartilage, the *epiglottis*, covers the opening of the larynx during swallowing and prevents food entering the lungs.

7.1.4 The trachea

The trachea (or windpipe) is just over 10 cm long and is kept open and protected by C-shaped pieces of cartilage. The trachea is lined with mucus-secreting and ciliated cells. These cells remove foreign particles by pushing them back up towards the larynx. The trachea divides at the bottom to form the left and right bronchi.

7.1.5 Bronchi

The right bronchus enters the right lung and the left bronchus enters the left lung. From there the bronchi subdivide to form smaller branches called bronchioles. This structure is known as the *bronchial tree* and carries the air deep into the lungs.

7.1.6 Bronchioles

The walls of the bronchioles, unlike those of the bronchi, are not reinforced with cartilage but do contain smooth muscle. When this smooth muscle contracts, as occurs during an asthma attack, it can create severe breathing difficulties. The bronchioles continue to divide, forming *terminal bronchioles* that supply each lobule of the lungs. The terminal bronchioles merge into *respiratory bronchioles* that lead to alveolar air sacs, which contain the alveoli (*Figure 7.2*).

Definition

LOBULE

Lobules are subdivisions of each lobe of the lung and contain terminal and respiratory bronchioles, alveoli and blood vessels. They are enveloped in sheets of elastic connective tissue.

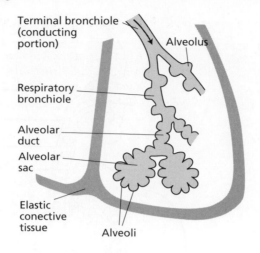

Figure 7.2 *Bronchioles within the lungs*

7.1.7 Alveoli

The alveoli are minute air-filled sacs. There are approximately 300 million alveoli in the lungs, providing a total surface area similar to that of a tennis court. The walls of the alveoli are extremely thin and are surrounded by capillaries. External respiration takes place here.

ACTIVITY

Rearrange the following terms so that they correctly show the passage of air from the atmosphere to the alveoli:

alveolar air sacs, trachea, nose, terminal bronchiole, epiglottis, pharynx, respiratory bronchiole, larynx, bronchi, alveoli

---

7.2 The lungs

The two lungs lie in the thoracic cavity. The right lung has three lobes and the left lung two. The heart nestles between the lungs in the mediastinum. Each lobe of a lung is further divided into lobules, which are completely separate units.

Each lung is surrounded by a serous membrane, known as the *pleural membrane*, which lines the *pleural cavity*. The outer layer of the membrane is called the *parietal pleura* and is attached to the wall of the thoracic cavity. The inner layer is known as the *visceral pleura* and covers the lungs.

The pleural cavity contains *pleural fluid*, which holds the two membranes together and acts as a lubricant, reducing friction.

The lower part of the lung is bordered by the *diaphragm*, which separates the thoracic cavity from the abdominal cavity. The diaphragm is a sheet of skeletal muscle and plays an important role in the mechanics of breathing.

The lungs receive deoxygenated blood from the heart via the right and left pulmonary arteries and return oxygenated blood to the heart via the pulmonary veins. The lung's own supply of oxygenated blood is delivered by the bronchial artery.

Definition
SEROUS MEMBRANE

Serous membrane forms the lining of cavities within the body and secretes serous fluid.

In practice

The response of the breathing mechanism to exercise is very similar to the heart rate response (see Chapter 5).

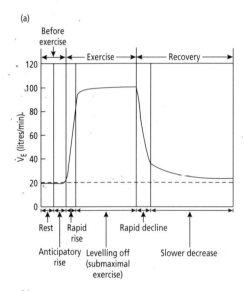

(a)

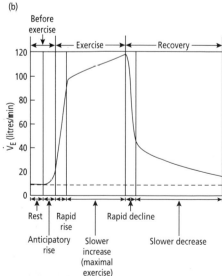

(b)

Figure 7.3 The changes in ventilation rate during (a) submaximal and (b) maximal exercise

7.3 Pulmonary ventilation

Movement of air into and out of the lungs is known as *pulmonary ventilation*. Taking air into the lungs is called *inspiration* and moving air out of the lungs is called *expiration*. The amount of air moved per minute (the *minute ventilation*, $\dot{V}_E$) varies, depending on the amount of work being performed. As more work is done more energy is required, increasing the demand for oxygen, and so the rate of pulmonary ventilation increases.

At rest, the average rate of breathing is 12–15 breaths per minute and the average amount of air taken in or out per breath (the tidal volume) is 0.5 litres, giving a minute ventilation of 6–7.5 litres per minute.

$$\dot{V}_E = \text{Frequency} \times \text{Tidal volume}$$

At rest,

$$\dot{V}_E = 12 \times 0.5$$
$$= 6 \text{ litres.}$$

ACTIVITY

Working in pairs, count how many breaths your partner takes in a minute. Why is it difficult to count your own rate of breathing and what does this imply about the breathing mechanism?

During strenuous exercise the volume of air breathed increases dramatically – up to 180 litres is not uncommon for male athletes. This increase is achieved by increasing the rate and depth of breathing. For example

$$\dot{V}_E = \text{Frequency} \times \text{Tidal volume}$$
$$= 45 \times 3.5$$
$$= 157.5 \text{ litres}$$

ACTIVITY

Complete as many sit-ups as you can in a minute. Get your partner to count the number of breaths you take in one minute after completing your exercise. Continue to monitor your rate of breathing until it returns to normal.

As with the heart, there is an *anticipatory rise* in ventilation rate, followed by a steep increase and a plateau (during steady-state exercise) or a steady increase to maximum (during maximal exercise). Recovery after exercise shows a substantial initial drop then a gradual levelling off to normal ventilation rates (*Figure 7.3*).

7.4 The mechanics of breathing

In order for air to move into the lungs the pressure of air within the lungs must be lower than the pressure of air within the atmosphere. The greater the pressure difference is, the faster the air will flow into the lungs. This is because air always moves from an area of high pressure to an area of low pressure. By changing the volume of your thoracic cavity you can alter the pressure of air in your lungs. Reducing the volume will increase the pressure within the alveoli; increasing it will decrease the pressure within the alveoli. The muscles involved in ventilation are shown in *Figure 7.4*.

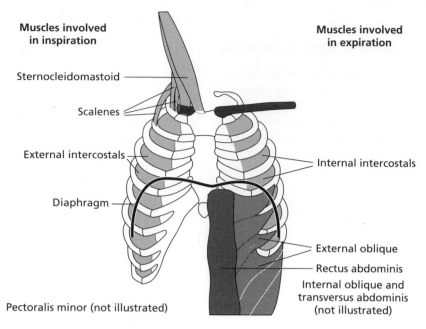

Muscles involved
in inspiration

Muscles involved
in expiration

Sternocleidomastoid

Scalenes

External intercostals

Internal intercostals

Diaphragm

External oblique

Rectus abdominis

Internal oblique and
transversus abdominis
(not illustrated)

Pectoralis minor (not illustrated)

Figure 7.4 The muscles involved in ventilation

7.4.1 Inspiration

During inspiration the volume of the thoracic cavity must be increased so that the pressure of air within the lungs is lowered. The pressure of atmospheric air is about 100 kPa (760 mmHg) and during inspiration the pressure within the alveoli is lowered to 99.74 kPa (758 mmHg), causing air to move into the lungs.

During quiet inspiration reduction of pressure in the thorax is achieved in part by contraction of the diaphragm. Usually dome-shaped, the diaphragm flattens during contraction, increasing the volume of the thoracic cavity. At the same time the external *intercostal muscles* contract, pulling the ribs upwards and outwards and helping to increase the volume of the thoracic cavity.

When exercising three more inspiratory muscles are involved as the rate and depth of breathing increases. *Sternocleidomastoid* lifts the sternum and *scalenes* and *pectoralis minor* both help to further elevate the ribs. As the parietal pleura is attached to the wall of the thoracic cavity and the visceral pleura is attached to the lung tissue, the lung tissue is stretched as the thoracic cavity increases in size.

7.4.2 Expiration

During quiet breathing expiration is passive. The diaphragm and external intercostal muscles relax, reducing the volume of the thoracic cavity and the lung tissue recoils to its normal position. This increases the pressure

Table 7.1 Summary of the muscles used in ventilation

Ventilation phase	Muscles used in quiet breathing	Muscles used in laboured breathing
Inspiration	Diaphragm, external intercostals	Diaphragm, external intercostals, sterno-cleidomastoid, scalenes, pectoralis minor
Expiration	Passive	Internal intercostals, abdominals

within the alveoli so that it exceeds atmospheric pressure and forces air out of the lungs.

When exercising expiration becomes active as air has to be forced out of the lungs quickly and effectively. The internal intercostal muscles help pull the ribs back downwards and inwards and the abdominal muscles contract helping to push the diaphragm back upwards. The net result of this is to reduce the volume of the thoracic cavity.

7.5 Respiratory volume

If you breathe normally for a few seconds and then at the end of expiration try to force more air out of your lungs, you will find you are able to breathe out a lot more air. Equally, if you breathe in normally and then continue to inhale as much air as possible you can take in considerably more air. This suggests that we have a 'working' volume of air that we ventilate normally, with a reserve volume available if we need it. This allows a great deal of flexibility in the amount of exercise we can perform, as we have the capacity to increase our ventilation in line with the increase in demand for oxygen. A normal healthy individual can easily ventilate more than enough air for any activity; the limiting factor is the amount of oxygen we can actually transport and use.

Several lung volumes have been identified (Table 7.2) using a spirometer to measure them (*Figure 7.5*). *Figure 7.6* shows an example of the trace that a spirometer produces. Lung volumes are measured in litres, ml or dm^3.

Table 7.2 Lung volumes

Volume	Resting value (ml/dm³)	Definition
Tidal volume	500/0.5	The amount of air breathed in or out of the lungs in one breath
Inspiratory reserve volume	3100/3.1	The amount of air that can be forcibly inspired in addition to the tidal volume
Expiratory reserve volume	1200/1.2	The amount of air that can be forcibly expired in addition to the tidal volume
Vital capacity	4800/4.8	The maximum amount of air that can be forcibly exhaled after breathing in as much as possible
Residual volume	1200/1.2	Even after maximal expiration there is always some air left in the lungs to prevent them from collapsing
Total lung capacity	6000/6.0	The vital capacity plus the residual volume

Lung volumes differ with age, sex, body frame and aerobic fitness – but, as already mentioned, in most cases pulmonary ventilation is not a limiting factor in sporting performance.

To summarise,

Vital capacity	= Tidal volume + Inspiratory reserve + Expiratory reserve

Total lung capacity	= Residual volume + Vital capacity

61

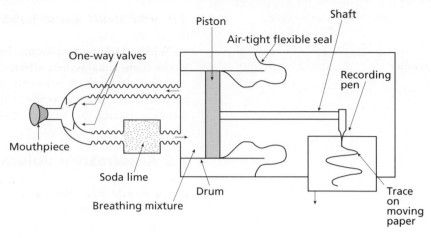

Figure 7.5 Use of a spirometer

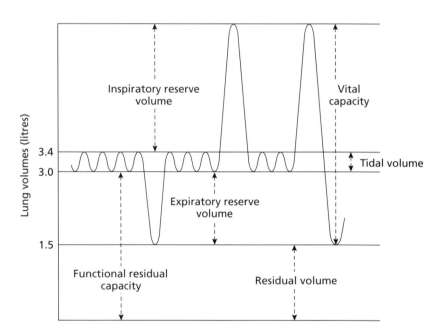

Figure 7.6 Spirometer tracing, showing the main lung volumes of a normal adult male

In practice

When you start to exercise, your 'working' volume (tidal volume) increases at the expense of your inspiratory reserve volume and your expiratory reserve volume, which decrease. You only rarely use your full vital capacity – for example, when taking a deep breath before swimming under water. Your tidal volume is usually increased in conjunction with an increase in breathing rate – it is not efficient to take fewer breaths and breathe to capacity.

ACTIVITY

● If, when you are resting, you inspire 500 ml and inhale every six seconds,
● if, when you forcibly exhale to a maximum having just breathed out, you blow out another 1850 ml,
● if, when you fill your lungs to capacity and breathe out as much as you can, you exhale 4300 ml,

what would be your

1 vital capacity
2 inspiratory reserve volume
3 expiratory reserve volume
4 minute ventilation?

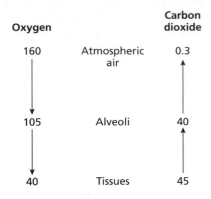

Partial pressure (mmHg) in:

Oxygen		Carbon dioxide
160	Atmospheric air	0.3
105	Alveoli	40
40	Tissues	45

Figure 7.7 Summary of the movement of gases during external respiration

---

7.6 External respiration

So far we have looked at how air is moved in and out of the lungs but we now need to consider what gaseous exchange happens at the lung's surface.

Gases flow from an area of high pressure to an area of low pressure. The term *partial pressure* is often used when describing the process of respiration: this refers to the pressure that a particular gas exerts within a mixture of gases and is linked to the concentration of the gas and the barometric pressure. At sea level the barometric pressure of air is 760 mmHg. Oxygen makes up 21% of air so oxygen in the atmosphere exerts a partial pressure of roughly 160 mmHg (21% of 760). By the time air reaches the alveoli the partial pressure of the oxygen has reduced to only 105 mmHg, but the partial pressure of oxygen in the alveoli is significantly higher than the partial pressure of the oxygen in the blood vessel surrounding the lungs, which is only 40 mmHg. This is because oxygen has been removed by the tissues so its concentration in the blood is lower, and its partial pressure is lower. The difference between the two pressures (105 – 40) is known as the *concentration gradient* or *diffusion gradient*. Oxygen will move from the area of higher pressure to the area of lower pressure (down the diffusion gradient) until there is a state of equilibrium. The greater the diffusion gradient is, the faster the diffusion will take place.

In the same way, carbon dioxide diffuses from the capillaries into the alveoli. The partial pressure of carbon dioxide in the alveoli is only 40 mmHg but it is 45 mmHg in the capillaries. Therefore carbon dioxide flows into the air in the alveoli and is expired.

A summary of the movement of the respiratory gases is given in *Figure 7.7*.

7.7 Internal respiration

The process described in the last section is reversed at the tissues because the cell is continuously using oxygen to produce ATP. This means that the partial pressure of oxygen is lower in the tissues than in the blood so it diffuses into the cell. At the same time, carbon dioxide is being continuously produced by the cell. This results in a higher partial pressure of carbon dioxide within the cell than in the blood, so it diffuses into the blood.

The lungs are designed to ensure that gaseous exchange takes place as quickly and effectively as possible. The most significant factor in terms of diffusion is the difference in the partial pressures of the gases, but the following factors all contribute to the efficiency of the process:

● the respiratory membrane is extremely thin
● the length of the diffusion path is very short
● the total surface area available for diffusion is very large.

7.8 Transport of respiratory gases

7.8.1 Oxygen

Oxygen diffuses into the capillaries, where 3% dissolves in plasma and about 97% combines with haemoglobin to form oxyhaemoglobin (see Chapter 6). Haemoglobin, when fully saturated, can carry four oxygen molecules and this easily happens at sea level where the pressure gradient between the alveoli and the blood is high. At the tissues the oxygen dissociates from the haemoglobin because of the relatively low pressure of oxygen in the tissues.

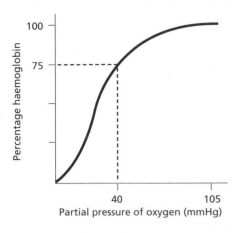

Figure 7.8 The oxyhaemoglobin dissociation curve, at 38°C and pH 7.4

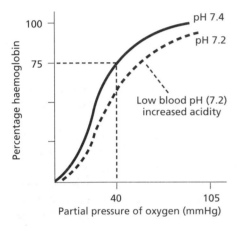

Figure 7.9 Effect of pH on haemoglobin saturation – the Bohr effect

7.8.2 Carbon dioxide

Carbon dioxide is transported one of three ways: 7% dissolves in plasma and 23% combines with haemoglobin. The remaining 70% dissolves in water to form carbonic acid. In the plasma this dissociates to hydrogen ions and bicarbonate ions.

7.8.3 Haemoglobin saturation

The relationship between oxygen and haemoglobin is often represented by the *oxyhaemoglobin dissociation curve* (*Figure 7.8*). The level of saturation of oxygen to the haemoglobin is affected by several factors.

● The *partial pressure of oxygen* influences the saturation of haemoglobin with oxygen. The partial pressure of oxygen at sea level is always high enough for full saturation of haemoglobin in the lungs. When the blood arrives at the tissues the partial pressure of oxygen drops, causing the oxygen to dissociate from the haemoglobin and diffuse into the cell. At high altitude the change in barometric pressure causes the partial pressure of oxygen to drop. This means that the haemoglobin is not fully saturated at the lungs and the oxygen carrying capacity of the blood is decreased. This can cause an athlete working at altitude problems.

● As *body temperature* increases the oxygen dissociates more easily from the haemoglobin.

● The *partial pressure of carbon dioxide*. As this increases the dissociation of oxygen from haemoglobin increases. During exercise the amount of carbon dioxide produced by the cells increases, which helps to increase the diffusion of much-needed oxygen into the cell.

● *Change in pH*. As more carbon dioxide is produced the concentration of hydrogen ions in the blood increases, lowering the pH. A drop in pH causes oxygen to dissociate more easily – this is known as the *Bohr effect* and is shown in *Figure 7.9*.

A combination of these factors means that as we start to exercise the rate of diffusion of oxygen into the cells accelerates and helps to maintain a good supply of oxygen to the working tissues.

7.9 Control of breathing

Two factors are involved in the control of breathing:

● neural control and
● chemical control.

7.9.1 Neural control

The respiratory centre in the medulla of the brain controls breathing. This centre is made up of three areas.

The rhythmicity area is responsible for the rhythmic cycle of inspiration and expiration.

The pneumotaxic area stimulates the rhythmicity area to alter the rate of breathing.

The apneustic area stimulates the rhythmicity area to alter the depth of breathing.

Neural control of breathing is summarised in *Figure 7.10*. In most circumstances the nervous regulation of breathing is involuntary. The respiratory centre sends out nerve impulses via the phrenic and intercostal

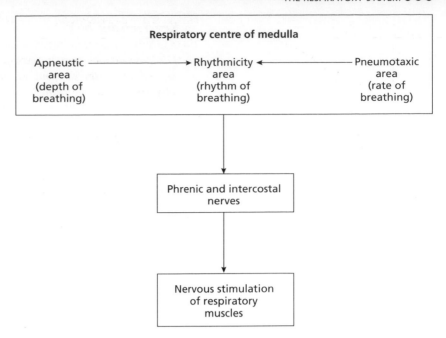

Figure 7.10 Neuronal control of breathing

nerves to the respiratory muscles. The muscles are stimulated for a short period, causing inspiration. Then, when the stimulus stops, expiration occurs.

The respiratory centre responds mainly to changes in the chemistry and temperature of the blood. The most significant factor is an increase in hydrogen ions in the blood (lowering of blood pH), which occurs when the amount of carbon dioxide being produced by the cells increases. This increase is detected by the respiratory centre and results in an increase in the rate and depth of breathing. A rise in body temperature will cause an increase in the rate of breathing but does not affect the depth of breathing.

Other factors influencing neural control of breathing include

● A large drop in oxygen tension. This is monitored by the chemoreceptors in the aorta and carotid arteries and results in an increase in the rate and depth of breathing.
● A rise in blood pressure, monitored by the baroreceptors in the aorta and carotid arteries, results in a decrease in ventilation rate.
● Proprioceptors in the muscles responding to movement stimulate the respiratory centre, increasing the rate and depth of breathing.
● The respiratory centre can also be affected by higher centres in the brain, for example emotional influences.

The lungs have a safety mechanism to make sure that they are never over-inflated. Stretch receptors located in the walls of the bronchi and bronchioles respond during excessive respiration by sending messages to the respiratory centre to inhibit inspiration. This is known as the *Hering-Breuer* reflex.

The response of the respiratory system to exercise should never really be considered in isolation – if a change occurs in the respiratory system then similar changes usually occur in the cardiac and vascular systems. For example, an increase in blood temperature will cause an increase in heart rate, an increase in ventilation and dilatation of the vessels supplying the skin and working muscles. The response of all three systems is coordinated to ensure efficient delivery of oxygen and removal of carbon dioxide and other waste products.

Key revision box

The amount of air required by the body varies considerably, depending on the amount of oxygen used by the cells. This is why we have a 'working' volume of air (tidal volume) plus a reserve volume available (inspiratory and expiratory reserve volumes). The respiratory control centre works in conjunction with the cardiac control centre and the vasomotor control centre to ensure a coordinated response to oxygen demand and delivery.

KEY TERMS

You should now understand the following terms. If you do not, go back through the chapter and find out.

External respiration
Internal respiration
Pulmonary ventilation
Alveoli
Minute ventilation
Pleural membrane
Inspiratory reserve volume
Tidal volume
Expiratory reserve volume
Partial pressure
Diffusion gradient
Bohr effect
Vital capacity
Respiratory centre

PROGRESS CHECK

1 Define respiration.
2 List the respiratory structures that air passes through from the nose to the alveoli.
3 How is air filtered?
4 Define pulmonary ventilation.
5 What is the relationship between minute ventilation, respiratory frequency and tidal volume?
6 What happens to minute ventilation during exercise?
7 Draw a graph to show the response of the respiratory system to ten minutes of submaximal exercise followed by a five-minute recovery period.
8 How does the movement of the ribs and diaphragm affect the volume of the thoracic cavity?
9 Which inspiratory muscles are used only during laboured breathing?
10 Describe the pressure changes that cause air to move into and out of the lungs.
11 What is meant by the term partial pressure?
12 List the ways that oxygen and carbon dioxide are transported in the blood.
13 What factors influence the oxygen saturation of haemoglobin?
14 Explain what is meant by the Bohr effect and describe what effect it has on the transport of oxygen during exercise.
15 How is respiration regulated during exercise?
16 Define tidal volume, inspiratory reserve volume and expiratory reserve volume.
17 What effect does exercise have on these three volumes?
18 Complete the following equation:

   Tidal volume + Inspiratory volume + Expiratory reserve = ?

Further reading

Glen F. Bastian. *An Illustrated Review of Anatomy and Physiology.* 1: The Skeletal and Muscular Systems. 2: The Cardiovascular System. 3: The Respiratory System. Harper Collins College Publishers, 1994.

R.J. Davis, C.R. Bull, J.V. Roscoe and D.A. Roscoe. *Physical Education and the Study of Sport.* Wolfe Medical Publishers, 1991.

D. Davis, T. Kimmet and M. Auty. *Physical Education: Theory and Practice.* Macmillan, Australia, 1986.

E. Fox, R. Bowen and M. Foss. *The Physiological Basis for Exercise and Sport.* Brown and Benchmark, 1989.

W. Kapit and L.M. Elson. *The Anatomy Colouring Book.* Harper Collins College Publishers, 1993.

David R. Lamb. *Physiology of Exercise, Responses and Adaptations.* Collier Macmillan Publishers, 1984.

H.G.Q. Rowett. *Basic Anatomy and Physiology.* John Murray, 1975.

R.R. Seeley, T.D. Stephens and P. Tate. *Essentials of Anatomy and Physiology.* Mosby Year Book Publishers, 1995.

Clem W. Thompson. *Manual of Structural Kinesiology.* Times Mirror/Mosby College Publishing, 1989.

Peter Walder. *Mechanics and Sport Performance.* Feltham Press, 1994.

R. Wirhed. *Athletic Ability and the Anatomy of Motion.* Wolfe Medical Publishers, 1989.

2

Exercise physiology

This part of the book contains:

Chapter 8   Energy

Chapter 9   Energy and exercise

Chapter 10   The recovery process

Chapter 11   Physical fitness

Chapter 12   Training: theory and practice

Chapter 13   Response to exercise

Whereas anatomy, biomechanics and physiology look at the structure and function of the human body, exercise physiology concentrates on the response of the body to exercise. In recent years this area of study has become very popular as teachers and coaches realise the benefits of a more scientific approach to exercise and training. As a consequence of today's increasingly sedentary lifestyles most people are extremely unfit. A knowledge of exercise physiology gives an understanding of the physiological benefits of exercise that can be applied to develop a healthier lifestyle and to significantly improve sporting performance.

Energy

Learning objectives:

- To understand the terms energy, work and power.
- To understand the role of ATP in energy production.
- To be able to describe the three methods of ATP production.

The body needs a constant supply of energy in order to perform everyday tasks such as respiration and digestion. When we start to exercise the rate at which our body uses energy increases and the efficiency of the energy supply is one of the major factors determining athletic performance. Production of energy for physical activity has to be able to cope with extreme situations – for example, during a 100 m sprint large amounts of energy are needed very quickly but during a marathon the energy must be made available over a prolonged period of time. Some people are physiologically better suited to certain activities than others because their bodies are more efficient at releasing energy in a particular way.

Energy is the capacity or ability to perform work, and is measured in joules or calories.

The more weight-conscious of us avidly study food labels to see how many calories food contains. Basically, the more calories food contains the more exercise we have to perform to burn off the energy provided. If you don't use the energy it is stored until it is required and you put on weight. We are all familiar with this process of energy exchange, but not so familiar with the more technical terms: food (*chemical* energy) is converted into movement (*kinetic* energy) or is stored as *potential* energy.

Work is defined as force × distance, but can be measured in the same units as energy (calories or joules). In most cases the force is equal to the performer's body weight, so if you ran 1500 m you would perform more work and would therefore use up more energy than if you ran 800 m. If two performers run 1500 m, but one is running twice as fast as the other, then the quicker of the two athletes is working harder and is exerting more power. *Power* is work performed per unit of time and is measured in watts.

The way energy is released in the body is quite complicated and in this chapter we give only a very simplified overview of the processes involved. Further reading is suggested at the end of Part two. There is only one usable form of energy in the body – *adenosine triphosphate* (ATP). All sources of energy, found in the food that we eat, have to be converted into ATP before the potential energy in them can be used.

ATP is a high-energy phosphate compound made up of one molecule of adenosine and three phosphates. The bonds that hold the compound together are a source of quite a lot of potential energy.

Definition

ELEMENT

An element is a simple substance that cannot be chemically split any further, such as oxygen or carbon.

COMPOUND

A group of elements combined together form a compound, for example carbon dioxide.

MOLECULE

A molecule is a small group of atoms with at least one atom from each element of the compound.

Definition

ENZYME

An enzyme is a biological catalyst which acts to bring about a specific reaction.

In practice

Most of the energy in the body is released as heat energy, which is why we get so hot when we exercise.

In practice

Movements that are fast and powerful rely on the alactic energy system as the predominant method of ATP resynthesis.

ATP = Adenosine–phosphate–phosphate–phosphate

When a compound is broken down (the bonds between the molecules are broken), then energy is released. A reaction that releases energy is known as an *exothermic reaction*. In the body a specific *enzyme* is used to break down a particular compound – the enzyme used to break down ATP is ATPase. ATP is broken down to adenosine diphosphate (ADP) and free phosphate (P), releasing the stored energy:

ATP → ADP + P + **Energy**

When a compound is built up (or synthesised) energy is needed to restore the bonds between the molecules. A reaction that needs energy to work is known as an *endothermic reaction*. Production of ATP from ADP and P is an endothermic reaction:

ADP + P + **Energy** → ATP

The energy released from the breakdown of ATP to ADP and P is converted to kinetic and heat energy.

Once the energy produced from the breakdown of ATP has been used we have a potential problem – what do we do when all the ATP has been broken down to ADP? Energy needs to be put back, in the form of an endothermic reaction, to reform ATP. There are three ways that this is achieved in the human body.

1 The phosphocreatine system (ATP/PC) or alactic system.
2 The lactic acid system or glycolysis.
3 The aerobic process.

As we cannot afford to run out of ATP all three methods take place very quickly. Each method is good at supplying energy for particular energy demands and duration, allowing us to cope with a variety of situations.

Systems 1 and 2 are anaerobic processes: they take place without oxygen. System 3 is aerobic: it requires oxygen to work.

8.1 Production of ATP by the phosphocreatine or alactic system

Phosphocreatine (PC) is a high-energy phosphate compound that is found in limited amounts in the sarcoplasm (muscle's equivalent to cytoplasm – see Chapter 3). Potential energy is stored in the bonds of the compound and when the enzyme *creatine kinase* breaks down the phosphocreatine to phosphate and creatine energy is released:

Phosphocreatine → P + Creatine + **Energy**

Creatine kinase is activated when the level of ADP within the muscle cell increases, when our stores of ATP start to diminish. The energy released by the breakdown of PC is used to convert ADP to ATP. The energy has to be liberated by the breakdown of PC before ATP can be formed. This is known as a *coupled reaction*. For every molecule of PC broken down sufficient energy is released to produce one molecule of ATP.

The stores of PC in the muscles are enough to sustain all out-effort for about ten seconds, which doesn't really seem very long. However, this is the only system that is capable of producing ATP quickly enough when we are performing activities that demand large amounts of energy over a short period of time, for example a short sprint or a triple jump.

This is because PC is a relatively simple compound that is very easy to break down. Breakdown of PC does not rely on the availability of oxygen and as PC is stored in the muscle cell it is readily accessible as an energy source. This means that energy for ATP synthesis can be obtained extremely quickly from PC and no fatiguing byproducts are released.

A javelin thrower relies on the alactic energy system

Definition

GLYCOGEN

A complex chain made up of a number of glucose molecules. It is used as energy storage in muscles and liver.

ACTIVITY

Using a team game of your choice identify three situations where you think that you would rely predominantly on the alactic system as a source of energy.

8.2 ATP production by the lactic acid system or glycolysis

This system is also an anaerobic process taking place in the sarcoplasm, but the energy needed comes from the food we eat. This process involves the *partial* breakdown of glucose – glucose can only be fully broken down in the presence of oxygen. The lactic acid system is sometimes called *anaerobic glycolysis*, as 'glycolysis' simply means the breakdown of glucose. Carbohydrate in the diet is digested to glucose, enters the bloodstream and travels to the muscles and the liver. Glucose is stored in the muscles and liver as *glycogen*.

Glycogen (chemical formula $(C_6H_{12}O_6)_n$, where n can be a very large number) is a much more complex compound than phosphocreatine and therefore stores more energy. Glycogen is broken down into glucose molecules (chemical formula $C_6H_{12}O_6$) by the enzyme *glycogen phosphorylase* and these glucose molecules are then broken down to produce the energy to make ATP. Glucose is broken down anaerobically (basically by breaking the molecule in half) by the enzyme *phosphofructokinase*. Phosphofructokinase is activated by a drop in the level of phosphocreatine and by increased levels of calcium (remember that calcium is secreted from the sarcoplasmic reticulum during muscle contraction – see Chapter 3). The glucose is broken down to two molecules of *pyruvic acid*. Then, because of the absence of oxygen, *lactic acid* is formed from the pyruvic acid (see *Figure 8.1*).

Breakdown of the bonds in glucose releases energy, which is used to synthesise ATP (two molecules of ATP for each molecule of glucose). This is another example of a coupled reaction. It should be remembered that the basic 'ingredients' of each compound are the same: we start off with a large compound containing carbon, hydrogen and oxygen and gradually break it into smaller compounds containing carbon, hydrogen and oxygen,

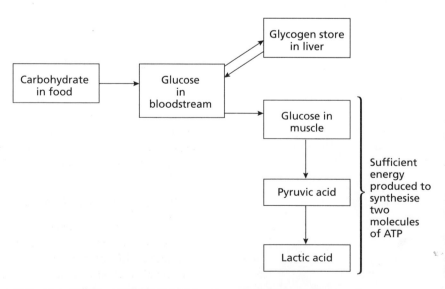

Figure 8.1 Outline of the lactic acid system of production of energy for resynthesising ATP

so that as much of the potential energy stored in the original compound as possible is released for ATP synthesis.

The lactic acid system takes longer to produce energy than the ATP/PC system because more reactions have to take place, but it is still a very quick process. Usually this method supplies energy for high-intensity activities for about a minute but it can last longer depending on the intensity of the activity.

The 400 m race is a good example of the possible effects of using this system to the maximum. If an inexperienced runner sets off too quickly, they will start to burn out or tie up before they finish. This is because when glycogen is broken down anaerobically lactic acid is produced. If the lactic acid accumulates it lowers the pH and the drop in pH directly affects the action of phosphofructokinase and also the lipoprotein lipase that breaks down fat, so the body's ability to synthesise ATP is temporarily reduced, causing fatigue.

In practice

A good example of an activity where glucose from glycogen is predominantly used for ATP resynthesis is a 400 metre race.

ACTIVITY

Using a team game of your choice identify three situations in which you think that you would rely predominantly on the lactic acid system for energy.

8.3 Production of ATP using the aerobic system

The aerobic system of energy production needs oxygen and, although oxygen is available at the onset of exercise, there isn't enough to break down food fuels at a rate that matches the breakdown of ATP, so for immediate energy production the two anaerobic systems are used. However, as soon as we start to exercise our heart rate and rate of ventilation increase and our vascular system distributes more oxygenated blood to the working muscles. Within 1–2 minutes the muscles are being supplied with enough oxygen to allow effective aerobic respiration.

The aerobic system has three stages in which glucose is broken down to carbon dioxide and water. These are just about the simplest compounds that can be made from carbon, hydrogen and oxygen, so by breaking the glucose molecule down this far nearly all the energy possible is being released from this compound.

8.3.1 Stage one: aerobic glycolysis

Aerobic glycolysis is the same as anaerobic glycolysis: glucose (a six-carbon compound), is broken down to pyruvic acid (a three-carbon compound). However, as oxygen is now present the reaction can proceed further than in anaerobic glycolysis and lactic acid is not produced. The reaction still takes place in the sarcoplasm and the energy yield is sufficient to synthesise two molecules of ATP.

8.3.2 Stage two: the TCA/citric acid/Krebs' cycle

The pyruvic acid produced in the first stage diffuses into the matrix of the mitochondria where it is broken down to a two-carbon acetyl group. This combines with coenzyme A (usually shortened to CoA) to form acetyl CoA. A complex cyclical series of reactions now occurs. Put very simply, acetyl CoA combines with oxaloacetic acid to form citric acid, which is changed into a number of different compounds in a series of reactions that produces more energy and results in the regeneration of oxaloacetic acid. The whole cycle can then repeat itself. The cycle is known as the *tricarboxylic acid (or TCA) cycle*, the *citric acid cycle* or *Krebs' cycle*.

During the cycle three important things happen:

1 carbon dioxide is formed
2 oxidation takes place – hydrogen is removed from the compound
3 sufficient energy is released to synthesise two molecules of ATP.

A summary of the cycle can be seen in *Figure 8.2*.

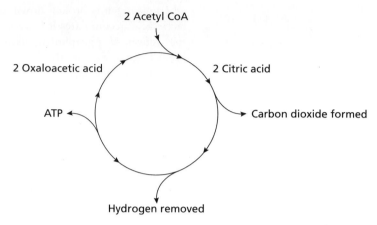

Figure 8.2 The TCA cycle

8.3.3 Stage three: the electron transport chain/electron transport system

The hydrogen atoms removed during the cycle in stage two are transported by coenzymes to the cristae of the inner membranes of the mitochondria. Here they enter the *electron transport system* and the electrons removed from the hydrogen are passed along by electron carriers, eventually combining with oxygen and the hydrogen ions to form water.

In an over-simplification of a very complex system, essentially high-energy carbon–hydrogen bonds are being broken (glucose) to form low-energy carbon–oxygen bonds (carbon dioxide) and hydrogen–oxygen bonds (water) and release energy to combine ADP and phosphate to form ATP.

The energy yield from the electron transport chain is sufficient to produce 34 molecules of ATP. This means that the total yield of aerobic respiration (from the three stages combined) is 38 molecules of ATP.

The aerobic system of synthesising ATP is the most efficient in terms of energy produced, and the byproducts (carbon dioxide and water) are easily expelled from the body. However, the reactions involved in this system depend on the availability of oxygen and at the onset of exercise and during very intense exercise the oxygen distributed to the cells just isn't enough for the body to rely on this system as a way of replenishing ATP stores. During submaximal exercise the aerobic system is the predominant method of ATP production as oxygen can be delivered at a rate to match the oxygen demand and unless you run out of carbohydrate, protein and fat stores, this system is unlimited.

8.3.4 Summary of the aerobic system of producing ATP

Glucose ($C_6H_{12}O_6$) + Oxygen (6 O_2) Æ Carbon dioxide (6 CO_2) + Water (6 H_2O) + Energy

Energy + 38 ADP + 38 P = 38 ATP

See *Figure 8.3*.

Stage one, aerobic glycolysis:	2 ATP
Stage two, TCA cycle:	2 ATP
Stage three, electron transport chain:	34 ATP
Total yield:	38 ATP

See *Figure 8.3*.

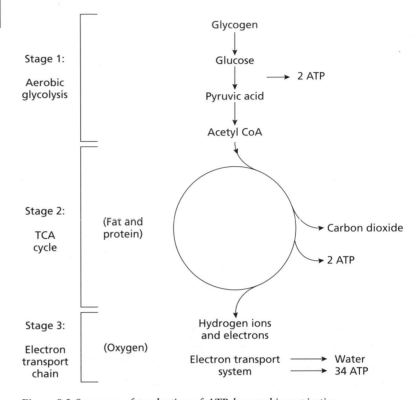

Figure 8.3 Summary of production of ATP by aerobic respiration

So far we have discussed how glycogen stores are broken down aerobically to produce ATP, but both fats and proteins may also be used as fuel for ATP synthesis.

8.4 Energy from fats

Fat is stored in *adipose tissue* in the form of *triglycerides*. Some fat is stored in the muscle cells and fats are also circulated in the blood.

The breakdown of fat is controlled by enzymes called *lipases* (e.g. lipoprotein lipase) and in the muscle cells the triglyceride is broken down to a two-carbon compound and enters the TCA cycle in a manner similar to the products of glycogen breakdown. Triglycerides contain a lot of high-energy carbon–hydrogen bonds, so when triglyceride is broken down to carbon dioxide and water a lot of energy is released. The amount of ATP synthesised by breakdown of fat is much higher than the amount obtained by breakdown of carbohydrate, which makes it a much more economical fuel in terms of energy yield than carbohydrate. However, the breakdown of triglycerides requires roughly 15% more oxygen than breakdown of glycogen, so when the supply of oxygen is limited glycogen stores will be broken down instead of triglyceride stores.

8.5 Energy from proteins

Although it *is* possible to use protein as an energy source for ATP synthesis we very rarely do so. Protein is only oxidised when the body is in a state

---

Definition

COENZYME

A molecule that can carry atoms, transporting them from one reaction to another. An example is coenzyme A.

Definition

TRIGLYCERIDE

A triglyceride molecule is made up of one molecule of glycerol and three fatty acids.

75

of starvation or near exhaustion. Two-carbon compounds produced by breakdown of proteins also enter into the TCA cycle.

ACTIVITY

Consider the following activities and decide which would be the predominant energy system used to resynthesise ATP.

1 Resting
2 A 30 m sprint
3 A 2 mile steady-state run
4 A gymnastic tumbling routine
5 A full-court man-to-man defence in basketball followed by a fast break attack.

Remember that the duration and intensity of the exercise dictates which system will be relied on most.

ACTIVITY

List the advantages and disadvantages of each energy system used to resynthesise ATP.

Table 8.1 Summary of the energy systems used to produce ATP

	Alactic system	Lactic acid system	Aerobic system
Site of reaction	Sarcoplasm	Sarcoplasm	Stage 1 sarcoplasm, stages 2 and 3 mitochondria
Presence of oxygen	Anaerobic	Anaerobic	Aerobic
Fuel used	Phosphocreatine	Carbohydrate	Carbohydrate and fat
Active enzyme	Creatine kinase	Glycogen phosphorylase and phosphofructokinase	Glycogen phosphorylase, phosphofructokinase, lipoprotein lipase (fat)
Enzyme activated by	Increase in ADP	Decrease in PC levels, increase in calcium levels	Decrease in insulin levels
Enzyme inhibited by	Increase in ATP levels	Increase in PC, reduction in pH	Increase in insulin, increase in lactic acid
Relative speed of reaction	Very fast	Fast	Slow
Brief outline	PC broken down to creatine, free phosphate and energy, which is used to convert ADP to ATP	Glycogen is broken down to glucose, then to pyruvic acid and then to lactic acid. Energy given off used to produce ATP	Stage 1: glucose broken down to pyruvic acid. Stage 2: cyclic series of reactions producing carbon dioxide. Hydrogen is removed from compounds in the cycle. Stage 3: in the electron transport system hydrogen ions and electron are recombined with oxygen to make water
Byproducts	None	Lactic acid	Carbon dioxide and water
Effects of byproducts	None	Lowers pH and inhibits action of enzyme	Easily expelled from body
Energy yield (molecules of ATP per molecule broken down)	1	2	Stage 1: 2, stage 2: 2, stage 3: 34
Threshold	approx. 10 seconds	1–2 minutes, depending on intensity of exercise	Unlimited during submaximal exercise

Key revision box

There are three ways of synthesising ATP from ADP and free phosphate to ensure a constant supply of energy. All three systems work together, the dominance of any one depending on the rate at which energy is used. When the demand for energy is high and immediate then the anaerobic processes are heavily relied on. When the demand for energy is low but sustained then the aerobic process is the main system used.

KEY TERMS

You should now understand the following terms. If you do not, go back through the chapter and find out.

Energy
Work
Power
Watt
Joule
Compound
Exothermic reaction
Enzyme
Endothermic reaction
ATP
Glycolysis
Coenzyme
Coupled reaction
Krebs' cycle
Electron transport system

PROGRESS CHECK

1 Define the following terms:
 (a) energy
 (b) work
 (c) power.
2 Joules are the units used to express …?
3 Watts are the units used to express …?
4 What is ATP? Where is it found?
5 How is energy released from ATP?
6 Name the three processes that are used to synthesise ATP.
7 Name the process that relies on the presence of oxygen.
8 What is meant by a coupled reaction? Give an example.
9 Which system is used to produce energy for very short bursts of intensive exercise?
10 During glycolysis glucose is broken down to pyruvic acid and energy is released. How much energy is released per molecule of glucose, and what is it used for?
11 Where in the cell does glycolysis take place?
12 What process takes place in the cristae of the mitochondria?
13 Name and briefly describe the three stages of the aerobic energy system.
14 What is the net energy yield of the aerobic process per molecule of glucose?
15 Which food fuel releases the most energy?
16 When you start to exercise why is carbohydrate broken down rather than fat?
17 During anaerobic glycolysis lactic acid is formed. What effect does a build-up of lactic acid have on the body?

CHAPTER 9

Energy and exercise

Learning objectives:

- To understand the concept of the energy continuum.
- To know how the energy systems are regulated.
- To be able to describe the effects of intensity and duration of exercise on energy supplies.
- To appreciate the affect of diet on performance.

9.1 The energy continuum

In Chapter 8 the three methods of synthesising ATP were looked at in isolation, which tends to give a distorted picture of what actually happens within the cell. We are constantly breaking down food fuels aerobically, and at rest nearly all our energy is provided this way. As there is no shortage of oxygen the main food fuel used is fat, although carbohydrate is also used.

If we suddenly start to exercise our demand for energy rises rapidly and, although the aerobic system still contributes to ATP synthesis, it cannot provide all the energy required. This is because it takes time to adjust the supply of oxygen to the working muscles. Until it can do so, another system is needed. The phosphocreatine system provides energy for a limited period of time (until stores run out) and the lactic acid system also contributes energy.

We can thus see that in some situations one or other of the systems will contribute nearly all the energy needed – for example, the aerobic system at rest or the phosphocreatine system during a 60 m sprint. In other situations a 'mix' of all three energy-production systems will be used and the athlete will continually move from one threshold into another system. An example of this occurs during a Fartlek session (see Chapter 12). This continual movement between and combination of the energy systems is known as the *energy continuum* (*Figure 9.1*).

A 1500 m race represents a mixture of energy sources used, and athletes should reflect this balance in their approach to training.

For some activities it is very easy to decide which of the energy systems is involved in the production of energy – for example during a marathon probably 99–100% of the energy will be released aerobically. In other activities it is not quite as clear because many other factors have to be taken into consideration.

A basketball game is usually accepted as being roughly 80% anaerobic, but this depends on several factors, such as

- the fitness of the player
- the standard of the game

Definition
THRESHOLD

The point at which the energy system being used is no longer effective in producing energy for ATP synthesis. The threshold for the phosphocreatine system is about 10 seconds. After this, the stores of phosphocreatine become depleted during intensive exercise.

78

Aerobic	0%		50%		100%
Anaerobic	100%		50%		0%
Activity	100 m sprint		1500 m race		Marathon

Figure 9.1 The energy continuum

- the tactics being employed, for example a full court press or a zone defence
- the commitment of the players.

Why is it important to identify the role of each energy system in relation to the total energy requirement of an activity? In order to optimise performance an athlete should make his or her training as specific as possible – to them as an individual and to their chosen activity. A knowledge of how intensity and duration of exercise affects the source of energy, along with how each system is regulated is therefore very important.

ACTIVITY

Consider the activities shown in the table below. By shading the appropriate areas indicate the involvement of each energy system in supplying the total energy requirements for each activity.

Marathon		
Basketball game		
1500 m swim		
50 m swim		
Hockey match		
Gymnastic floor routine		
Total energy	0% 50% 100%	

- Compare your answers with those of others in your group.
- Discuss any differences in opinion and be prepared to justify your answer. For example, what factors did you consider as significant for each activity when you decided the contribution of each energy system?

9.2 Exercise and energy supplies

As already mentioned, in order to perform work we need *energy*. Energy is measured in joules or kilocalories. The more work we perform the more energy we need and some activities use up more energy per hour than others (examples are given in Table 9.1).

The amount of energy used is directly related to the amount of oxygen consumed, as the breakdown (oxidation) of glycogen or fat requires a certain amount of oxygen. At rest we consume 0.2–0.3 litres of oxygen per minute (expressed as $\dot{V}O_2$, where $\dot{V}$ stands for volume per minute and O_2 stands for oxygen). During maximal exercise this can increase to 3–6 litres. This is the maximum amount of oxygen a person can utilise, or the $\dot{V}O_2$(max).

In practice

If you weigh 60 kg and go for a 30 minute walk you will use about 90 kCal.

Definition

AEROBIC CAPACITY

The maximum amount of oxygen that can be taken in and used by the body in one minute. This is known as a person's $\dot{V}O_2(max)$ and is expressed in millilitres per minute per kilogram of body weight.

Table 9.1 Energy requirements for several activities

Activity	Energy requirement (kCal/h/kg body weight)
Sitting	1
Walking	3
Playing tennis	4–9
Basketball	7–12
Running a mile in 8 minutes	12.5

When a given amount of oxygen breaks down a given amount of fuel a specific amount of energy is released. It is too difficult to monitor the amount of energy released, but it is possible to monitor how much oxygen is consumed. If you collect the expired air of an athlete you can determine how much oxygen has been used by comparing the percentage of oxygen in the expired air with that of atmospheric air. The amount of energy required to perform an activity can be estimated from the amount of oxygen consumed. When one litre of oxygen is used to oxidise glycogen then 5 kCal are released.

In practice

If during a run you used 0.2 ml of oxygen per kilogram of your body weight per minute and you weighed 70 kg and ran 1500 m you will have used 21 litres of oxygen. This is the equivalent of expending 105 kCal.

ACTIVITY

If you weighed 55 kg and you ran 5 miles in 40 minutes, roughly how many kCal of energy would you have used? Assuming that you are using only carbohydrate to produce energy, approximately how many litres of oxygen would you have consumed during the run?

Although there is no shortage of oxygen in the atmosphere there is a limit to how much oxygen can be taken into the bloodstream and delivered to the muscles. A person's $\dot{V}O_2(max)$ depends on the efficiency of their cardiac, respiratory and vascular systems along with their physiological make-up in terms of fibre type. Remember that it is the slow oxidative muscle fibre that works aerobically (Chapter 3). A person may improve their $\dot{V}O_2(max)$ up to 20% by training aerobically, but they still might be more physiologically suited to anaerobic activities.

When sufficient oxygen can't be delivered to the muscles to supply the total energy required aerobically, the anaerobic systems are used. This occurs either at the start of exercise or when the exercise is very intense. The most reliable way of monitoring the contribution of the lactic acid system to energy production is to measure the amount of lactic acid in the blood. A small amount of lactic acid is always present in the blood, but when the level starts to rise rapidly the body is relying heavily on the lactic acid system for energy production.

9.2.1 Carbohydrate compared with fat

The amount of oxygen available not only has a direct effect on whether energy is released aerobically or anaerobically but also affects the type of food fuel used. The body requires about 15% more oxygen to oxidise fat than to break down carbohydrate. Although fat produces more ATP than carbohydrate, when oxygen is in limited supply the body has to burn carbohydrate. This explains why carbohydrate is the major source of fuel for at least the first 20 minutes of exercise. When activities continue for 45 minutes or more the balance of fat to carbohydrate used changes, with fat being predominantly oxidised after an hour.

This is also the case as the intensity of exercise increases and as an athlete reaches the anaerobic threshold. The body is struggling to deliver sufficient oxygen to keep pace with the amount of energy required so

Definition

AEROBIC THRESHOLD

The point at which the intensity of an exercise leads to a dramatic increase in the anaerobic production of energy.

In practice

The best way to lose weight is to perform any submaximal, continuous exercise for a long period.

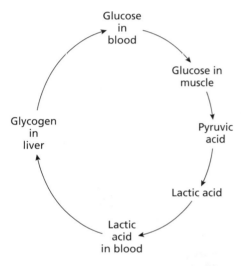

Figure 9.2 The Cori cycle

Definition

HYPOGLYCAEMIA

A condition caused by low blood sugar levels. At best hypoglycaemia can result in loss of concentration and sweating. If blood glucose levels are not returned to normal then the person's condition will quickly deteriorate. In extreme situations this can result in coma or death.

Definition

METABOLISM

The sum of all the chemical reactions that take place within the body.

cannot afford to oxidise fat. Once the anaerobic threshold has been reached only carbohydrate can be broken down anaerobically, which further depletes the body's store of carbohydrate.

A good way of judging the intensity of an activity is to monitor your heart rate because there is a direct relationship between heart rate and oxygen consumption and therefore exercise intensity. You should not exercise too close to your anaerobic threshold so you should work at about 75% of your maximum heart rate (this is calculated as 220 minus your age) or about 65% of your $\dot{V}O_2(max)$. The body has only a limited supply of carbohydrate, stored in the liver and muscles as glycogen and circulating in the blood in the form of glucose. During exercise glycogen from the liver is broken down to glucose and is transported in the blood to the muscles. During anaerobic energy production this glucose is broken down to lactic acid, which enters the bloodstream and is carried back to the liver where it is converted back to glycogen. This process is known as the *Cori cycle*, and is shown in *Figure 9.2*.

It is possible to severely deplete glycogen stores while performing prolonged periods of exercise like a triathlon. When liver glycogen stores run low the blood glucose is used. If blood glucose levels drop the athlete can suffer from *hypoglycaemia*. This condition can be avoided if the athlete consumes a glucose-based drink during the activity.

Taking a glucose drink shortly before the onset of prolonged exercise will have a negative effect on performance, because elevated levels of blood glucose result in an increase in insulin levels. Insulin helps to regulate blood glucose levels by converting excess glucose in the blood to glycogen in the liver. An increase in insulin levels inhibits the enzyme that controls the oxidation of fat, so the body will have to rely more heavily on the breakdown of carbohydrate, depleting stores even quicker.

Similarly, if an athlete starts a triathlon at a faster pace than he or she can cope with in an attempt to keep up with the leaders, he or she may also encounter difficulties. This is because during the early stages of exercise you rely on anaerobic energy production and if you are working hard lactic acid will accumulate early in the race. Lactic acid also inhibits the enzyme responsible for the breakdown of fat, so you are delaying the use of your most economical fuel. Another related problem is that if you deplete your glycogen stores early in an event you may not have enough left to produce a sprint for home – remember that only carbohydrate can be broken down anaerobically. Pacing in long distance events is therefore very important.

9.3 Diet and exercise

We need to eat to obtain enough energy to complete our daily tasks; we have to keep pace with our body's *metabolism*.

A term that is commonly used is the *basal metabolic rate* (BMR). The BMR is a measure of the amount of energy we would use if we remained at rest. Our daily intake of food has to cover the BMR plus any additional energy for other activities such as a 20 minute walk to work or a 45 minute game of squash, as well as the more functional activities of the body such as digestion and excretion.

Men can usually consume 2800–3000 kCal a day and women 2000–2200 kCal a day without putting on weight. If you are particularly active or train regularly you will probably need to eat 5000–6000 kCal a day. By eating the same amount of energy as you use you will maintain a constant body weight. Metabolic rates vary between individuals, and your metabolic rate will slow down as you get older – so don't expect to eat the same amount of food when you are 40 as you do now and not put on weight.

Body weight is referred to in terms of *body fat* and fat-free weight or *lean body mass*. The body fat is the amount of fat stored in the adipose tissue, the lean body mass being equivalent to the weight of the rest of the body. Men carry an average of 12–15% of their body weight as fat, whereas women carry about 20%. To lose weight we need to lose some of the fat stores and we can achieve this by going on a low-fat diet and by increasing the amount of submaximal exercise we perform. Athletes, particularly endurance athletes, tend to carry far less fat.

A balanced diet contains

- 15% protein
- 30% fat
- 55% carbohydrate.

You also need to make sure that you have enough vitamins and minerals, fibre and water in your diet. If you do a lot of endurance work you might need to increase your carbohydrate intake to 60–65%. After a heavy training session it can take up to 24 hours to fully replenish the glycogen stores, so the following day's training needs to be relatively light.

ACTIVITY

From the following list decide which foods are high in protein, high in fat, high in carbohydrate:

tuna, pasta, potato, chocolate, eggs, nuts, mayonnaise, butter, chicken, bread, cream cheese, rice.

The choice of food before exercise or competition is very personal, and the psychological benefits of food should be considered along with the physiological benefits. However, one form of dietary manipulation that has been proved successful is *carbo-loading* or *glycogen-loading*. Before an event an athlete depletes their stores of glycogen by training on a diet high in protein and fat for three days. Then they do light training on a high-carbohydrate diet for a further three days leading up to the competition. This form of diet significantly increases the stores of glycogen in the muscles and helps to offset fatigue in endurance events. Although this method does work for some athletes it should be noted that some people suffer more psychologically by having their routine changed than they benefit from the carbo-loading.

ACTIVITY

Write down your typical daily diet and try to work out how much carbohydrate, fat and protein you eat. Most food packaging provides extensive nutritional information so you should be able to estimate your calorific intake as well.

9.3.1 Some food facts

- Endurance training helps the body to use more fats during submaximal exercise
- Protein supplements are not needed for body-building, providing a balanced diet is eaten.
- Caffeine helps to mobilise fatty acids in the blood.
- Carbohydrate drinks are not much use for activities that last only for about 40 minutes.

- Any meal before an activity should be eaten at least two and a half hours before the start time and should be high in carbohydrate.
- Go for the 'feel good' factor: if you have a favourite food that gives you a psychological boost, take it.
- Regularly drink small amounts of water or glucose drinks during long endurance events to avoid dehydration and hypoglycaemia. Don't wait until you feel thirsty.

Key revision box

In most activities we use a 'mix' of all three systems of producing energy. This is reflected in the amount of oxygen we consume and the food fuels we use. By regulating the intensity we work at we can optimise our use of oxygen and fuel supplies to enhance performance.

KEY TERMS

You should now understand the following terms. If you do not, go back through the chapter and find out.

Energy continuum
Threshold
Aerobic capacity
$\dot{V}O_2$(max)
Anaerobic threshold
Cori cycle
Hypoglycaemia
Basal metabolic rate
Carbo-loading
Lean body mass

PROGRESS CHECK

1 What is meant by the term energy continuum?
2 List three activities that would predominantly use the aerobic system as a means of energy production.
3 Compare the energy demands of a goal keeper in football with a midfield player. Estimate the contribution made by each of the three energy systems for both positions.
4 How much oxygen do we consume at rest?
5 Define the term $\dot{V}O_2$(max).
6 How much oxygen is needed to break down sufficient glycogen to produce 15 kCal of energy?
7 When you start to exercise why don't you oxidise fats?
8 How can you estimate your maximum heart rate?
9 What is hypoglycaemia? How can it be avoided?
10 Why should you avoid taking a glucose drink less than an hour before you exercise?
11 Name three foods that are high in carbohydrate.
12 What happens to blood lactic acid when it reaches the liver?
13 What should a balanced diet consist of?
14 Briefly describe how you would carbo-load before a competition.
15 How can you estimate the amount of energy needed to perform a particular activity?

10

The recovery process

Learning objectives:

- To understand the role of the energy systems during the recovery process.
- To understand the concept of the oxygen debt.
- To be able to describe the alactacid and lactacid components of the oxygen debt.
- To be able to apply the major concepts of the recovery process to aid training and performance.

10.1 The recovery process

During any form of exercise changes occur in the body that need to be reversed once the exercise has stopped. The recovery process involves returning the body to the state it was in before exercise. The reactions that need to take place and how long the process takes depends on the duration and intensity of the exercise undertaken and the individual's level of fitness.

The changes that take place within a muscle cell during a period of exercise are summarised in Table 10.1.

Table 10.1 Changes that occur in muscle cells during exercise

Factor	Levels increased	Levels decreased
ATP		✓
Phosphocreatine		✓
Glycogen		✓
Triglycerides		✓
Carbon dioxide	✓	
Oxygen/myoglobin stores		✓
Lactic acid	✓	

We must also consider what is required to reverse these changes. During exercise our demand for energy greatly increases and, not surprisingly, all our energy stores are depleted to some extent. At the same time more of the byproducts of respiration have been produced and need to be removed. Energy is needed to reverse these changes.

When we stop exercising our demand for energy returns to its resting level, so why doesn't our cardiac output (calculated as heart rate × stroke volume – see Chapter 5) and our tidal volume (the amount of air breathed in or out in one breath – see Chapter 7) immediately also return to normal? The body continues to take in elevated amounts of oxygen and transport

Definition
OXYGEN DEBT
The amount of oxygen consumed during recovery above that which would have ordinarily been consumed at rest in the same time.

it to the working muscles where elevated rates of aerobic respiration are maintained. So what are we doing with the surplus energy? It is being used to help return the body to its pre-exercise state – this is known as the *oxygen debt*.

At rest we consume 0.2–0.3 litres of oxygen per minute, which is sufficient to meet the body's demand for energy. During recovery the body takes in far more oxygen than is actually required for several minutes after completing the exercise.

10.1.1 The oxygen deficit

When we start to exercise insufficient oxygen is being distributed to the tissues for all the energy production to be met aerobically, so the two anaerobic systems described in Chapter 8 have to be used. This is known as the *oxygen deficit* – and should not be confused with the oxygen debt. Phosphocreatine stores have to be broken down to phosphate and creatine and the energy produced used to synthesise ATP. Once these stores have been broken down they cannot be built up again until sufficient energy is available to do so during recovery. Glycogen is also being broken down anaerobically, producing lactic acid. The lactic acid accumulates in the blood and lowers its pH, which eventually results in inhibition of the important enzymes controlling breakdown of fats and carbohydrates (lipases and phosphofructokinase). The lactic acid must be removed during recovery so that the blood pH will return to normal.

10.1.2 The oxygen debt

The oxygen debt is made up of two components

● the alactacid component,
● the lactacid component.

The alactacid component

This is the more rapid of the two processes and is involved with restoration of the muscle phosphagen stores (ATP and phosphocreatine). As shown in Table 10.1, the levels of both ATP and phosphocreatine have been depleted as they have been broken down and the energy released has been used.

Both reactions are reversible, provided that energy is made available. During the alactacid component of the oxygen debt oxygen consumption remains high to allow elevated rates of aerobic respiration to continue. The energy released aerobically is used to continue ATP production and then to reform the stores of phosphocreatine that were depleted by exercise. The alactacid component uses up to 4 litres of oxygen and takes 2–3 minutes to complete restoration after intense exercise. However, the stores are replaced to 50% of normal levels after only 30 seconds of recovery and if the exercise was submaximal replenishment is even quicker. Table 10.2 shows the relationship between recovery time and replenishment of muscle phosphagen.

Table 10.2 Replenishment of muscle phosphagens after exercise

Recovery time (seconds)	Percentage of phosphagen replenished
<10	Negligible
30	50
60	75
90	87
120	93
150	97
180	98

In practice

Tennis players are well advised to make the most of the time available when changing ends. Participants in team games have many opportunities during a match to replenish muscle phosphagen stores – for example while a free kick is being taken.

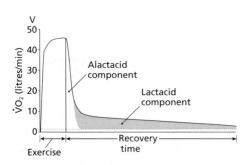

V
$\dot{V}O_2$ (litres/min)
50 — V
40 —
30 — Alactacid component
20 — Lactacid component
10 —
0 —
Exercise ← Recovery time →

Figure 10.1 The lactacid and alactacid components of the oxygen debt

In practice

By training anaerobically you can improve your body's tolerance to lactic acid and speed up the removal of this toxin during recovery.

ACTIVITY

Using the information in Table 10.2 draw a graph to show the rate of phosphagen restoration during recovery.

As the muscle phosphagen stores provide the energy for short intensive bouts of exercise it is useful to know that the stores can be replenished so quickly. In a game that relies heavily on the anaerobic energy systems, such as basketball, the coach may want to schedule time-outs to help his or her team recover.

The time available may not be sufficient to gain full recovery, but the athlete will be able to offset fatigue as at least some stores will still be available for energy production. Any phosphocreatine stores available will reduce the contribution made by the lactic acid system and will therefore reduce the amount of lactic acid being produced.

The lactacid component

This is the process responsible for the removal of lactic acid. It is the slower of the two processes and full recovery may take up to an hour, depending on the duration and intensity of the exercise (*Figure 10.1*). Lactic acid accumulates in the working muscles and the blood but may be removed in four ways.

Most (over 60%) of the lactic acid is removed from the cells by using it as a metabolic fuel. Within the muscle and some other organs, such as the heart, lactic acid is converted to pyruvic acid. This reaction requires energy (it is an endothermic reaction) but once it has occurred the pyruvic acid formed enters the TCA cycle and is metabolised aerobically to carbon dioxide, water and energy. The energy needed to convert the lactic acid back to pyruvic acid is made available aerobically because of the elevated rate of respiration during recovery. This is one of the reasons why an active recovery is recommended. The exercise performed during recovery should be submaximal (or you would be producing more lactic acid than you would be removing) and helps to flush the lactic acid out of the fast-twitch muscle fibres.

Other fates of lactic acid are conversion to protein or to glycogen in muscle and liver, or excretion via urine and sweat.

The processes involved in the oxygen debt are summarised in *Figure 10.2*.

ACTIVITY

Select three members of your group to perform three 10 m × 10 m shuttle runs. The first performer is allowed a 10 second recovery between each shuttle, the second performer 60 seconds to recover and the third performer is allowed 120 seconds. Each shuttle must be timed. Record the shuttle times in a table like the one below.

Performer	Rest interval	Time 1	Time 2	Time 3	Overall drop/ increase in performance
Subject 1					
Subject 2					
Subject 3					

Discuss your results in relation to the rest interval allowed and each subject's performance.

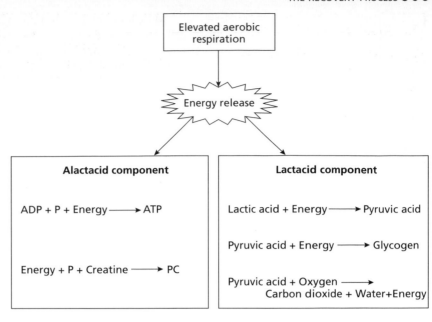

Figure 10.2 Summary of the processes involved in the oxygen debt

Usually 50% of lactic acid can be removed during the first half hour of recovery and 5–8 litres of oxygen is required.

Contrary to popular opinion, lactic acid is not responsible for the muscle soreness and stiffness often felt a day after intensive exercise. This discomfort is more likely to be due to damage to connective tissue and a closer look at technique, muscle strength and warm-up routines may be called for.

10.2 Myoglobin and replenishment of oxygen stores

Myoglobin is found in the sarcoplasm of the cell and is very similar to haemoglobin in that it has a high affinity for oxygen. It acts as a temporary store for oxygen and helps to transport oxygen from the capillaries to the mitochondria. Slow oxidative muscle fibre contains more myoglobin than the other fibres (remember that type 1 fibres produce energy aerobically) and the amount of myoglobin increases with aerobic training, helping to improve the supply of oxygen to the mitochondria.

ACTIVITY

Basketball is a game that relies heavily on the anaerobic energy systems. Using basketball, or another predominantly anaerobic activity, as your example:

1 List the opportunities that occur within the game that allow partial recovery of the anaerobic systems.
2 How can a coach help to maximise their teams energy output by providing as much time for recovery as possible?

After intense exercise the myoglobin stores of oxygen are depleted – it takes about 0.5 litres of oxygen and 1–2 minutes to replenish these stores. No energy is required for this process, but it will happen only when a 'surplus' of oxygen is being delivered to the muscles. During recovery the elevated rate of ventilation and heart rate means that additional oxygen is available for myoglobin replenishment.

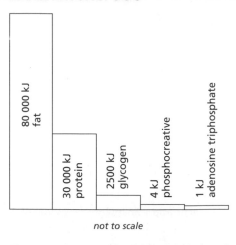

Figure 10.3 Proportions of food fuels stored in the body used to produce energy

---

In practice

Training schedules should provide a rest day after a particularly hard training session or competition – at the most do only a light session or work on technique the day after. Repeated sessions of intensive exercise will not allow the body to recover and can lead to chronic exhaustion.

Myoglobin stores are important because if oxygen is present within the cell then some energy can be produced aerobically and the body does not have to rely solely on the anaerobic systems. This means that valuable stores of phosphocreatine can be maintained for supplying additional bursts of energy – for example for a sprint finish – and that production of lactic acid is slowed down, delaying overall fatigue.

10.3 Glycogen

The stores of glycogen in the body are small relative to the stores of fats and proteins (*Figure 10.3*)

As glycogen is used as a metabolic fuel for both aerobic and anaerobic work its stores can very quickly become depleted. Certainly, after two hours of intensive exercise the stores are running low. If, for example, you have taken part in a tournament or have completed a triathlon, then you must make sure to replace your glycogen stores. This is achieved very easily – by eating – although it is advisable to eat a high-carbohydrate meal, such as a baked potato or pizza followed by banana pudding and custard. Most of the glycogen is replaced within ten hours of recovery but complete recovery can take up to two days.

Glycogen stores can be conserved if

- an athlete learns how to pace him- or herself properly, so that they do not cross their anaerobic threshold unnecessarily
- the athlete takes any opportunity available to recover muscle phosphagen and myoglobin stores
- he or she regularly takes small amounts of a glucose drink during the exercise.

Aerobic training also improves the body's ability to oxidise fat and therefore helps to conserve glycogen stores during submaximal exercise. If an athlete follows a high-carbohydrate diet and carbo-loads before an event (see Chapter 8), the stores of glycogen in the body will increase. All of these factors combine to enhance overall endurance performance.

Some glycogen is used when an athlete takes part in short periods of intense exercise, but a high-carbohydrate diet is not necessary to replace these stores. In fact, some of the stores are replaced by the conversion of lactic acid and pyruvate to glycogen (see earlier this chapter). The energy for this process is made available aerobically during the lactacid component of the oxygen debt.

Triglyceride stores are also used during prolonged periods of activity but because of the large amounts of fat available in the body no other measures need to be taken to replace them other than to eat a normal balanced diet. Similarly, the increased production of carbon dioxide during exercise does not cause any problems. Carbon dioxide enters the blood, by dissolving directly or as carbonic acid in the plasma, or attaching to haemoglobin, and is transported to the lungs and expelled in expiration.

Key revision box

The recovery process returns the body to its pre-exercise state. Replenishment of ATP and phosphocreatine stores and removal of lactic acid will take place only when additional energy is available. Elevated rates of respiration during recovery provides the energy for these processes.

KEY TERMS

You should now understand the following terms. If you do not, go back through the chapter and find out.

Oxygen debt
Oxygen deficit
Alactacid component
Lactacid component
Myoglobin
Elevated respiration
Metabolic fuel

PROGRESS CHECK

1 What is the purpose of the recovery process?
2 Define the term 'oxygen debt'.
3 What is the function of the alactacid component of the oxygen debt?
4 What is the function of the lactacid component of the oxygen debt?
5 How long does the body take to recover from exercise? Explain your answer fully.
6 What is the role of myoglobin?
7 What factors affect muscle glycogen replenishment after exercise?
8 Why should you cool down actively after exercise?
9 How does the oxygen deficit differ from the oxygen debt?
10 How long does it take to replace 50% of the muscle phosphagen stores?
11 Why is it important to try to replace myoglobin stores during activity?
12 List three opportunities within a game when players can partially or fully recover their muscle phosphagen stores.
13 Outline the process involved in the resynthesis of lactic acid.
14 Name an organ of the body that uses lactic acid as a metabolic fuel.
15 What is the probable cause of muscle soreness after exercise?
16 Why should athletes rest for a day after a particularly intense and prolonged period of exercise?

Physical fitness

Learning objectives:

- To understand the concept of fitness.
- To be able to identify the different fitness components.
- To be able to differentiate between health-related and skill/motor-related fitness.
- To know how to evaluate the different fitness components.

The fitness industry has exploded over the last few years as people have more leisure time and more disposable income. Most local papers carry pages of advertisements enticing you to 'move it with Mandy', 'step with Sarah', or 'pump iron with Brian' and Lycra-clad examples of bodily perfection encourage you to 'go for the burn' and remind you 'no pain no gain'. Looking beyond all the rhetoric, most people who join a class or visit a gym are attempting to improve their level of fitness for one reason or another. However, one person's concept of fitness may differ considerably from that of someone else.

11.1 What is fitness?

Fitness is the ability to cope effectively with the stresses of everyday life. Fitness cannot be stored so it should be considered as a continuum of fluctuating levels. As everyone's lifestyle (and therefore the stress that they have to cope with) differs, so do their levels of fitness. If you lead a very sedentary life then two or three walks a week will probably be enough exercise to maintain your level of required fitness but if you play regular competitive sport you will need to train quite hard to maintain the level of fitness needed to perform well.

Fitness should not be confused with *health*, although the two are commonly interchanged. To be healthy means to be in a state of well-being and free from disease – in other words, you are physically, mentally and emotionally in good shape. Being fit can add to your feeling of well-being and make you less likely to suffer from ill health, but fitness only contributes to an overall healthy lifestyle.

Fitness is made up of several components (outlined in *Figure 11.1*), which can be subdivided into

Health-related components: aerobic capacity, strength, flexibility and body composition. These contribute towards a healthy body. Everyone would benefit by developing these components of fitness to some degree.

Skill-related components: these include speed, power, balance, reaction time, coordination and agility. The skill-related aspects of fitness are far more

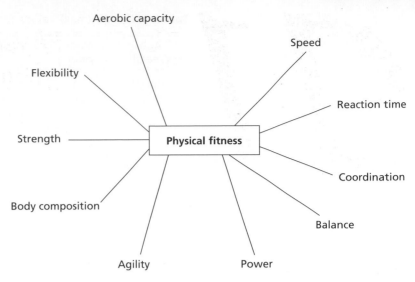

Figure 11.1 *Factors affecting physical fitness*

appropriate to the sports performer who may wish to develop some of them through additional training.

11.2 Health-related fitness

11.2.1 Aerobic capacity

Aerobic capacity is the ability of an athlete to take in and use oxygen, allowing participation in prolonged periods of continuous submaximal activities, such as swimming, running, cycling and rowing.

A person's aerobic capacity depends on three factors:

1 Effective external respiration.
2 Effective oxygen transport from the lungs to the cells.
3 Effective use of oxygen within the cell.

Your aerobic capacity therefore depends on the efficiency of your respiratory, cardiac and vascular systems. Your aerobic capacity is mostly genetically determined, for example you will be able to use far more oxygen if you have a high percentage of slow oxidative muscle fibres, but training can improve your aerobic ability.

Aerobic capacity is referred to as $\dot{V}O_2(max)$. Various values for $\dot{V}O_2(max)$, obtained experimentally by Professor Astrand, a famous Swedish sports physiologist, are shown in Tables 11.1 and 11.2.

A person with a high $\dot{V}O_2(max)$ isn't necessarily going to be outstandingly good at endurance events. A much better indicator is the percentage of their $\dot{V}O_2(max)$ an athlete can work at for prolonged periods of time without crossing their anaerobic threshold. Elite endurance athletes can usually work at about 85% of their $\dot{V}O_2(max)$, but non-athletes will

Swimming is a good way to develop your aerobic capacity

Definition

$\dot{V}O_2(MAX)$

The maximum volume of oxygen that can be consumed and used by the body per unit of time. It is usually expressed as millilitres per minute per kilogram of body weight.

Table 11.1 $\dot{V}O_2(max)$ values for men (ml/min/kg body weight)

Age (years)	Very poor	Poor	Average	Good	Very good
20–29	38	39–43	44–51	52–56	57+
30–39	34	35–39	40–47	48–51	52+
40–49	30	31–35	36–43	44–47	48+
50–59	25	26–31	32–39	40–43	44+
60–69	21	22–26	27–35	36–39	40+

Table 11.2 $\dot{V}O_2$(max) values for women (ml/min/kg body weight)

Age (years)	Very poor	Poor	Average	Good	Very good
20–29	28	29–34	35–43	44–48	49+
30–39	27	28–33	34–41	42–47	48+
40–49	25	26–31	32–40	41–45	46+
50–65	21	22–28	29–36	37–41	42+

struggle to maintain a workload of about 65% of $\dot{V}O_2$(max). Most male endurance athletes have a $\dot{V}O_2$(max) in excess of 70 ml/min/kg and female endurance athletes have a $\dot{V}O_2$(max) in excess of 60 ml/min/kg.

ACTIVITY

Why do you think that the values for $\dot{V}O_2$(max) of men and women differ? Suggest reasons why a person's $\dot{V}O_2$(max) deteriorates with age.

11.2.2 Evaluation of aerobic capacity

The most accurate way to assess an athlete's $\dot{V}O_2$(max) is under laboratory conditions. The athlete runs on a treadmill and all the air they expire is collected in a Douglas bag. The athlete works to exhaustion and then the volume and oxygen content of the expired air is measured. We know the percentage of oxygen in atmospheric air so it is possible to calculate how much oxygen has been consumed by the athlete, and therefore to calculate their $\dot{V}O_2$(max).

To measure a person's $\dot{V}O_2$(max) directly relies on the availability of expensive equipment and technical assistance. It is also time consuming, especially if you want to assess the whole of your football or rugby team. Other field tests have been developed that need very little equipment and allow large numbers of athletes to be tested at any one time. The results of these tests may be compared with standardised nomograms or tables to obtain an estimate of the athlete's $\dot{V}O_2$(max). One such test is the *multi-stage fitness test*, developed by the National Coaching Foundation, in which an athlete performs a progressive 20 m shuttle run to exhaustion. The level that the athlete reaches is compared with the standard results table. Although this produces only an estimate of the athlete's $\dot{V}O_2$(max) it is a useful guide and can be repeated in future training sessions to monitor progress.

Definition
DOUGLAS BAG
A rubber-lined bag used to collect expired air.

ACTIVITY

Offer to test the $\dot{V}O_2$(max) of a school team or a local club team using the multi-stage fitness test. Analyse your results in terms of age, sex, frequency and type of training and position. You may need to devise a short questionnaire to supplement your data.

11.2.3 Strength

Strength is a general term for applying a force against a resistance. In most team sports the resistance you are working against is your own body weight and, although you are not using your maximum strength, you do need to keep working for long periods of time. In other activities, such as weightlifting, you are applying more force and working to maximum. In sport we therefore need to state more specifically the type of strength being used.

Three types of strength have been identified:

- maximum strength
- dynamic strength (power)
- endurance strength.

Maximum strength

This is the greatest force the neuromuscular system is capable of exerting in a single maximum voluntary contraction. Men tend to be able to exert a greater maximum strength than women because they have a larger muscle mass – the greater the cross-sectional area of the muscle, the greater the force that can be generated. Fibre type also affects strength, fast glycolytic fibres being able to produce more force than slow oxidative fibres, so once more it's down to the genes. Some muscle groups are stronger than others, not only because of their size; muscle shape also plays an important role. The *fusiform* muscle shape (for example the biceps) allows most movement, the *multipennate* shape (such as the deltoid) provides more strength but less movement.

Most people do not need to work on improving their maximum strength as they rarely need to exert maximum strength in everyday life.

ACTIVITY
List three sporting activities where the maximum strength that an athlete can exert is essential for good performance.

Dynamic strength or power

The ability of the neuromuscular system to overcome resistance with a high speed of contraction is the dynamic strength.

This aspect of strength is more appropriate to sport than to general health-related fitness. Dynamic strength is essential for any activities involving sprinting, throwing, jumping or hitting and an athlete needs a high percentage of fast glycolytic muscle fibres to perform well. The motor neurones that stimulate fast-twitch muscle fibres have a thicker myelin sheath than those stimulating the slow oxidative fibres, which speeds up the rate of conduction of the stimulus and therefore the speed of contraction.

Endurance strength

This is the ability of the muscle to withstand fatigue. This is the type of strength most appropriate to health-related fitness. We are often called upon to do tasks requiring this kind of strength – digging the garden, carrying home the shopping, etc. It is also essential to the sports performer. For example towards the end of a game or when a game goes into extra time, the team whose players have better muscular endurance will be in the more favourable position.

11.2.4 Evaluation of strength

The easiest way to assess someone's maximum strength is to find out the maximum weight that they can lift in a single contraction. Free weights or a multi-gym can be used and more than one muscle group can be tested. A dynamometer (see *Figure 11.2*) can be used to measure hand grip and leg strength.

Definition

FUSIFORM

The fibres run the length of the muscle.

MULTIPENNATE

The fibres run off either side of small tendons that are attached to the main tendon of a muscle.

In practice

Any continuous submaximal activity relies on endurance and athletes with a high percentage of slow oxidative fibres will be at an advantage as they can work for prolonged periods of time. Remember that slow oxidative muscle fibres release energy aerobically and do not produce fatiguing by-products.

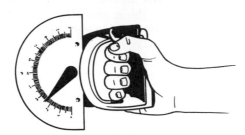

Figure 11.2   The Dynamometer

Endurance can be measured by the sit-up test that has been developed by the National Coaching Foundation, but any repetitive exercise such as pull-ups, squat thrusts or dips can be performed over 1–2 minutes and the number performed recorded.

Dynamic strength or power is an indication of an athlete's *anaerobic power* or *capacity*. Dynamic activities such as sprinting and jumping require a lot of energy quickly and have to rely predominantly on the alactic and lactic acid energy systems (see Chapter 8). A simple and easy test of dynamic strength is the vertical jump, but a more sophisticated test of an athlete's anaerobic capacity is the Wingate test.

The Wingate test

This test is performed on a cycle ergometer, and requires maximum effort by the athlete over a period of 30 seconds. The athlete warms up and then the relevant load is added to the bike – for men this load is 0.083–0.092 kg per kg of body weight, for women and children the load is 0.075 kg per kg. As soon as all the weights have been added to the bike the athlete must pedal as fast as possible. Someone must count the number of pedal revolutions for every five seconds of the test. Using the following formula the athlete's power output (in Watts) can be calculated.

Output (Watts) = Load (kg) × Revolutions (per 5 seconds) × 11.765

The Wingate test is a maximal test and it is very important that the athlete cools down after completing it. A heart rate monitor is not required but as a guide the athlete should cool down until their heart rate has dropped to at least 120 beats per minute.

In practice

By increasing the range of movement possible around a joint you are potentially increasing the amount of power that your muscles can generate. By improving your dynamic flexibility you are reducing the risk of connective tissue damage.

11.2.5 Flexibility

Flexibility (or static flexibility) is the range of movement possible around a joint and depends on the amount of stretch allowed by the ligaments, joints, tendons and muscles. Dynamic flexibility is slightly different – it is the resistance of a joint to movement. Flexibility has only recently been considered as an important component of physical fitness for all athletes. In the past it was assumed that girls are naturally more flexible than boys and that you need to be flexible to participate in gymnastics or to dance, but that flexibility isn't important for footballers or other male-dominated activities. This attitude has changed considerably – increasing your flexibility aids performance and helps to avoid unnecessary injury.

It is impossible to have the same degree of flexibility around all joints as the joint structure itself limits flexibility, for example a lot of movement is possible at the shoulder joint because it is a ball and socket joint, but movement at the hinge joint of the knee is more limited. Other factors affecting flexibility are the amount of stretch allowed by the antagonistic muscle and the length of the surrounding connective tissue. Increasing body temperature helps to improve flexibility, which is a good reason why an athlete should always warm up. Our range of movement deteriorates as we get older, due to shortening of the connective tissue and general joint degeneration caused by wear and tear.

11.2.6 Evaluation of flexibility

A widely used test of flexibility is the sit and reach test shown in *Figure 11.3*. The athlete sits on the floor with their legs straight, their toes pointing upwards and their feet in contact with the box. He or she then reaches forward as far as possible and the distance from the toes is measured. The range of joint movement may be measured using a double-arm goniometer or a 360° angle measurer, as shown in *Figure 11.4*.

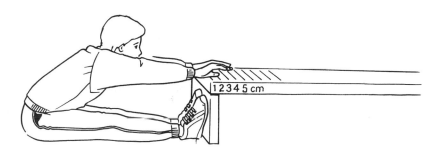

Figure 11.3 The sit and reach test

Figure 11.4 The angles of movement can be measured using a double-arm goniometer

---

ACTIVITY

Perform the sit and reach test without a warm-up. Thoroughly warm up and perform the test again. Can you suggest any physiological reasons for the difference in performance?

11.2.7 Body composition

As mentioned in Chapter 9, your body mass is made up of lean body mass plus body fat. On average men carry 12–15% fat and women 18–20% fat. When people start to carry more fat they become overweight and in some cases obese. This can lead to health problems as the additional weight puts a strain on the cardiovascular system and can cause cardiovascular disease and high blood pressure. Overweight people are less likely to exercise because they get tired very quickly and put a lot of strain on their joints, causing injury and discomfort. In general, most athletes carry less fat than average, mainly because their energy expenditure is quite high and they use their fat stores. If you establish a routine of regular exercise and sensible eating habits when you are young, you are less likely to 'go to seed' as you approach middle age.

11.2.8 Evaluation of body composition

The percentage of body fat is usually estimated by measuring skin folds at specific sites on the body. Common sites measured include the triceps, scapula and abdomen and usually the sum of all three sites is calculated. A skin fold caliper is needed; the ones made from metal tend to be more accurate than those made of plastic. The person measuring should hold the skin fold, place the caliper over it and measure the fold in millimetres. Care should be taken not to include muscle tissue.

Many health and fitness texts include nomograms to help you estimate your percentage of body fat, but their validity depends on the accuracy of the measurements taken.

To stay reasonably fit and healthy athletes and non-athletes alike should be aware of the health-related components of fitness and do the exercise appropriate to maintain an active lifestyle. Many texts outline exercise programmes which are suitable for all ages and standards, but you should select a regime that is realistic and which will fit into your daily routine. Athletes need to be more specific in their approach to fitness because different activities require different mixes of fitness components. A gymnast needs to be very flexible, have good dynamic strength and strength endurance, but does not need a lot of aerobic fitness. A marathon runner, on the other hand, needs good aerobic capacity and a lot of strength endurance, but doesn't need to be particularly flexible. An athlete should analyse the requirements of their speciality very closely and make sure that their training reflects the demands that will be made on them.

11.3 Motor/skill-related fitness

11.3.1 Speed

Speed is basically how fast you can move part of your body or the whole of your body, and is measured in metres per second. Speed is an important factor in all explosive sports and activities that require sudden changes in pace (remember that power is work performed per unit of time). How fast you are depends on the percentage of fast glycolytic fibres in particular muscle groups as these fibres receive stimuli quicker and release energy anaerobically. You need fast reactions to be able to respond to the right cue and also need to be able to select the necessary motor units. Increased speed doesn't always result in an improved performance if you go too quickly and make mistakes.

Evaluation of speed

A 60 metre timed sprint is commonly used to measure an athlete's speed.

11.3.2 Reaction time

This is the time between a stimulus being detected and the first movement made in response to it – for example the time taken between the gun going off and the sprinter starting to move. Reaction time is affected by conduction of the nerve impulse and the speed of muscle contraction, therefore people with a high percentage of type 2b fibres respond quicker. It also depends on how long you take to process the information, and this can be improved with practice.

Evaluation of reaction time

A number of reaction timers are available. Mostly they involve pushing a button when a light comes on. Pushing the button breaks an electrical circuit and stops a timer, consequently measuring the time it takes to respond to the stimulus.

11.3.3 Agility

Agility is the combination of speed and coordination. It allows you to efficiently change direction and body position at speed, for example a goal keeper needs to have fast reactions and to be very agile.

Evaluation of agility

The Illinois Agility Run involves an athlete lying face down at the starting line. On the word 'go' they get up and complete the agility course outlined in *Figure 11.5* as fast as possible.

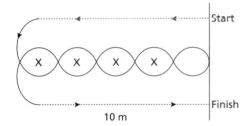

Figure 11.5 Course for the Illinois Agility Run. X = obstacle

11.3.4 Balance

Balance is the ability to maintain equilibrium – in other words, something is balanced when its centre of gravity is over its area of support. A balance that is held, such as a headstand in gymnastics, is known as a *static balance*. Balance also has a *dynamic* dimension as athletes need to retain their balance while in motion.

Evaluation of balance

A balance board can be used to evaluate balance. This is a circular piece of wood about 60 cm in diameter with a small hemispherical piece of wood attached to one side as a base (*Figure 11.6*). The athlete stands on the board and tries to prevent the sides of the board making contact with the floor. How long the athlete can retain their balance on the board is recorded.

Figure 11.6 Balance board

11.3.5 Coordination

Coordination involves putting the relevant motor programmes in the right order, and effectively using the neuromuscular system to produce smooth and efficient movement.

Evaluation of coordination

The alternate hand wall toss is an easy test to administer, requiring little space or equipment. An athlete stands 2 m from a wall, holding a tennis ball in the right hand. He or she tosses the ball underarm against the wall and must catch the ball with the left hand. They then throw the ball from the left hand and attempt to catch it in the right – and so on. The number of successful catches made in 30 seconds is recorded.

The rationale behind fitness testing is not necessarily to compare your performance with others, but to give you an indication of your strengths and weaknesses so that your training can be tailored to your requirements. The tests can be repeated at a later date to monitor improvement.

EXERCISE PHYSIOLOGY ● ● ●

Complete the following fitness evaluation.

On the table below mark the appropriate rating (1 = very low and 10 = very high) for each fitness component in relation to your present state of fitness and the ideal state of fitness for your chosen activity.

Date

Percentage body fat

Individual sport

Team sport

Fitness component	1	2	3	4	5	6	7	8	9	10
Aerobic capacity										
Flexibility										
Maximum strength										
Strength endurance										
Anaerobic capacity										
Speed										
Balance										
Coordination										
Agility										
Reaction time										

Key revision box

Physical fitness cannot be stored but must be maintained by following a programme designed with both your physiological make-up and the demands of your sport in mind. Fitness can be divided into health-related components and skill-related components. An athlete should evaluate each component before embarking on a training schedule.

98

KEY TERMS

You should now understand the following terms. If you do not, go back through the chapter and find out.

Anaerobic capacity
Health
Capacity
$\dot{V}O_2(max)$
Aerobic capacity
Coordination
Reaction time
Wingate test
Strength endurance
Flexibility
Maximum strength
Agility

PROGRESS CHECK

1 Define health.
2 Define fitness.
3 What is the usual measurement of aerobic capacity?
4 What three main factors affect aerobic capacity?
5 List the four components of health-related fitness.
6 Briefly describe the multi-stage fitness test.
7 List the three different types of strength.
8 Which type of muscle fibres are stimulated when you perform strength endurance activities?
9 What does the Wingate test measure?
10 How is energy released when you are performing dynamic strength exercises?
11 List three factors that limit flexibility.
12 How can flexibility aid performance?
13 What is the difference between static balance and dynamic balance?
14 Identify the main fitness components that are required by
    (a) a gymnast
    (b) a goal keeper
    (c) a 400 m hurdler
    (d) a 10 000 m runner
    (e) a prop forward.
15 How would the flexibility required by a swimmer differ from that required by a gymnast?

Training: theory and practice

Learning objectives:

- To understand the principles of training.
- To know the training methods used to develop specific fitness components.
- To be able to describe the physiological benefits of a warm-up and a cool-down.
- To be able to apply the principles of training and training methods to the development of a personal fitness programme.

It is doubtful that your present state of fitness will match the specific demands of your chosen activity. You can either accept your shortcomings or you can decide to improve your fitness by training.

Most 'recreational' athletes have a very inconsistent approach to training. Usually it takes the form of a couple of frenetic weeks in early January, as penance for excesses over Christmas and as part of yet another New Year's resolution to get fit, and another two weeks before the season starts to make up for the fact that you haven't done anything for the previous three months. Such erratic behaviour has almost no physiological benefit – it just eases your conscience. For training to be effective it should be planned well, and the athlete should follow the basic principles of training. Everyone benefits from training, not just top-class athletes, providing the programme you follow is specifically geared towards your level of fitness and lifestyle.

12.1 The principles of training

The *principles of training* help ensure that sensible, realistic and safe training programmes are developed.

12.1.1 The principle of overload

The whole point of training is to improve your level of fitness but you will only improve your level of fitness if you 'overload' your body. In other words, you make your body work harder than normal by increasing the amount of work it has to perform. The body will then gradually *adapt* to the new level of work and your level of fitness will improve. The physiological adaptations that occur through training are discussed in detail in Chapter 13.

Overload can be achieved by

1 Increasing the number of times (the *frequency*: F) that you train.
2 Increasing the *intensity* (I) of the activity you are doing, for example running faster or lifting more weight.

3   Increasing the *duration* (time: T) of each individual session, for example go for a 40 minute run rather than a 30 minute run.

12.1.2 The principle of progression

Your body will only improve if it is put under stress, but the principle of progression underlines the fact that the amount of overload attempted should be *progressively* made more difficult. The workload should be increased only once some adaptations have occurred, therefore it is important to monitor your performance closely so that you don't put too much stress on the body too soon. The term *moderation* is often used – meaning that you should be realistic and reasonable about the demands you make on your body. By being over-ambitious you could over-train and seriously damage your muscular and skeletal systems.

12.1.3 The principle of specificity

Every activity requires a specific mix of fitness components and the training you undertake needs to reflect the contribution made by each component. However, before you attempt any specific training you must have developed a general level of fitness. There is a lot of truth in the saying 'don't play squash to get fit, get fit to play squash'.

Three main factors must be considered:

● *The individual.* Training should be specific to the individual. It is important to assess your initial state of fitness so that the workload can be accurately estimated. Everyone has limitations, as much of our physical capacity is genetically determined. Being aware of your physiological make-up will help you make the most of your strengths rather than highlight your weaknesses.
● *The activity.* First identify the mix of fitness components required and then identify the major joints and muscles that are used. Make sure that your training uses these joints and muscle groups and try to reproduce the movement patterns that you would use in competition.
● *The energy systems.* Identify the energy systems used during the activity and their overall contribution to total energy expenditure. Make sure that your training reflects the same balance by manipulating the intensity and duration of your work.

12.1.4 The principle of reversibility

Fitness cannot be stored for future use and your level of fitness is constantly changing. Any adaptations that take place as a consequence of training will be reversed when you stop training.

12.1.5 The principle of variance

Variety is the spice of life! If you do the same thing week after week it becomes monotonous and boring. The principle of variance is very simple – it suggests that a training programme should include a variety of training methods. This will help to maintain interest and motivation, and makes sure that the loads you work against are varied. It is very easy to develop overuse injuries and if you do not give your body sufficient time to recover you can develop chronic exhaustion.

12.2 Warming up and cooling down

Integral parts of any training session are the warm-up and the cool-down. Both physiological and psychological benefits are to be gained from these two activities. Outlined below are some of the physiological reasons why it is extremely important to warm up and cool down properly.

12.2.1 The warm-up

The warm-up helps to prepare the body for the physical exertion to come. By gently raising your pulse you are beginning to increase your cardiac output and your rate of ventilation. Your vasomotor centre is making sure that more blood is being distributed to the working muscles. The combined effect is to increase the amount of oxygen being delivered to the muscle cells, which will help to reduce the oxygen deficit when you start your activity for real.

The muscle works better when it is warm for several reasons:

- oxygen dissociates from haemoglobin more readily as muscle temperature increases
- the activity of the enzymes responsible for cellular respiration increases, making energy more readily available
- the conduction of nerve impulses is quicker, improving contraction speed and resulting in faster reaction times
- blood vessels within the muscle dilate, further increasing the blood flow
- an increase in muscle temperature allows greater stretch in the muscles and connective tissue, increasing flexibility.

The warm-up has three phases. Phase one involves a continuous, submaximal whole body activity, such as jogging, to gently raise your pulse. This is followed by a stretch session in which particular attention should be paid to the joints and muscles that will be most active. Finally you should specifically rehearse the movement patterns that will be performed, for example performing skill practices.

As well as helping you to prepare mentally and physically for your activity, a warm-up considerably reduces the risk of injury.

ACTIVITY

Outline a warm-up session that would be suitable for a 110 m hurdler.

12.2.2 The cool-down

As mentioned in Chapter 10, your body returns to its pre-exercise state more quickly if you perform light exercise during the recovery period. The increased blood flow helps to flush out waste products such as lactic acid and carbon dioxide, reducing your overall recovery time. A cool-down also prevents blood pooling – remember that about 85% of the blood volume is distributed to the working muscles and one of the main ways of maintaining blood flow back to the heart is by the skeletal pump mechanism. If muscle action stops suddenly the amount of blood returning to the heart drops dramatically. This in turn reduces the stroke volume and causes a drop in blood pressure, making in the athlete feel dizzy and light-headed.

A cool-down allows the muscles to return to their normal temperature slowly because a sudden drop in temperature could cause muscle damage. The cool-down is also a good time to perform flexibility exercises as the muscles are still warm and at their most pliable. In conclusion, a cool-down allows you to physically and mentally relax. It aids recovery and helps to prevent muscle soreness and injury.

12.3 Methods of training

Having outlined the guidelines to follow when developing a fitness programme we will now look at what you should actually do during a training session. Numerous training methods have been developed, and here we only intend to outline a few suggestions for each component of health-related fitness. Further reading is suggested at the end of Part 2.

12.4 Improving your aerobic capacity

In order to improve your aerobic capacity you need to take part in continuous, submaximal activity involving the whole body. Activities such as brisk walking, jogging, running, cycling, swimming and rowing are ideal, as they will all put stress on the cardiovascular and respiratory systems.

The duration of the training session will depend on your initial level of fitness but you should work for a minimum of 12 minutes. This is because for the first couple of minutes of exercise the major contributors to energy production are the anaerobic systems, as your body needs time to adjust to the increased oxygen demand. You need to work long enough to put the aerobic system under stress – if you keep stopping and starting your body will have time to recover and you would not be applying the principle of overload. Usually 30–40 minutes is sufficient for recreational athletes, whereas elite endurance athletes will work for considerably longer periods.

The intensity of work will depend on your level of fitness. One of the easiest guides to intensity of work is heart rate because during aerobic activity your heart rate increases in proportion to the amount of work undertaken. It is important that you work at an intensity that overloads your system, but at the same time keeps you below your anaerobic threshold. Remember that if you go beyond your anaerobic threshold the predominant method of producing energy is the lactic acid system. If you rely heavily on this system lactic acid will accumulate in the tissues and cause fatigue.

A researcher from Finland named Karvonen suggested that we should always train above a point that he called the 'critical threshold' for 20 minutes. The critical threshold is calculated in the following way.

Critical threshold = Resting heart rate + 60% of (maximum heart rate – resting heart rate)

Remember that your maximum heart rate is roughly 220 minus your age. If you are 20 and your resting heart rate is 65 then

your critical threshold = 65 + 60% of (200 – 65)

= 65 + 60% of 135

= 65 + 81

= 146 beats per minute

See *Figure 12.1*.

Jogging and running will put stress on the cardiovascular and respiratory systems

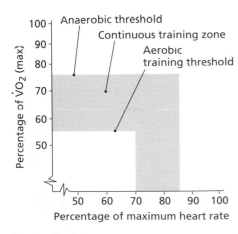

Figure 12.1 Working within the aerobic threshold

ACTIVITY

Calculate your critical training threshold using Karvonen's principle. The critical threshold in the case above is about 75% of the athlete's maximum heart rate, but elite endurance athletes can usually work at 80–85% of their maximum heart rate and still be working aerobically.

The other aspect of overload is frequency, and in order to gain any long-term physiological benefit you need to train aerobically at least twice a week; elite athletes will do at least five sessions a week. You will begin to notice an improvement in your aerobic capacity after 3–4 weeks, but it is recommended that you continue the programme for at least 12 weeks. During that time you need to monitor your performance and increase the overload as and when required. When your heart rate response to the same workload begins to drop, your body has begun to adapt to that intensity of work and you need to increase the workload. Always remain above the critical threshold.

Types of aerobic training include continuous running, Fartlek and interval training.

12.4.1 Continuous running

This involves jogging or running continuously at a steady pace. However, any continuous activity can be used – from swimming to step aerobics.

12.4.2 Fartlek

Fartlek means 'speed play' in Swedish and the idea of this activity is that the athlete varies the pace of the run and also the terrain they run over. A typical run will include some steady-state running interspersed with sprints and slow recovery work and should include uphill and downhill work. Fartlek involves the athlete working aerobically and anaerobically and it is a much more demanding form of training. Fartlek training helps to improve an athlete's $\dot{V}O_2(max)$ and recovery process. It is ideal for athletes who need to be able to change pace during an activity and it is also good for games players.

ACTIVITY

Devise a 30 minute Fartlek session that would be appropriate for your level of fitness. Plan a route near your home or college and attempt the session. If possible, wear a heart rate monitor to assess the intensity you are working at. During steady-state work your heart rate should be above the critical threshold and during the sprints you should raise your heart rate over 180 beats per minute.

12.4.3 Interval training

Interval training is popular because it can be used for both aerobic and anaerobic training. It is a form of training in which periods of work are interspersed with periods of recovery. Four main variables can be manipulated to ensure specificity of training:

1 The duration or distance of the interval.
2 The intensity of the interval.
3 The duration of the recovery period.
4 The number of work/recovery intervals.

Anaerobic training would be based on short-distance, high-intensity intervals and aerobic sessions would involve long-distance, submaximal-intensity intervals. If the athlete is concentrating on developing speed the recovery periods need to be long enough to ensure full recovery, if he or she wants to improve their level of endurance and resistance to fatigue the recovery periods need to be shortened accordingly. Interval training adds variety to training sessions and allows quality work to be maintained. The recovery intervals reduce the oxygen debt and therefore the onset of fatigue is delayed, allowing more work to be completed than in an equivalent continuous session.

Interval training can also be adapted for games players by using repetitive skill practices and circuit training. This not only improves fitness levels but also allows practice of individual skills.

Successful interval training depends on the coach or athlete being able to correctly identify the initial fitness level of the athlete, the fitness components required by the activity and the energy systems used in the activity. He or she must then manipulate the four variables to ensure that the interval training session devised is specific to the activity and the athlete.

Examples of intervals used in training:

10 × 60 m @ 8 seconds with 90 seconds recovery
10 × 200 m @ 30 seconds with 90 seconds recovery
5 × 400 m @ 80 seconds with 160 seconds recovery

12.5 Improving strength

In order to improve your strength you need to work against some form of resistance, but in order to make your training programme as specific as possible you need to consider the following.

● The type of strength you want to develop – maximum strength, strength endurance or dynamic strength?
● Which muscle groups you want to improve.
● The type of muscle contraction performed – concentric, eccentric or isometric?

The athlete should also

● follow a general strength conditioning programme before specialising
● exercise large muscle groups before smaller ones
● perform the exercises in such a way as to use the energy system required during the activity
● overload movements that are as close as possible to the movements to be strengthened
● allow appropriate recovery between individual exercises and training sessions.

Any strength training programme refers to the number of *repetitions* and the number of *sets* performed.

The number of repetitions performed will depend on the type of strength being improved. If you are developing maximum strength you may perform only six repetitions per set because you will be working to maximum and will fatigue very quickly. Remember that the fast twitch muscle fibres will be recruited for maximum strength work, and they rely on the anaerobic energy systems and fatigue quickly. If you are developing strength endurance you may do anything from ten to twenty repetitions per set.

The intensity that you work at will also depend on the type of strength you wish to develop. To develop maximum strength you need to determine the maximum weight that you can successfully lift six times (six repetition maximum: 6RM). As a general guide the session will include low repetitions of high weights. In contrast, to develop strength endurance the number of repetitions will be high and the resistance will be relatively low (15–20RM).

You might need to develop the strength to hold a particular body position, for example the crucifix position on the rings. In this case the muscles act as fixators and perform an isometric contraction (remember that during an isometric contraction there is an increase in muscle tension, but no movement occurs). It is possible to improve strength using the static

---

Definition

REPETITION

Repetition is the number of times that an athlete repeats a particular exercise, for example 10 arm curls. The number of repetitions performed is one set.

SET

A set is a certain number of repetitions. Usually three sets are completed in a session.

resistance method (working isometrically) but you will only improve your strength at the specific joint angle used in training. Most methods of strength training involve concentric and eccentric muscle contraction, where the whole range of muscle movement is improved.

To improve strength you should train two or three times a week and should continue the programme for at least ten weeks. As with aerobic training, you will begin to notice improvements in your strength due to muscular adaptations after 3–4 weeks. It is important to continually monitor your performance so you can progressively increase the resistance you work against in line with your level of improvement.

ACTIVITY

For your individual and/or team activity identify

- the types of strength you need to improve
- the major muscles used
- the type of muscle contraction employed.

Strength can be improved using circuit training, weight training, pulleys and plyometrics.

12.5.1 Circuit training

In circuit training the athlete performs a series of exercises (8–10) arranged in a circuit (*Figure 12.2*) usually used for general conditioning. The resistance used is the athlete's body weight and each exercise concentrates on stressing a particular muscle group. It is important to order the exercises to alternate the muscles being used and allow for recovery. Typical exercises include press-ups, sit-ups, squat thrusts, step-ups, shuttle runs, star jumps, astride jumps, dips, burpees and pull-ups.

Sit-ups

Press-ups

Shuttle run

Dips

Figure 12.2 Exercises for circuit training

ACTIVITY

Arrange the above-mentioned exercises into a circuit, making sure that the major muscle groups being used are rotated to allow recovery.

Dribbling

Lay-up

Figure 12.3 Combining circuit training with skills training

Circuit training can be adapted to include skill training while still developing strength (*Figure 12.3*); this is ideal for the games player. For example, a basketball circuit might include

1 a 5 metre shuttle dribbling the ball
2 chest passes against the wall
3 right-handed lay-ups
4 free throws
5 figure-of-eight dribble around two cones
6 rebounding drill (using a crash mat for the landing surface)
7 left-handed lay-ups
8 overhead throw using a medicine ball.

ACTIVITY

Devise a skills circuit for your team activity that would develop strength endurance.

Once you have decided what exercises you are going to perform, you must decide on the length of the work and rest intervals. A typical circuit involves the athlete working to maximum for 30 seconds with a 30 second recovery period. This makes it ideal for working in pairs, with one of each team recording how many repetitions their partner performs in the 30 seconds. If strength endurance is to be stressed it is more appropriate to work for one minute at each station. As a circuit is usually repeated three times in a session you should be realistic about the amount of work you can perform until your level of conditioning has improved.

12.5.2 Weight training

Instead of using the athlete's body weight as the resistance, additional weights, in the form of free weights or a multi-gym, are used. The athlete will perform a number of repetitions and sets at prescribed weights, depending on the type of strength being improved and the athlete's level of fitness. Typical exercises are shown in Table 12.1.

Table 12.1 Typical weight-training exercises

Exercise	Body part worked
Arm curl	Upper and lower arm
Bench press	Chest
Heel raise	Lower leg
Squat	Back and upper leg

Weight training is good for developing strength, but rarely allows the athlete to reproduce the same movement pattern that is performed during an activity.

12.5.3 Use of pulleys

To allow an athlete to train against a resistance and still perform the actual movement pattern used in the activity pulleys can be used (see *Figure 12.4*). This idea is used quite a lot by swimmers and throwers, but can be adapted for most activities. Another method of applying resistance during skill practices is to wear ankle or wrist weights.

Figure 12.4 Using pulleys to improve strength

12.5.4 Plyometrics

Plyometrics is a form of training that has been developed to improve dynamic strength. It involves jumping, hopping or bounding, in which muscle groups have to work eccentrically. To be most effective the athlete starts from the top of a bench or box and jumps down. During the landing the muscle groups are working eccentrically, acting as a brake to help control the movement. The athlete should then immediately take off and jump up, performing a concentric muscle contraction (see *Figure 12.5*).

A muscle will contract concentrically with more force if it has been stretched under tension before the contraction. This concept can easily be demonstrated with a piece of elastic – the further you stretch it, the more strongly it will recoil; remember that one of the properties of muscle is its elasticity. Any athlete needing to perform explosive movements will benefit by doing some plyometric work, but should not attempt plyometrics until they have a reasonable amount of leg strength.

Figure 12.5 Plyometrics helps to improve dynamic strength

12.6 Improving flexibility

Flexibility is improved by stretching, moving a joint to *just beyond* its point of resistance. Flexibility is limited by the joint itself and the muscles, ligaments and tendons acting on it. We cannot change the bony structures or the type of joint, but we can stretch the soft tissue surrounding the joint. Women have a natural advantage because their body structure allows greater flexibility, but both male and females can significantly improve their flexibility through training.

For improvement to occur a stretch should be held for a minimum of ten seconds and a mobility session should last for at least ten minutes. For the best results the body should be warm, so the exercises should be performed after a warm-up or during the cool-down phase of the training session. Flexibility training needs to be undertaken at least three times a week, but improvement is rapid and will be obvious after five or six weeks of training. An athlete should identify the joints where increased flexibility is required and concentrate their efforts on these joints. However, it is not always beneficial to increase the amount of flexibility around a joint as this can lead to lack of stability – and in contact sports this could result in injury.

Types of flexibility training include static and ballistic stretching and PNF.

Figure 12.6 Active static stretching

Figure 12.7 A passive static stretch is performed with the aid of a partner

12.6.1 Static stretching

This can be achieved *actively* by an athlete moving into a position that takes the joint beyond its point of resistance, lengthening the soft tissue around the joint. The position is held for a minimum of ten seconds (see *Figure 12.6*). In a *passive* stretch a partner is used to move the joint beyond its resistance point and holds the position – see *Figure 12.7*.

12.6.2 Ballistic stretching

This involves the athlete using momentum to move a body part through its extreme range of movement. The exercises involve swinging or bouncing movements, as shown in *Figure 12.8*. This type of stretching should be undertaken only by athletes who are very flexible, as it is very easy to over-stretch and damage connective tissue.

12.6.3 Proprioceptive, neuromuscular facilitation (PNF)

This relatively new method of stretching is extremely effective. The athlete moves the joint to just beyond its resistance point and then performs an isometric contraction (a partner can be used to provide the resistance). The muscle is relaxed and stretched again, and will usually stretch further the second time.

ACTIVITY

Design a programme that will improve your flexibility in line with the demands of your individual or team activity.

Figure 12.8 Ballistic stretches

Key revision box

The main principles of training include overload, progression, specificity, reversibility and variance. Any training programme should be closely monitored and evaluated and every session should include a warm-up and a cool-down. Training should be specific to the athlete and the sport they participate in but a general fitness programme needs to be completed before any specialisation.

KEY TERMS

You should now understand the following terms. If you do not, go back through the chapter and find out.

Overload
Variance
Plyometrics
Progression
Critical threshold
Specificity
Fartlek
Warm-up
PNF
Reversibility
Cool-down
Moderation

PROGRESS CHECK

1 Briefly outline the principles of training.
2 What happens when you overload a system?
3 Why is it important for overload to be progressive?
4 How can you ensure that your training is specific to your activity?
5 What does FIT stand for?
6 Give two reasons why training should be varied.
7 List three physiological benefits of a warm-up.
8 List three physiological benefits of a cool-down.
9 Describe two methods of improving your aerobic capacity.
10 How can you calculate your critical threshold?
11 What intensity can an elite athlete normally train at?
12 Explain what 'Fartlek' means.
13 What four variables can be changed in interval training?
14 What is meant by the term repetition maximum?
15 Explain the general guidelines used when planning
   (a) a maximum-strength programme
   (b) a strength endurance programme.
16 What types of exercise would you be performing in a plyo-metric session?
17 Explain the difference between a general conditioning circuit and a skill circuit.
18 What is the difference between an active static stretch and a passive static stretch?

Response to exercise

Learning objectives:

○ To be able to describe the short-term physiological response of the body to exercise.

○ To understand the relationship between the responses of the cardiovascular system and the respiratory system.

○ To be able to differentiate between a short-term response and a long-term adaptation.

○ To be able to describe the chronic physiological response of the body to training.

13.1 The body's response to exercise

The body is continually responding to the demands made on it by the individual and by the environment in an attempt to maintain a stable internal environment, known as *homeostasis*.

The body functions best when body fluids, temperature, oxygen levels etc. are at specific levels. Any change in the body's internal environment usually prompts an immediate response in an attempt to redress the balance.

The internal regulatory systems of the body cause the changes in the body that we experience when we begin to exercise. When we begin to work harder we use up more energy and produce more carbon dioxide. Increases in carbon dioxide concentrations cause an increase in blood acidity, which is an unwelcome change to the body's internal environment. The increase in carbon dioxide is detected by the brain, which responds by increasing the rate and depth of breathing (remember that the respiratory control centre in the medulla of the brain is sensitive to an increase in carbon dioxide levels). This response helps to expel carbon dioxide and also helps to increase the supply of much-needed oxygen.

In this chapter we look at the short-term physiological response of the body to exercise and the long-term physiological adaptations that occur as a result of training. Short-term physiological responses are the changes that occur in the body during an exercise session, such as an increase in heart rate, that return to normal shortly after the period of exercise has finished. Long-term physiological adaptations, sometimes referred to as a chronic response, are long-lasting changes that take place in response to training, making the body more efficient at dealing with the demands made on it. A good example is the increase in stroke volume that occurs after a period of aerobic training. This makes the heart more efficient (it supplies more blood per beat) so that it doesn't have to work as hard.

If no long-term physiological adaptations took place no improvements would be gained and there would be little point in training. The adaptations

Definition
HOMEOSTASIS
Maintenance of a stable internal environment.

that do occur are very specific in that they depend on the physiological make-up of the individual and the type of training that he or she performs. A well planned fitness programme will very quickly cause long-term adaptations, making you fitter, healthier and more able to cope with the demands of your chosen sport.

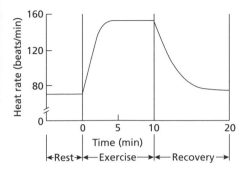

Figure 13.1 Change in heart rate with exercise

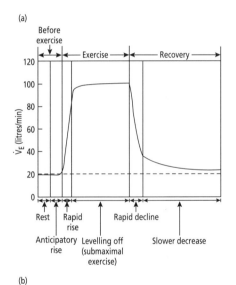

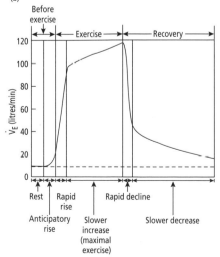

Figure 13.2 The changes in ventilation rate during (a) submaximal and (b) maximal exercise

13.2 Short-term physiological response to exercise

The following changes will take place to a greater or lesser extent during exercise. The degree of change will depend on the intensity and duration of the exercise. As soon as the athlete stops exercising then the recovery process begins as the body works to return to its pre-exercise state.

13.2.1 The heart

The onset of exercise causes changes in the levels of lactic acid, carbon dioxide, oxygen and body temperature. Information about these changes is relayed to the cardiac control centre located in the medulla.

Neural control

The cardiac control centre responds to exercise by increasing the activity of the sympathetic nerve acting on the sinuatrial node of the heart (the pacemaker), causing an increase in heart rate.

Hormonal control

Even before the start of exercise the regulatory systems of the body have a way of pre-empting the changes that are likely to occur and start to prepare the body by releasing adrenaline. Adrenaline increases heart rate and the strength of the contraction of the myocardium.

Intrinsic control

As the heart rate increases so does the stroke volume. During exercise more blood is returned to the heart (venous return is increased) and more blood enters the heart during diastole. The combination of more blood in the heart and greater strength of contraction leads to an increase in stroke volume. The raised heart rate and stroke volume causes an overall increase in cardiac output, so that more oxygen can be delivered to the muscles and the waste products of respiration can be removed. *Figure 13.1* shows the heart rate response to exercise.

13.2.2 The lungs

Changes in oxygen and carbon dioxide levels are detected by the respiratory centre of the brain. The respiratory centre responds by increasing the minute ventilation.

Changes to lung volumes

The minute ventilation is the product of the number of breaths taken and the tidal volume. As the tidal volume increases both the inspiratory reserve volume and the expiratory reserve volume decrease.

Changes to the mechanics of breathing

For more air to be taken into the lungs the respiratory muscles must work harder to change the volume of the thoracic cavity and expiration becomes an active process. *Figure 13.2* shows the response of the respiratory system to exercise.

13.2.3 The blood

Blood is the major transport medium of the body. Its constituents change during exercise. Receptors in the aortic and carotid bodies detect any changes that occur and relay the information to the brain.

Blood volume

During strenuous exercise blood plasma volume can be reduced by sweating, and blood glucose levels will drop as carbohydrate stores run low. This is why during endurance events athletes are encouraged to drink water or glucose-based drinks.

Blood acidity

The blood acidity increases as more lactic acid and carbon dioxide are produced. If levels are not controlled the athlete will have to slow down or stop as enzyme activity will be affected.

Blood oxygen

There is less oxygen in the blood returning to the heart and this increases the oxygen diffusion gradient at the lungs. This in turn speeds up the rate of diffusion.

Blood pressure

Exercise causes a rise in systolic blood pressure, mainly because of the changes in cardiac output. Diastolic pressure remains unchanged.

13.2.4 The vascular system

The vasomotor centre in the medulla controls the flow and pressure of blood.

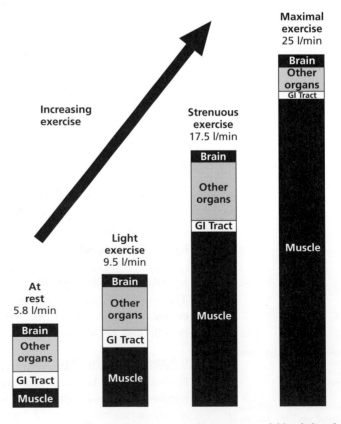

Figure 13.3 Effect of exercise on cardiac output and blood distribution

Vasodilatation

During exercise more blood is distributed to the working muscles as arterioles supplying the working muscles are dilated. At the same time the precapillary sphincters of the capillary networks supplying the working muscles are opened, further increasing the flow of blood.

Vasoconstriction

Arterioles supplying blood to the kidneys and other organs are constricted, reducing the blood flow.

The net effect is to supply more oxygen to the muscles and to aid removal of the waste products of respiration. *Figure 13.3* shows the response of the vascular system to exercise.

13.2.5 The muscles

As a muscle works harder it uses up more energy, so the rate of respiration in the muscle cell has to increase. The changes in the muscle cell stimulate the rest of the body to respond in order to ensure that the energy supply meets the energy demand and that waste products are disposed of before the internal balance can be disturbed.

Energy stores

During exercise the cell's energy stores (phosphocreatine, glycogen and triglyceride) are slowly depleted. Depending on the intensity and duration of the activity they may become completely exhausted.

Oxygen stores

Less oxygen is stored in the myoglobin during exercise as mitochondrial demand for oxygen increases. This increases the rate of diffusion of oxygen into the cell, as the partial pressure of oxygen is reduced in the cell relative to the partial pressure of oxygen in the capillary. Other changes (increase in blood acidity and rise in body temperature) also help to speed up the rate of dissociation of oxygen from haemoglobin.

Carbon dioxide and lactic acid levels

Owing to the elevated rate of respiration more carbon dioxide and lactic acid enter the bloodstream and are removed from the muscles. Carbon dioxide is taken to the lungs to be expired and the lactic acid is taken to the liver, where it is changed back to glycogen.

Body temperature

Another change brought about by the increase in respiration is an increase in body temperature. Most of the energy released by the muscle is in the form of heat energy. In order to maintain a constant body temperature the body begins to sweat more and blood vessels near the body's surface are dilated.

ACTIVITY
Produce a table summarising the short-term responses of the body to exercise.

13.3 Long-term physiological response to exercise

As already mentioned, physiological adaptations take place as a result of training. The type of training undertaken determines what adaptations will take place and every individual responds differently because of their physiological make-up. We should remember that our physical capabilities are mostly genetically determined and no amount of training will change slow oxidative fibres into fast glycolytic ones. All we can do is to maximise our existing potential.

13.4 Aerobic adaptation

After following an aerobic training programme for 12 weeks you would probably find your initial training session is now very easy. A task that once left you tired and out of breath is now accomplished with relative ease – so what has happened? You will have improved your $\dot{V}O_2(max)$, and for that to happen the following adaptations will have taken place.

13.4.1 The heart

Hypertrophy of the myocardium

When any muscle is made to work harder it responds by increasing in size. The strength of a muscle relates to its cross-sectional area, so as it gets larger it also gets stronger.

The heart reacts in the same way as any other muscle, and after endurance training is able to contract with more force, enabling it to push more blood out of the heart per beat.

Increase in stroke volume and maximum cardiac output

As the heart increase in size it can hold more blood and the contractility of the myocardium improves. This means that the resting stroke volume of an endurance athlete, along with the maximum stroke volume achieved during exercise, is increased.

During submaximal exercise the heart of an endurance athlete doesn't have to beat as often as that of an untrained individual to deliver the same amount of blood to the working muscle. During maximal exercise the cardiac output will increase, meaning that more oxygen reaches the muscles and helping to improve $\dot{V}O_2(max)$.

For example, a 20 year old has an estimated maximum heart rate of 200 beats per minute.

Cardiac output = Maximum stroke volume × Maximum heart rate

For an untrained individual   = 120 ml × 200

         = 24 litres

For a trained athlete   = 160 ml × 200

         = 32 litres

Decrease in resting heart rate

The cardiac output required at rest remains the same, as the demand for oxygen is unchanged. As the resting stroke volume has increased the heart doesn't have to beat as many times to produce the same cardiac output, so the resting heart rate decreases.

Definition

HYPERTROPHY

An increase in cell size leads to an increase in tissue size.

For example,

Cardiac output	=	Stroke volume × Heart rate
Before training at rest	=	70 ml × 72
	=	5.04 litres
After training at rest	=	100 ml × 50
	=	5 litres

The combined effect of these changes to the heart means that the heart is far more efficient at pumping blood round the body, helping to distribute more oxygen to the muscles.

13.4.2 The lungs

Maximum minute ventilation

The maximum minute ventilation of endurance athletes is greater than that of untrained individuals due to an increase in the frequency of breathing and the tidal volume.

Respiratory muscles

The respiratory muscles become more efficient with training, making ventilation more efficient.

Lung volumes

After training an increase in resting lung volumes (apart from tidal volume) takes place. This is because you use more of your existing lung capacity.

Diffusion

Diffusion rates improve with training because the increase in lung volume creates a greater surface area, allowing more diffusion to take place.

These changes don't really have a direct effect on an athlete's VO_2(max), as healthy lungs are always capable of ventilating more than enough oxygen. Improved ventilation may be linked more to the need to expire the greater volume of carbon dioxide produced due to the increased rate of respiration in the cells.

13.4.3 Blood

Blood volume

Blood volume will increase as a result of endurance training. Although most of the increase is due to an increase in the volume of blood plasma, there is also a small increase in the number of red blood cells. This means that more haemoglobin is available, increasing the oxygen-carrying capacity of the blood.

Blood acidity

During submaximal exercise the blood of trained athletes is less acidic because their aerobic system is more effective and they produce less lactic acid. During maximal exercise the reverse is true – as endurance athletes have a greater tolerance to lactic acid, more accumulates in the blood and increases acidity.

13.4.4 The vascular system

Endurance training increases the elasticity of the arterial walls, which helps the arteries withstand greater fluctuations in blood pressure. The number of capillaries at the lungs and skeletal muscle increase, helping to improve the rate of gaseous exchange.

13.4.5 The muscles

Several changes occur within the muscles, all helping to improve the use of oxygen once it reaches the cell. The muscle itself increases in size and strength (undergoes hypertrophy) and the following other changes also occur.

Myoglobin

The amount of myoglobin in the muscle cell increases, helping to transport oxygen from the capillary to the mitochondria more effectively.

Mitochondria

The number of mitochondria increases, allowing greater rates of aerobic respiration and using more oxygen.

Enzyme activity

Increased activity of the respiratory enzymes further adds to the efficiency of the aerobic energy system.

Energy stores

The muscle cell stores more glycogen and triglycerides, plus fat stores are mobilised more efficiently.

13.4.6 Overall benefits

The overall effect of all these changes means that the following processes all become more efficient:

● external respiration
● oxygen transport from the lungs to the cells
● use of oxygen within the cell.

These factors lead to an improvement in $\dot{V}O_2(max)$ of up to 20% and therefore significantly improve the performance of activities that rely heavily on the aerobic energy system.

Aerobic activity also has beneficial effects on connective tissue:

● tendons become stronger
● ligaments are stretched, increasing flexibility
● exercise stimulates deposition of calcium to bony tissue, strengthening the bones
● the lines of stress on bone are varied.

Although these last four changes don't affect a person's aerobic capacity, they help to reduce the risk of injury and offset the effects of ageing on connective tissue.

ACTIVITY

Produce a table summarising the long-term responses of the body to aerobic training.

13.5 Anaerobic adaptations

Nowhere near as many adaptations take place due to anaerobic work as do to aerobic work. This is because the important adaptations occur *within* the muscle, as the anaerobic system does not rely on the availability and transport of oxygen. Any adaptations to anaerobic training tend to last longer once training has stopped than aerobic adaptations.

The changes outlined below allow the athlete to work at increased levels of intensity and for longer periods of time, as they increase the threshold of anaerobic energy systems. Just as importantly the ability to recover from anaerobic work improves, allowing more work to be performed during a training session or activity.

13.5.1 Muscle hypertrophy

The fibre type recruited during the exercise will hypertrophy, in this case type 2a and type 2b fibres.

13.5.2 Enzyme activity

Activity of the enzymes responsible for the breakdown of ATP, phospho-creatine and glycogen increases. In addition activity of the enzymes responsible for synthesis of ATP and phosphocreatine during recovery speeds up, shortening recovery time.

13.5.3 Energy stores

Anaerobic training stimulates the muscle to store greater amounts of ATP, phosphocreatine and glycogen, increasing the thresholds of the anaerobic energy systems.

13.5.4 Lactic acid

The fast-twitch muscle fibres can tolerate higher levels of lactic acid and are also better at removing lactic acid during recovery.

13.6 Flexibility adaptations

The soft tissue surrounding a joint (the ligaments, tendons and muscles) can be stretched and their resting length increased. This is because they have elastic properties that allow a change in length – providing flexibility training is carried out correctly.

ACTIVITY

Refer back to the skills circuit you developed for your games activity in Chapter 12. Outline the adaptations you would expect to occur if you followed your programme for three months.

Key revision box

The body responds to exercise on both a short-term and a long-term physiological basis. A short-term response, such as an increase in heart rate, takes place during the actual training session and will return to normal shortly after the athlete stops exercising. A long-term response, such as a drop in resting heart rate due to aerobic training, is an adaptation to the body that takes place over a period of time.

KEY TERMS

You should now understand the following terms. If you do not, go back through the chapter and find out.

Homeostasis
Short-term response
Chronic response
Adaptation
Hypertrophy
Myoglobin
Mitochondria

PROGRESS CHECK

1 Explain what is meant by 'homeostasis'.
2 What is the major difference between a short-term physiological response to exercise and a long-term physiological response to exercise?
3 List three adaptations that occur to the heart after aerobic training.
4 What is the main reason for the drop in resting heart rate following aerobic training?
5 List three of the changes that occur to the blood during exercise which help to increase the rate of diffusion of oxygen from the capillary to the muscle cell.
6 When does expiration become active?
7 Name two lung volumes that decrease during exercise.
8 Name the energy stores that are increased by aerobic training.
9 Define hypertrophy.
10 How does aerobic training affect cardiac output?
11 Why doesn't anaerobic training result in major adaptations to the heart?
12 List three changes occurring within the muscle cell after aerobic training that help to improve the cell's ability to use oxygen.
13 By how much can you improve your $\dot{V}O_2$(max)?
14 What are the benefits of exercise on connective tissue?
15 Describe three changes within the muscle cell that can help to increase the threshold of your anaerobic energy systems.
16 Outline the physiological adaptations you would expect to happen if you followed a programme designed to improve your maximum strength.

Further reading

R.J. Davis, C.R. Bull, J.V. Roscoe and D.A. Roscoe. *Physical Education and the Study of Sport*. Wolfe Medical Publishers, 1991.

D. Davis, T. Kimmet and M. Auty. *Physical Education: Theory and Practice*. Macmillan Australia, 1986.

F. Dick. *Sports Training Principles*. A & C Black, 1989.

E. Fox, R. Bowen and M. Foss. *The Physiological Basis for Exercise and Sport*. Brown and Benchmark, 1989.

R. Hazeldine. *Fitness for Sport*. Gowood Press, 1985.

David R. Lamb. *Physiology of Exercise, Responses and Adaptations*. Collier Macmillan Publishers, 1984.

W. Paish. *Training for Peak Performance*. A & C Black, 1991.

Peak Performance Magazines. Available by subscription only from Stonehart Leisure Magazines Ltd, 67–71 Goswell Road, London EC1V 7EN.

B. J. Sharkey. *Physiology of Fitness*. Human Kinetics Books, 1990.

Motor learning

This part of the book contains:

Chapter 14   Skill and its characteristics
Chapter 15   Theories related to the learning of skills
Chapter 16   Theories related to the teaching of skills

In this part of the book we will investigate how we learn movement skills associated with physical education and sport. The process of motor learning can only be understood by studying the nature of skill and its characteristics. The more we know about a particular skill, the better we are placed to devise teaching strategies to teach that skill. We will also look in detail at theories related to the learning of skills. There are no 'watertight' theories about learning because the human brain is such a complex organ, but this part highlights the relevant theories widely accepted by sports psychologists. Finally, this part deals with theories related to the teaching of skills. Effective teaching is dependent on a number of factors, including the personality and ability of the teacher, but to optimise the learning environment the teacher or coach must consider the research underpinning good practice – including the structure of training sessions, the type of guidance given and the possible teaching styles that can be adopted.

CHAPTER 14

Skill and its characteristics

Learning objectives:

- To be able to explain what we mean by the term skill.
- To be able to differentiate between skill and ability.
- To be able to classify skill in a number of different ways.
- To link our ideas to practical situations.

14.1 The concept and nature of skill

ACTIVITY

Study the photograph above. We would probably all agree that this performer is skilled. Before you read on, write a list of words and phrases which you feel would describe a skilled performer.

You will probably have thought of *fluent, coordinated* and *controlled* and phrases like *'seems effortless', 'looks good'* and *'good technique'*.

We often comment that an experienced sports person is 'skilful', but what do we actually mean by the word 'skill'? We use it to describe a task such as kicking a ball, but often we use it to describe the overall actions of someone who is good at what they do. There are two main ways of using the word 'skill':

In practice

If a tennis player often serves 'aces' in a match, we would label that player as skilled. If we watched him over a number of matches and he continued to serve aces, we would be more justified in labelling him as skilled. A squash player whom we might regard as skilled would anticipate where the ball is going to land and would put herself in a position to receive the ball early so that she could hit it early, thus putting her opponent at a disadvantage.

- to see skill as a specific task to be performed
- to view skill as describing the quality of a particular action, which might include how consistent the performance is and how prepared the performer is to carry out the task.

When we see top-class sportsmen and sportswomen we are often struck by the seemingly effortless way that they perform, and it is not until we try to perform ourselves that we realise just how difficult it really is! We know that these performers are very fit but they don't seem to exert themselves and we are aware that whatever the skill – whether it is a somersault in gymnastics or a perfectly timed rugby tackle – the end product looks good and is aesthetically pleasing. A skilled performer knows what he or she is trying to achieve and more often than not is successful, which is annoying if you are their opponent! A beginner, or novice, will seem clumsy and slow and will lack control. The novice will also tire quickly and expend more energy than is necessary.

When an accomplished hockey player, for instance, performs a skilful pass, he or she shows a technically good movement. This movement is called the *motor skill*.

A skilled hockey player needs both motor skills and perceptual skills

Definition

MOTOR SKILL

An action or task that has a goal and that requires voluntary body and/or limb movement to achieve the goal.

Definition

PERCEPTION

A complex concept that involves interpretation of stimuli. Not all stimuli are perceived and what is perceived depends on past experience and attention ability. For a detailed explanation of perception see the section on Information Processing on page 135.

The player also has to assess the position of the opponents and the players on the same team and will have to decide where to pass the ball and how hard to pass it. This interpretation of information or stimuli is called *perception* and the skill required is called *perceptual skill*.

When we talk of skill, we usually mean a combination of perceptual and motor skills.

Skilled performers are not born with these skills already programmed in their minds – they have to learn them in a number of different ways. The ways in which we learn skills are investigated in Chapter 15.

'Skill' has been defined in the following way:

A skilled movement is one in which a predetermined objective is accomplished with maximum efficiency with a minimum outlay of energy.

Key revision box

The main characteristics of skilled movement: learned, goal directed, pre-determined goals, consistent achievement, economy of movement, efficiency, coordinated, precise, aesthetically pleasing, fluent, controlled.

In practice

The abilities of balance, strength and flexibility are necessary before you can perform a head-stand. A Frisbee catch needs the underlying abilities of hand–eye coordination and perceptual awareness.

14.2 Ability

We often talk about improving our own abilities and those of other people, but we probably usually mean 'skills' rather than 'abilities'. Skills are, as we now know, learned and involve often pre-planned movements which are goal directed. To carry out skills, we need certain underlying factors such as strength and hand–eye coordination. These factors are known as *abilities*.

Our abilities are largely determined genetically – they are *natural* or *innate* – and they tend to be enduring characteristics. This is bad news for some of us who would like to get to the top of our sport but who don't have the natural ability to do so because, no matter how hard we try, we may never reach those giddy heights. We simply may not have the necessary innate qualities. However, research has revealed that some abilities can be enhanced to a certain extent, especially in early childhood.

In the previous activity you may have listed hand–eye coordination for tennis, strength for rugby, fine motor control for snooker, flexibility for golf and speed for netball. All of these abilities are found in most sports but their importance to the execution of skills and techniques varies with the particular sport. It would be nice to suppose that there is a general 'sporting ability' which underpins most sports, but research to date does not support this. Several specific abilities help form the foundation for certain sporting skills – two of the most important are *psychomotor* and *gross motor* abilities.

Certain skills require specific abilities or sets of abilities but most motor skills involve the abilities of strength, speed and coordination.

14.2.1 The general and specific views of abilities

Top sports people are popularly thought to possess an overall single ability to perform well. Many researchers believe in many different specific motor abilities but if these abilities were very closely related then a 'general' motor ability could exist. Some individuals seem to be very good at many different sports, which seems to back the idea of a general motor ability. The presence of a general motor ability could be explained by viewing the performer as having a high degree of prowess in *groups* of abilities. For example a good all-round sports person may have good balance, speed

---

Definition

PSYCHOMOTOR ABILITY

Our ability to process information regarding movement and then to put our decisions into action. Psychomotor abilities include reaction time and limb coordination.

GROSS MOTOR ABILITY

Ability involving actual movement – strength, flexibility, speed.

KINESTHESIS

This is the information we hold within ourselves about our body's position. The information comes from receptors found in the muscles, tendons and joints. The term proprioception is often used in the same way.

Certain skills require specific abilities

Catching a Frisbee

and hand–eye coordination. It would therefore follow that this person is likely to be good at a wide range of sports involving these abilities. However, there is no firm evidence to support the notion that there is such a thing as general motor ability.

Some researchers have looked into ways of predicting athletic prowess after an individual's abilities have been identified. Tests have been performed on young people to find out their abilities and then to link these abilities to certain sports. This has not been very successful, because different abilities are needed at different stages of skill learning. For instance, good vision and the ability to process information rapidly are important when beginning to learn a complex task, but kinesthesis is more important in the later stages. Ability tests cannot, therefore, be used to accurately predict sporting prowess.

Key revision box

We are all born with certain abilities. Before we can be proficient at skills we must have the abilities that help us to perform these skills. There is no single 'general' motor ability but there are many specific abilities – such as manual dexterity, physical strength. A good all-round athlete probably develops through many complex and interlinking factors, such as body type, innate ability, personality, parental support and other socialising factors.

14.3 Classification of skill

In order to understand the nature of a particular skill, we need to analyse it. The traditional way of doing this is by classification but this can be very unsatisfactory and inaccurate because skills have many characteristics, which can change in different situations. For example, catching a Frisbee involves large and small muscle movements and involves the catcher adjusting their movements according to the varied flight of the Frisbee. It is very difficult to classify skills neatly, but to make teaching and learning more effective it is essential that we fully understand skills.

14.3.1 Analysis of skills

If we accept that skills cannot be neatly labelled the best means of analysis is to use a scale or continuum which will illustrate that skills have different characteristics to a greater or lesser extent. The skill in a tennis serve, for instance, has elements of fine muscle movements and gross muscle movements but we would probably agree that it involves more gross muscle movements. We might place the skill of the tennis serve at X on a continuum like that in *Figure 14.1*.

Gross ·············· **X** ··· **Fine**

Figure 14.1 Skills should be assessed on a continuum

Most skill classification systems are based on the view that motor skills are affected by three factors:

1. how precise a movement is
2. whether the movement has a definite beginning and end
3. whether the environment affects the performance of the skill.

127

The following words and phrases are often used in the classification of skills. Always remember to classify skills according to a continuum because this reflects the true, although complex, nature of skill.

The gross–fine continuum

This is concerned with the precision of movement.

Gross skills involve large muscle movements. These skills are not very precise and include many of the fundamental movement patterns such as walking and jumping. An example of a skill which is predominantly gross is the shot putt.

Fine skills involve more intricate movements using small muscle groups. These skills tend to be precise in nature and generally involve a high degree of hand–eye coordination. An example of a fine motor skill is a snooker shot.

The open–closed continuum

This continuum is concerned with the effects of the environment on skills.

Open skills are affected by the environment and are, therefore, predominantly perceptual. Movements have to be adapted to the environment and the skill is mostly externally paced – for example, a pass in football.

Closed skills are not affected by the environment and are predominantly habitual. Movements follow a set pattern and have a definite beginning and end. These skills tend to be self-paced. An example of a closed skill is a free throw in basketball.

The 'pacing' continuum

This is often used in conjunction with the open–closed continuum and refers to the timing of movements.

Self-paced skills. The performer controls the rate at which the skill is executed. Self-pacing involves proaction by the performer. Self-paced skills are usually closed skills – an example is a javelin throw.

Externally paced skills. The environment, which may include your opponent, controls the rate of performing the skill. This type of skill involves reaction and is usually an open skill such as receiving a serve in badminton.

The discrete–serial–continuous continuum

This is concerned with how well defined the beginning and end of the skill are.

Discrete skills have a clear beginning and a clear end. The skill can be repeated but the performer must start again from the beginning. It is a single, specific skill. A penalty flick in hockey is an example of such a skill.

Serial skills have several discrete elements which are put together to make an integrated movement or sequence of movements – for example the sequence of skills in a triple jump.

Continuous skills have no obvious beginning or end – the end of one cycle of movement is the beginning of the next. The skill is repeated as a set pattern, for example cycling.

In practice

A tennis serve is a skill which involves a set pattern of movement. It is not greatly affected by the environment, so it is more closed than open. If the server perceives some movement of their opponent the serve will need some adjustment and therefore there are open elements to the skill – but it still remains predominantly closed.

ACTIVITY

Draw an open–closed continuum and place the following skills on it: long jump, netball catch, hockey penalty flick, pistol shooting, basketball dribble, receiving a serve in badminton, a vault in gymnastics.

14.4 Using our knowledge of skill classification

In practice

Choose a skill from either soccer or netball and attempt to classify it. Remember to use a continuum.

The coach or teacher and the performer must be able to identify the important aspects of skills. A better understanding of the nature of the task is essential if the task is to be completed skilfully. A knowledge of which stimuli to attend to and which to ignore will help the performer to ignore irrelevant information. The coach can also guide the performer towards making the right decisions.

Knowing how to classify skills can help to decide on the type of teaching/learning strategies that will optimise performance – it might be appropriate to split a skill up into its component parts (its sub-routines) if it is serial in nature, or to build strength of large muscles if the skill is predominantly gross in nature. Knowledge of the perceptual requirements of a skill will also help the performer to take in the correct amount and type of information so that there is no *attentional wastage*.

The importance of knowing all there is to know about the skill to be attempted cannot be overstated. It is particularly important at the top level of performance, where only a small difference in technique or tactics can mean the all-important advantage over your opponent.

Coaches who work with performers with disabilities can make important differences to physical performance using their knowledge of skill composition to ensure effective instruction (see Chapter 16).

The server uses a pattern of movement but can perceive the movement of his opponent

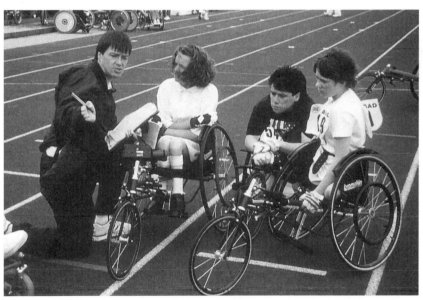

Knowledge of skill will help to optimise performance

Definition

ATTENTIONAL WASTAGE

The performer's concentration can be misdirected to irrelevant cues. This can damage the effectiveness of their performance, and will particularly affect the way a novice learns.

In practice

A novice rugby player who is about to tackle an opponent is not concentrating fully on the movement of the opponent, but will be distracted by the movement of other players.

Key revision box

Skills are classified on a continuum. Knowledge of the task/skills gives good insight into movement requirements and teaching strategies. For example, receiving a pass in lacrosse is predominantly perceptual and therefore more of an open skill. A coach would adopt the strategy of giving a player experience in a variety of different situations (see section on schema, p.141).

KEY TERMS

You should now understand the following terms. If you do not, go back through the chapter and find out.

Motor skill
Perceptual skill
Perception
Stimuli
Ability
Psychomotor ability
Gross motor ability
Kinesthesis
Continuum
Gross and fine skills
Open and closed skills
Discrete, continuous and
    serial skills
Self-paced and externally
    paced skills
Attentional wastage

PROGRESS CHECK

1 What are the main characteristics of a skilled performer?
2 What is meant by a motor skill?
3 What is a perceptual skill?
4 Give the main differences between skill and ability.
5 Why is there no such thing as general sporting ability?
6 What is meant by the term psychomotor ability?
7 What is meant by the term gross motor ability?
8 Why are ability tests unable to predict sporting prowess?
9 Define kinesthesis.
10 How could early childhood experiences influence abilities?
11 Why can't we classify skills accurately?
12 What does the term 'continuum' mean in skill classification?
13 What is the gross/fine continuum?
14 Why are open skills predominantly perceptual?
15 If discrete is at one end of a continuum, what should be at the other?
16 Why is a triple jump a serial skill?
17 What is meant by an externally paced skill?
18 How can a skill be a closed skill in an open situation?
19 Why would a teacher or coach split a skill up into sub-routines?
20 How can knowledge related to skill classification help a coach of a disabled athlete?

CHAPTER 15

Theories related to the learning of skills

Learning objectives:

○ To understand the associative and cognitive theories of learning.

○ To understand the theory of information processing, including the role of memory.

○ To understand the concepts of motor programmes and schema.

○ To investigate different types of feedback.

15.1 The associationist or connectionist view of conditioning

A sprinter driving off the blocks is a response which is closely 'bonded' to the stimulus of the gun

The term *associationist* is given to a group of theories related to connecting *stimulus* and *response*. These theories are often referred to as *S-R theories*. An individual is *conditioned* by stimuli which are 'connected' or 'bonded' to appropriate responses.

15.1.1 Classical conditioning

In classical conditioning an existing S-R connection is replaced by a new bonding. The most famous example of classical conditioning was carried out by Pavlov. Pavlov's experiments with dogs show that pairing an unconditioned stimulus with a conditioned stimulus can eventually result in a conditioned response. Pavlov gave food to his dogs (this is the unconditioned or natural stimulus) and the dogs' natural response (the unconditioned response) was to salivate. Pavlov then rang a bell at the same time as presenting the food. The dogs salivated because of the food, but were unknowingly connecting the arrival of food with the sound of the bell. When the bell was rung again later the dogs still salivated even if no food was presented. The dogs' natural behaviour had now been changed through manipulation of the stimulus – their response became conditioned.

This process is also known as a *conditioned reflex*.

In practice

A coach shouts 'now' to a performer when it is time to open out from a somersault. The performer learns to connect the word 'now' with the kinesthetic 'feel' of the movement at that exact time. Eventually, the word 'now' becomes redundant because the performer has been conditioned by associating the unconditioned stimulus (kinesthesis) with the conditioned stimulus ('now') to get the conditioned response (opening out at the right time). In the teaching of motor skills the practice of motor drills, where movements become almost habitual and bad habits are kept to a minimum, is common.

Key revision box

Unconditioned stimulus (food) → *Unconditioned response (salivation)*
Unconditioned stimulus + Conditioned stimulus (bell) → *Unconditioned response*
Conditioned stimulus → *Conditioned response*

Conditioning is important in the natural environment – for instance, animals learn to recognise other dangerous animals by certain characteristics such as skin colour and avoid coming into contact with them. Conditioning usually allows modification of behaviour to ensure maximum rewards and to avoid punishment. In human behaviour phobias are often the result of conditioning in childhood, including the concept of learned helplessness in sport (see p.180). By punishing their children parents could cause conditioned fear. It has been suggested that when this fear cannot be overcome aggression may result, becoming displaced and directed towards other targets. This may explain aggression in sports performers and some spectators. It is difficult to relate classical conditioning with sports performance, but there are times when a stimulus is manipulated to get a desired response.

ACTIVITY
Try to think of another example in the teaching of motor skills of a response that has been conditioned using another stimulus. What are the drawbacks of this type of teaching?

The main problem with the 'drill' style of teaching motor skills is that the performer can't gain a real understanding of why he or she is doing something. This lack of understanding can have a detrimental effect on future development of skills.

15.1.2 Operant conditioning

Work undertaken by Skinner in 1964 revealed that conditioning was more effective through manipulation of behaviour towards a stimulus than through modification of the stimulus. Skinner used a box with a rat inside it. If the rat hit a lever inside the box a food pellet would be released. Through trial and error the rat eventually learned that hitting the lever would produce food. This has become known as *operant conditioning* or *trial and error learning*. Hitting the lever gave food and therefore a reward, which *reinforced* the hitting action. Operant conditioning is concerned with actions being 'shaped' and then reinforced. Conditioning of this type will only take place if reinforcement is present.

Definition

REINFORCEMENT

The process which increases the probability of a behaviour occurring. Reinforcement strengthens the S-R bond.

POSITIVE REINFORCEMENT

A stimulus which increases the probability of a desired response occurring.

NEGATIVE REINFORCEMENT

The stimulus is withdrawn when the desired response occurs.

PUNISHMENT

Giving a stimulus to prevent a response occurring. Not to be confused with negative reinforcement.

In practice

If you wished to teach the long high serve in badminton, you could draw a large chalk circle at the back of the opposing service box and ask the performer to try to serve into the circle. After several trials (and eventual success) you would make the circle smaller and ask the performer to serve into this smaller circle. Once they are successful at this, wipe out the circle altogether. The performer should have been conditioned to serve long to the back of their opponent's service box. This is the operant method of conditioning: the performer's behaviour had been shaped by targets which became progressively more realistic to the game situation and the correct actions reinforced by praise. The actions were also reinforced through the player's perceived success in hitting the target. How would you go about teaching the same performer to serve high as well as long, using the operant method of conditioning?

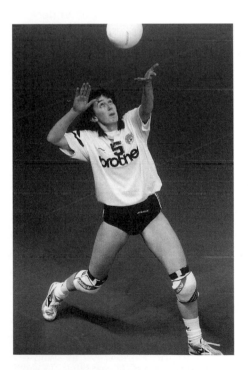

Operant conditioning, a process of shaping behaviour using reinforcement, is useful for teaching skills such as serving

ACTIVITY

Give examples in sport of positive reinforcement, negative reinforcement and punishment.

An example of operant conditioning may be a parent who gives a child a sweet to stop it crying. This reinforces the behaviour and the child cries to get another sweet.

Learning is faster if a reward is given on every occasion – this is known as *complete reinforcement*. Research shows that if a reward is given after a number of correct responses learning takes longer but lasts longer – this is known as *partial reinforcement*. Operant conditioning is commonly used in teaching motor skills.

Rewards are used extensively in skills teaching because they reinforce the type of behaviour required, but there are problems associated with the use of rewards. These will be addressed in Chapter 17.

> ### Key revision box
>
> *Operant conditioning/trial and error learning is a process which involves modification of behaviour. Behaviour is shaped and then reinforced. For conditioning to take place, reinforcement must be present but partial reinforcement is more effective in the long term than complete reinforcement.*

15.1.3 Thorndike's 'laws'

Thorndike developed a theory based on strengthening the S-R bond. He developed some 'laws' which he thought should be taken into consideration when trying to match a response to a particular stimulus.

Law of exercise

Repeating or rehearsing the S-R connections is more likely to strengthen them. If the desired response occurs, reinforcement is necessary.

Law of effect

If the response is followed by a 'satisfier', then the S-R bond is strengthened. If the response is followed by an 'annoyer', then the S-R bond is weakened. This means that pleasant outcomes are likely to motivate the performer to repeat the action.

Law of readiness

The performer must be physically and mentally able to complete the task effectively.

ACTIVITY

Choose a sport and using Thorndike's Laws state how you would teach a specific closed skill.

In practice

A hockey player who has been drilled to perform a particular penalty flick may become predictable and demotivated by inhibition. Practice should be stopped for a while – perhaps new strategies should be discussed and practised later. New targets should be set and the practice resumed.

| Definition |

INTERVENING VARIABLES

Mental processes occurring between the stimulus being received and the response.

| Definition |

INSIGHT LEARNING

Problem solving involving memory. Previous experiences are used to help solve new problems.

| Definition |

GESTALTISTS

A group of German scientists (including Wertheimer, Kohler and Koffka) who established many principles or laws of perception. They extended these laws to provide accounts of learning and problem solving.

15.1.4 Hull's drive theory

Hull pioneered the 'drive theory'. He stated that if the S-R bond is to be strong a performer must be motivated to do well. He warned against too much repetition of practice, because he thought that it could lead to 'inhibition', which would demotivate the performer and weaken the S-R bond.

The inhibition, or drive reduction, can be overcome after a rest interval or when new and more motivating goals are determined.

15.2 Cognitive theories of learning

The cognitive theories go beyond the associative or S-R theories. Many psychologists feel that there are *intervening variables*.

Cognitive theories are concerned with thinking and understanding rather than connecting certain stimuli to certain responses. Trial and error has no place in cognitive theory. It is sometimes known as *insight learning*.

Kohler used chimpanzees to illustrate this concept. The chimpanzee was placed in a cage with a box and a banana was hung from the roof of the cage. The chimp could reach the banana only by putting the box underneath the banana and standing on it. Only one in seven chimpanzees were able to solve this problem without help. Problem solving of this kind involves memory, because chimpanzees who had previous experiences of boxes seemed to be able to solve the problem quicker.

According to cognitive theorists, we are continually receiving information from our surroundings and we work out what has happened using our memories and by our previous knowledge and general understanding (or perception). This cognitive view is often known as *Gestaltist* theory. The word 'gestalt' means 'entirety' or 'wholeness of form'. The *Gestaltists* think that we perceive objects as a whole, rather than a collection of parts.

In practice

A cricketer who learns to swing the ball when bowling by understanding the basic mechanics of this movement is using cognitive theory, although she might not know it. A basketball player who has the benefits of the zone defence explained to him and therefore understands when it is necessary to play this tactic is another example.

The cognitive view lends support to 'whole practice' teaching, rather than part practice – playing the game, so that the participants understand what is required, is more effective than simply learning skills separately, according to the cognitive approach. Giving young children lots of sporting experiences may also help with their future learning and motor development because the child can draw from these experiences to understand a problem and then solve it – gaining insight into the learning process.

ACTIVITY

To illustrate that you understand the differences between the S-R (associative) approach and the cognitive approach, create two different training practices for teaching the front crawl in swimming. Try to integrate both approaches by creating a third training session.

A wide variety of experience in childhood can have enormous benefits in future skill learning

15.3 Information processing

In this theory the brain is viewed as working like a computer. Stimuli entering the brain are known as *information* or *input*, which is then *processed*, decisions are made and a response (known as *output*) takes place:

Input → Decision-making process → Output

A more detailed model than this would help us to understand the cognitive processes involved and therefore give us valuable clues to make skill learning more effective. This can be seen in *Figure 15.1.*

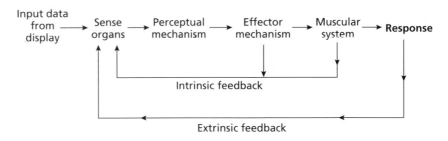

Figure 15.1 Information processing

Models which set out to explain human behaviour are meant only to be illustrative and should not be taken as a factual representation of what actually happens. The environment is constantly changing, as is the nervous system controlling the body's actions. The model of information processing must be taken as dynamic.

To understand what happens at each stage of information processing, we will look at each part of the model from the environment, before information is processed, right through to the feedback immediately after the response.

● The *display* represents the environment surrounding the performer. For instance a basketball player's display might be her opponents, the ball, the basketball, the crowd, the noise and the score board.
● *Sensory input* is the way information is taken in – vision, audition, proprioception, smell, etc.
● The *sense organs* are receptors which pick up the information and transport it to the brain.

Definition

MOTOR PROGRAMME

Sometimes called an executive programme, this is a generalised series of movements stored in the long-term memory that can be retrieved by making one decision.

- In the *perceptual process* the relevant information is selected, interpreted and then used to make a decision. Memory is also used in the perceptual process.
- *Decision-making* process or *translatory mechanism*. Once information has been interpreted a motor plan is formed for movement to take place.
- Using the *effector mechanism* the decisions that have been made are put into action and impulses are sent to the muscles for a response to be made. This plan of action may well be in the form of a '*motor programme*'.
- *Feedback* may be *extrinsic* via knowledge of results or *intrinsic*, which arises via proprioception.

The whole process of information processing is complex but one way of understanding the process is to divide it into three stages:

1 stimulus identification stage
2 response selection stage
3 response programming stage.

In practice

Stimulus identification: A netball player who is about to catch the ball detects the movement of the ball, including its speed and direction.
Response selection: The netball player now decides to change direction to get into line with the ball and catch it.

Stage 1: stimulus identification

In this part of the process the sense organs pick up information from the environment and recognise them for what they are.

Stage 2: response selection

This stage involves making a decision about how to respond to the information that has just been received.

Stage 3: response programming

When the decision to move has been made, the appropriate response is selected. At this stage a motor programme may be used to initiate muscle movement.

15.3.1 Reactions

The speed with which we process information is known as *reaction time*. The process of attending to relevant stimuli, making a decision and responding involves all three of the stages outlined above.

Several factors affect response time:

- whether the reaction involves making a choice
- your age
- your sex
- whether you were expecting the stimulus or not
- previous experience
- how quickly one stimulus follows another
- whether you can anticipate what is going to happen.

Let us look at each of these in more detail.

Definition

REACTION TIME

The time between first presentation of a stimulus to the very start of the movement in response to it.

MOVEMENT TIME

The time between starting and finishing a movement.

RESPONSE TIME

The time between first presentation of the stimulus to completion of the movement (reaction time plus movement time).

Simple or choice reactions

A performer will take a lot less time to react to only one stimulus or to a stimulus that requires a simple response than to more than one stimulus or if more than one response is possible. According to *Hick's Law*, the more responses that are possible, the longer the reaction time will be.

In practice

Think of situations in your own sport where reactions are important. Identify the stimulus or stimuli which trigger your information processing system into action. When does the response finish?

Quick reactions are often crucial if a skill is to be successful

---

Definition

HICK'S LAW

'Choice reaction time is linearly related to the amount of information that must be processed to resolve the uncertainty about the various possible stimulus response alternatives.'

In practice

An activity involving simple reaction time is the start of a sprint race. The sound of the gun is the only stimulus which needs attention. An example of choice reaction time is waiting to receive a tennis serve – there are several possible responses that could be made to the stimulus of the ball.

Definition

SINGLE-CHANNEL HYPOTHESIS

This states that when handling stimuli from the environment the brain can deal with only one stimulus at a time. This is because the brain is thought of as a single-channel organ – it can only deal with one piece of information at a time, which has to be processed before the next stimulus can be dealt with. This is often referred to as the 'bottleneck'.

Age

Your reaction time gets quicker, up to an optimum age and then deteriorates.

Sex

Males have generally quicker reactions than females but the reaction times of females deteriorate less quickly than those of males.

Stimulus–response compatibility

If the response demanded by a stimulus is the one you were expecting, you are likely to react more quickly than if the response demanded is not what you expected.

In practice

An example of stimulus–response compatibility could occur in squash, when the position of your opponent's feet indicates that he is going to make a drive down the wall, but he then executes a boast on the side wall. Your reactions may well be slower because the response required is different from the one you were expecting to make.

Previous experiences

If you have had to react to the same stimulus, or a similar one, in the past your reactions may be quicker, particularly if choice reaction time is involved. Motor programmes may be formed and can be 'run' automatically, cutting down the decision-making requirements.

Psychological refractory period

If a second stimulus follows quite closely behind the first, reaction time is slowed because of the increased information processing time needed. The *single-channel hypothesis* underpins this phenomenon.

Anticipation

As we discussed earlier, skilled performers seem to have more time available to complete the actions necessary. This is because he or she has drawn

In practice

'Selling a dummy' is a typical way of delaying an opponent's tackle. The opponent has to clear the initial decision to tackle before dealing with the realisation that a 'dummy' has taken place. This can give a player valuable time to change direction or make an unexpected pass.

In practice

A basketball player might be able to predict that an opponent is about to make a shot and jumps to block the shot (spatial anticipation). He or she may also use clues given by particular movements of the opponent to predict that a shot is about to be taken (temporal anticipation).

Anticipation can save valuable time in reacting to a situation

on past experience to anticipate what is about to happen, and has processed information before the event actually happened, which saves them time. Anticipation can set a pattern of movement in advance, which can then be used when it is required – this is called *spatial* anticipation. Using anticipation to predict what is about to happen is called *temporal* anticipation.

However, anticipation *can* be wrong and could lengthen reaction time instead of shortening it. The delay could be caused by the psychological refractory period coming into play because the first decision was the wrong one. For example, the basketball player who is perceived to be going for a shot could well be 'faking' the movement.

ACTIVITY

Imagine that you are about to receive a tennis serve. List the cues that you could take notice of to anticipate effectively and cut down your reaction time. Identify the spatial anticipation and temporal anticipation processes.

Other factors affecting reactions

Other factors, such as the intensity of the stimulus, the presence of warning cues and the type of stimulus/stimuli may also affect the speed of information processing.

Key revision box

Information processing is only one of many different ways of understanding how we learn skills. The basic model involves input, decision-making and output. According to Schmidt, there are three stages in processing stimuli: stimulus identification, response selection and response programming. A short reaction time is essential in many sporting activities. There are two types of reaction time: simple and choice. Many factors affect reaction time and the key to shortening reaction time is to optimise the positive effects of these factors.

15.3.2 Memory

The memory is very important in processing information. Our previous experiences affect how we judge and interpret information and the course of action we take.

The memory process is very complex and, although there has been much research in this area, it is still not fully understood. It is useful to try to simplify the process by using the information processing approach

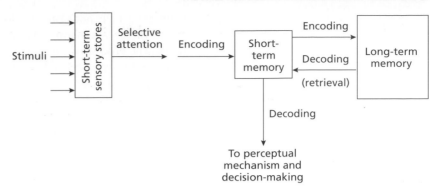

Figure 15.2 Model representing the memory process

Definition

SELECTIVE ATTENTION

In selective attention relevant information is filtered through into the short-term memory and irrelevant information is lost or forgotten. This process is particularly important in sport, where quick reactions depend on being able to concentrate on important information and to shut out distractions.

discussed above. The model in Figure 15.2 seeks to explain the components of memory.

Short-term sensory stores

Information in the form of stimuli enters the brain from the environment. Each store has a large capacity but information is only stored for between a quarter and one second before it is *filtered*. This filtering takes place in the stimulus identification stage. *Selective attention* takes place in the short-term sensory stores.

Short-term memory

This has been named the 'workspace' or the 'working memory' because this is where the information is used to decide what needs to be done. Only a limited amount of information can be stored in the short-term memory (research is ambiguous but points to about 7 pieces of information and is only held for a short time (about 30 seconds). To extend the time that the information is stored in the short-term memory, the performer would have to rehearse the information, through imagery or sub-verbal repetition (by talking to yourself). Information can also be held in short-term memory through a process called *chunking*.

If information is considered important enough and is rehearsed it can be passed into the long-term memory. This process is called *encoding* the information. Information that is not considered important, or is not rehearsed, is usually lost because it does not go into the long-term memory.

Selective attention involves concentration

Definition

CHUNKING

Different pieces of information can be grouped (or chunked) together and then remembered as one piece of information. For example, instead of trying to remember each separate move made by each player in a line-out in rugby or a penalty corner in hockey a player might remember the whole drill as a single number.

In practice

When practising a serve in table tennis, a player would use the short-term memory to store the last shot so that they could compare it with the next to help improvement. The coach may give information to the player, but only a small amount because of the limited capacity of the short-term memory.

Long-term memory

This store of information has almost limitless capacity and holds information for long periods of time. The information which is stored has been encoded (see above). Information is stored in the long-term memory, possibly by associating it with other information or with meaning. Meaningless items are usually not stored for long periods of time. Motor programmes are stored in the long-term memory because they have been rehearsed many times. The process of continued rehearsal leads to a skill being almost automatic and the process of learning by rehearsal is often referred to as 'over-learning'. If you are regularly using particular motor skills you are more likely to remember them – for example, once you have learned to swim you are unlikely to forget.

ACTIVITY

If you were about to receive a serve in badminton, how would selective attention help you? List the items of information that you would use your short-term memory to process and those you would use your long-term memory for.

Key revision box

The memory process is still largely a mystery but simplified models have been developed to try to explain the process. The basic model describes memory as essentially a three-stage process: short-term sensory store → short-term memory → long-term memory. All information that is selected passes through the short-term memory. The process of chunking (organisation of information) can help a performer deal with larger amounts of information. Items of information need to be rehearsed before they can be stored in the long-term memory.

15.3.3 Motor programmes

Open loop control

Motor programmes are generalised series of movements stored in the long-term memory and each is retrieved by a single decision. They usefully explain how we perform very quick actions in sport, especially closed skills. Some almost automatic movements do not seem to be under conscious control – if a decision had to be made about every single muscle action to catch a ball the information processing would take far too long. This kind of control over our actions is known as *open loop control*, and a model of open loop control is shown in *Figure 15.3*.

There is no feedback involved with open loop control. If the environment remains constant and predictable then a motor programme can be used or 'run' effectively.

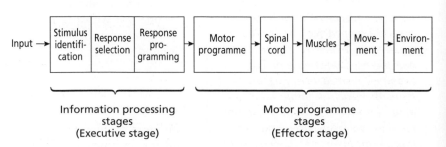

Figure 15.3 Model of open loop control

The more a performer practices a series of movements, the more likely it is that a motor programme will be formed. Most movements that we make in sport are a mixture of open loop control and closed loop control.

Closed loop control

This involves the process of feedback (which is discussed in Section 15.3.5). The feedback for this type of control is internal – information is received from the proprioceptors which detect and correct errors in movement. A model of closed loop control is shown in *Figure 15.4*.

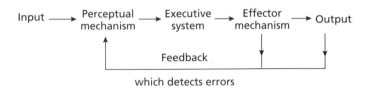

Figure 15.4 Model to show closed loop control

15.3.4 Schema theory

Some people feel that the open loop and closed loop theories do not fully explain how we perform so many actions in sport with relatively little conscious control – there simply cannot be enough storage space for so many motor programmes. Under the schema theory a motor programme is seen as only a generalised series of movements that can be modified by taking in information as a skill is performed.

The theory usefully explains how we can immediately learn a new skill, and also solves the storage problem. When a movement takes place we perceive information about where we are (knowledge of the environment), what we have to do to perform successfully (response specifications), what the movement feels like (sensory consequences) and what happens when we respond (response outcomes). These items of information, called 'schema' are then stored and used to update the motor programme when we next want to use it.

Recall schema

Recall schema are the information stored about the production of movement – the environment and the response specifications. The recall schema starts the appropriate movement.

Recognition schema

These include information stored about evaluating the response – the sensory consequences and the response outcomes. The recognition schema control the movement.

Teachers and coaches who want their students to be successful in a variety of situations must bear the schema theory in mind. If information about many different situations is to be stored, the performer must be exposed in training to as many of these different situations as possible and must be aware of both recall and recognition schema.

In practice

An experienced basketball player probably has developed a motor programme for making a shot at the basket, but will not have a programme for shooting from every possible position on the court or for dealing with every possible position of a blocking opponent. However, she will have had many different experiences from which to draw. These will have become schemas stored in the long-term memory which she can use to modify her shooting programme.

In practice

A teacher or coach *must* give feedback to the performer – he or she may not be able to detect errors on their own because of limited kinesthetic awareness. For example, a novice gymnast might not be aware of what a good handstand feels like and therefore feedback related to the end result would help him or her detect errors. The coach could use a video of the performance to show the novice how he performed.

15.3.5 Feedback

Feedback involves using the information that is available to the performer during the performance of a skill or after the response to alter the performance. There are several forms of feedback:

Continuous feedback – feedback during the performance, in the form of kinesthesis or proprioception.
Terminal feedback – feedback after the response has been completed.
Knowledge of results – this is a type of terminal feedback that gives the performer information about the end result of the response.
Knowledge of performance – this is information about how well the movement is being executed, rather than the end result.
Internal/intrinsic feedback – this is a type of continuous feedback that comes from the proprioceptors.
External/extrinsic/augmented feedback – feedback that comes from external sources, for example from sound or vision.
Positive feedback – reinforces skill learning and gives information about a successful outcome.
Negative feedback – information about an unsuccessful outcome, which can be used to build more successful strategies.

Two of these types of feedback are more important than the others in sports performance: knowledge of results and knowledge of performance.

ACTIVITY
Think of a practical example for each of the types of feedback listed above, using one of the sports that you are involved with.

A gymnast can gain knowledge of performance through kinesthetic awareness or external feedback

Knowledge of results

This feedback is external, and can come from the performer seeing the result of their response or from another person, usually a coach or teacher. It is extremely important for the performer to know what the result of their action has been. There can be very little learning without this type of feedback, especially in the early stages of skill acquisition.

Knowledge of performance

This is feedback about the pattern of movement that has taken, or is taking, place. It is normally associated with external feedback but can be gained through kinaesthetic awareness, especially if the performer is highly skilled and knows what a good performance feels like.

In practice

The coach of a trampolinist should use simple verbal feedback, and playing a video of the performance in slow motion is a good teaching aid. Once the major errors have been corrected the feedback would become less frequent. Any feedback given must be as accurate as possible and should not contain too much information. The trampolinist needs to develop her own awareness of what movement is good and what movement is poor.

The coach should give simple, accurate and brief information

Both knowledge of results and knowledge of performance can help with the motivation of a performer but if used incorrectly they can also demotivate. Reinforcement, as we discovered earlier in this chapter, is essential for effective skill learning and feedback serves as a good reinforcer. If the movement and/or the result is good then the performer will feel satisfaction, and the S-R bond is strengthened. Knowing that the movement and results are good will help the performer form a picture of what is correct and to associate future performance with that picture, image or model.

External feedback should be used with care because the performer may come to depend too heavily upon it and will not develop internal feedback. The type of feedback that should be given depends on the ability of the performer, the type of activity being undertaken and the personality of the performer – different performers respond differently to different types of feedback.

Feedback and setting goals

There is an important link between feedback and setting goals and future motivation and performance. In research carried out by Bandura and Cervone in 1983, 20 cyclists were given performance goals, 20 cyclists received performance feedback but were not set goals, 20 were set goals and received feedback and a further 20 acted as a control group (they were given no feedback and were not set goals). The results of this experiment are set out in *Figure 15.5*, and clearly show that the effects of feedback are enhanced by goal setting.

ACTIVITY

Give examples of performance feedback. Choose a sport and identify the goals that you might set a novice. How would you link goal setting with performance?

When performance is measured and is given to performers as feedback, their motivation can be enhanced and their performance improved. Sports performers often set themselves targets from their previous performances

Figure 15.5 The relationship between performance, feedback and goal-setting

Control group

Goals and feedback

Feedback only

Goals only

0   20   40   60   80

Percentage increase in performance

Mental rehearsal can help the performer concentrate

but teachers and coaches can help by constructing performance/goal charts that the performer updates as necessary. These charts serve as feedback on current performance and set clear and progressive targets. This is another useful way of strengthening the all-important S-R bond.

Key revision box

Feedback occurs both during and after movement. The two main types of feedback are knowledge of results and knowledge of performance. Feedback can help to reinforce effective movements and to detect and correct errors. When intrinsic feedback is involved in the detection and correction process, it is known as closed loop control. In order to motivate a performer it is very important to give the appropriate feedback and to set relevant goals.

15.3.6 Mental rehearsal

This is sometimes called *mental practice* and is a strategy adopted by many sportsmen and women. By mentally rehearsing you form a mental image of the skill or event that you are about to perform. No physical movements are involved in mental rehearsal. Some performers find mental rehearsal easier than others but the ability can be improved with practice. Mental rehearsal is used either to learn a new skill or to improve existing skills. It is important in the cognitive stage of skill learning.

In practice

Before performing the serial skill of a floor routine a gymnast will go through the routine in his mind by creating a mental image of each stage of the routine. Before taking a penalty kick a soccer player may visualise the kick and the desired result. A demonstration will help the novice tennis player to form a mental picture of a serve before actually serving.

Figure 15.6 The effects of mental practice on performance

Mental rehearsal and skill learning

The cognitive stage of skill learning (identified by Fitts in 1967) involves the performer understanding what is required to perform the skill. This understanding is associated with building a mental image. Mental rehearsal is thought to involve going through possible movements and mentally experiencing the possible outcomes. This process can help to eradicate unnecessary and energy-consuming movements.

For the novice, mental rehearsal may well improve confidence and help to control arousal levels. Research has shown that if a performer concentrates on successful movements rather than unsuccessful ones, a degree of optimism is experienced.

Figure 15.6 clearly shows the positive effects of mental practice on the performance of a fine motor skill.

By combining physical and mental practice all performers, especially ones who are already skilled, will be able to improve their performance.

In practice

To maximise the effects of mental rehearsal, teachers and coaches should encourage the performer to mentally rehearse successful movements away from the heat of competition. Mental rehearsal should include as much fine detail as possible. The performer should also be encouraged to mentally rehearse during rest periods between practice sessions.

KEY TERMS

You should now understand the following terms. If you do not, go back through the chapter and find out.

Associationist/Connectionist
Classical conditioning
Operant conditioning
Reinforcement
Drive reduction theory
Cognitive theory
Insight learning
Information processing
Reaction time
Hick's Law
Psychological refractory period
Short-term sensory store
Short-term memory
Long-term memory
Selective attention
Motor programme
Open loop control
Closed loop control
Schema
Feedback
Mental rehearsal

PROGRESS CHECK

1 What is the S-R bond?
2 Why is operant conditioning different from classical conditioning?
3 What is meant by the term reinforcement?
4 What is the difference between negative reinforcement and punishment?
5 Give a practical example, other than the one cited in this chapter, to show operant conditioning in action.
6 What are Thorndike's three laws which help to strengthen the S-R bond?
7 According to Hull, what is wrong with too much repetition in practice situations?
8 What did the Gestaltists say about the learning process? Give a practical example of the cognitive theory in action.
9 Draw a detailed information processing model.
10 What are the three stages in information processing?
11 Define reaction time.
12 Choose an example in sport when the time to respond needs to be short. Write down as many factors affecting the performer's response time as you can.
13 Draw a simple model of the memory process.
14 What is meant by the term selective attention?
15 How can a teacher ensure that information is stored in the performer's long-term memory?
16 What is meant by a motor programme?
17 How does Schema theory help with the problems of the programme theory?
18 What are the two most important types of feedback and how can they help in future performances?
19 What is mental rehearsal?
20 What are the main effects of mental practice on skill learning?

16

Theories related to the teaching of skills

Learning objectives:

- To recognise the different stages in the learning process.
- To understand the concept of transfer.
- To be able to investigate the most effective ways of structuring practices.
- To be able to apply different types of guidance to practical situations.
- To be able to identify different teaching styles, along with their advantages and disadvantages.
- To understand the need to adopt different teaching styles in different situations.

16.1 Stages or phases of learning

Fitts and Posner identified several different stages in the learning process, although it must be remembered that learning is a complex process and the stages, or *phases* as they were labelled, are not clear cut. However, it is useful to try to identify the different levels of understanding that each phase represents because we are then better able to create successful teaching strategies throughout the learning process.

16.1.1 Phase 1: the cognitive phase

The *cognitive phase* is the earliest phase of learning, when the performer understands what needs to be done. There is quite a lot of trial and error in this phase, the beginner trying out certain movements which may be successful or may fail. The successful strategies can be *reinforced* by the performer experiencing success or being told by their teacher that the move has been successful. Unsuccessful strategies should not be dismissed because all experiences can be worthwhile. The performer should understand why failure occurred in order to avoid the same experience in the future. To establish understanding teachers may use demonstrations or other methods of guidance (these are discussed later in this chapter). It is important that relevant cues are highlighted by the teacher and recognised by the performer.

16.1.2 Phase 2: the associative phase

In the associative or motor phase of learning the performer practises, and compares or associates the movements produced with the mental image. This is the stage at which feedback occurs and the learner gradually becomes more aware of increasingly subtle and complex cues. During this stage a vast improvement in performance usually occurs. Motor programmes are

In practice

If a novice badminton player is in the cognitive phase of learning and needs to understand the serve, her teacher could demonstrate the correct technique and highlight important points (this is called *cueing*) so that the player builds up a mental picture of what needs to be done. This 'visualisation' of the movement is more effective if the teaching is simple, clear and concise.

In practice

The novice badminton player who is now aware of what needs to be done for the serve has tried various strategies and is now entering the associative phase. Her service is now more consistent and most serves fall into the service box. The performer is concentrating on getting the service lower and into different areas of the service box and the teacher is giving feedback. The performer is starting to detect and correct errors, even without her teacher's help.

The skilled performer who is in the autonomous phase can disguise intentions more effectively

said to be formed in this phase of learning, although skills have probably not been 'grooved' automatically yet.

16.1.3 Phase 3: the autonomous phase

This is the final phase of the skill learning process. Movements are becoming almost automatic, with very little conscious thought. Any distractions are largely ignored and the performer is able to concentrate on more peripheral strategies and tactics. It is said that during this stage motor programmes are completely formed in the long-term memory and reaction time is short. Some performers may never reach this stage or may reach it with only the basic movement patterns. For performers to stay in this phase they must continuously refer back to the associative phase, where practise ensures that motor programmes are reinforced.

In practice

The performer of the badminton serve is now confident and able to consistently perform an accurate serve with the minimum amount of thought. The performer can use more sophisticated strategies such as disguising the nature of her serve, putting her opponent at a disadvantage. The performer can now also take into consideration more peripheral cues such as her opponent's position on court and, in doubles, the position of the other opposing player.

Key revision box

Three phases of learning have been identified. In the cognitive phase the learner understands the requirements of the task. There is some trial and error learning in this phase. The associative phase is the practise phase in which the learner receives feedback and starts to build motor programmes. In the final, or autonomous, phase execution of the skill is almost automatic. There is apparently little conscious control and the skill is speedily executed. The performer can now concentrate on more complex responses.

16.2 The concept of transfer

Transfer in skill acquisition is the influence of the learning and/or performance of one skill on the learning and/or performance of another. If this influences a skill yet to be learned or performed it is called *proactive* transfer, if it influences the performance of a previously learned skill it is called *retroactive* transfer.

One skill can help in the learning or performance of another, in which case it is known as *positive* transfer, or may hinder the learning or performance of another skill, when it is called *negative* transfer.

It is important that teachers of skills maximise the effects of positive transfer and minimise the negative aspects. Throughout this chapter we will be investigating the best ways of presenting and teaching skills, always bearing in mind the important concept of transfer. In order to do this we must first understand this complex concept.

Identify whether the following situations are examples of proactive or retroactive transfer, and whether positive or negative transfer are involved.

1 Practising overarm throwing of a ball, then learning the basic cricket bowling action.
2 A novice badminton player spends a day playing tennis, then returns to badminton and finds that many of his shots lack control.

In practice

To teach a straddle vault in gymnastics, the coach may well use the following sequence of activities:

1 star-jumps with legs wide and straight
2 running with 'two feet take-offs'
3 straddle vault over a partner
4 straddle jump onto a low vault, with support
5 make the vault higher and gradually reduce support.

This encourages transfer of skills in a logical fashion, increases confidence, ensures safety and gives kinesthetic awareness.

Teach basic skills first and then build up to more complex actions

16.2.1 Basic to complex

In all areas of education it is common practice to teach basic skills first and then to build upon these skills to achieve more sophisticated skills. In physical education in primary schools, basic throwing and catching, kicking and striking activities are encouraged so that these basic skills can be transferred to more complex activities such as passing in football and netball or the serve in tennis. Skill teaching is therefore progressive and involves a step-by-step approach from basic 'foundation' actions to more finely tuned complex skills.

16.2.2 Situational influences

Positive transfer is only likely to occur if practice conditions are as realistic as possible. If the response to a training stimulus is not consistent with the response demanded in the real situation, negative transfer could take place and bad habits could be encouraged. For instance, a teacher may use traffic cones to coach dribbling skills in hockey, but the method used to go around the cones is very different from the way a player will go around a real opponent – you don't meet many traffic cones on a hockey pitch! Land drills are often used in the coaching of swimming because it is assumed that positive transfer will take place from the 'dry' situation to the water. However, use of land drills may involve some negative transfer because the different situations have different kinesthetic experiences. The real situation should be used as much as possible to maximise the transfer effects.

16.2.3 Positive transfer

To ensure that any transfers are helpful, the coach must bear in mind that positive transfer will take place only if the structure and context in which the skills are performed are similar to those used in teaching. Positive transfer is also more likely if the information processing requirements in practice are similar to the ones of the actual skill.

For example, an overarm throw and the tennis serve are both similar skills and therefore positive transfer is likely if the throw is used to learn the serve (the context is not similar but cannot be confused). The information processing requirements are different in some ways – in the tennis serve, for instance, the position of the receiver must be taken into account – but this difference is unlikely to interfere with successful execution of either skill. The 'identical elements theory' (developed by Thorndike in 1914) suggests that the greater the number of components of practice that are relevant to the 'real' situation, the more likely positive transfer is to take place and for future responses to be correct. The term 'transfer-appropriate processing' is given to the idea that a new skill may be different from any skill performed before, but if the cognitive, information-processing requirements are similar then positive transfer could occur.

It is important to remember that the amount of positive transfer that takes place often depends on how well previously performed skills have been learned. If a skill is broken down and taught in parts, each part must be learned thoroughly before positive transfer can be maximised.

ACTIVITY

Using your own sport, give examples of skills which could be used to positively influence the learning of new skills. Identify any movement or motor elements which may be useful and also identify similar information processing requirements.

16.2.4 Negative transfer

Fortunately negative transfer is rare, and mostly temporary. It is more often than not associated with the performer misunderstanding the movement requirements rather than having problems with movement control. Negative transfer must be minimised, and coaches must understand the strategies to avoid it occurring. Negative transfer often occurs when a familiar stimulus requires a new response, particularly if the demands of the new response are so similar to the old demands that the player becomes confused. For example, a tennis player may misjudge her shots when playing indoors because the techniques needed are subtly different from those required in outdoor play. Such problems are usually short-lived and, once the performer gets used to the new requirements, normally disappear. If the coach understands that initial performance may be hindered because of negative transfer and draws the performer's attention to the problem negative transfer can be eliminated.

Key revision box

Transfer in skill acquisition involves one skill influencing the learning and performance of another. Transfer that helps to learn and perform other skills is known as positive transfer. If it hinders other skills it is known as negative transfer. Factors affecting transfer include the structure of practice sessions, situational influences and awareness of possible negative effects. Other types of transfer are listed below:

Bilateral transfer – *transfer between one limb and another.*
Intertask transfer – *the influence of one skill on a new skill.*
Intratask transfer – *the way different conditions in practice can influence the learning of a skill.*
Near transfer – *when the tasks given in training are very similar to the 'real game' situation.*
Far transfer – *the training tasks are very different from the 'real game' tasks but give general experiences which could be used in a variety of situations.*

16.3 The structure and presentation of practices

To optimise skill learning teachers and coaches must create the best possible practice conditions. Using what we learnt of Schmidt's Schema theory in Chapter 15, we know that variety in training is very important – not

In practice

In hockey the reverse stick tackle is a complex skill. The information which needs to be processed includes the position and speed of the opponent, the tackler's position, the position of the ball, and an awareness of other players. This skill may be best taught using a slow demonstration, followed by practice at walking pace. The pace of both players may then be increased and then put into a small game situation before coaching within the full game.

just to build up schema in the long-term memory but also to increase motivation.

For practice to be meaningful and relevant the following factors need to be taken into consideration:

1 The nature of the skills involved – are they open or closed for instance?
2 The amount of technical knowledge needed.
3 The amount of information the performer needs to process.
4 Environmental factors.
5 The previous experience of the performer.
6 The performer's personality and how well they are motivated.

The teacher or coach should analyse carefully the nature of the task involved. A *complex* task involves skills which require a lot of information processing. The perceptual requirements are therefore quite high and the decision-making process depends on feedback and previous experience. The performer needs to fully understand the task and therefore careful explanation is needed. The task may be broken down into easier subunits and as the performer improves is made more complex, until the complete task can be performed. This technique is most effective in learning open skills which need high levels of information processing.

The organisation level of the task must also be taken into consideration. A *highly organised task* involves skills that are difficult to split into sub-routines – it is often a continuous skill, such as cycling. A skill which has *low organisation* is easily broken down into its constituent parts – for example the tennis serve. The serve involves preparation, throwing up the ball, striking it and finally following through.

A skill which is highly organised is best practised as a whole but with the support of mechanical or manual aids – like these stabilisers

In practice

The highly organised skill of cycling would have to be taught as a whole movement, because of the difficulty of splitting it into sub-routines. The use of stabilisers is common; these enable the novice to experience the action safely and effectively. The novice will eventually be able to cycle without the stabilisers, first with manual support and then without any help. The low organisation of the tennis serve is best practised by splitting the skill up into its constituent parts. The throwing action of the arm could be practised first, followed by throwing the ball up, hitting it and following through. Eventually the separate actions could be brought together.

16.3.1 Teaching skills using the 'whole' method

In the 'whole' method a skill is taught without breaking it down into sub-routines or parts. If possible this method should be employed more than any other because the player experiences the true 'feel' (or kinesthetic sense) for the skill and transfer from practice to the real situation is likely to be positive. The player is also likely to execute the skill fluently and can appreciate the relationships between each part of the movement. If a task is rapid or ballistic in action, the 'whole' method of teaching is best because the components of the skill interact closely with one another.

The golf swing is a good example of this. For the swing to be effective, the action as a whole must be practised because each part of the swing interacts closely with the next. If a motor programme, like a golf swing, is to be built up, then again it is better to practise the movement as a whole.

In practice

A gymnast will benefit from concentrating on one element of a floor routine at a time but must remember that one part of the routine interacts with another. For instance the way in which he finishes the 'round-off' will affect the start of the back somersault in a sequence.

16.3.2 Teaching skills using the 'part' method

The 'part' method is often used when the skill is low in organisation and can be split up into sub-routines. If the skill is complex this method is useful because it allows the performer to make sense of the skill and to achieve initial success with basic movements before progressing to the more complex movements. Part practice can also be useful in learning a dangerous skill.

The performer can gain confidence by learning each element of the skill separately and then, when the separate parts are brought together, the performer will have a better idea of the technique involved and more confident of success. This practice technique is particularly useful when trying to teach serial skills.

16.3.3 Progressive-part method

This is often referred to as 'chaining' in the teaching of skills. The skill, usually serial in nature, is broken down into sub-routines which are thought of as the links of a chain. The performer learns one link at a time, then adds on a second link. She practises the two links together, then adds on a third link – and so on, until the links can be practised together as a whole. This process is sometimes referred to as the 'gradual metamorphosis' process.

ACTIVITY

Think of a serial skill. Write down how you would break the skill down and use the progressive-part technique to teach it to a novice.

Many skills are best practised using a mixture of part and whole methods. For instance, a performer may well benefit from trying out the skill as a whole, to get the idea of the complete movement and to understand the interrelationships between the various components. Each component could then be practised separately and the skill is then brought together and performed as a whole. This mixture of methods highlights weak areas, which can then be isolated for more intensive practice.

16.3.4 The operant method

This method was described in Chapter 15. It involves 'shaping' behaviour using trial and error followed by reinforcement. The operant method is particularly effective in teaching complex skills. The performer will be able to understand the interrelationships between the components of the skill and also to build strategies of avoiding errors in the future.

In practice

If we take the penalty kick in football as an example, it is clear that the actual conditions of a penalty should be held constant in practice. Stimuli that will vary in the game situation, such as crowd noise, fatigue on the part of the penalty-taker and the different pressures associated with the scoreline must be varied.

16.3.5 Variable practice

Practice needs to be varied so that the performer can come into contact with a range of experiences (in line with Schmidt's schema theory, discussed in Chapter 15). Relevant experiences are stored in the long term memory and can be used to modify motor programmes in the future. With closed skills it is important that practice conditions closely resemble the 'true life' situation. Stimuli which are irrelevant to the closed skill should be varied but those that *are* relevant should *not* be varied.

With open skills, each situation will be different from the last – the conditions, unlike those in closed skills, are not constant. It is essential, therefore, that practice involves many different situations so that the performer can draw from the strategies in long-term memory that he or she has learned in previous practice.

In practice

Primary school physical education places emphasis on giving each child a wide variety of experiences, involving gymnastic, dance and game activities. The child then builds a 'bank' of experiences which he or she can draw on when faced with new situations.

ACTIVITY

Choose an open skill related to your sport. Devise a practice session which would allow the performer to develop a number of strategies that he or she could draw on in the future. Remember the factors which affect positive transfer, especially the 'identical elements' theory.

16.3.6 Massed and distributed practice methods

The structure of the practice session is important when considering the most effective way of teaching skills. There are many different definitions of what is meant by 'massed' and 'distributed' practice, but we will take 'massed' practice to mean practice which involves very short, or no, rest intervals within the practice session. Massed practice, then, is a continuous practice period. 'Distributed' practice involves relatively long rests between trials. The 'rest' intervals could involve tasks which are unrelated to the main practice activity. For example, between basketball drills players could go and play table tennis. It is important to remember the theory of transfer – these rest periods should not involve activities which could lead to negative transfer. Many performers, particularly the experienced ones, use the intervals between activities to practice mental rehearsal, the effects of which have already been discussed.

Research has shown that distributed practice is generally best because massed practice can lead to poor performance and hinder the learning process because of fatigue and demotivation. Massed practice may help learn discrete skills which are relatively short in duration but distributed practice is best for learning continuous skills because the player rapidly becomes tired. With tasks which are potentially dangerous, distributed practice is also best because it ensures that physical and mental fatigue does not negatively affect performance and put the performer in danger.

16.3.7 Overlearning

The word 'overlearning' suggests that this is a negative concept but it is usually positive, although in some situations it can be detrimental to skill acquisition. Overlearning is extremely helpful in retention and retrieval of the information needed to perform motor skills.

ACTIVITY

Construct two training sessions using your knowledge of whole and part practice and massed and distributed practice conditions, along with the concept of overlearning.

Session 1 – A one hour session teaching a novice a skill such as a tennis serve, a basketball shot or a gymnastic sequence.

Session 2 – A one hour session with an advanced-level performer – in an athletic field event, an advanced swimmer or an advanced badminton player for instance.

The definition that is often used for overlearning is 'the practice time spent beyond the amount of practice time needed to achieve success'. This 'extra' practice time can help to strengthen motor programmes and schema. If a skill has been learned so well that it is almost automatic, a performer can concentrate on other variables – for instance a basketball player may have learned to dribble so well that he or she can direct attention to other aspects of the game, such as the position of colleagues and opponents.

There is, however, an optimal level of practice – too much practice could result in demotivation and fatigue. The teacher or coach must ensure that good performers stay in the autonomous phase of learning by rehearsing skills, but must also be aware of the plateau effect and the costs of doing too much.

The actual structure of the practice session is important when considering the most effective way of teaching skills

Key revision box

Practice sessions must be well planned, taking into consideration the skill to be learned, the performer and the environment. If the skill is complex, with many items of information to process, the skill should be split up into sub-routines and each part taught separately. If the skill is highly organised, and the sub-routines closely interrelated, then it is better to teach as a whole. If the skill is serial in nature, then the progressive-part method may be appropriate. Using this method each section is taught and linked or 'chained' to the next. The operant method of teaching allows learning by trial and error and reinforcement of appropriate responses. Variable practice is important to build up schema in the long-term memory. Massed practice is generally not as effective as distributed practice and involves a practice session with no or very few rest intervals. Massed practice is better for more able performers and can help with overlearning. Distributed practice involves relatively long rest periods. It can help with motivation and delays fatigue. Mental rehearsal is facilitated through this approach. Overlearning generally helps the performer to retain information in the long-term memory. Overlearning helps to ensure that the performer reaches and stays in the autonomous phase of learning.

In practice

The following points should be considered before using visual guidance.

- Demonstrations must be accurate and should hold the performer's attention.
- Demonstrations must be repeated but should not be too time consuming.
- Videos can be useful, especially if they have a slow motion facility, but the student must be able to copy the model presented.
- For a learner to gain maximum benefit, their position during training should be considered. For example, the demonstration of a swimming stroke is best viewed from above on the poolside.

16.4 Types of guidance in the teaching of motor skills

When a teacher or coach presents a new skill to a student or seeks to develop the skills of an experienced performer he or she needs to decide the best way to transmit the knowledge necessary for effective performance. There are four main types of guidance:

- visual
- verbal
- manual
- mechanical.

The type or combination of types chosen depends on the personality, motivation and ability of the performer, the situation in which learning or development of skills is taking place and the nature of the skill being taught or developed.

16.4.1 Visual guidance

Visual guidance is widely used when teaching motor skills. During the cognitive phase of skill learning visual guidance (often a demonstration by the instructor of another competent performer) helps the learner develop a mental image of what needs to be done. Some instructors use videos, charts or other visual aids to build up the 'ideal' picture of what is required to successfully perform a new skill. The demonstration must be accurate so that there is no possibility of the learner building up an incorrect picture. To avoid confusing the learner and overloading him or her with information in the early stages of learning, it is important to concentrate on only a few aspects of the skill. The teacher may therefore only 'cue' the performer onto one or two aspects of the whole movement. One way of ensuring that the learner cues on to the right stimuli is to change the 'display'. The instructor may highlight certain features of the display to help the learner to concentrate on relevant and important information.

ACTIVITY

Choose a skill from any sport. How would you teach this skill with visual guidance only? Include any ideas about modifying the display.

16.4.2 Verbal guidance

This is often associated with visual guidance, being used to describe the action and explain how to perform the activity. Verbal guidance has limitations if used on its own – motor skills are very difficult to describe without a demonstration of some kind. Remember that the instructor is trying to create an image in the learner's mind of what needs to be done. Verbal guidance of the more advance performer is effective when the more perceptual information, such as tactics or positional play, needs to be conveyed.

16.4.3 Manual and mechanical guidance

This involves two factors:

1 Physical support for the performer by another person or a mechanical device. This is commonly known as 'physical restriction'. An example of this is supporting a gymnast over a vault or the use of a twisting belt in trampolining.

During the cognitive phase of skill learning visual guidance is important for the learner to develop a mental image of what needs to be done

154

In practice

When using verbal guidance the teacher/coach needs to be aware of the following points.

- Do not speak for too long – sports performers have notoriously short attention spans!
- Some movements simply cannot be explained – stick to visual guidance in these cases.
- Direct (or didactic) verbal guidance is better in the early stages to ensure that the learner has a clear idea of what needs to be done.
- Questioning techniques can encourage personal development and develop confidence if handled in the right way – especially for the more advanced performers. Feedback from the performers will also test understanding.

In practice

The following points should be considered before using manual or mechanical guidance.

- Manual/mechanical guidance can reduce fear in dangerous situations. For instance, wearing arm bands will help in learning how to swim.
- This method of guidance can give some idea of kinesthetic awareness of the motion.
- However, it could give unrealistic 'feeling' kinesthesis of the motion. For example, it is advisable to remove the arm bands as soon as possible to be able to teach stroke technique in swimming.
- The intrinsic feedback received could be incorrect and may instil bad habits or negative transfer.
- There is a reduction in the learner's participation, which could negatively effect motivation.

Manual/mechanical guidance can reduce fear in dangerous situations e.g. arm bands in swimming

2 The response of the performer being directed physically by another person. This is commonly known as 'forced response'. Holding the arms of a golfer and forcing his or her arms through the movement of a drive is an example of forced response.

Key revision box

Visual guidance is used in early stages of teaching a skill. Demonstrations are the most common form. Important cues must be highlighted through this guidance.

Verbal guidance is not very effective if used on its own, except with very able performers, but with visual guidance it can be very effective, especially to help identify important cues.

Manual and mechanical guidance is important in the early stages of learning. It can help a performer cope with fear and can help with safety. This type of guidance helps to give kinaesthetic awareness but should not be overused.

16.5 Teaching styles related to the acquisition of motor skills

There are many different styles that can be adopted by teachers and coaches. Each instructor has his or her own way of presenting information and the style each chooses depends on several variables.

- The teacher's personality and abilities.
- The type of activity to be taught.
- The ability of those being taught.
- The level of motivation of those being taught.
- The age range of the students.
- Environmental factors.

ACTIVITY

Think of some of your instructors. Write down the characteristics they display – are they humorous in their approach? Are they strict? Do they let you have a say in what happens?

Is coaching like acting on a stage?

An effective style takes into account all of these variables. Some teachers are far more extrovert in their approach than others and may adopt a style which is far more open and sociable. Teachers who are more introverted may adopt a style which ensures they don't get into situations where they feel uncomfortable. Teachers who are very able physically may adopt a style to use their physical prowess for demonstration purposes. Some teachers are naturally more charismatic than others and so they tend to use a more teacher-centred approach. Coaches need to be aware of their own personality characteristics and abilities before they decide on the approach they will take. Some feel that teaching is an act and that a 'performance' is required – they create an artificial 'persona', masking their own personality and abilities. Others believe that if they act out a role, their pupils will eventually find out and the learning that has been achieved will be devalued. Both arguments are valid, and each individual must decide on the style they will adopt.

ACTIVITY

Think of some teaching/coaching situations where the teacher needs to 'act out' a role, rather than be themselves. Give reasons for your choices. Think of some situations when it is better for the teacher to be truthful about their own thoughts and feelings.

Environmental situations need to be taken into account when adopting a teaching style!

The type of activity being taught also has an influence over the style the teacher adopts. For instance, if the activity is dangerous the coach is more likely to adopt a strict, authoritarian style. If the activity is complex and the perceptual demands are high, a more explanatory style will be appropriate. We have already looked at how to analyse and classify motor tasks. Once the instructor has analysed and classified the motor tasks involved, he or she will be in a position to choose an appropriate style of delivery.

The characteristics of the group or individuals being taught is another important element to take into account.

Experience – a novice may need a more direct style to begin with so that he or she gains a clear understanding of what needs to be done. If the individual is experienced, a more consultative or democratic style will allow the individual to give some valuable contributions and share in the decision-making process.

Motivation – if the performers are highly motivated the coach can concentrate on the task rather than attempting to increase motivation. If motivation is low, the teaching style adopted should be more enthusing and reward-based.

Age – With very young children a non-threatening style should be adopted, with the emphasis on fun. As the performer gets older the emphasis could be more democratic and more responsibility could be shifted onto them. There is nothing worse than the teacher or coach treating responsible adults like children and not valuing their input. Similarly, too much responsibility should not be placed on young people. A key to successful teaching is to know the characteristics of those who are trying to learn and then to adopt a suitable approach.

Environment – Teaching approaches may be affected by the situation. For instance, the weather may dictate the style adopted: a consultative, democratic approach is the last thing that is needed on a cold, wet day! In a dangerous, hostile environment a more task-oriented approach could be called for. Instructors should assess each environmental situation as it arises and adopt the appropriate approach.

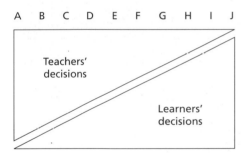

Figure 16.1 The spectrum of teaching styles

16.5.1 Mosston's spectrum of teaching styles

In 1986 Mosston and Ashworth identified a range of styles, which are characterised by the amount of decisions that the teacher and learner make in the teaching/learning process. This is shown in *Figure 16.1*.

When more decisions are made by the teacher, the style is said to be more 'command'. When the learner makes nearly all the decisions the style is said to be 'discovery'. The spectrum includes many styles between these two extremes. At about C or D the style is said to be more 'reciprocal' – this style is characterised by the learners becoming 'teachers' themselves and teaching their peers. This style involves both the instructor and the pupils making decisions. The 'discovery' method is essentially pupil-centred; the performers are largely self-motivated and have the experience and creative ability to work largely without help and guidance.

ACTIVITY

The command, reciprocal and discovery styles are all relevant to the teaching of motor skills. List the advantages and disadvantages of each of these styles.

Successful teachers and coaches are able to adopt a range of styles, depending on the variables identified above. It is important to ensure an enjoyable and productive atmosphere and motivation can be enhanced if personal achievements are recognised. The teacher should analyse the variables in each situation so that performance and motivation can be optimised.

In practice

The best style to use if the teacher has good discipline and the group is large, or if the situation is dangerous, is the command style. This style does not allow social interaction or individual involvement in learning. The learner can simply end up being a clone of the teacher, which may be useful up to a point but does not allow development of new ideas and is not a dynamic process. The reciprocal style of teaching allows more social interaction and encourages a sense of responsibility. Group members must be mature enough to handle the responsibility and have reasonable communication skills. This style is not recommended for complete beginners. The discovery style allows individual creativity but the performer must be well motivated. The instructor must be prepared to step in and guide if the performer runs out of strategies or is beginning to develop bad habits. It can be difficult to 'unlearn' incorrect practices, and the learning process could be severely delayed.

Key revision box

There is a range of teaching styles possible. The teacher or coach should adapt their approach to the type of activity, the age, ability and motivation level of the performer, environmental factors and their own personality and capability. Mosston's spectrum of teaching styles takes into consideration the proportion of decisions made by the learner and the teacher in the learning process. The more decisions that are made by the teacher, the more authoritarian the style. Each style in the spectrum has its advantages and disadvantages and should be chosen, bearing in mind the factors just mentioned. Successful teachers use a wide range of styles, and know how to adapt to changing environmental circumstances and the different needs of performers.

The teacher or coach must know what teaching technique motivates each individual in the team if performance is to be optimised

KEY TERMS

You should now understand the following terms. If you do not, go back through the chapter and find out.

- Cognitive phase
- Associative phase
- Autonomous phase
- Proactive transfer
- Retroactive transfer
- Positive transfer
- Negative transfer
- Identical elements theory
- Organisation of a task
- Whole method
- Part method
- Progressive part method
- Variable practice
- Massed practice
- Distributed practice
- Overlearning
- Visual guidance
- Verbal guidance
- Manual and mechanical guidance
- Spectrum of teaching styles

PROGRESS CHECK

1 Name the three main stages or phases of learning that were identified by Fitts and Posner.
2 What are the characteristics of each of these phases?
3 Why is it important to know what happens in each phase of the learning process?
4 Define what is meant by the term transfer in skill acquisition.
5 Give a practical example of how negative transfer can inhibit effective skill performance.
6 How can a teacher or coach ensure that only positive transfer takes place?
7 What factors must be taken into consideration when structuring a practice session?
8 What is meant by a complex task? Give a practical example.
9 When is it best to use the 'whole' method of teaching a skill?
10 Give a practical example of using the 'part' method of teaching a skill.
11 Why is the 'variable practice' method so important for building up schema?
12 Why is distributed practice usually better than massed practice?
13 What is meant by 'overlearning'?
14 Identify the four main types of guidance.
15 Choose any skill and describe how you would teach it, selecting only one type of guidance.
16 What variables should be taken into consideration when adopting a particular teaching style?
17 Choose one of these variables and justify the 'discovery' approach of teaching it.
18 What could be the problems of adopting a reciprocal approach to teaching?
19 What did Mosston take into account when he developed his spectrum of teaching styles?
20 Give as many advantages and disadvantages as you can for the 'command' style of teaching.

Further reading

D. Davis, T. Kimmet and M. Auty. *Physical Education: Theory and Practice*. Macmillan, 1986.

P. M. Fitts. *Human Performance*. Brooks/Cole, 1967.

C. L. Hull. *Principles of Behaviour*. Appleton-Century-Crofts, 1943.

R. A. Magill. *Motor Learning, Concepts and Applications*. Brown and Benchmark, 1993.

M. Mosston and S. Ashworth. *Teaching Physical Education*. Merrill, 1986.

M. Robb. *The Dynamics of Skill Acquisition*. Prentice Hall, 1972.

R. A. Schmidt. *Motor Learning and Performance*. Human Kinetics, 1991.

R. Sharp. *Acquiring Skill in Sport*. Sports Dynamics, 1992.

B. F. Skinner. *Science and Human Behaviour*. Macmillan, 1953.

E. L. Thorndike. *Educational Psychology: Briefer Course*. Columbia University Press, 1914.

Psychology of physical education and sport

This part of the book contains:

Chapter 17   Individual differences
Chapter 18   Social influences
Chapter 19   Stress and its management

The field of sports psychology is of increasing interest to performers and their teachers or coaches. A performer might have a body that is finely tuned physically for performance, but without mental strength will never reach the top of their sport. Every individual is different, and this part first deals with these differences and how they can affect performance in sport. Every person is affected by other people and their environment. We will be investigating the social influences on the performer of sport and how we can harness the positive aspects and limit the negative ones. Finally, we deal with the concept of stress and how it can help the performer to achieve the best performance possible. Stress is also very destructive in its effects, and we will be studying research related to the management of stress and what this means in practical terms for sports participants and their coaches.

17

Individual differences

Learning objectives:

- To understand what is meant by personality and how it is measured.

- To be aware of the links between personality and performance in physical education and sport.

- To understand how attitudes are formed and the influences upon attitudes.

- To know the links between attitudes, participation and performance.

- To understand what is meant by the term aggression.

- To comprehend what makes performers aggressive.

- To know the ways of harnessing aggression for optimum performance.

- To understand the concept of motivation.

- To understand the different motives held by performers in sport and young people in physical education.

- To be able to describe the links between attribution and motivation.

- To understand the concept of self-efficacy and relate it to participation and performance.

17.1 Personality

The study of personality and its relationship to performance in sport has been wide ranging, and yet solid conclusions are hard to find. Some researchers think that someone's personality is an enduring trait that can influence behaviour in all situations – this is known as the *trait approach*.

In psychology there is an approach to personality called the 'narrow band' approach. This approach splits personalities into two types: type A is characterised by impatience, intolerance and high levels of stress, type B personalities have a relaxed, tolerant approach, with lower personal stress.

Whether the distinction between type A personality and type B personality is helpful when related to sport is not clear. A study undertaken by Hinckle, Lyons and Burke is quite interesting. They identified 96 runners aged between 16 and 66 years as either type A or type B personalities. The runners were compared for levels of competition anxiety, forceful behaviour and response to the challenge of training and racing. The two groups were not significantly different, except type A runners ran more often when they were not motivated than type B runners. This research backs up the argument that one particular personality type is not preferable to another, although the persistence of type A may point towards their behaviour being more aggressive in a sports context.

Definition

TRAIT

Personality traits are seen as generalisable and behaviour can be predicted in various situations. There is, however, much contradictory evidence with this perspective. The traits most commonly referred to are extroversion, introversion, stability and neurosis. All opposing traits should be viewed on a continuum.

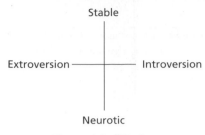

Extrovert: likes social affiliation
Introvert: avoids social contact
Stable: reliable and predictable
Neurotic: extreme emotions and unreliable

Figure 17.1 Trait dimensions for personality

ACTIVITY

Copy out the two dimensions shown in *Figure 17.1* and plot – by drawing an X – where you think your personality profile should lie. Use any well known personality test, such as Eysenck's personality inventory, and compare the result to your own assessment. Try to account for any possible differences. It might be interesting to repeat the process for a larger sample. Can you see any reliability/ validity problems here?

The way to get the best from an individual is to get to know them well

<table>
<tr><td>

Definition

SOCIAL LEARNING

This involves the way the behaviour of one person is influenced by the behaviour of others. We often observe and imitate others – but only others who are significant to us or whose behaviour is reinforced. There is a comprehensive review of this important theory in Chapter 18.

</td></tr>
</table>

Some psychologists think that a person's personality changes with the situation and that the environment (including the behaviour of other people) influences behaviour. This is known as the *social learning* approach.

Most sports psychologists feel that both the trait and the social learning approaches have some value – we are all born with certain personality characteristics but some of these can be modified by interacting with the environment. This has resulted in the *interactionist* approach. The interactionist approach agrees that we do have certain traits which appear consistently, but on many other occasions our traits interact with environmental factors in a given situation.

This has been stated simply by Lewin as

$$B = f(PE)$$

where B is behaviour, f is the function, P is personality trait and E the environment. This formula is a simplistic but useful way of understanding the interactionist approach. The interaction between personality and the situation determines our behaviour.

Eysenck (1960) stated that personality is 'the more or less stable and enduring organisation of a person's character, temperament, intellect and physique which determines the unique adjustment to the environment.' When teaching and coaching individuals it is important that we treat each person as an individual with different feelings and motives. The key to getting the best from each person is to get to know them well.

Personality also involves (among many other factors) how anxious a person becomes in a particular situation and whether he or she can concentrate in any given situation. Gill gives a very good summary of personality: 'Personality is an overall pattern of psychological characteristics that makes each person a unique individual.'

17.1.1 Measurement of personality

There are many methods of assessing the personality of an individual. All methods have problems with reliability and validity.

163

| *Definition* |

RELIABILITY

Reliable research achieves consistency of results after two or more applications of tests.

VALIDITY

There are two types of validity. Internal validity assesses whether the research measures what it is supposed to measure. The research instrument or method must be scientific and unwanted variables that are peripheral (nuisance or confounding variables) are kept to a minimum. External validity assesses whether the results of the research can be generalised to the population as a whole. If the sample used is not representative, then the research has low external validity. Laboratory experiments generally have much lower external validity values than field experiments (which are carried out in real-life situations).

| *Definition* |

PROJECTIVE TESTS

Early in the twentieth century, Freud's ideas about the unconscious led to measuring methods that were based on the premise that an individual will reveal their personality characteristics under the appropriate conditions. If the subject is given ambiguous stimuli, according to this approach, he or she will be caught off guard and will reveal their true self.

Interviews

This method seeks to assess the personality of someone through discussions with them. Projective measures, such as the Rorschach inkblot test, have been popular with clinical psychologists. In this test the subject is presented with an ink blot and he must say what he thinks the picture represents. The responses are then scored and analysed. For example, intelligence is associated with the use of the whole blot and obstinacy is thought to be associated with use of the white space.

ACTIVITY

Read about the Rorschach inkblot test in any basic psychology book. Assess its reliability and validity. What value does it have for assessing someone's sporting capabilities?

Questionnaires

These are sometimes referred to as objective psychological inventories. The use of questionnaires is the most common way of assessing personality. The most common questionnaires used for sports personality research are Cattell's 16PF and Spielberger's Sport Competition Anxiety Test (SCAT). The latter test is discussed in more detail in Chapter 19.

Observing behaviour

The subject is watched and their behaviour characteristics recorded. The validity of this method can be very low – if the subject knows that they are being observed, then that in itself will modify the subject's behaviour. The researcher may be too subjective in analysing what he or she sees. What one person reads into a situation may be completely different from another researcher's assessment. Observation of behaviour can, however, be valuable in conjunction with other research instruments.

ACTIVITY

Ask someone to observe with you a person involved in a sporting activity, live or from the television or video. Both of you write down the personality characteristics being displayed (e.g. aggression, extroversion, determination). How can you account for any differences in your assessments?

17.1.2 Personality research and sports performance

There is an abundance of research articles on the links between personality and sport – many contradict each other and almost all are too general in their treatment and their conclusions. Many sports psychologists feel that personality traits have little or no bearing on whether someone will be a good sports person or not.

Two different groups of psychologists have emerged (Morgan 1980): the 'skeptical' group, who feel that the study of personality and its link with sport is of little value, and the 'credulous' group, who feel that there is some link between personality, participation and performance in sport.

Various personality tests have been used to screen and select performers for teams but very few coaches would put much emphasis on this type of

There may well be a link between physical exercise and mental health

screening alone for selection. The ambiguity of the available research points towards this type of screening being foolhardy.

Some research has been undertaken to study the effects of sport on personality, rather than the other way around. It is often stated that physical education is character-building and that sport can develop social qualities like teamwork which could then be transferred to other situations. Many outdoor pursuits courses are being marketed as helping to build leadership qualities and teamwork but unfortunately the claims made for these courses are not backed up by valid research – although many people involved in sport would say that it has enriched their lives. A link has been suggested between physical exercise and psychological well-being (Gill 1986).

Students who are interested should do some further reading about the links between personality and performance. Suggested further reading is listed at the end of Part 4.

Key revision box

The trait approach to personality research sees personality as a relatively enduring characteristic which can predict a person's behaviour in a variety of different situations. Traits can be generalised. The social learning approach sees personality as being affected by the environment, including the actions of others. The interactionist approach combines both sides of the argument and can be summarised as B = f(PE). There are many different ways of measuring personality but to be worthwhile research must be reliable and valid. The most valid research instrument (although a combination of many is to be recommended) is the objective questionnaire, which is usually self-report. Personality research is mostly confusing and many contradictory conclusions have been drawn. It is very dangerous to assume that particular traits suit particular sports. The claims that physical education and sport can affect personality can be backed up anecdotally but there is little scientific evidence to prove the claims.

Definition

PREJUDICE

This is a prejudgement – someone evaluates a situation before receiving adequate information. It is possible to be prejudiced in favour of something, although psychological research has focused on negative prejudice. Prejudice in a sports context has been seen in crowd behaviour at football matches, for instance. There is a tendency to overvalue the 'in group' and to undervalue the 'out group' and there is pressure for conformity and group cohesion. Allport (1935) stated that prejudice is 'An antipathy based upon a faulty and inflexible generalisation.'

17.2 Attitudes

We often refer to sports people or participants in physical education as having a particular 'attitude', whether positive or negative – but what do we mean by 'attitude'? Attitudes can be seen as a part of someone's personality but they tend not to be regarded as a particular trait. Attitudes are normally directed towards a particular situation, although they are fairly enduring once they have been formed.

Triandis (1977) defines an attitude as 'An idea charged with emotion which predisposes a class of actions to a particular class of social situations.' Mednick (1975) states that an attitude is 'A predisposition to act in a certain way towards some aspect of a person's environment, including other people.'

Whatever definition is chosen there seems to be agreement that we take our attitudes around with us and apply them to particular situations, objects or people. The focus of one's attitude is called the *attitude object*. Attitudes are learned rather than innate and tend to be judgmental. If an attitude is based on false information and is unfair, then it becomes *prejudice*.

Prejudice is unfair and decisions are made without adequate or accurate information

---

ACTIVITY

Choose an attitude object – a particular sport, or physical education in general. Express your attitude by writing down how you feel about the attitude object. Where have these feelings and beliefs come from?

In practice

Your attitude to fitness training could be made up of the belief that fitness training will keep you fit and will enhance your body-image – this is the *cognitive* element of your attitude. You enjoy fitness training and you have fun being with others who are training with you – this is the *affective* element of your attitude. You go fitness training twice a week – this is the *behavioural* element of your attitude.

17.2.1 The triadic model of attitudes

As the name suggests, this model has three elements to it:

1 beliefs – this is the *cognitive* element
2 emotions – this is the *affective* element
3 behaviour – this is the *behavioural* element.

This model states that attitudes are formed through influences on these three elements.

Our beliefs are formed through our past experiences and by what we have learned from others. Many of our beliefs are learned from our parents or peers. People who are significant to us are more likely to influence our beliefs.

Our emotional reactions to an attitude object, whether we like or dislike it, also depend on past experiences. If we have previously experienced satisfaction and enjoyment, then if we find ourselves in a similar situation we are more likely to look forward to liking the experience.

Our behaviour is not always consistent with our attitude, for instance we may believe that exercise is good for us and may enjoy participating but we may not exercise very much. We are, however, more likely to behave in a way that reveals our attitude.

There is continued support for the notion that attitudes are not always linked with behaviour, but the triadic model is still relevant as long as we are not inflexible in its use. All elements must be consistent if an attitude is to be stable and this interdependence is the key to changing attitudes.

17.2.2 Attitudes and behaviour

Although the triadic model views behaviour as being closely linked with the other two components, this has not always been evident in observable behaviour. The famous study by La Piere in 1934 is often used to demonstrate the weak link between attitudes and behaviour and although the study is nothing to do with physical education and sport directly, we can apply his findings.

La Piere's study

For two years, during the early 1930s, La Piere travelled around the USA with a Chinese couple, visiting 251 hotels and restaurants. At this period prejudice against the Chinese in America was particularly high, but they were turned away from only one establishment. Six months later La Piere wrote to each of the establishments they had visited and asked if they would accept Chinese customers – 92% indicated that they would not welcome Chinese visitors. There is clearly much inconsistency between attitudes and behaviour.

Fishbein's theory

In 1975, Fishbein and Ajzen tried to resolve the problem of the link between attitude and behaviour and demonstrated that only specific attitudes can affect specific behaviours. For instance, a schoolgirl may have a positive attitude to physical education but this may not mean that she participates very often; she also has a positive attitude to specifically playing five-a-side football, and is more likely to participate.

The theory they developed states that the best predictor of behaviour is the individual's 'behavioural intention'. To predict whether a school child is likely to participate in five-a-side football, we should ask him whether he intends to participate. Research has consistently revealed that if a person intends to participate in a particular activity, then they are more likely to do so.

We can learn from Fishbein that if we develop positive attitudes to physical education and sport, participation is more likely because the intention to participate is present. Fishbein also highlighted the importance of the influences of family and friends and also the environmental setting. If a young person's family supports participation in sport and the facilities are good, then his or her positive attitude to sport is more likely to result in actual participation.

17.2.3 Changing attitudes

As a physical educationalist, sports coach or any person involved with promoting the benefits of exercise, you are probably trying to develop positive attitudes and change negative attitudes. Our knowledge of what makes up attitudes and their influences gives us some useful information about how we might go about changing negative attitudes into positive ones.

Persuasion is important in changing attitudes or an element of an attitude. For instance, if you can persuade someone that exercise is fun, then you are on the way to getting them to participate.

The effectiveness of persuasion depends on

● the person doing the persuading
● the quality of the message
● the characteristics of who is being persuaded.

In order to promote exercise and change the attitudes of those that are 'non-exercisers', the person doing the persuading should have high status. Teachers or coaches have been given authority – a position – therefore they are more likely to be of high status. They may be fit themselves and become role models and they may have good communication/leadership skills. See the later section on leadership (p.189) for more information.

For persuasion to be successful, the message must make sense and be believable. The information given must be accurate, unambiguous and clear.

A positive attitude can lead to participation

In practice

A teacher wants to promote gymnastics to a group of boys. Their attitudes are generally negative because many of them believe that gymnastics is a feminine activity (belief 1). The teacher introduces the class to an older boy, who clearly has high muscle definition and who shows a number of exercises showing strength and courage. The boys are now starting to believe that gymnastics is far more masculine than they previously thought (belief 2). Belief 2 may cause many of the boys to experience dissonance or a disagreement within their own minds. It may take over and dominate belief 1 for many of the boys, whose negative attitude changes to a positive one.

The effectiveness of persuasion depends on the leader, the message and the audience

The people you are trying to persuade may be intelligent enough to understand the message, but may not accept it. They may put up counter arguments such as 'I haven't got the time to exercise' or 'I might get injured.'

ACTIVITY

If you are a student, think of a sport which is not represented in your institution. Seek to persuade the person that has the power (the Head of PE) to run the activity. Think about how you would present your case and the evidence you could use to support your arguments. If you are involved in promoting sport, think of ways in which you can promote physical activity in your local community. Who would front the campaign? What information needs to be put across? Who is your target audience?

Attitudes towards an activity – for example, gymnastics – can be changed through cognitive dissonance

The most popular theory related to attitude change is Festinger's theory of *cognitive dissonance* (1957). This theory states that all of the three elements involved in an attitude, according to the triadic model, should be consistent if the attitude is to remain stable and the individual to be content. If a change of attitude is desired the individual must experience two or more opposing beliefs. This causes the individual to feel uncomfortable because of the disharmony or dissonance that has been created in the mind. To be comfortable once again, one of these beliefs needs to be dominant, which is where teachers and coaches can influence the attitude of the individual.

17.2.4 Attitudes associated with physical education and sport

In physical education, recreation and sport some people possess positive attitudes because

Definition

SOCIAL NORMS

These are behaviours that are deemed 'normal' within a culture and are created through a process called socialisation, which is dealt with later in this part of the book. Some people feel that participation in physical activity is important to be accepted as part of their peer group or in a wider context to be accepted within society. Others may feel that physical activity is not essential for acceptance.

- they believe in the value of exercise
- they enjoy the activities and have fun or enjoy competition
- they are good at the activity
- they experience excitement because of the physical challenge
- they enjoy the physical sensations and personal expression
- they experience relaxation and see it as an escape from stress (catharsis)
- they see participation as a social norm.

Some have negative attitudes to physical activity because

- they believe that it is harmful or that they are better off doing other activities
- they dislike the experiences involved
- they lack the physical or perceptual skills necessary for success
- they are frightened of the activity
- they experience stress and anxiety when they participate
- they see the social norm as being non-participation.

Differences in attitudes between boys and girls

Smoll and Schutz (1980) investigated the differences in attitudes towards physical activity between boys and girls. They found that girls were more positive towards the aesthetic activities (e.g. dance). Boys were more positive than girls towards activities that obviously involved physical challenge (e.g. wrestling). It was also found, however, that these attitudes changed over time – showing that attitudes are not necessarily enduring.

Boys and girls are often attracted to different activities because of their attitudes

---

ACTIVITY

Try to account for the differences highlighted by Smoll and Schutz.

17.2.5 Expected behaviour

There is often enormous social pressure on people to behave in a particular way and to hold certain attitudes. Research has shown that expectations of others on a particular individual can lead to those expectations being fulfilled. A teacher who has high expectations can influence the pupils' expectations and this in turn can motivate them to achieve more. *Stereotyping* can also influence our expectations.

There are many stereotypes in sport, and these can influence our attitudes. For instance, 'boys are no good at dance-type activities or creative movements', 'strength activities are less suited to girls', 'black people are no good at swimming' or 'white people are not so good at sprinting'. These stereotypes are constantly being challenged but they persist and can influence expectations – which, as we have seen, can influence attitudes.

Teachers, coaches and all who try to promote exercise and sport must continue to challenge stereotypes and the prejudice that results from them. Many people have talents that are as yet undiscovered or feel unable to express themselves because of stereotyping. As we have seen, although attitudes do not necessarily predict behaviour, they can certainly influence it.

Definition

STEREOTYPE

A belief held by a collection of people about traits shared by a certain category of person is called a stereotype. Brown (1986) simply defines a stereotype as 'a shared conception of the character of a group'.

We must continue to challenge stereotypes to give equal opportunities

Key revision box

Attitudes are learned and are made up of beliefs, emotions and the way we behave (cognitive, affective, behavioural) – this is called the triadic model. Prejudice is an extreme form of attitude – it is judgmental and inflexible. Attitudes are not always linked to behaviour but are more likely to be if the attitude is specific towards a specific attitude object. Attitudes can be changed through persuasion and through cognitive dissonance. Attitudes depend largely on previous experience and social learning – we tend to follow social norms. Expectations of behaviour can influence actual behaviour. Stereotyping persists in sport and physical education but is constantly being challenged and equal opportunities are now more realisable.

17.3 Aggression

ACTIVITY

After reading the following paragraphs on aggression, identify which of the following examples show aggression and which show assertion:

- an athlete shoulder pushing another on the final bend in a 1500 metre race
- a boxer landing the final knock-out punch
- a rugby forward player punching a member of the opposition in a scrum
- a cyclist in a race cutting up another rider and causing a pile up
- a squash player smashing her racquet against the wall with frustration
- a football player pulling another player off the ball by the shirt
- a netball player verbally abusing another player.

The term aggression is used widely in sport but it is important to distinguish between the aggression that is desirable and what is unacceptable. Let us first define what we mean by 'aggression'. Dollard (1939) defined aggression as 'a response having for its goal the injury of a human organism'. Baron (1977) states that 'aggression is any form of behaviour directed toward the goal of harming or injuring another living being who

Aggression is the intent to harm outside the rules of the game

is motivated to avoid such treatment.' Most definitions agree that it is the *intent to harm* which makes an action aggressive. For the purposes of this book we will take aggression as being the intent to harm *outside the laws of the event*. In sport it is often very difficult to distinguish between what is aggressive behaviour and what is not.

Seemingly, aggressive behaviour that is controlled within the laws of the game is seen as assertion rather than aggression. *Assertion*, instrumental or channelled aggression, is preferable in sport and pure aggression, or reactive aggression, should be discouraged. A player who is aggressive as defined in the previous paragraph is likely to underachieve, to get injured themselves or to be removed from the game.

17.3.1 Theories related to aggressive behaviour

Instinct theory

This theory views aggression as being a natural response. Aggression is clearly instinctive and is important in the well-being and evolutionary development of the species. Defending the territory is a common expression of aggression in animals. Human behaviour, however, is far more complex and there are problems in relating the animal instinct to the behaviour of a human being. The fundamental problem with the instinct theory is that you would expect all humans (even from different cultures) to display similar tendencies, but this is not so. The major advocate of this theory, after Freud, is Lorenz (1966), who applied the instincts of animals to humans and said that humans generate aggressive energy that needs to be released. Freud stated that aggressive impulses would build up inside an individual and if not released through aggressive acts would become dangerous to the individual's well-being. Lorenz believed that the natural build-up of aggression needs release, either through an antisocial act or via more acceptable behaviour.

The following arguments may be made against this theory:

- early humans were not warriors but 'hunter-gatherers'
- close evolutionary relatives, such as gorillas, would also be expected to be highly aggressive – they are not
- human aggression is often not spontaneous
- human aggression is often learned, and many cultural differences back this up.

Modern psychologists feel that this simplified view is too generalised, that in human aggression more reasoning is involved and that aggression is often a learned response rather than a purely instinctive one.

Frustration has been seen as one of the causes of aggression

Frustration–aggression hypothesis

This hypothesis was devised by Dollard and co-workers in 1939. It is closely allied to the instinct theory but has more evidence to back it up. The hypothesis states that frustration will always lead to aggression, because any blocking of goals that an individual is trying to reach increases that individual's drive, which in turn increases aggression. Aggression, once initiated will then reduce the frustration, leading to *catharsis*.

ACTIVITY

Look at the model of the frustration–aggression hypothesis in *Figure 17.2*. Use an example from sport to explain each part of the model.

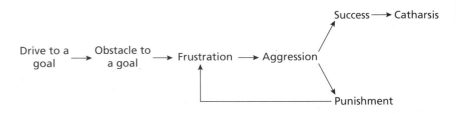

Figure 17.2 The frustration–aggression hypothesis

The problem with this theory is that frustration does not always lead to aggression and aggression often occurs with no evidence of frustration. Berkowitz (1974) brings this theory closer to the social learning view (see next section), when he states that frustration can make an individual potentially aggressive but is not sufficient on its own to cause aggressive behaviour.

Social learning theory

Bandura (1977) is one of many who have advocated that aggression is a learned response, rather than instinctive. The social learning theory states that we learn by observing the behaviour of others (sometimes known as vicarious processes) and/or by direct reinforcement of our own behaviour. There is more information about Bandura's research in Chapter 18. In sport and physical education individuals will learn to be aggressive if they see *significant others* being aggressive or if their own aggression is reinforced by significant others.

The social learning theory disputes the idea that we have natural aggressive drives towards goals. This view is known as an optimistic one. If sports people can learn aggressive behaviour, then it must be true that they can learn non-aggressive tendencies.

Definition

SIGNIFICANT OTHERS

Those people who are held in high regard by an individual, for instance parents, top sports people or influential peers.

In practice

Identify practical examples of how a young person might learn to be aggressive in sport. Now write down a few strategies that you could employ to combat this aggression.

17.3.2 Eliminating aggressive tendencies in sport and physical education

The following strategies could be employed to combat aggression.

1 Control the arousal level of the participant, via stress management techniques such as relaxation or by focusing attention on the job in hand – this is sometimes called channelling aggression. (More about these types of techniques in Chapter 19.)

2 Avoid situations that initiate aggressive responses – for example by changing the sport or changing positions in the team.

3 Remove the aggressive player completely from the situation – for instance, a basketball coach may substitute an aggressive player out so that he or she can experience a period of calm.

4 Reinforce non-aggressive acts – if a player is successful by being assertive rather than aggressive, then reward them.

5 Show non-aggressive role models and highlight successful sports people who are not aggressive.

6 Punish an aggressive participant – for instance, use a fine system or drop the player from the team. The coach and the player could draw up a contract, setting out what would happen if the player lost control and became aggressive during a match.

7 Increase peer pressure to be non-aggressive. If significant others are seen not to reinforce aggressive acts, the aggression may not reoccur.

8 Give or highlight the player's position of responsibility. Show that aggression could let the rest of the team down.

You may be able to think of other ways of dealing with aggressive players.

An aggressive player can let the rest of the side down

Key revision box

Aggression is the intent to harm outside the rules of the game. Another phrase for aggression is reactive aggression and channelled aggression is also known as instrumental aggression and assertion. The instinct theory states that aggression is innate and it is natural to express it. Although there may be some truth that there are naturally aggressive responses, the instinct theory has been largely discredited. The frustration–aggression hypothesis is a drive theory, which states that blocking goals can cause frustration to build up. This can then result in aggression which leads to catharsis. This theory seems to be valid if aggression is seen as potential rather than actual. The social learning theory states that we learn to be aggressive by watching significant others be aggressive and also if the aggression of significant others is reinforced. This is known as an optimistic approach. Strategies to combat aggression include internal control of arousal levels, punishment and reinforcement of non-aggressive behaviour. All three of these theories probably have some bearing on why aggression occurs.

17.4 Motivation

Motivation is one of the main issues in sports psychology. The problems of motivating people to participate in physical education, recreation and sport and getting the most out of them when they do participate are central to our area of study. The study of motivation has been wide, and it could take a whole book to cover each aspect of motivational research in any detail. We will investigate here what is meant by 'motivation', the different types of motivation and the main theories related to this important topic.

Sage (1974) stated that motivation is 'The internal mechanisms and external stimuli which arouse and direct our behaviour'. This definition has three key points.

1 Motivation involves our *inner drives* towards achieving a goal.
2 Motivation depends on *external pressures* and rewards that we perceive in our environment.
3 Motivation concerns the *intensity* (often referred to as our *arousal level*) and the *direction* of our behaviour.

The motivation to participate and to perform well in sport can come from internal drives or from external pressures

17.4.1 Intrinsic motivation

Intrinsic motivation is a term used for the internal drives to participate or to perform well. Such drives or emotional feelings include fun, enjoyment in participating and the satisfaction that can be felt through playing a particular game. Personal accomplishment and a sense of pride are also intrinsic factors, as well as the physical feeling of well-being when exercising (sometimes referred to as *muscular sensuousness*).

ACTIVITY

Choose a sports activity or hobby that you are involved in and write down all the reasons why you participate. Next to each write either 'external' or 'internal', depending on whether you feel that the reason is a result of inner drives or external pressures. You will see that it is not a clear-cut exercise – some external pressures lead to inner drives and vice versa.

Martens (1987) gives the following as examples of intrinsic motivation: inner striving to be competent and self-determining, a sense of mastery over a task and a sense of achievement. Csikszentmihalyi (1975) described the intrinsic 'flow' experience of many participants in sport. The characteristics of this 'flow' experience are total concentration on the activity, loss of self-consciousness and the feeling of total control. Duda (1989) identified three motivational factors: to have mastery over a task, to display superiority (ego) and to gain social approval (thereby gaining a sense of belonging).

17.4.2 Extrinsic motivation

External factors can be extremely powerful in determining what sport we choose, whether we participate and how well we perform. External factors often come in the form of rewards such as medals, badges and prizes. The pressures from other people can also be extrinsic motivators – some young people participate in a particular activity to please their parents, for instance, or you may continue to play for a team once you have lost interest, simply to not let the team down.

As we know from the theories related to learning, reinforcement from others can ensure that an action is repeated. This is relevant to extrinsic motivation – rewards act as the reinforcers. Rewards can be *tangible* or *intangible* and can encourage people to participate or to strive to improve performance.

Definition

TANGIBLE REWARDS

Badges, medals, prize money, etc.

INTANGIBLE REWARDS

Praise from peers, gaining a world record, national recognition, etc.

In practice

A child who learns to swim and who enjoys swimming can be motivated to swim further by giving them swimming badges. After a time, when the child has achieved the full range of badges, he could lose interest in swimming because he may feel that there are no more rewards to be had. This is an example of rewards assuming too much importance. The intrinsic motives of the swimmer have mainly been lost because there is no longer a sufficient reason to continue. A similar example could also enhance intrinsic motives. The young swimmer may experience more enjoyment in swimming because of the inner drive to achieve something worthwhile (a badge), which may give a lifelong love of swimming.

17.4.3 Relationship between intrinsic and extrinsic motivation

There has been much debate among sports psychologists about whether external rewards undermine or enhance intrinsic motives.

The need to win could be seen as both intrinsically and extrinsically motivating. The performer could be striving for success to gain a sense of satisfaction or to achieve recognition. In nearly all cases motivation is a mixture of both. Weinberg (1984) makes the key point that 'Rewards do not inherently undermine intrinsic motivation.' Many people feel that it is not the presence of extrinsic rewards that motivates but rather the way the performer perceives the reward. In other words, performers should put rewards into the proper perspective and the people that have influence over the performer (coaches, teachers or parents) must be aware that the performer's perspective can be influenced greatly by their own. If there is too much emphasis on winning the performer will only concentrate on that goal and will not think about the pleasure of taking part.

Deci (1985), with his *cognitive evaluation theory*, sees two ways to increase intrinsic motivation by using rewards:

1 Try to get the performer to feel responsible for progress.
2 Try to enhance the performer's feelings of competence.

Deci's theory states that reinforcement (e.g. giving rewards) will affect both of these factors.

17.4.4 Theories related to arousal levels

Motivation is related to the intensity and direction of behaviour. *Arousal* represents the intensity aspect of motivation. The effects of arousal can be positive or negative. The physiological effects of arousal, which occur along with the psychological reactions, include an increase in heart rate, breathing and production of sweat. In this chapter we are concerned with the psychological reactions. High arousal can cause us to worry and become anxious, which is a negative aspect if it is not controlled. Raising arousal level can also cause a state of 'readiness' to perform – this is largely a positive aspect and can enhance performance.

As a performer's arousal level increases (often referred to as getting 'psyched up') the state of readiness and expectation increases, but if the level of arousal gets too high a performer can lose concentration and feel over aroused, which we may refer to as being 'stressed out'. This relationship between arousal and performance is often explained through the *drive theory* or the *inverted U theory*.

Drive theory

This was first developed by Hull in 1943. The drive theory sees the relationship between arousal and performance as linear: performance increases in proportion to arousal. A very high arousal level would result in a high performance level. Hull saw that performance depends on how a dominant learned response is intensified. Learned behaviour, according to Hull, is more likely to occur as the intensity of the competition increases. The formula often used to explain this theory is

$$P = f(H \times D)$$

where P represents performance, f the function, H habit and D drive

If the dominant learned response is correct then the performance will be enhanced. The dominant response for a beginner, however, may be an incorrect action and if this was intensified performance levels would actually decrease.

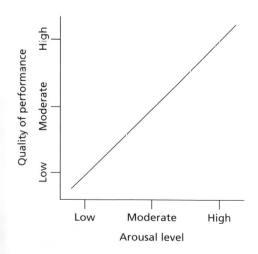

Figure 17.3 The relationship between arousal and performance: drive theory

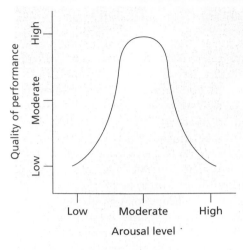

Figure 17.4 The relationship between arousal and performance: inverted U theory

Inverted U theory

This theory is more popular among sports psychologists, although it does have drawbacks because of its simplicity. It was first put forward by Yerkes and Dodson (1908) and has since been applied to sports situations. According to this theory, as arousal level increases so does the level of performance – but only to an optimum point, which occurs usually at moderate arousal level. Once past a moderate arousal level, performance decreases. Participants in sport can become anxious if they are over aroused and their performance usually suffers.

This theory fits many observations of sports performers, although it needs modification to apply it to different types of activities, skill level-sand personalities.

Types of activities. If the activity to be performed involves many fine controlled movements, then the arousal level of the performer needs to be fairly low for optimum performance. Pistol shooters and archers, for example, go to great lengths to control their emotional arousal levels. If the activity is much more gross, such as weightlifting, arousal levels need to be fairly high to expend so much dynamic strength. Rugby forwards have often been seen 'psyching themselves up' before a match.

Skill levels. If the performer is highly skilled, many movements are controlled by motor programmes (see Chapter 15). Many of their actions need little conscious attention and therefore they can cope with higher levels of arousal. A performer who has low skill levels will need to attend to many details related to movement and consequently will need to consciously process much more information. If the arousal level is even moderate, a novice may lose concentration or become anxious, and so a low level of arousal is likely to produce optimum performance.

Personality. Personality types who enjoy high levels of excitement and are generally more extrovert can cope in a high arousal situation. People who are more introverted are generally more likely to perform well under low arousal conditions. This is backed up by the link between the *reticular activating system* and personality.

Definition

RETICULAR ACTIVATING SYSTEM (RAS)

This is located in the central core of the brainstem and maintains our levels of arousal. It can enhance or inhibit incoming sensory stimuli. According to the theories linked to the biological basis of personality, extroverts tend to inhibit the intensity of stimuli and introverts tend to increase the intensity. According to Eysenck (1970), introverts dislike high arousal conditions because their RAS is already stimulated. Extroverts seek high arousal levels because their RAS lacks stimulation.

ACTIVITY

Figure 17.5 shows three inverted U relationships between arousal and performance. What types of task, ability levels and personalities are represented by A? Now attempt to do the same with B and C.

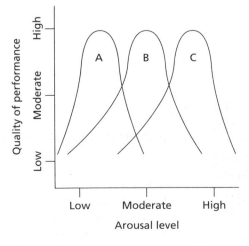

Figure 17.5

In practice

A novice is best taught basic skills in a low arousal environment. It is better if no-one else is watching and if competition is not applied in the early stages of learning.

For gross, dynamic activities, arousal levels are likely to improve performance

The relationship between arousal and performance is more complex than the inverted U theory infers, but this theory remains a good starting point for us to prepare the right conditions for optimum performance.

Key revision box

Motivation involves inner drives, external pressures, intensity and direction of behaviour. There are two main types of motivation: intrinsic, which involves internal drives and extrinsic, which involves rewards. Sometimes one type of motivation can affect the other, either positively or negatively. Rewards do not necessarily undermine intrinsic motivation but rewards must be used carefully so that enjoyment of the activity is not lost. Rewards must be put into their proper perspective. There are two main theories about the relationship between arousal level and performance. The drive theory ($P = f(H \times D)$) is a linear relationship and involves the dominant response being more likely to occur in high arousal situations. The inverted U theory states that optimum performance is reached at moderate arousal level, but at low and high arousal levels performance decreases. The inverted U theory should be modified to take into account the nature of the task, the ability of the performer and the personality of the performer. Stimulation of the reticular activating system can be related to personality, arousal level and performance.

Extroverts tend to do well in high-arousal situations

17.5 Achievement motivation

We have already looked at the some of the links between personality, motivation and performance. One important aspect which needs more detailed investigation is why some people are more motivated to compete than others. Competition is an important aspect in sport, and some people are more competitive than others. *Achievement motivation* is a concept that sports psychologists have developed to link personality to competition.

If the performer is an expert, high arousal levels are likely to improve performance

The theory of achievement motivation is an interaction model, the characteristics of which we have discussed in Section 17.1. According to this model behaviour is determined by the person's interaction with their environment. Some people have a greater need to achieve ('Nach') than others and have what is known as 'approach behaviours'. People at the other end of the scale seem to avoid competitive situations because they need to avoid failure ('Naf') and have what is known as 'avoidance' behaviours. Either type of behaviour is more likely to occur when an individual is in an evaluative situation – when someone feels that they are being judged. In sport, evaluation of performance is often occurring and sport is thought to attract more 'Nach' than 'Naf' personalities.

'Nach' personality types are characterised by

● high task persistence (they stick to the job in hand)
● the ability to complete a task quickly
● a willingness to take reasonable risks
● having a liking for challenging situations
● being able to take responsibility for their actions
● welcoming feedback about their results and their performance.

'Naf' personality types tend to

● give up easily
● take their time to complete the task or do not complete the task at all
● seek situations that present little challenge
● avoid personal responsibility
● not want to receive feedback about results or performance.

17.5.1 *Application of achievement motivation theory*

Recent work has revealed weaknesses in this view of achievement motivation. It has been suggested that success is interpreted by different people in different ways. Some may see success as beating someone else and showing their superiority – these people are known as 'ego' oriented. Others may see success as being internal, a kind of self-competition (e.g. a personal best is seen as being successful) – these people are known as 'task oriented'. Ego-oriented people are thought to believe that ability is most important for success, whereas task-oriented people regard effort as being more important.

An understanding of the type of motive that drives a particular individual can help to formulate a relevant motivational strategy and improve performance.

Tests have been developed which are claimed to determine the achievement orientation of any individual. An example is Gill and Deeter's sport-specific inventories. These tests can be unreliable and there is no substitute for finding out what motivates someone by talking to them and observing their behaviour in different situations. Most people have a mixture of motives but usually some motives are stronger than others.

In practice

When setting goals, decide whether to concentrate on enhancing the mastery of skill or to be predominantly competitive. If a performer is motivated mainly by achieving mastery over a problem, goals should be set that are related to personal standards. If the motives are more ego related (the performer likes competing against others), then goals that allow for comparisons with others should be used.

Key revision box

Achievement motivation is related to a performer's reaction to competition. There are two types of motives – need to achieve ('Nach') and need to avoid failure ('Naf'). Both types of behaviour are more likely to occur in an evaluative situation. Ego-oriented types believe that ability is important but task-oriented people regard effort as more important. Recognition of types of motive can help with motivational strategies such as goal-setting.

'Need to achieve' personalities like a challenge and will take risks

The reasons we give for winning or losing can affect our future motivation

Locus of causality

	Internal	External
Stable	Ability	Task difficulty
Unstable	Effort	Luck

(Stability)

Figure 17.7 Weiner's classification for causal attributions

17.6 Attributions

Attributions are the perceived causes of a particular outcome. In sport these are often the reasons we give for the results we achieve. For example, a team member may cite the bad weather conditions as a reason for the team losing.

ACTIVITY
Think back to your last competitive experience. Write down the reasons that you can think of now for the result you achieved.

Attributions are important because of the way in which they affect motivation, which in turn affects future performances, future effort and even whether the individual continues to participate. A young person who is told that they failed because they do not have enough ability to succeed is unlikely to try again. If the same individual is given reasons that he or she can work on, such as 'need to try harder' is more likely to continue and to heed the advice.

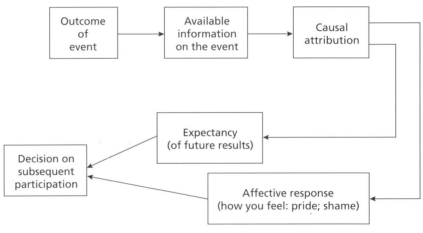

Figure 17.6 The attribution process

The model in *Figure 17.6* is a well known representation of the process of attribution.

At times inappropriate attributions are given and, for the sake of future success, it is important to change these to ones that are going to be far more helpful. This is known as *attribution retraining*.

Weiner (1974) identified four main reasons given for examination results: ability, effort, task difficulty and luck. He then constructed a two-dimensional model which he called the *locus of causality and stability*. The locus of causality refers to whether the attributions come from within the person (*internal*), or from the environment (*external*). Stability refers to whether the attribution is changeable or unchangeable. Weiner's classification for causal attributions is shown in *Figure 17.7*.

17.6.1 Attribution theory related to sport

Weiner's model is not sports specific, which causes problems when trying to apply it to sports situations. For instance, task difficulty changes frequently in sport, especially in team games because the opposition changes. Roberts and Pascuzzi (1979) related Weiner's model to sport. They found that the two-dimensional model was still relevant but that far

Locus of causality

	Internal	External
Stable	Ability	Coaching
Unstable	Effort Unstable ability Psychological factors Practice	Luck Task difficulty Teamwork Officials

Stability (label on vertical axis)

Figure 17.8 The attribution model of Roberts and Pascuzzi

Instructors tend to criticise lack of effort and controllable failures

> **Definition**
>
> **CONTROLLABILITY**
>
> *This refers to whether attributions are under the control of the performer or under the control of others. Coaches and teachers tend to praise effort and controllable success and punish or criticise lack of effort and controllable failures. Concentrating on uncontrollable external and stable factors is not of much use if you want to turn failure into success.*

In practice

Specific learned helplessness –
'I am a hopeless football player'.
Global learned helplessness –
'I am hopeless at all sport'.

more attributions were given than Weiner's main four. Their model is shown in *Figure 17.8*.

People who lose tend to attribute their failure to external causes and those who succeed usually attribute their success to internal causes. This is known as the *self-serving bias*. This bias limits the sense of shame due to failure and highlights personal achievement in success. The stability dimension of the model will affect achievement motivation. If the reasons given for winning are stable reasons, the individual is motivated to achieve again. If failure is attributed to an unstable factor the individual is more likely to try again because there is a good chance that the outcome will change.

A third dimension has recently been added to this attribution model – the dimension of *controllability*.

17.6.2 Learned helplessness

This phrase was first used by Dweck in 1978. It refers to a belief that failure is inevitable and a feeling of hopelessness when faced with a particular situation (*specific learned helplessness*) or groups of situations (*global learned helplessness*).

Low achievers often attribute their failure to uncontrollable factors, which can lead to learned helplessness. Dweck saw high achievers as people who are oriented towards mastery and see failure as a learning experience, and who will attribute failure to controllable unstable factors. This fits into Atkinson's model of achievement motivation – the Nach performers are not afraid of failing and will persist with a task until they succeed (see Section 17.5).

ACTIVITY

Imagine you are a coach of a sports team. Read the following scenarios and write down what attributions you would encourage. Justify your answers by using the theories that we have investigated.

1 Your team won and played well.
2 Your team won but played badly.
3 Your team lost and played well.
4 Your team lost and played badly.

In practice

A person who fails in a task should be encouraged to attribute to controllable unstable factors. For example, a team of 12-year-old girls who have just narrowly lost a hockey match should be encouraged to give attributions such as 'must try harder next week' (these are internal, unstable and controllable).

17.6.3 Attribution retraining

Many attributions that are given are subjective and are therefore not desirable for future progression. For instance, I used to play for a team that constantly blamed the officials for their poor results. Although this helped to draw the team together, they got a bad reputation with most officials and they were not attributing to changeable or (in this case) realistic factors. Attributions often need to be reassessed in order to succeed in the future.

To help those who have failed and are starting to experience learned helplessness, teachers and coaches should concentrate on the positive attributions. If the performer feels that they lack ability he or she will inevitably fail, but their attribution could be changed to 'having the wrong tactics' or 'slight alteration of technique needed'. The performer may then be disappointed rather than frustrated and will persist with the task rather than avoid it altogether. This process is known as *attribution retraining*.

> *Key revision box*
>
> *Attributions are the reasons we give for winning or losing. Attributions can affect motivation and therefore future performance. Weiner's model of attribution is two-dimensional, including where the attributions have come from (the locus of causality) and whether they are stable or not (the locus of stability). A third dimension (controllability) has been added, which refers to whether the performer has control over the causes of failure. Low achievers can suffer from learned helplessness, which can be global or specific. Attributing to uncontrollable, stable and internal factors can lead to learned helplessness. Attribution retraining can help to change attributions and minimise the effects of learned helplessness.*

17.7 Self-efficacy

Motivation is often affected by the degree of self-confidence that an individual has. *Self-confidence* is a rather global term which infers a general disposition. According to Bandura (1977) self-confidence can often be specific to a particular situation – Bandura called this *self-efficacy*. This specific confidence can vary from situation to situation and, according to Bandura, can affect performance if the individual is skilful enough. People who expect to be confident in a particular situation are more likely to choose that activity. Conversely, people who expect to have low self-efficacy in a situation will avoid that particular activity.

ACTIVITY

Write down as many situations in your sport where you feel a low sense of self-efficacy. How do you account for these feelings of low self-confidence?

Our expectations of whether or not self-confidence is going to be high or low may determine the activity we choose, the amount of effort we put into it and whether we stick with the task or give up easily.

In practice

Here are a few strategies that you could use to raise the level of self-efficacy of the athlete in the last activity.

1 Try to give him initial success by lowering the bar to start with, or using some flexi-rope.

2 Demonstrate how it can be done or, if you are much better than him, use someone of similar ability. An actual demonstration (live modelling) can be more effective in raising self-confidence than a video recording.

3 Verbally encourage the athlete. Tell him that he should 'have a go', that you think that he will succeed – even that the mat is nice and soft!

4 Tell him that to be worried is a natural, very positive response because it prepares the body well. Alternatively, teach him some relaxation techniques or how to mentally rehearse the activity (but be aware that this could increase his anxiety).

Being worried is a natural response and can help to prepare the body for action

17.7.1 Factors affecting self-efficacy

Our expectations of self-efficacy depend on four types of information.

Performance accomplishments. These probably have the strongest influence on self-confidence. If success has been experienced in the past, especially if it has been attributed to controllable factors, then feelings of self-confidence are likely to be high.

Vicarious experiences. This refers to what we have observed before. If we watch others perform and be successful, then we are more likely to experience high self-efficacy, as long as the performers we are watching are of a similar standard.

Verbal persuasion. If we are encouraged to try a particular activity, our confidence in that situation may increase. The effectiveness of this encouragement depends upon who is encouraging us and in what ways. Significant others are more likely to persuade us to 'have a go' than strangers.

Emotional arousal. Our perceptions of how aroused we are can affect our confidence in a particular situation. If you have effective strategies to control physiological and psychological arousal levels (perhaps the ability to relax or to use mental rehearsal) then you are more likely to have high self-efficacy. These are illustrated in *Figure 17.9*.

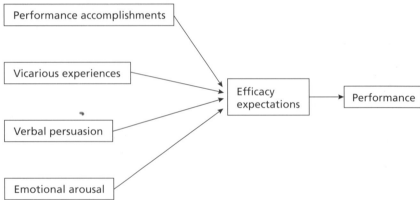

Figure 17.9 Information affecting self-efficacy

ACTIVITY

You would like a fellow student to attempt a high jump but he has low self-confidence. Using Bandura's four factors which influence self-efficacy, state how you would try and raise the athlete's self-efficacy in this situation.

Key revision box

Self-efficacy is self-confidence in a specific situation. Expectations of self-efficacy are closely linked to motivation and can affect the choice of activity, the amount of effort expended and persistence at the task. The factors affecting expectations (according to Bandura) are performance accomplishments, vicarious experiences, verbal persuasion and emotional arousal.

KEY TERMS

You should now understand the following terms. If you do not, go back through the chapter and find out.

Trait
Social learning
Interactionist
Reliability
Validity
Skeptical group
Credulous group
Prejudice
Triadic model
Cognitive dissonance
Social norms
Stereotypes
Aggression
Assertion
Instinct theory
Frustration–aggression
    hypothesis
Intrinsic motivation
Extrinsic motivation
Arousal
Drive theory
Inverted U theory
Reticular activating system
Nach
Naf
Attribution process
Attribution retraining
Learned helplessness
Self-efficacy
Vicarious experiences

PROGRESS CHECK

1 Outline the trait approach to personality research.
2 What approach brings together trait and social learning perspectives?
3 Explain B = f(PE).
4 Using an example from personality research, explain what we mean by validity when we investigate research conclusions.
5 Give a definition of attitudes and describe the triadic model.
6 Do attitudes predict behaviour? Explain your answer using examples from sport or physical education.
7 What makes persuasion an effective way of changing attitudes?
8 Outline the cognitive dissonance theory of attitude change.
9 What is a stereotype? Give an example in a sporting context.
10 Define what is meant by aggression in a sports psychology context.
11 Draw a model to explain the frustration–aggression hypothesis.
12 Using social learning theory, who are we more likely to imitate and why?
13 List five ways of combating aggression in sport.
14 Define motivation and give examples of intrinsic and extrinsic motivation.
15 Explain the positive and negative aspects of the relationship between intrinsic and extrinsic motivation.
16 Draw a graph to show the drive and inverted U theories. Why is the inverted U theory so much more popular than the drive theory?
17 What are the characteristics of a person whose motive is primarily the need to achieve?
18 Why is attribution theory important in sports psychology?
19 Draw Weiner's model of causal attributions and explain it using examples from physical education or sport.
20 What creates learned helplessness and how can it be avoided?
21 Define self-efficacy and, using examples from physical education or sport, list the factors which affect it.

CHAPTER 18

Social influences

Learning objectives:

○ To understand what is meant by social learning theory.

○ To be able to relate social learning to physical education and sport.

○ To be able to discover what makes a group or team successful.

○ To understand the nature of and qualities related to leadership.

○ To know the theories related to leadership styles and be able to apply them to situations in sport and physical education.

○ To understand the effects of social facilitation on performance.

○ To know how to develop strategies for coping with the effects of social facilitation.

18.1 Social learning

In Chapter 17 we came across the concept of social learning. Social learning is a theme which runs throughout psychology. The opposing view, that behaviour is largely a result of innate responses, is also a common theme in psychology. The debate of 'nature versus nurture' is always active in the field of psychology. The social learning view has gained in popularity over the last 20 years.

Most sports activities are set within a social situation, where interaction with others is inevitable. When we investigated the sources of aggressive behaviour (Chapter 17) we learned that observation can lead to imitation. Social learning underpins *socialisation* and therefore dominates all our behaviours.

Social learning theorists state that we learn by observing other people – this is known as *observational learning*.

18.1.2 Observational learning

In observational learning the person who is being observed is the *model*. What we learn depends not only on what we see but also on the identity of the model. Social learning is not just about imitating actions – it is also about adopting moral judgements and patterns of social organisation.

In a classic study by Bandura (1961), young children were exposed to a display of adult aggression. The children saw, in isolation from one another, an adult attacking a life-size doll (a 'bobo doll'). When each child was given a similar opportunity to imitate this behaviour, many of them showed patterns of behaviour similar to those they had observed in the adults. This study demonstrated several important points.

Definition

SOCIALISATION

The process through which children acquire the many behaviours they need to have as adult members of their culture. Socialisation is the process of adopting the norms and values of a culture. Children learn many important responses, including attitudes, values and aspects of self-control, through exposure to their parents and the people around them. Many studies reveal that we learn more from the deeds we witness than from the words we hear. Parents who have the 'do as I say and not what I do' approach often find their children imitating what they actually do.

1 If the model shows behaviour that is more *appropriate* according to social norms, it is more likely to be copied. For example aggressive male models are more likely to be copied than aggressive female models.
2 The *relevance* of the model's behaviour is also important. Boys are more likely to imitate the aggressive model than girls, because boys, through socialisation, see aggressive behaviour as being relevant to them.
3 The *similarity* of the model to the child (age, sex) is also important.
4 Warm and friendly adults are more likely to be imitated by children than aggressive and unfriendly ones.
5 Models whose behaviour is *reinforced* in some way by significant others are more likely to be copied.
6 More *powerful* models are more likely to be imitated.
7 If a model's behaviour is *consistent*, it is more likely to be copied.

ACTIVITY

Suppose you are a teacher or a coach needing to demonstrate a skill, or series of skills. Taking the research findings mentioned above into account, use the concept of observational learning to plan your demonstration. Who is going to demonstrate and how? Give reasons for your choices.

Social learning is often based on copying what we see, especially if that behaviour is reinforced

Social learning through observation and imitation is very relevant to physical education and sport. Many of us find ourselves in situations where we can influence the views and behaviour of others, especially children – this may be because we are in a position of authority or because we are good at a particular sport. Top sports people sometimes forget that they are avidly watched by many young viewers who will try to copy their every move – they are *role model*s, whose behaviour is seen as acceptable and preferable to others.

When teaching skills, it is the demonstration process which is particularly important. According to Bandura (1977), copying or modelling can affect our performance through four processes (*Figure 18.1*):

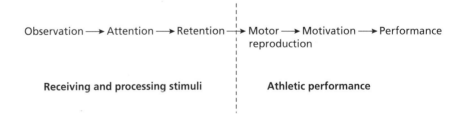

Observation ⟶ Attention ⟶ Retention ⟶ Motor ⟶ Motivation ⟶ Performance
reproduction

Receiving and processing stimuli   **Athletic performance**

Figure 18.1 Bandura's analysis of observational learning

Attention. To be able to imitate a demonstration, the performer must pay attention to the demonstration and focus on important cues (this is called cueing). The amount of attention paid will be influenced by the perceived attractiveness of the model, the competence of the model and the status of the model. The personal characteristics of the observer (such as personal attention span) and the incentives that are present are also important influences.

Retention. The observer must be able to remember the model that is presented. Therefore he or she needs to create a mental picture of the process (see Chapter 15). Mental rehearsal can improve retention of this mental image.

Observational learning depends on the competence, status and attractiveness of the model

Motor reproduction. The observer must be physically able to imitate the skill being observed. Demonstrations should therefore be matched to the capabilities of the observer. Feedback during future practices would be important if motor reproduction is to eventually match the model.

Motivation. The level of motivation of the observer is crucial if they are going to imitate the performance. External reinforcement of the model will increase the motivation to imitate it.

There are important links between observational learning and aggression – see Chapter 17.

Key revision box

Social learning is a leading theory to explain human behaviour. In sport nearly all behaviour is set in a social setting. Socialisation is the adoption of the norms and values of a culture and is learned mostly in childhood, although it goes on all through life. Observational learning is the main way in which we learn behaviour. We observe others and will imitate them if the conditions are right. We are more likely to imitate the model if the behaviour of the model is reinforced and if the model is of high status. Demonstrations are very important in the acquisition of new skills. Imitation of the demonstration depends on the observer's attention, retention, motor reproduction and motivation.

Definition

GROUP

A group is a number of people who need to communicate with each other in many different ways and who work to some common objective or goal. Therefore a collection of people who just happen to be weight training in the same sports centre is not a group. Shaw (1976) defined a group as 'two or more persons who are interacting with one another in such a manner that each person influences and is influenced by each other person.' Carron (1980) sees a group as having 'a collective identity, a sense of shared purpose or objectives, structured patterns of interaction, structured modes of communication. personal and/or task interdependence and interpersonal attraction.' The model in Figure 18.2 represents this theory.

The two main characteristics of a group or team are interaction and the sharing of common goals

18.2 Groups

Group behaviour is of particular interest in physical education and sport because there are many situations where participants and spectators operate within groups. The most common form of a group in sport is the team. To ensure that a team works together well and all the individuals within it maximise their potential, we must understand why and how people work together. The processes within a group and between groups are called *group dynamics* and the relationships within a group are extremely complex because of the many internal and external influences on group performance.

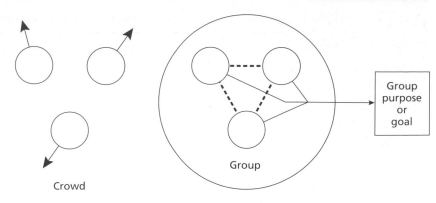

Figure 18.2 Carron's theory. The broken lines represent group processes such as interaction, personal and task interdependence and communication. The large circle represents a collective identity, while the sense of shared purpose in groups contrasts with the independent behaviour of separate individuals

In practice

The South African rugby union team that won the 1995 World Cup was made up of individuals who had a high regard for all other members of the team and who resisted any break up of the team after the competition finished. This is an example of group cohesion.

Group cohesion can help group performance and performance can help group cohesion

18.2.1 Cohesion

Cohesion is a term that is widely used when discussing group dynamics. It concerns the motivation which attracts individuals to the group and the resistance of those members to the group breaking up. Festinger (1963) states that cohesiveness is 'the total field of forces which act on members to remain in the group.'

According to Carron (1980) cohesion has two dimensions:

group integration – how the individual members of the group feel about the group as a whole
individual attraction to the group – how attracted the individuals are to the group.

Widmeyer (1985) saw that these two dimensions could be either *social* motivation or *task* motivation. An individual might want to be part of a team because he likes the personal interaction, or he might want to just play the game and succeed and not be involved in social interaction. Of course, the reasons for joining a group are usually a mixture of these two dimensions, but many people fall on one side or another. For a group or team to be cohesive all members must have similar reasons for being attracted to the team.

There has been much debate about whether good performance is a result of a cohesive team or whether a cohesive team develops as a result of good group performance. A team that is on a winning run is nearly always a cohesive team, but a team on a losing streak may also be cohesive, especially if the team members' motives are predominantly social.

18.2.2 Group performance

If you bring the best individual performers together you are likely to get the best team, but this is not always the case. It is important to look in more detail at the processes that operate within a team. In 1972 Steiner proposed a model which is helpful when looking at the relationship between the individuals in a group and group performance. Put simply,

Actual productivity = Potential productivity – Losses due to faulty processes

Potential productivity refers to the best possible performance of the group and must take into account the resources available to the group and

Definition
PROCESS
The interaction behaviours within a group to target resources to group objectives: 'putting it all together'.

In practice

A hockey team penalty corner drill continues to break down because the timing of the players involved does not match (losses in performance due to coordination fault). A water polo team are not playing very well because one particular player is not trying very hard (losses in performance due to motivational fault).

Definition
SOCIAL LOAFING
Some individuals in a group seem to lose motivation. It is apparently caused by the individual losing identity when placed in a group. Individual efforts may not be recognised by those who are spectating or by those that are taking part.

In practice

Observe a team game either live or on video. Try to identify any individuals who do not seem to be trying as hard as they should. What are the possible reasons for this?

the abilities of the individual members. Steiner's model proposes that groups fall short of their potential because of *process* faults.

The losses due to process faults are mainly caused by two factors:

1 Coordination problems – if coordination and timing of team members don't match, team strategies that depend on them will suffer, and therefore so will team performance.
2 Motivation problems – if individual members of a team are not motivated to the same extent, they will be 'pulling in different directions' and the potential of the team will not be realised.

The Ringelmann effect

This arises when the average individual performance decreases as the group size increases. Ingham and colleagues (1974) continued the research of a psychologist called Ringelmann, who found that in a rope-pulling task groups pulled with more force than an individual, but not with as much force as each individual pulling force put together – eight people pulled only four times as hard as one, not eight times as hard. Ingham showed that this loss in performance was due to both coordination and motivational problems but was mainly caused by individuals within the group losing motivation.

Latane

Latane (1979) also studied group performance. Latane also found that performance suffered as groups got larger and concluded that both coordination and motivational problems were the main causes. He called the motivational losses *social loafing*.

Social loafing is undesirable in teams and should be eliminated as far as possible. If lack of identity is the main cause and the individual feels 'lost in the crowd', strategies should be developed to highlight individual performance. Examples of giving credit to individuals in team situations to make them feel important include 'tackle counts' in rugby or the number of 'assists' in basketball. Feedback to individuals about performance can also help to combat social loafing. Support from others in the team can also help – this is known as *social support*. Peer pressure will aid elimination of social loafing and can serve to reinforce individual effort. A team whose players get on well socially will be more cohesive, which also helps to limit social loafing.

Key revision box

Groups are characterised by individuals within them interacting and having common goals. A sports team is a typical group and those within it have a collective identity, a shared purpose, patterns of interaction and communication and interpersonal attraction. A team that is cohesive is one where the members are motivated to work together. Team cohesion depends on the motives of team members. Some may be socially motivated, some may be task motivated. A team can become cohesive because of good performance or a cohesive team can help to produce good performance – research is inconclusive on this point! Group performance depends on team coordination and motivation. The Ringelmann effect and research by Latane show that losses in team performance increase as team size increases. Motivational losses can be due to social loafing, which is caused by lack of identity of individuals within a team. Strategies should be developed to limit the effects of poor coordination and lack of individual motivation.

Social loafing can lead to losses in group performance

To cut down on losses in team performance due to coordination difficulties, individuals should be selected on their interactive skills. Teachers and coaches should also emphasise that good coordination will eventually lead to better performance. Games using small teams, for instance, may help to coordinate the actions of different sets of players within a team.

18.3 Leadership

Leadership is important in influencing behaviour in sport. Team captains, managers, coaches, teachers all need leadership qualities. Barrow (1977) saw leadership as 'the behavioural process influencing individuals and groups towards set goals.' The key words in this definition are *influencing* and *set goals*. Leadership involves personal relationships and affects the motivation of individuals and groups.

ACTIVITY
Think of a 'good' leader that you know – a captain, a coach or simply one of your friends. Write down all the characteristics of this person which contribute to him or her being a 'good' leader.

An effective leader has a number of qualities, no single quality will ensure effectiveness on its own. Qualities of leadership include:

- good communication skills
- high motivation
- enthusiasm
- having a clear goal or a vision of what needs to be achieved
- empathy (an ability to put yourself in the position of others to understand how they feel)
- being good at the sport themselves or having a good knowledge of the sport
- charisma – this is a quality that is difficult to analyse but the person who has charisma is someone who is hard to ignore, has a certain 'presence' and great powers of persuasion.

Some of these qualities may be learned, some may be seen as natural – it is commonly thought that a leader is born, not made.

Is a leader born or made?

The early instinct theory related to leadership has been called the *Great Man theory*. This states that leaders are usually male and are born to be leaders because they have certain personality traits. This theory ignores situational factors and interactions with others and on its own has little value. It is, however, still quite a popular view outside psychological research.

Carron (1981) suggested that an individual can become a leader in one of two ways:

Emergent leaders come from within the group because they are skilful or because the rest of the team selected them.
Prescribed leaders are appointed from an external source to a team.

There are advantages and disadvantages in both methods of becoming a leader.

189

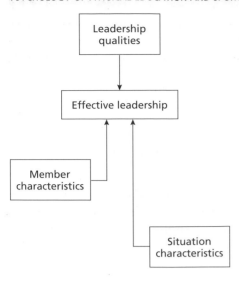

Figure 18.3 *The three main influences on effective leadership*

18.3.1 Influences on leadership

The most popular view of leadership is that leaders learn to be leaders through social learning and interactions with their environment. Chelladurai's multidimensional model of leadership (outlined in *Figure 18.3*) is a popular approach to the study of leadership among sport psychologists.

ACTIVITY

Outline the advantages and disadvantages of an emergent leader, and a prescribed leader. State which situations would suit which type of leader.

Chelladurai identified three factors that affect leadership.

1 The characteristics of the situation.
2 The characteristics of the leader.
3 The characteristics of the people who are to be led (the group members).

The more the elements of this model match each other, the more effective the leadership is likely to be. If the leadership qualities are what the group want and expect, then they are more likely to follow the leader. If the leadership style matches the situation, again leadership is likely to be more effective.

In practice

A team manager's leadership style will be different when talking to the team as a whole before a big match from when she is talking to one member of the team in a training situation (situation characteristics). A captain may adopt different leadership styles with different players, according to the personalities involved (member characteristics). A coach who is extroverted and confident may adopt a dominant leadership style (leader characteristic).

A leader is likely to be more effective if his qualities match the expectations of the group

18.3.2 Leadership styles

Many different styles of leadership have been identified, but most fall into two types. One is concerned with the task demands of the group – *task oriented* – the other is concerned with interpersonal behaviour of the group members – *person-oriented* leadership. These are not mutually exclusive, and effective leadership requires both qualities. Lewin and colleagues (1935) divided leadership into three styles:

In practice

Coaches and teachers should not rely too heavily on the autocratic approach. It may result in hostility and if the coach is not present the athletes may not take on personal responsibility. A democratic approach may result in less work being done but will increase the positive effects of interaction. The laissez-faire approach should be actively avoided.

Authoritarian leaders are task-oriented and are more dictatorial in style. They make most of the decisions and tend to have commanding and directing approaches. They show little interest in the individuals making up the group.

Democratic leaders are person-oriented and value the views of other group members. These leaders tend to share decisions and show a good deal of interest in the individuals of the group.

Laissez-faire leaders take very few decisions and give very little feedback. The individual group members mostly do as they wish.

Lewin looked at the styles of leadership that group members preferred. He studied a group of 10-year-old boys attending after-school clubs, which were led by adults using the three different styles. Boys with an autocratic leader became aggressive towards each other when things went wrong and were submissive in their approach to the leader. If the leader left the room, they stopped working. Boys with a democratic leader got on much better with each other. They did slightly less work than the group with an autocratic leader but their work was comparable in quality. When the teacher left the room the boys carried on working. With the laissez-faire leader, the boys were aggressive towards each other, did very little work and were easily discouraged.

18.3.3 Preferred styles of leadership

Quite a lot of research has been undertaken on the styles of leader that group members prefer. A good leader will not shy away from making unpopular decisions, but should consider the preferences of the group when making decisions. Chelladurai listed five categories of leadership.

Training and instruction behaviour improves performance and emphasises hard training – it is a very structured approach.

Democratic behaviour allows group participation in decision making.

Autocratic behaviour – the coach makes the decisions and stresses his or her personal authority.

Social support behaviour – the coach has concern for individuals and there is a positive and warm atmosphere in the team.

Rewarding behaviour recognises and reinforces good performances.

Chelladurai's results (shown in *Figure 18.4*) suggest that, from the group members' perceptions, ideal coaching behaviour emphasises skill development, positive feedback and a concern for personal development.

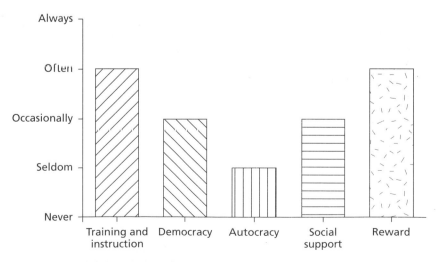

Figure 18.4 Athlete preferences for teaching styles

Your response to the last activity will probably depend on who you are coaching or being coached by and the situation you are in. Some generalisations may be made from the available research findings.

1 Novice athletes prefer more rewards and experts prefer more democratic and social support coaching.
2 Team members prefer more training and instruction, autocratic coaching and rewards. Individual sportspeople prefer democratic coaching and social support.
3 Male athletes prefer a more autocratic style of coaching and females prefer a democratic style.
4 Older athletes prefer democratic coaching, social support and training and instruction. Athletes of all ages seem to value rewards equally.

18.3.4 Fiedler's contingency model of leadership

Fiedler (1967) proposed a model which looked at the way the leader interacts with the situation. He used the two classifications of leader for his model that we described earlier – the task-oriented leader (focus on performance) and the person-oriented leader (focus on personal relationships). He saw that the effectiveness of these leaders depends on the *favourableness* of the situation, which itself depends on

● the relationship between the leader and the group members
● the structure of the task
● the leader's power and position of authority.

The situation is most favourable if the relationships between leader and group members are warm and positive, the task clear and unambiguous and the leader is in a strong position of authority. If a situation is unfavourable the opposites apply.

According to Fiedler task-oriented leaders are more effective in situations that are at the extremes (most favourable or least favourable). Person-oriented leaders are most effective in situations that are moderately favourable.

Leadership is a very complex area because it deals with group dynamics – that, we have already discovered, has many diverse influences. Good

Good leadership can positively affect team performance

leadership can positively affect motivation and performance and bad leadership can inhibit the performance of a team and demotivate individual players.

> ### Key revision box
>
> *Leadership involves encouraging people towards set goals. Leaders may be born or made but research points to social learning aspects. Leaders can fill positions of responsibility, either by emerging or being prescribed. Effective leadership depends on situational factors, the characteristics of the leader and the expectations and nature of the group members. The main styles of leadership are the authoritarian, task-oriented style or the democratic, person-oriented style. Most leaders have a mix of both but tend towards one or the other. There are preferred styles by sports people but again this depends upon situational and group characteristic variables. Fiedler's theory states that the favourableness of the situation must be taken into consideration before adopting a particular style.*

18.4 Social facilitation

This has been defined by Zajonc (1965) as 'the influence of the presence of others on performance'. In many physical education and sports settings an audience or a crowd is watching the performers. The effect of this audience and the presence of other performers forms the basis of *social facilitation*. Zajonc's theory is outlined in *Figure 18.5*.

The earliest study in this area was made by Triplett in 1897. Triplett investigated official bicycle race records under three different conditions:

● alone (unpaced)
● paced against time
● paced in competition with others.

Over different distances performance improved consistently under all three conditions, but paced times tended to be faster than unpaced times. Triplett attributed the increase under paced conditions to a raising

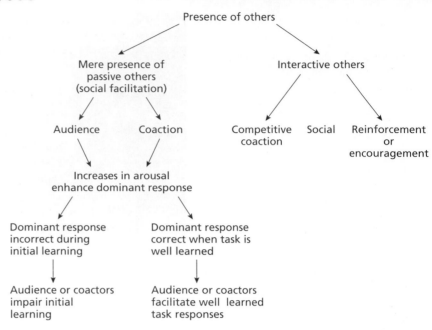

Figure 18.5 *Zajonc's theory of social facilitation related to drive theory*

AROUSAL

This is the 'energised state' or the 'readiness for action' that motivates us to behave in a particular way.

of 'competitive instinct' and suggested that the sight of other cyclists 'facilitated' a faster pace.

Although Triplett's work was far from conclusive, even with his follow-up experiments under laboratory conditions, it pointed the way for others to investigate the effects of the presence of others on performance.

Researchers label the effect of others performing the same activity as the *coaction* effect – the other performers are known as *coactors*. The spectators are known as the *audience*.

Zajonc has more recently identified the following factors as affecting performance:

1 The presence of an audience or coactors increase the arousal level of a performer.
2 This increase in arousal makes it more likely that the performer's dominant response will occur (see the section on drive theory in Chapter 17 for a further explanation of this).
3 If the skill to be performed is simple or if the performer is an expert, the dominant response is likely to be the correct one and performance will improve.
4 If the skill to be performed is complex or if the performer is a novice, the dominant response is likely to be incorrect and performance may decline.

ACTIVITY

Although Zajonc used the drive theory to back up his arguments, the inverted U theory is also relevant here. Look back at the explanation of this theory, then try to relate it to social facilitation and the concept of high arousal level.

18.4.1 Evaluation apprehension

Cottrell (1968) stated that it was not just the presence of the audience or coactors that raised arousal levels and that at times the presence of others had a calming effect, rather than raising anxiety. Cottrell went on to state

An increase in arousal level, caused by the presence of the crowd, can affect performance

In practice

The presence of an audience may cause a tennis player, for instance, to be anxious. This anxiety is likely to be heightened if the tennis player is inexperienced. If the tennis player also knows that she is being judged in some way (e.g. watched by her parents), her anxiety could increase because of evaluation apprehension.

A performer's anxiety can be increased if he or she thinks the performance is being evaluated

that arousal level increases only when the others who are present evaluate, or are perceived by the performer to evaluate, the performance. Cottrell labelled this rise in performer's arousal level *evaluation apprehension.*

18.4.2 Effects of social facilitation on performance

The presence of others will spur some athletes onto greater performances but may 'choke' others, adversely affecting their performance. We have already seen that the psychological effects can be caused by the complexity of the task and the ability of the player but the situational influences must also be taken into consideration – such as whether the player is playing in familiar surroundings or away from their home base. Research on the 'home' and 'away' effects has shown that teams win more often at home than they do away. This may have something to do with the nature of the audience – whether they are hostile, whether the team has its own supporters in any numbers – and whether the team feels alienated by the environment. However it would be very difficult to narrow the effects down to a particular aspect. Some research suggests that playing at home can be a disadvantage – a performer may suffer increased pressure in front of people that he or she knows or feels that he or she is being evaluated more as an individual.

The following factors may have some influence on performance.

- High anxiety (type A) individuals perform less well in the presence of others than individuals with a low anxiety trait (type B individuals).
- Extroverts tend to seek situations with high arousal levels (see RAS theory, p.176), and they therefore perform better with an audience.
- Previous experiences in front of an audience affect future responses. If an individual has failed before in front of an audience, he or she may expect to fail again. Conversely, having been through the experience before may have removed the threat of an audience and future performances may be better.
- Age and gender may have some effect (research is particularly unreliable in this area).
- The crowd's knowledge of the sport may increase evaluation apprehension, or the performer may feel supported because of the crowd's well informed empathy.

The effects of an audience on performance can be influenced by personal, situational or audience characteristics

195

- Performing in front of people you know can increase anxiety levels and hinder performance. If the performer is an expert the presence of peers can increase the sense of pride, thus enhancing the performance.
- The nature of the audience can affect the arousal level of the performer. For example if the crowd is noisy and very competitive, the performer may feel more anxious and possibly more aggressive.
- The physical proximity of the audience can also affect arousal level and in turn affect performance. If the crowd is very close, the performer may feel very threatened (conversely they may feel reassured by the closeness of the crowd).

Even top sportsmen find it difficult to ignore those who are watching them perform

18.4.3 Coping with the effects of an audience

There is no easy way of predicting the behaviour of a sports performer in front of an audience. However, it is very difficult to ignore those who are watching you perform. Many sports people try to do exactly that – they try to shut out the audience so that they can mentally prepare for the task in hand, some using imagery techniques, some using relaxation techniques. A number of coaches prepare their athletes to cope with an audience by getting them used to people watching during training.

Teachers and coaches should be aware that an audience can impair performance in the early stages of skill learning and so it is best to teach skills in a non-evaluative atmosphere. The athletes must be aware of the negative effects of distractions and must be prepared to deal with the potentially negative reactions of coactors, as well as hostile spectators. Instructors can help by being calm and focused, reassuring the athlete – there may well be a case for decreasing the importance of the event. Other team members also play a part in supporting their fellow players.

Whatever strategies are chosen, there is little doubt that all sports performers should be aware of the potentially positive and negative effects of the presence of others during performance.

> ### Key revision box
>
> *Social facilitation is the influence of others (an audience or other performers – coactors) on performance. The presence of others raises arousal levels which can have a positive or negative effect on performance. According to drive theory, the dominant response is more likely in high-arousal situations – this will be positive for experts, for simple/gross skills and for extroverts but negative for the novice, for complex/fine skills and for introverts. The presence of others can cause evaluation apprehension – when there is perceived judgement of performance. Coping strategies should be developed to cope with the negative effects of social facilitation.*

KEY TERMS

You should now understand the following terms. If you do not, go back through the chapter and find out.

Social learning
Nature/nurture
Socialisation
Observational learning
Cohesion
Process faults
Ringelmann effect
Social loafing
Emergent
Prescribed
Task-oriented
Person-oriented
Situation favourableness
Social facilitation
Coactors
Arousal
Evaluation apprehension

PROGRESS CHECK

1 What is meant by the 'nature versus nurture' debate?
2 Using an example from physical education or sport explain the concept of socialisation.
3 Using Bandura's research explain observational learning.
4 What makes a group?
5 What factors affect group cohesion?
6 Potential productivity of a group depends on what factors?
7 Explain the Ringelmann effect.
8 What is meant by social loafing?
9 How may the effects of social loafing be minimised?
10 What makes a good leader in physical education or sport?
11 In what two ways could a person assume the position of leader?
12 What are the three main influences on the style of leadership?
13 Choose one leadership style and describe it, using an example from sport.
14 What makes a situation favourable according to Fiedler?
15 What leadership styles do different types of participant in sport prefer?
16 Define social facilitation.
17 Draw a model explaining the effects of an audience on a sports participant using drive theory.
18 Using an example from physical education explain what is meant by evaluation apprehension.
19 What are the positive aspects of the presence of an audience?
20 Outline the coping strategies that could be adopted when an audience is present.

CHAPTER 19

Stress and its management

Learning objectives:

- To understand the nature of stress.
- To understand anxiety and why it occurs.
- To know the effects of stress and anxiety on performance.
- To be aware of the techniques used to manage stress.
- To understand goal setting and the factors which influence it.
- To be able to apply goal setting to practical situations.

Definition

EUSTRESS

A type of stress that has a positive effect. The performer actively seeks the thrill of the danger associated with the stressor. A typical activity of this type is bungy jumping.

Some people actively seek out stressful situations – for example, bungy jumping

19.1 The nature of stress

There is much confusion over the terminology associated with stress. We will attempt to clarify the position. Stress can be extremely beneficial to the sports performer – many people say they thrive under stress and some participants even seek stressful situations. This is known as *eustress*.

Stress can also have an extremely negative effect on a performer's readiness to perform and subsequent performance.

The concept of stress can be split into:

stressors – the environmental changes that can induce a stress response
stress response – the physiological changes which occur as a result of stress
stress experience – the way we perceive the situation.

An experience which is potentially stressful is affected by how each of us view that particular experience and so stress is not inevitable. We might view the experience with excitement (*Figure 19.1*).

Stressors ⟶ **Stress response** ⟶ **Stress experience**

| Environmental changes that create stress, such as crowd noise | Physiological changes, such as raising of arousal level | How we feel about the situation |

Figure 19.1 How we perceive stress

ACTIVITY
Try to identify what makes you feel under stress in your sport. Do you think that the same stressors will affect someone else the same way? If not, why not?

198

When we experience stress, according to Lazarus (1991), we judge how threatening the stressor is and then how able we are to cope with the threat. This concept of coping is important when we investigate stress management techniques.

19.1.1 Stressors

In physical education and sport there are many types of stressors. However, an experience that is stressful to one person may not be stressful to another.

Competition itself is a powerful stressor. It puts performers into an evaluative position, and we saw in Chapter 18 that this can cause apprehension. We will look at competitive anxiety later in this chapter.

Conflict, with other players or the opposition, can be a stressor. A sports person can bring with them to the sport social stressors from everyday life, causing conflict within the individual about the choices and decisions that have to be made.

Frustration can also be a stressor. When we investigated aggression in Chapter 17, we saw that frustration can build up if we are prevented from reaching a goal. Frustration can be caused by our own inadequacies, by a number of external influences over which we have little control.

Climate can be a stressor. If a sports person has to train under very hot or very cold conditions, this can produce a stress experience.

In sport the stressor of being physically hurt (not just through injury but through fatigue that hard training or demanding competition often produces) is very common.

Definition

STRESSOR

A stressor generally arises when there is an imbalance between the person's perception of the demand being made on them by the situation and their ability to meet the demand.

In practice

A golfer has just reached the third tee and is feeling under stress. The stressors include frustration because he made some poor earlier shots, frustration because he was late due to his car not starting and frustration because the people in front of him are making slow progress. How could we help him cope with all this?

One of the main causes of stress in sport is frustration, which can occur if goals are not reached

---

ACTIVITY

List as many stressors as you can think of that sports people could experience.

19.1.2 The stress response

The general adaptation syndrome (GAS) (devised by Selye in 1956) is the most widely accepted theory to explain how our bodies respond to stress. Selye saw GAS as being made up of three stages:

The *alarm reaction* involves physiological changes such as increased heart rate, blood sugar levels and adrenaline release.

Resistance – if the stressor is not removed, the body begins to recover from the initial alarm reaction and starts to cope with the situation. Adrenaline levels fall.

Exhaustion – the body now starts to fail to cope. Blood sugar levels drop and at this stage physiological disorders can develop such as heart disease.

19.1.3 The stress experience

Psychological symptoms are likely to accompany the physiological symptoms of stress identified above. People under stress often feel worried and unable to make decisions. The worry over feeling stressed can cause even more stress and anxiety. Many people who are experiencing stress feel a sense of losing control and not being able to concentrate.

In practice

Experiences of some elite performers (adapted from Jones and Hardy, 1990):

Steve Backley (a javelin thrower) stated that he looked forward to competition and that, for him, stress before a competition is positive. He has been in the position where he has had to impose stress upon himself. His physiological arousal builds up to the competition and he experiences strong physiological changes on the day of competition. 'I'm off to the toilet every ten minutes, and I'm very active and chattering away.' Steve saw one source of stress as being in a winning situation and then someone throwing further than him.

Sue Challis (a trampolinist) became very anxious, even to the point of crying, when she felt under pressure. Her stress levels seemed to be linked with her confidence level at that particular time – if training was going well, her stress levels were consequently low. She described symptoms such as loss of appetite and sleeplessness during her build up to a competition. She also tended to become mentally exhausted because of her fear of failing. 'On a good run up to a competition I suffer from panic a week beforehand then I'm alright from then on in – it gets better towards the day.'

Definition
TRAIT ANXIETY
A trait that is enduring in an individual (also known as A trait). A performer with high trait anxiety has the predisposition or the potential to react to situations with apprehension.

Key revision box

Stress can be positive or negative. The process of actively seeking positive stress is called eustress. Stress involves stressors, stress response and stress experience. Coping strategies help us to control the negative effects of stress. Conflict, competition, frustration and environmental factors such as climate are all stressors. The stress response can be explained by GAS, which has three stages: alarm, resistance and exhaustion. The stress experience is characterised by worry and anxiety.

19.2 Anxiety

Anxiety is the negative aspect of experiencing stress and can be caused by worry experienced due to the fear of failing in a competitive situation. Arousal levels are high, due to emotional responses. We may be under intense stress in sports situations because of the importance of winning or because of the presence of a large crowd. Anxiety describes our feelings of being threatened: threat of physical harm, threat to our self-esteem, threat of letting other people down or the fear of being punished.

Some competitors seem to be able to cope with anxiety and remain calm. Others, including some expert performers, can become extremely stressed and even physically ill. Martens (1977) developed the Sport Competition Anxiety Test (SCAT) to try to identify performers who were likely to suffer from anxiety in competitive situations. We will investigate what the SCAT tells us about stress later in this chapter.

19.2.1 Competitive anxiety

Martens identified four major factors that are related to competitive anxiety.

1 Individual differences in the ways people *interact* with a *situation* (see Chapter 18). Important games will generate more anxiety than 'friendly' games.
2 Different types of *anxiety*, which can be treated in different ways. Spielberger (1966) identified *trait anxiety* and *state anxiety*. Performers who have high trait anxiety are more likely to experience high state anxiety in stressful situations but other situational factors can also cause high state anxiety.
3 General or specific anxiety. High A trait performers are likely to become anxious in highly stressful situations but are not equally anxious in all stressful situations: their anxiety levels may vary. Some performers may, for instance, be extremely anxious when in a training situation but in a match, with a large crowd watching, they are not as anxious. Martens identified a particular trait anxiety, which he called *competitive trait anxiety*.
4 The *competition* process. This involves the interaction between personality factors, competitive trait anxiety and the situation. This interaction will affect behaviour and may cause state anxiety.

Sport competition anxiety test (SCAT)

Martens gave competitors a self-report questionnaire to assess the anxiety they felt during competition. This test measures competitive trait anxiety. The test is reliable and, because it tests tendencies to become anxious about competition, it should be useful in predicting how anxious a performer

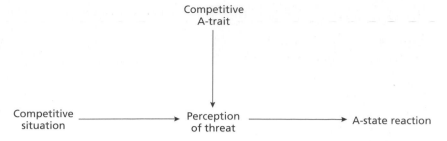

Figure 19.2 Relationship between the situation and personality factors

will be in future competitions – their state anxiety. The results of the SCAT are closely related to the state anxiety a performer feels before competition and is therefore valid in predicting competitive state anxiety (see *Figure 19.2*).

The SCAT is a personality measure but it is not just aspects of personality which determine anxiety levels – situational factors also need to be taken into consideration.

Key revision box

Anxiety is a negative form of stress. Four factors affect levels of anxiety in competition: individual differences, nature of the anxiety experienced, general or specific anxiety and the process of competition. There are two types of anxiety: A trait – the enduring characteristic of potential anxiety – and A state – the actual anxiety experienced in a particular situation. The SCAT is a test of competitive trait anxiety and proves that high trait anxiety can lead to competitive state anxiety.

19.3 Stress management

Considerable importance is placed on managing stress to eliminate anxiety and optimise performance. One of the most important factors separating the very best from the merely good is the ability to control anxiety at crucial moments.

Two types of state anxiety have been recognised:

● *Somatic* anxiety (stress response of the body).
● *Cognitive* anxiety (stress response of the mind).

Management of cognitive anxiety can affect the somatic anxiety, and vice versa. Controlling the heart rate by relaxation methods can make us feel more positive about performing. Positive thinking can, in turn, control our heart rate. Setting goals can affect anxiety levels (we will deal with goal setting later in this chapter). The following techniques are useful for controlling both types of anxiety.

19.3.1 Imagery

The technique of imagery can help to improve concentration and develop confidence, and to ensure the correct response. Imagery has a number of uses.

● To create a mental picture to get the feeling of movement or to try and capture an *emotional feeling* (see the section on mental rehearsal in Chapter 15).

Some sports people may become extremely anxious in competitive situations

It is important to manage anxiety levels to improve concentration

In practice

Imagery evaluation: imagine a situation, providing as much detail from your imagination as possible to make the image as real as you can. Then rate your imagery according to:

1 how vividly you saw the image
2 how clearly you heard the sounds
3 how vividly you felt the body movements
4 how clearly you felt the mood or emotions of the situation.

● Imagery can also create *pictures of escape* – we could imagine ourselves in a much more relaxed place, like lying on a beach in a far away place. The creation of mental pictures is called *visualisation*, and many top sports people use this method to help them control anxiety.

ACTIVITY

Visualisation: close your eyes and visualise yourself performing your sport. Try to just imagine performing one skill, such as hitting a forehand in tennis or kicking a ball in football. *Imagery – to escape*: close your eyes and imagine that you are in a comfortable place, such as lying on a deserted beach under the warm sun: mmmm!

● Imagery can also be used to recall *sounds* as well as pictures – to hear the sound of the cricket ball being hit by your bat or the 'swish' of the ball as it goes through the net in basketball.
● To try to *feel* what it is like to perform a skill – a successful tackle in rugby or the exhilaration of running fast.
● Finally, imagery can be used to try to imagine your *emotions* – to feel the happiness and sense of achievement by saving a penalty or holing a putt in golf.

There are two forms of imagery:

External imagery – seeing yourself from outside your body, as if you were in a film.
Internal imagery – seeing yourself from within.

Internal imagery is probably more effective than external imagery, but most people prefer to use one method over the other. To be effective in using imagery the following points should be taken into consideration.

● Relax in a comfortable, warm setting before you attempt to practise imagery.
● If you want to improve skill by using imagery, practise in a real life situation.
● Imagery exercises should be short but frequent.
● Set goals for each session, for example concentrate on imagining the feel of a tennis serve in one short session.
● Construct a programme for your training in imagery.
● Evaluate your programme at regular intervals. Use the sports *imagery evaluation* described on the left to help to assess your training.

19.3.2 Self instructions/self talk

Being positive about your past performances and your future strategies by talking to yourself (no, it is not a sign of complete madness) can help your performance. Many sports performers use negative self-talk: 'I will never get any better'; 'I am going to drop this catch'. Instructions aimed at yourself can be directed towards technique or towards your emotions.

ACTIVITY

Write down three examples of negative self-talk and three of positive self-talk related to: technique; emotions.

When sports people become more anxious they are less able to distinguish between positive and negative thoughts. The negative thoughts become the focus of attention. Negative thoughts, according to Martens (1980), can be placed into five categories:

1 Worry about performance, especially about comparing with others.
2 Inability to make decisions because there is too much going on in your mind.
3 Preoccupation with physical feelings such as fatigue.
4 Thinking about what will happen if you lose and the consequences (e.g. disapproval).
5 Thoughts of not having enough ability to do well – too much self-criticism.

As performers become more skilful, they tend not to consciously talk to themselves so much, so it is best to use self-talk in training that is positive. Words or phrases can be used in training to help skill development – in rugby it could be 'fast hands', in hockey it could be 'steady'.

Positive self-talk can increase confidence and improve performance

In practice

Mace (1993) identifies key words that could help top netball players in a variety of situations:

To maintain motivation when winning easily: 'Liven up'; 'kill'.
When losing or when opponents score: 'Fight'; Concentrate ... think about the strategy to win the game'; 'Let's go England'.
When anxiety/tension is affecting performance: 'Stay sharp but steady'; 'Accurate ... accurate ... accurate'.
To overcome fatigue: 'Strong'.
Specific position statements: 'Defence'; 'Keep steady' (shooters); 'It's my line'; 'It's my circle'.

19.3.3 Relaxation

Relaxation mainly controls somatic anxiety but can also control cognitive anxiety. It is useful to go through some relaxation exercises before attempting to train yourself in mental exercises such as imagery. Relaxation can help players adopt a calm and positive attitude before a game, but you do not want to go to sleep! It is important, therefore, to avoid a long session of relaxation just before competition.

Relaxation needs practice, just as mental imagery needs practice and practices are best if they are progressive.

Self-directed relaxation

Positive thinking helps performance

This needs lots of practice to be effective. The athlete concentrates on each muscle group separately and relaxes it, with help from the coach. Eventually the athlete can perform this without help, or perhaps the aid of a prerecorded tape. The aim of self-relaxation is to take as little time as possible to become fully relaxed so that eventually it will only take a few moments. This time factor is crucial if the athlete is to be able to use the strategy just before or during competition. This technique is effective if the athlete is able to be aware of the muscles to be relaxed – some have more self-awareness than others, although this can be improved over time.

Progressive relaxation training (PRT)

This technique was developed by Jacobsen in 1932 and is sometimes referred to as the Jacobsen technique. It is a much lengthier process initially than self-relaxation but can be very effective. The technique is concerned with learning to be aware of and to 'feel' the tension in the muscles and then to get rid of this tension by 'letting go'.

In practice

(Adapted from Jones and Hardy, 1990.) David Hemery (athlete) said that just before the Olympic Final in 1968 (he won the gold medal) 'I lay on the bench and the others started jogging around, while I just stayed there, because that was what my plan was, trying to bring my pulse rate down. At will, I tend to be able to relax the whole body without going through the progressive bits.' Hemery went on to explain that this relaxation had come about through relaxation training, which was integral to his other training.

ACTIVITY

Sit on the floor with your legs out straight in front of you. Now with your right leg, tense the muscles by a dorsiflex action of your ankle joint (pull your toes up towards your knee using your leg and foot muscles). Develop as much tension as possible and hold it for about five seconds, concentrating on what it feels like. Now completely relax your leg muscles and let your foot go floppy, concentrating on what the relaxed muscles feel like. Now try to relax your muscles even more. How does your leg feel now? It should feel far more relaxed.

PRT becomes more effective with practice. The idea is to combine muscle groups, so that eventually the entire body can be relaxed at one time. Although this technique may take longer to master, many top sports people have found it most helpful, especially leading up to competition. It has also helped many to achieve a better night's sleep before competition and can be good preparation for imagery exercises.

Key revision box

Stress management deals with somatic and cognitive anxiety. Imagery helps with concentration and confidence. It can recreate the task about to be performed or can help to visualise successful movements. It can also help the mind escape reality. Imagery can represent sounds, feelings and emotions. There are two forms of imagery: external and internal. Positive self-talk can help with reducing anxiety. In anxious situations athletes are unable to distinguish easily between positive and negative self-talk. Relaxation helps to control somatic anxiety. Relaxation can be self-directed or through progressive relaxation training (PRT). Like all stress management techniques, PRT becomes more effective through practice.

19.4 Goal setting

The setting of goals is an important strategy to be adopted by teachers, coaches or performers. Goal-setting is often used to increase a performer's motivation and confidence. Participants in sport are often faced with complex and threatening situations and may feel anxious. Goal-setting can help to alleviate this anxiety and ultimately to enhance performance.

According to Lock and Latham (1985) goal-setting can affect performance in four ways:

1 by directing attention
2 by regulating the amount of effort that is put into a given task
3 ensuring effort is sustained until the goal is reached
4 by motivating people to develop a variety of strategies to reach their goals.

19.4.1 Different types of goals

Different types of goals will affect the performer in different ways.

Outcome goals are related to the end result. Sports people and their instructors often set goals to win or are concerned with the outcome of the competition.

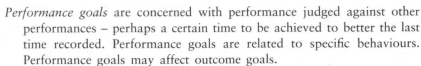

In practice

To help a sports person deal with anxiety over the outcome, success may have to be redefined. Personal performance goals may be less stress inducing than outcome goals and will put the participant into a position of control. Emphasis could shift towards more process-type goals. A move away from outcome goals may make losing bearable and less stressful, thus reducing anxiety. Setting goals such as personal bests can help to focus on performance and process-type goals.

Performance goals are concerned with performance judged against other performances – perhaps a certain time to be achieved to better the last time recorded. Performance goals are related to specific behaviours. Performance goals may affect outcome goals.

Process-oriented goals concentrate on the performer's technique and tactics – in other words, what a performer has to do to be more successful.

Setting goals such as a personal best can help to focus on performance rather than the outcome

19.4.2 Goal difficulty

Research has shown that setting difficult goals led to better performance than setting medium or easy goals. There is evidence to suggest that goals that are set *just beyond reach* produce a better performance than those that are achieved with ease. If the task to be achieved is complex, with many perceptual requirements, goal-setting becomes less effective in the short term, but the strategies that have been tried and failed could be useful in the long term. Generally speaking, goals must be achievable but challenging. If goals are set too easy, motivation will soon decline.

19.4.3 Goal specificity

Clearly defined goals usually leads to better performance. Simply saying 'do your best' is not good enough – targets need to be better defined. Evaluation of goals is also difficult if the goals have not been clearly defined. Sports involving objective measurements, such as time, are easier to make specific but it is possible to set specific goals in most activities.

19.4.4 Other factors affecting goal-setting

Long-term and short-term goals

Achievement of long-term goals is a *progressive* process and must start with achieving short-term goals. Many athletes use realistic target dates to help them achieve their short-term goals. Short-term goals provide a greater opportunity for success, which can reinforce positive feelings, which in turn helps to control anxiety levels.

Evaluation

Goals need to be *measurable*. The measurement of goals will give information about success, in itself a motivating factor, and will also give useful information about setting further goals. There is nothing worse for a performer not to know how he or she is progressing, so accurate feedback is essential.

Goals need to be measurable to be effective

Key revision box

Goal-setting can help motivation, boost confidence and help with anxiety control. There are three different types of goals: outcome goals, performance goals and process-oriented goals. Goals should be challenging, but not too difficult. They should be well-defined so that goal evaluation can take place. Long-term goals should be preceded by short-term goals to help with motivation and to control anxiety. Goals must also be measurable for evaluation to take place. If there is a sharing in decisions about goals, then those goals are more likely to be achieved, and anxiety is less likely.

Sharing decision-making

Goals which are set through negotiation and agreement are far more effective than externally set goals. The participant will have a sense of ownership over the goal-setting and will be better motivated to achieve. Goal-setting is also likely to be fairer and more realistic if all parties involved have an input.

ACTIVITY

Write down some long-term goals that you might have related to your sport, your coaching or even your studies. Now try to identify some short-term goals or objectives that might help you achieve your long-term goals. Use all the guidance that has been set out in this last section. Are the goals you have set measurable, achievable, specific? Are they outcome goals, performance goals or process-oriented goals?

KEY TERMS

You should now understand the following terms. If you do not, go back through the chapter and find out.

Stress
Eustress
Stressor
Conflict
General adaptation syndrome
Anxiety
Sport competition anxiety test
A state
A trait
Somatic anxiety
Cognitive anxiety
Competitive A trait
Imagery
Self-directed relaxation
Progressive relaxation training
Performance goals
Process-oriented goals
Long-term goals
Short-term goals

PROGRESS CHECK

1 Define the term stress and explain what is meant by eustress.
2 Give three examples of typical stressors in a physical education or sports context.
3 Describe Selye's GAS theory of stress response.
4 Define the term anxiety.
5 Using examples from physical education or sport explain what is meant by trait anxiety and state anxiety.
6 What is meant by competitive trait anxiety?
7 Outline the SCAT.
8 Draw a model to show the relationships between competitive trait anxiety, situation and personality factors.
9 What are the two types of state anxiety?
10 Describe the imagery process of stress management. What are the main effects of this process?
11 How do you make imagery more effective?
12 Outline the five categories of negative thoughts, according to Martens.
13 What are the main effects of somatic relaxation?
14 What makes a situation favourable according to Fiedler?
15 What leadership styles do different types of participant in sport prefer?
16 Define social facilitation.
17 Draw a model explaining the effects of an audience on a sports participant using drive theory.
18 Using an example from physical education explain what is meant by evaluation apprehension.
19 What are the positive aspects of the presence of an audience?
20 Outline the coping strategies that could be adopted when an audience is present.

Further reading

G. W. Allport. *Attitudes*. Clarke University Press, 1935.

A. Bandura. *Social Learning Theory*. Prentice Hall, 1977.

R. A. Baron. *Human Aggression*. Plenum, 1977.

J. L. Barrow. The variables of leadership. *Academy of Management Review*, 1977.

L. Berkowitz. Some determinants of impulsive aggression. *Psychological Review*, 1974.

S. J. Bull. *Sport Psychology, A Self Help Guide*. Crowood, 1991.

A. V. Carron. *Social Psychology of Sport*. Mouvement Publications, 1980.

P. Chelladurai. Multidimensional model of leadership 1984. In: J. M. Silva and R. S. Weinberg. *Psychological Foundations of Sport*. Human Kinetics, 1984.

N. B. Cottrell. *Performance in the Presence of Other Human Beings*. Allyn & Bacon, 1968.

B. J. Cratty. *Social Psychology in Athletics*. Prentice-Hall, 1981.

M. Csikszentmihalyi. *Beyond Boredom and Anxiety*. Joey-Bass, 1975.

F. L. Deci. *Intrinsic Motivation and Self-determination in Human Behaviour*. Plenum Press, 1985.

J. Dollard. *Frustration and Aggression*. Yale University Press, 1939.

J. L. Duda. The relationship between task and ego orientation. *Journal of Sports Psychology*, 1989.

C. S. Dweck. *Learned Helplessness in Sport*. Human Kinetics, 1980.

H. J. Eysenck. *The Structure and Measurement of Personality*. Routledge, 1969, 1970.

L. A. Festinger. *A Theory of Cognitive Dissonance*. Harper & Row, 1957.

L. Festinger. *Social Pressures in Informal Groups*. Harper & Row, 1963.

F. E. Fiedler. *A Theory of Leadership Effectiveness*. McGraw-Hill, 1967.

D. L. Gill. *Psychological Dynamics of Sport*. Human Kinetics, 1986.

D. L. Gill and T. E. Deeter. Development of the Sport Orientation Questionnaire. *Research Quarterly for Sport*, 1988.

A. G. Ingham *et al*. The Ringlemann effect. *Journal of Experimental Psychology*, 1974

J. G. Jones and L. Hardy, editors. *Stress and Performance in Sport*. Wiley, 1990.

B. Latane *et al*. Many hands make light work. *Journal of Personality*, 1979.

K. Lewin. *A Dynamic Theory of Personality*. McGraw-Hill, 1935.

K. Lewin. *Psychological Theory*. Macmillan, 1951.

K. Lorenz. *On Aggression*. Brace & World, 1966.

R. Martens. Science and sport psychology. *The Sports Psychologist*, 1987.

R. Martens, R. S. Vealey and D. Burton. *Competitive Anxiety in Sport*. Human Kinetics, 1990.

W. P. Morgan. *Sport Personology*. Mouvement, 1980.

J. Radford and E. Govier, editors. *A Textbook of Psychology*. Routledge, 1991.

G. C. Roberts, editor. *Motivation in Sport and Exercise*. Human Kinetics, 1992.

K. C. Roberts and D. Pascuzzi. Causal attributions in sport. *Journal of Sports Psychology*, 1979

C. G. Roberts, K. S. Spink and C. L. Pemberton. *Learning Experiences in Sport Psychology*. Human Kinetics, 1986.

G. H. Sage. *Sport and American Society*. Addison-Wesley, 1974.

M. E. Shaw. *Group Dynamics*. McGraw-Hill, 1976.

J. M. Silva and R. S. Weinberg, editors. *Psychological Foundations of Sport*. Human Kinetics, 1984.

F. L. Smoll and R. W. Shutz. Children's attitudes towards physical activity. *Journal of Sports Psychology*, 1980.

I. D. Steiner. *Group Process and Productivity*, Academic Press, 1972.

H. C. Triandis. *Interpersonal Behaviour*. Brooks/Cole, 1977.

R. S. Weinberg. The relationship between extrinsic rewards and intrinsic motivation. In: J. M. Silva and R. S. Weinberg. *Psychological Foundations of Sport*. Human Kinetics, 1984.

J. D. Willis and L. F. Campbell. *Exercise Psychology*. Human Kinetics, 1992.

R. M. Yerkes and J. D. Dodson. The relation of strength of stimulus to rapidity of habit formation. *Journal of Neurological Psychology*, 1908.

PART 5

Sociocultural aspects of physical education and sport

This part of the book contains:

Chapter 20   The history of sport
Chapter 21   The organisation of sport in the United Kingdom
Chapter 22   Sport in society

This final part investigates how society can affect the sports performer and how society can be influenced by physical education and sport. In order to understand what is happening today, it is useful to look back at what has happened before and this part deals with historical factors. The terms we use when describing the activities related to sport differ, which can lead to confusion. We encourage readers to analyse these different terms to develop a better understanding of why people get involved in physical education and sport at different levels and the factors which influence and restrict their choices. This part compares physical education and sport in the UK with that of other countries so that we can learn from the experiences of other cultures. Many social issues surround physical education and sport and this section of the book takes an in-depth look at the main issues affecting the performer. It is hoped that the reader will base any future decisions and attitudes on careful consideration of the facts surrounding a particular issue, not on hearsay or stereotypes. Discrimination of all forms is unfortunately a feature of our society, in sport as in other aspects. We must strive for equality of opportunity and we hope that this part of the book will help all of us consider the issues surrounding physical education and sport intelligently and without prejudice.

20

The history of sport

Learning objectives:

- To develop knowledge of the history of sport.
- To be able to discuss the role of the study of sport.
- To be able to define the concepts involved in the study of sport.
- To understand the role that concepts such as outdoor recreation play in society.
- To know the factors that affect sport and recreation in Britain.

In human activity, the invention of the ball may be said to rank with the invention of the wheel

In the Haka, the Maoris are really saying 'today we get our own back!'

Sports are developmental – they develop from *conquest* or from *social hierarchy*.

For example, rugby was introduced by the upper classes at Rugby public school in the early 1800s and then spread with the British Empire around the world. The game was taken to Western Samoa from New Zealand by plantation farmers and merchants at the beginning of the twentieth century. The Western Samoans play the game by the same rules as everyone else, but to them rugby is a *war game* – this is very evident in the ferocity of their tackling. The New Zealand Maoris (and even the national team) play the modern game but have incorporated parts of their own culture into it with the ritual Haka, performed before the game.

20.1 The origins of sport

The oldest sports were probably gymnastic displays. One of the earliest recorded forms of sport is evident in Minoan Crete – this is bull leaping, in which slaves leapt over the horns of a bull. Records of bull leaping give us a glimpse of the function of this ancient form of sport, mainly as a spectacle with some ritualistic or religious element. To the Minoans the bull symbolised God because it was the biggest, most ferocious and strongest animal known to them and by challenging the bull they honoured the God. However, bull leaping was also a *test of physique and temperament* – which is the essence of sport. The Minoans did not actually perform the bull leaping themselves – they used servants to represent them. This leads us on to another important element of sport, that of *spectacle*.

The modern game of lacrosse originated in a game that the Iroquois Indians of North America played, called Baggataway, in which they threw a bag containing the head of an enemy or rival to each other. The South American civilisations had a similar bloody use for the heads of their enemies – ritual games of football, which they played in purpose-built stadiums that can still be seen today. It has been suggested that the great British game of football has its origins in a game called 'Daneshead', played by men who had defeated Scandinavian raiders.

Wrestling originated in Graeco-Roman times. Wrestling was considered as the 'ultimate' sport because it was (and still is) one-on-one and could end in the death of one participant.

These examples point to another characteristic of sport – you often put your life on the line: *there is no sport without risk*.

20.1.1 Historical links of various sports

The many sports played today derive from five main historical areas:

● invasion games
● target games
● court games
● field sports
● religious rituals.

Invasion games

These games, such as rugby and football, are warlike games, where the object is to invade the opponent's territory. The origin of these games lies in mob games in which one part of a community played against another part, usually to defend or steal something.

Target games

These games involve use of marksmanship and include sports such as archery, with its clear link to war/defence and also sports such as golf and bowls. The urge to aim and hit targets is almost innate in humans. Think about how you put a piece of scrap paper into the wastebasket – no doubt you screw it into a ball and 'fire' it at the bin.

Court games

Court games originally reflected culture – sophisticated games were thought to represent sophisticated culture. Such games include real tennis, fives, rackets, squash and lawn tennis. The sports are non-contact because the opponents are on opposite sides of a net. Because of the sophistication and expense these games were often confined to the upper classes.

Field sports

Sports such as hunting, shooting and fishing are associated with finding food and survival but also the enjoyment of the chase. The fox is thought to represent man (French man), master of the environment and so a challenge. These sports have also been associated with the upper classes, although the working classes found a similar satisfaction in 'coarse fishing' and in animal baiting.

Games involving ritual

These games included baiting animals such as badgers and bulls with dogs. The bull was seen as 'bad', man showed his supremacy over the animal, and everybody could own a dog. Baiting the bull before slaughter was often a legal requirement. This is another example of sport reflecting the society in which it exists – but this sport shows an uncivilised society limited in its development.

In bull baiting the bull represented evil, over which man showed his supremacy

20.1.2 A brief overview of the historical development of modern sport

Modern sport may be seen to have passed through four stages of development.

1 Popular recreation (before 1790)
2 Public school athleticism (1800–1860)
3 Rationalisation of sport (1860–1919)
4 Twentieth century of sport (1920 onwards)

The transition between the phases represents not only development in sport but also major developments in society.

Popular recreation

In pre-industrial Britain, sports clearly reflected the society. In the main sports were of two types:

● the sports of the aristocracy – complex and refined, such as real tennis and fencing
● the sports of the peasants – the so-called 'mob' games.

The mob games and other 'people's' sports were closely associated to the church calendar of holy days and wakes and to the farming year of spring and harvest. These sports were a chance for the people to meet as a community and 'let off steam'. They were not really sport in the modern sense – there were very few (if any) rules, the game being a kind of free-for-all. They were also not played often – sometimes only once a year (for example the annual Ashbourne Football game was played once a year on Shrove Tuesday).

Street football in the Middle Ages

Sports involving animals were also popular. Hunting was mostly the domain of the upper classes, and at this time there was still a great deal of 'quarry' available. The royal deer forests are a good example of the exclusivity of this 'sport' – these forests were protected for the sport of the king and those to whom he was pleased to grant a similar privilege. Rigorous Game Laws were enforced in every county, keeping the common people from catching animals on these lands.

For the lower classes this hunting drive was satisfied by the bloody spectacle of animal baiting. Cock-fighting was a huge gambling sport and bulls, bears and even horses were trained to fight dogs. Special arenas were built to house these events.

Public school athleticism

At the beginning of the nineteenth century, public schools began to appear for the upper classes. Very quickly these became an essential element of training to be a gentleman – they were also to play a very important role in the development of modern sport.

Initially the boys took the rural sports into the schools and with some adaptation carried on the sporting traditions of an upper-class gentleman. The games of hare and hounds or cross-country running became substitutes for hunting, but games and sports were increasingly used for educational purposes. Football is the most popular example of this transformation. With its roots in the mob festivals of the populace, football was transformed by public schools into an organised regular game with rules and played an essential role in the education of a gentleman whose destiny was to lead and develop the Empire.

Sport was used as social control in the reformation of the public schools, which led to concept of 'muscular Christianity' – the idea that moral understanding could be developed through athletics.

The public schools were the first bodies to *codify* sport – to give it rules. This process extended sports and ultimately gave us the concept of sport as we know it today.

213

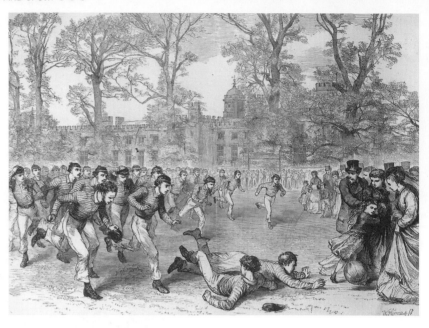

Rugby School – the birthplace of rugby football

Rationalisation of sport

From 1860 onwards the development of sport began to spiral. We can chart the development, codification and administration of all the major sports from this time on. Important changes occurred in society that would determine the image modern sport would portray. It is important that you know a little about the impact of Industrialisation and the effect that this had on the people, their work, homes and leisure (space does not allow a deeper investigation but we recommend the book by Holt, listed in the Further Reading at the end of Part 5).

Most people now lived and worked in urban areas and the influence of the rural elements in sport declined – modern sport is also urban sport.

As boys left their public schools they played an important role in developing sport at the universities of Oxford and Cambridge. They began to unify the various strands and develop national sports, wrote rules and set up governing bodies to oversee these unified sports. These young men then spread their love of games around the world.

The university boat race, 1829

Sport in the twentieth century

Several factors have affected the development of sport through the twentieth century. There has been a steady move away from participation in sport to the phenomenon of watching sport, initially through spectatorism but increasingly through the media. Spectatorism generated money, which led to professionalism in virtually all sports. Many sports performers are now full-time paid entertainers.

Sport has become a mass consumer spectacle unavoidably linked to commercialism, a point which is discussed further in Chapter 22.

Key revision box

Ancient sports had the following characteristics: ritual/symbolism, function and spectacle. These elements are still visible in many modern sports. Popular recreation took place in pre-industrial Britain, the games being played having close links to the social background of the players. Sport in public schools was based on the concept of athleticism. Schoolboys adapted the popular games at these schools. Later schools used sports to develop character ('muscular Christianity') and as a means of social control. A great deal of development and codification of modern sports occurred at universities in the late nineteenth century, which was also a period of great change in society. By the end of the nineteenth century the games ethic was being carried all around the world. In the twentieth century spectatorism, professionalisation and the media have had great influence on sport.

20.2 An introduction to the study of sport

The rest of this chapter involves sociocultural study of the environment in which sports take place. This area is concerned with a family of activities:

● sport
● leisure
● physical recreation
● play
● outdoor recreation
● physical education.

We will take each of these separately and discuss them in their correct context.

20.3 Sport

20.3.1 A brief history

In the middle of the nineteenth century the word 'sport' referred to the 'field' sports of hunting, shooting and fishing which the upper classes enjoyed. Gradually it became more widely applied to all games played in the open air.

Sports (plural) was the name given to a series of athletic contents, often held at rural festivals or gatherings. The Scottish Highland Games and the Basque Games in southern France are good examples of events of this type which still take place.

Definition

SPORT

According to the dictionary 'to sport' means 'to play, or frolic'. A more appropriate definition for this book is 'Institutionalised contests, using physical exertion between human beings or teams of human beings'.

Competitive mountain biking is an example of a modern sport

The modern meaning of sport was born during the industrial revolution at the public schools such as Rugby. Gradually these games were passed on to the lower classes and new pastimes of playing, watching and reading about sport developed. The number of activities that come under the name of 'sport' is ever increasing. Some of the latest additions to this list are speed climbing and mountain biking.

20.3.2 What is sport?

We can identify certain characteristics that are shared by all sports.

ACTIVITY

Look at the following list of sports and make a list of the characteristics they have in common.

Hockey, rugby, cricket, cycle pursuit, orienteering, netball.

From your answers to the activity above, you will have probably discovered the following points:

- they all contain an element of *chance*
- they all involve *competition* between *distinct sides*
- *physically strenuous activity* is involved
- the *clear outcome* has *winners* and *losers*
- games are *spontaneous* and *enjoyable*
- *special equipment* is usually needed to play.

From this list we may develop the hypothesis that all sports must have the features in this list.

ACTIVITY

Would you consider the following activities sports?

1 Darts
2 TV's *Gladiators*
3 Jogging
4 Competition ballroom dancing

The essence of sport?

To check the effectiveness of this hypothesis let us study a particular activity – recreational swimming, for example. Although this activity certainly involves physical exercise and some (very basic) equipment, there is no real competition in swimming a few lengths of a pool. We could argue that there is an element of competition against self, but there are no clear winners and losers, nor any distinct 'sides'. Consequently we may conclude that recreational swimming is not a sport, according to our hypothesis.

Therefore, for a theoretical approach to the study of physical activity, sport can best be defined as an activity that involves competition, which is physically strenuous and enjoyable.

20.3.3 Why study sport?

In Britain, sport holds a special place in education and culture. According to Winston Churchill, 'sport was the first of all the British public amusements'. We have a long tradition of sport in Britain. Several sporting events have become national pastimes – Derby Day, the Boat Race, the FA Cup, the Grand National, Wimbledon.

Sport and education

Education has long been associated with sport. Through sport you can learn a lot of life's moral issues and experiences – it also has the advantage of making you healthy!

Sport and social control

Sport has been used to control the masses – a concept called *social control*. If people are playing or watching sport they are not getting themselves into trouble. Social historians have often said that Britain never had a social revolution because its people were too busy playing games!

Britain has a unique position in the history of world sport. Most of the modern games played throughout the world were invented and developed here, and then taken to the extremes of the British Empire.

Sport and international relations

Sport can be used to keep up morale in times of war. For example the Kuwaiti soccer team toured Britain during the Gulf War. It can also be used to promote trade and cement allegiances or offer an olive branch to nations that are in conflict with each other. For example England and Argentina played rugby and soccer internationals soon after the Falklands conflict as a means of peace making.

Sport and the media

Perhaps the best illustration of the importance sport plays in our culture is the amount of time and space the media devote to it. The BBC alone devotes at least 20 hours each week, and most national newspapers donate 10–20 per cent of their space to reporting sport.

The armchair sports enthusiast

> ### Key revision box
>
> *Sport is a complex concept, the true meaning of which has been distorted by its use in the media. Sport is best seen as any physical activity that includes competition with a clear winner, which is strenuous and enjoyable. As Samuel Johnson concluded in 1756, above all, sport is 'Tumultuous merriment'.*

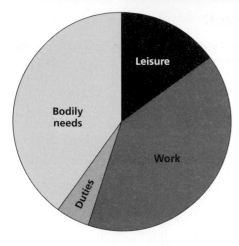

Figure 20.1 Average split of a person's daily activities

20.4 Leisure

If we listed all the particular things we do in a day, we would probably end up with a very long list. However, most of our activities could be categorised under the following headings:

● work
● bodily needs
● duties
● leisure.

We need to *work* to earn a living. Work consumes a large amount of our time. This definition of work includes related activities such as housework, school and college work, travel to work. Our *bodily needs* include sleeping and eating. *Duties* include the tasks we must perform in relation to family pets and the home. If we exclude from our day the time required for these three activities we are left with *free time* – this is the time we have available for *leisure*. The average split of a person's daily activities may be represented in a pie chart, as shown in *Figure 20.1*.

ACTIVITY

Make a record of your time over the next few days, put the activities in to the categories described above and produce your own pie chart.

The key to leisure time is that you perform the activities that you *choose* to do. *Figure 20.2* shows how the various activities involve choice.

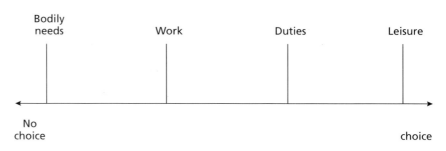

Figure 20.2 The continuum of choice in activities

20.4.1 What exactly is leisure?

We use the word leisure in two ways:

1 as the period of free time which is left after work.
2 to describe an activity or something we do. A leisure activity is freely chosen.

A great many definitions of leisure are available. Perhaps the best suited to our study are given in the definition box on this page.

Any attempt to fully answer the question 'What is leisure?' reveals it to be a frustrating and elusive concept whose definition changes depending on the context in which it is used. However, leisure does have positive connotations of enjoyment, freedom of choice, self-fulfilment and self-actualisation. These keywords are our criteria for a definition of leisure.

Definition

LEISURE

'Time in which there is an opportunity for choice.' (Arnold, 1978). 'An activity, apart from the obligations of work, family and society, to which the individual turns at will, for either relaxation, diversion, or broadening experiences and his spontaneous social participation, their free exercise of his creative capacities.' (Dumazedier, 1967).

Definition
WAKE
Initially derived from the ceremony honouring the dedication of the local Parish church, extended into first a one-day holiday after the all-night vigil and then in the industrial northern towns to an annual weekly holiday based on the Saint's day of the parish church.

20.4.2 Is leisure a new concept?

We often hear talk of increasing leisure time and we are said to be living in a leisured society. Increasing automation and development of labour-saving devices, along with the general decline of manufacturing, have meant that most people have more spare time than they used to. However, there has always been leisure time – Roman Britain had 156 'Holy' days (equivalent to our bank holidays), then there were wakes and fairs, half days on Saturdays and other days (e.g. shopkeepers and their half days on Wednesdays). In Sheffield the shop owners formed a sports club so that they could play cricket and football on Wednesday afternoons. They called their club Sheffield Wednesday – a name that is retained by today's Premier League soccer team.

Leisure has historically been compensation for work done, an escape from drudgery. Clearly the most simple definition of leisure is time away from work. This of course raises the question of what is work – and it is wrong to consider work as only a job one is paid for. Over half of the population are not in paid employment and therefore are not included in the conceptual boundaries of such a definition.

ACTIVITY

Is housework a leisure activity? To help you answer the question look at the definitions above and the key words we have identified.

The essence of leisure is that it is not so much the activity but whether it is freely chosen that counts. For example, a person may hate cutting the lawn and will therefore look at it as a duty. However, if she spends hours feeding the grass, talking to it and cutting it so that it resembles the pitch at Wembley, this is obviously a freely chosen leisure activity.

Other problems arise when we look at high sport – sport undertaken by top performers. To these people, amateurs and professionals alike, sport is not simply time away from work (it takes up most of their time). Their chance for spontaneous participation in a range of leisure interests is also severely limited. A professional footballer may well be under contract not to take part in any other contact sports or activities such as ice skating because they involve too high a risk of injury.

Key revision box

Key words for leisure: free time, choice, not work. Definitions of leisure tend to infer that it is time not at work, but work can include many things. Although there has always been some form of leisure throughout history, we all have more leisure time and can choose from a far greater list of activities than people in the past.

20.5 Recreation

The word recreation stems from the Latin word *recratio*, which means 'to restore health'. Recreation is an active aspect of leisure, something useful, not simply a time left over after work, duties and so on.

Keywords that are appropriate for recreation include:

- *relaxation* – a chance to escape
- *recuperation* – recovering from stress
- *re-creation* – to be creative.

Definition

RECREATION

According to Lumpkin, 'Recreation, refreshes or renews one's strength and spirit after toil.'

Kaplan defines recreation as '. . . activity voluntarily engaged in during leisure and motivated by the personal satisfactions which result from it . . . a tool for mental and physical therapy.'

Parker says about recreation: 'In its literal sense of re-creation, it may be seen as one of the functions of leisure: that of renewing the self or preparation for work.'

These are often referred to as recreation's 'three rs'

In modern life, stress is one of the greatest dangers to health. Worry about work or unemployment, difficulties at the home or in the family can make people ill. Recreation does not usually solve any of these problems but it will enable the individual to relax and get 'away from it all' for a while.

ACTIVITY

Make a list of your own recreational activities. What do you do to relax? To recuperate?

20.5.1 The history of physical recreation

The term physical recreation is closely linked with middle-class culture. Its modern usage has been shaped by the public schools and industrial philanthropists of the nineteenth century. In the last century people in the middle and upper classes were very concerned about the moral well-being of the working masses – mainly about how the working classes amused themselves in their increasing leisure time. Recreation was considered as positive use of leisure time and the middle classes promoted parks, fresh air, recreation grounds and 'muscular sports' to combat the appeal of the gin palaces and ale houses. Religious movements were also quick to seize on the idea that recreation could be used as a form of social control (keeping the masses in check). This was highlighted by the expansion of church soccer teams, YMCA clubs and organisations such as the Boys' Brigade at the turn of the last century. Holt reports how the Boys' Brigade lured the youth of Glasgow off the corrupting streets by the prospect of 'banging drums, blowing whistles and kicking balls!'

20.5.2 Physical recreation and outdoor recreation

Traditionally, *physical recreation* has been used to describe physical activities within the concept of leisure. The term is now better known as 'Sport for All', which describes physical performance opportunities for all members of the community, and places emphasis on participation rather than performance standards.

Outdoor recreation is associated with tradition and the romantic movement. Outdoor recreation usually involves an individual undertaking a challenging activity in the natural environment. Again, many such activities are available.

20.5.3 Physical recreation now

Playing for the sake of playing, or playing sport for intrinsic rather than any extrinsic rewards, is the key to understanding the true meaning of physical recreation.

ACTIVITY

List the possible rewards that may arise from taking part in a physical recreation under the headings of intrinsic or extrinsic rewards.

However, this also accounts for the low status which sport often achieves in our society – if an activity has no external value it serves little function. This is certainly the view of sport that many politicians and leaders adhere to.

Jogging, step aerobics, a knock-up in tennis and visiting a water 'splash' theme pool are all recreational activities. They all involve physical exercise and the participants gain something from doing them. However, they are not sport as we have defined it, because there is no definite outcome, extrinsic reward or stringent organisation.

A new range of activities are developing, which are associated with this idea of taking part in sporting activities for fun – the 'Life-time sports'. Activities such as badminton and walking can be carried on throughout life, and all generations are being encouraged to get involved. It is hoped that this will break the myth that sport is only for the young – you are not really a veteran at 35, as is currently the rule in sports such as hockey and rugby.

> ### Key revision box
>
> *Physical recreation is physical activity of a relaxing nature, with limited outcome and organisation. It is a positive use of leisure time, involving an activity worth doing. Physical recreation has a strong link with middle-class moral guidance of the nineteenth century. Intrinsic rewards dominate in physical recreation.*

20.6 Outdoor recreation

In the last section we defined and discussed the term recreation, and in particular physical recreation. We also identified another term: *outdoor recreation*. This is associated with challenge in the natural environment, but due to the popularity of such activities and the importance the 'great outdoors' plays in our culture the term deserves more detailed investigation.

The simplest and most straightforward definition of outdoor recreation is simply the participation in any enjoyable, holistic activity in the outdoors, where the term outdoors refers to the natural, or at least rural, environment.

Definition
HOLISTIC ACTIVITY
Participation involves immersing your whole body in the activity, a complete commitment to the activity.

20.6.1 A brief history of outdoor recreation

The term really developed from two movements that occurred as Britain became an Imperial nation and the leading industrial centre of the world in the nineteenth century:

● The Naturalist movement
● The Romantic movement

Both these middle-class cults saw England as 'God's own country' and believed that every Englishman had the right to go out and breathe the fresh air of the country.

Rambling and fishing are our most popular outdoor recreations, and both retain a link with our rural past and the seemingly inherent need to seek out rural roots. The oldest of outdoor recreations, the so-called 'field sports' (a collection of various forms of hunting and other rural pursuits) have in the main been available only to the upper classes.

Rambling, the most popular of modern outdoor recreations, is a much more open activity. It is free and the general development in transport has increasingly opened up the countryside to all. From about the 1850s onwards walking clubs were set up by a variety of organisations. Holt reports how the Manchester YMCA were 'truly muscular Christians'

Fishing – Britain's most popular hobby

organising weekend rambles of up to 70 miles. Great emphasis was placed on this flight from the rigours of urban life into the more natural pacing of the countryside – a theme the French call *rustic simplicity*. The descendants of these Manchester walkers were no doubt among the working-class ramblers who in 1932 helped cement the status of outdoor recreation with their mass trespass on Kinder Scout – this led to the setting up of our National Parks and to other measures which helped open up the countryside to all.

Cycling followed rambling as a popular form of enjoying the outdoors and has continued to develop – the latest boom being in mountain biking.

Most people now have the use of a car – and this is the way that most of us now enjoy some 'fresh air'. Unfortunately, much of the benefits of outdoor recreation seem limited by the fact that few people move more than 200 yards of our car when we do get out into the natural environment.

ACTIVITY

William Wordsworth (an influential member of the Romantic movement) wrote that the Lake District of Cumbria was: '. . . a sort of national property in which every man has a right and would interest anyone who had an eye to perceive and a heart to enjoy.' Do you agree with Wordsworth's idea? What do you think are the advantages and disadvantages of developing outdoor recreation and tourism in such areas?

The challenge of the environment

Some countries have used outdoor recreation as a central part of nation building and even as a political tool. This usually is concerned with fostering a love of the 'Mother country' as seen in the Soviet concept of tourism. The French actively promote 'Le Plein Air' in a country steeped in rural heritage, instilling a love of the outdoors in the young which lasts throughout life. The Americans quest the Frontier Spirit, a concept related to the history of the country and a counter-culture to the urban 'win at all costs' society.

20.6.2 The boom in outdoor recreation

In recent years there has been a boom in outdoor sports. Activities such as windsurfing and mountain biking have become extremely popular and part of 'fashion' culture. This expansion has been linked to the greater availability of transport, particularly ownership of cars which has meant that more and more people can get out into the outdoors. Developments in technology and manufacturing have allowed the mass production of cheap equipment (mountain bikes for example), opening these sports up to more and more of the population.

Key revision box

Outdoor recreation involves challenging activities in the natural environment. Most people in Britain partake in some form of outdoor recreation frequently. For most people, the essential element is an escape from the urban environment. The most popular outdoor recreations are walking and fishing.

20.7 Play

One important concept we have not yet looked at and one which has an important part in our society is *play*.

Play is a term with a number of meanings:

- it is an issue in itself, as in *I Play*
- it is also part of the morality of sport, as in the phrase *Fair Play*.

Huizinga suggests that our ability to play has formed the basis for all human cultures and civilisation – mankind has always played and it could be argued that all inventions and discoveries have been a product of play. Our children learn about life through play and adults use play to relax and escape from the 'seriousness' of everyday life.

Play is the base from which sport begins. All sports have their origins in play – as children we first play, then move on to more sophisticated games and eventually to sport.

> **Definition**
>
> ### PLAY
>
> *According to Huizinga: 'Play is a quality of experience within an activity. It is fun.' Armitage says, 'Play is only true, if it is performed with free will, for fun, and only as long as the participant wants it to go on.'*

> **Definition**
>
> ### INTRINSIC REWARDS
>
> *Merits such as enjoyment and self-satisfaction that come from an activity.*
>
> ### EXTRINSIC REWARDS
>
> *Material benefits, such as cups, medals and money that some sports performers receive for their activities.*

20.7.1 What is play?

Play is considered to be a free activity, generally non-serious and outside the maintenance of life. There is certainly a large play element in sport – at the lower level sport is fun and we play to escape and relax. However, the higher you get the more competitive and serious the activity becomes. Sport is not play when there are extrinsic rewards such as money: it becomes too serious.

We can pick out the following keywords that characterise play activities:

- spontaneous
- childlike
- self-fulfilling
- intrinsic.

20.7.2 The concept of play

As we have seen above, play is not connected with material interest or profit – so do professional sportsmen *play*?

ACTIVITY

List in the terms of play the differences between an amateur and a professional sportsman, using the keywords to help you.

Play creates an order of its own and often symbolises overtly and covertly aspects of the real world. If we study children at play, it is easy to identify aspects such as competition, dominance and leadership. Gender differences are also obvious, often the boys' football games will dominate the play space, with the girls being confined to the edges.

As mentioned above, we play to learn about life and we usually associate the term with younger people but adults *do* play. Adults play to escape the rigours of work and the stresses of life – paintball or laser arcades are clearly older, if a little more sophisticated, forms of the shooting games that all children play.

20.7.3 The functions of play

What role do play activities have in our lives? It has been suggested that play has three functions:

Biological – play is an instinctual part of the learning process. It forms a crucial part in the development and refinement of many skills.

Psychological – play allows us to learn about ourselves; we direct it and it allows us to gain experience. We need to learn how to make decisions and control our emotions and arousal levels, which we usually develop through role plays and games when we are young.

Sociological – play enables children (and to some extent adults) to practice future social roles. We acquire a knowledge of how other people respond to us and how they react to us when we try different roles.

Play also helps to diffuse conflict – because of its non-serious nature it can be used to dispel aggression and frustration.

Key revision box

Children play to increase their mastery of reality. Adults play to escape from reality. Because of its non-serious quality a number of dimensions of play can be identified:

1 *Play must be freely undertaken. If constrained it is less playful.*
2 *Play is non-instrumental. It is an end in itself, you do not play for an outcome.*
3 *Play generally has its own set of rules and regulations. It is very informal and any rules will be agreed by the participants and may well change during the activity.*
4 *Play activities involve uncertainty. Play is open ended and has no limits.*

20.8 Physical education

In Britain, physical education takes place only in educational institutions (schools, colleges and universities). It always involves a 'teacher' passing on knowledge to a group of 'pupils' and is almost always concerned with bodily movement. However, it is a wide concept with many different interpretations. Even with the National Curriculum for physical education, no one school's programme is the same as another's. In recent years the academic study of physical education has grown greatly and it is now studied at many levels.

The values developed through physical education are twofold:

Practical skills, which will enable players to take part in a variety of sports.
Social skills such as leadership, discipline and cooperation, which will help a individual develop independence and at the same time produce a love of sport that will continue throughout life and reverse the *Post 16 gap*.

Physical education occurs within the school curriculum, although other physical activities may also take place in schools.

Definition

PHYSICAL EDUCATION

The formal inculcation of knowledge and values through physical activity/experience.

Definition

POST 16 GAP

It is estimated that after young people leave education over 60% of them will never take part in any physical activities.

ACTIVITY

The following scenarios may occur in schools, but can you link the correct definition to the scenario?

Scenario	Definition
Impromptu game of football during dinner break	Sport
Playing for school team	Physical education
Attending aerobics club after school	Play
Year 9 football lesson	Recreation

The activities actually undertaken vary from school to school, but most of the time is spent on the traditional team games such as football, netball and hockey. Swimming and athletics are the main individual activities and now new innovations such as 'health-related fitness' and the 'life-time' sports such as badminton and table tennis are gaining in popularity.

20.8.1 A brief history of physical education

Physical education is a modern phenomenon, less than 100 years old. However, its origins go back further than this and it developed from many different strands. Two main pathways can be identified, which developed from the two traditions of education in England in the nineteenth century.

Public school sports education

In the public schools of the upper classes organised games began to appear, at first as spontaneous recreations played by the boys and for the most part disapproved of by the teachers. However, as they became more developed it was recognised that educational objectives could be passed on through participation in games.

Sports became an important feature of all public schools and were regarded as a powerful force in the education of the sons of the upper classes. Team games formed the central core, particularly football and cricket (and rowing at the schools situated near a river). These games were physically strenuous, demanding and relied on cooperation and leadership – all characteristics that a gentleman needed to acquire.

The term 'Games Cult' has been used to describe the influence of sport in these schools, as have the phrases 'athleticism' and 'muscular Christianity' (see further reading suggestions at the end of Part 5).

Sports education outside public schools

Outside the public schools, a different type of physical education grew up, springing from several roots: military drill, callisthenics and gymnastics. From these grew the system of physical training, which at the end of the century was adopted in the Elementary schools of the lower classes.

From 1902, the government began producing and prescribing a National Syllabus in Physical Training. The 1902 Model Course was composed by the War Office in an attempt to rectify the poor levels of fitness of the lower classes, which had been identified from the performance of recruits during the Boer War (1899–1902). The emphasis of these *drill* exercises was on discipline and obedience – they were aimed at creating a fit, disciplined workforce and army. These drill exercises were compulsory for schoolchildren up to the age of 12 years, and were carried out in the schoolyard

Table 20.1 Part of the 1933 syllabus for physical education

SECTION 1

1. Here, There, Where. Leap-frog practice in three's.

2. 4 Astride jumps with rebound, 4 Skip jumps without rebound.

3. (*Astride*) **Trunk bending downward** with 2 taps forward, 2 backward, 2 pulls on ankles and **Trunk stretching forward** with Hands on hips. (1–8). (Later, with Arm bending upward and Arm stretching upward.)

4. **Upward jump in three's.** Free Practice. Fig 39.

5. i. (*Arm Sideways*) **Arm bending and stretching** sideways alternately in one count and two counts.
   ii. ([*Astride*] *Arms Crossed*) **Rhythmical Arm swinging** mid-upward (Heels raising). Fig 40.
   iii. (*1 Arm Sideways supported at wall*) **Informal Leg circling**.

6. ([*Astride*] *1 Arm Mid-Upward Support*) **Trunk bending sideways** with outer arm raising sideways-upward to touch other hand. (Rhyth.) Figs. 41 and 42.

7. Move to team files, **hopping** with leg swinging forward.

8. (*Knees Full Bend*) **Jump** to "*Astride, Heels Raise*" position with arm bending upward or swinging mid-upward.

9. **Riders and Horses**.

SECTION 2

10. (*Kneel Sitting, Trunk Forward, Arms Upward Rest*) **Rhythmical Trunk pressing downward**. (Bench.) (.) Fig. 43.

11. (*Kneel Sitting, Trunk Downward, Forehead Rest*) **Trunk stretching forward** with Elbow swinging sideways. Fig. 44.

12. **Hand-standing**, in pairs, one supporting. (Benches.) Fig. 45.

13. Race round bench twice and mount in "Knee Raise, Upward Bend" position. Leg stretching backward with arm stretching upward. Race round twice in opposite direction and repeat balance exercise standing on other leg. (Bench top.)

14. (*Astride High Sitting, 1 Arm Sideways Clenched*) **Trunk and Head turning** to side of raised arm. (Bench.)

15. (*Low Front Support*) **Head turning**. (Benches, 2 high) Fig 45.

16. Free March on toes, six counts; Knee springing with Knee forward, six counts.

17. (*Front Standing, Trunk Downward, Hands on bench*) **Bouncing up and down**, i.e. pushing off 2 feet and raising hips high. (Benches, 2 high.)

18. **Face vault** with bent knees. (Benches, 2 high.) See Fig 13, page 39.

19. **Running Thro. vault** to High Standing. (Benches, 2 high, and supporters.)

with instructions barked out by instructors. Many of the activities involved wooden staves in clear imitation of guns. The instructors were peripatetic, and non-commissioned officers were paid 6d a day by the school to drill the children. This military influence and view of children as 'young soldiers' persisted well into the 1920s.

Some examples of exercises in the 1933 syllabus

The course was revised periodically and gradually became a little more educational. The Board of Education took control of the national syllabus and produced a new syllabus in 1904 with revisions in 1909, 1919 and 1933. With each revision the military influence was reduced and slowly 'physical education' grew into something that we would recognise today. However, in 1933 physical education lessons were very formal; instructions were given to teachers in a set of tables and very little variety was allowed. An example of the 1933 syllabus is shown in Table 20.1.

ACTIVITY

Your grandparents could well have experienced some of the above syllabuses. Ask one of them, or another older person you know, about their physical education. Compare this with the physical education lessons your parents experienced and your own physical education programmes.

227

Physical education in the last 50 years

After 1944, the move towards a free comprehensive education for all was reflected in the development of physical education. The two pathways began to come together, many of the state schools programming both games and physical education into their curriculum. Team games had been adapted by the Grammar schools and, with the widespread popularity of sports such as football, became central to all schools. Other activities such as swimming, cross-country and athletics are universally accepted in all physical education programmes.

In the last 30 years physical education has also become an all-graduate profession. Since the introduction of the non-commissioned officers as instructors in the early 1900s the profession has always had a low status in schools, but now the training and career paths of physical education teachers are on a par with those of other subjects. The other great step has been the development of physical education as an academic subject – courses are currently available at GCSE and 'A' level. This has again raised the status of the subject and greatly advanced the study of sports science. We also now have a National Curriculum for physical education, which has given the subject a little more formality and has attempted to bring uniformity to physical education across the country.

Extracurricular sport (sport outside the actual curriculum) still continues and in most schools is an important part of the school culture. In the main extracurricular sport involves teams representing the school in fixtures against other schools, but increasingly sports clubs are being used to involve more people in sport. The main problem is that most physical education teachers supervise extracurricular sport in their own time, and are not paid for the extra work. With the increasing demands on all teachers it is difficult to say how long many of them will continue this goodwill activity.

Key revision box

Physical education takes place only in schools, colleges and at university. In schools a variety of activities can take place – physical education is included within the curriculum and involves learning through practical activities. Modern physical education has developed from two differing systems – the games of the public schools and the drill of the elementary schools. Teaching physical education is now an all-graduate profession and academic courses in physical education are now available.

20.9 Outdoor education

One other activity that takes place in schools that can also involve some form of physical activity is outdoor education. We will briefly look at some of the main characteristics of this concept.

The National Association for Outdoor Education gives the following definition of outdoor education 'A means of approaching educational objectives through guided direct experience in the environment using its resources as learning materials.' According to Passmore, 'Outdoor education is learning in and for the outdoors.'

Outdoor education also is a concept which has a number of meanings and has been used to embrace all educational activities that take place out of doors. Education out of doors includes many disciplines – geography, biology, history and art as well as physical education. Where do outdoor

Definition
OUTDOOR EDUCATION
All those activities concerned with living, moving and learning in the outdoors.

pursuits fit in? These achieve particular educational objectives: overcoming challenges and the total emergence of one's self in the natural environment.

The definition of outdoor education given in the definition box on this page is probably the best one. It covers all the activities above and involves learning many skills, the learning environment is outside, and preferably the natural environment.

20.9.1 The aims of outdoor education

To heighten awareness of and foster respect for

Self – by giving yourself a challenge and overcoming that challenge. A good example of this is climbing a rock face.
Others – to gain group experiences, share decisions and work together as a team. Canadian canoeing demonstrates this well.
The natural environment – through direct contact with it.

In outdoor education the emphasis is on holistic experiences and relationships rather than specific skills.

If you want to stay afloat and go in a straight line, teamwork is the key

---

ACTIVITY
We discussed earlier the development of both practical and social skills through physical activity. Identify four outdoor activities you have experienced and link them with the type of skills that you may have developed within them.

Outdoor education forms some part of most school curricula and is now a stated aim of the National Curriculum. However, in most schools it is only an extracurricular activity. The problems are that outdoor pursuits are very expensive in terms of transport and equipment needed, and many safety precautions must be considered, especially in light of several recent tragedies. Time is another major problem – most schoolchildren have to travel some distance before they can experience the 'natural environment', which makes it very difficult to include such activities within a normal school day. In attempts to solve these problems 'trim trails' are being developed, schools setting up orienteering courses around their grounds and artificial climbing walls are being put up in sports halls and playgrounds.

A keyword for outdoor education is *adventure*. In 1984, Mortlock introduced the concept of the 'adventure alternative', believing that we have an instinct for seeking adventure and that outdoor education is one way of fulfilling this drive.

It can be argued that outdoor activities have an advantage over more conventional games in that the decisions that have to be made are much more real. These activities always contain an element of risk because the unpredictability of the natural environment means that there are many uncontrollable (and sometimes life-threatening) factors that need to be taken into consideration.

Key revision box

Outdoor education is learning in the natural environment. The objectives of outdoor education are the development of the individual through scenarios and experiences that are very novel. Challenge is the essential element, and risk makes the experiences so novel.

KEY TERMS

You should now understand the following terms. If you do not, go back through the chapter and find out.

Conquest
Invasion games
Target games
Court games
Field games
Popular recreation
Athleticism
Rationalisation
Social control
Romanticism
Intrinsic values
Life-time sports
Escapism
Post 16 gap
Games cult

PROGRESS CHECK

1 Taking Minoan bull leaping as an example, what were the functional aspects of primitive sport?
2 Invasion games have has an important role in Britain's sporting tradition. Suggest reasons for this importance.
3 Why were the court games limited to the upper classes in the early years of their development?
4 What are the main characteristics of a sport?
5 Why, for some people, is leisure not free from the obligations of work, family and society?
6 Why is recreation a more positive use of free time than leisure?
7 What are intrinsic values in relation to a sports activity?
8 Why is badminton a 'life-time' sport?
9 Why is outdoor recreation a holistic activity?
10 What factors have led to an increase in participation of outdoor sports?
11 Do professional footballers play?
12 Why do adults play? Give some examples of adult play.
13 How might a school's physical education programme reverse the Post 16 gap?
14 Why was drill an essential component of elementary schooling in the early part of this century?
15 'Extracurricular sport tends to be elitist.' What does this statement mean?
16 What advantages might outdoor education have over normal lessons in the inculcation of social skills?
17 What are the unpredictable parts of the natural environment?
18 What were the key characteristics which the Games Cult developed in its pupils?

The organisation of sport in the United Kingdom

Learning objectives:

- To have an overview of the structure of sport in the UK.
- To know the key organisations in this structure.
- To understand the role of the government in the organisation of British sport.
- To be able to construct a brief historical analysis for the present structure of sport.
- To be able to compare the structure and organisation of sport in the UK with that in other countries.
- To understand the organisation of sport at the local level.

Definition
OPEN OLYMPICS

The modern Olympic Games were set up in 1896, and the International Olympic Committee stated that sports performers should not make a living or any form of profit from sport. The games were encased in the Olympic Ideal – the important thing was to take part, not win. However, the dramatic rise in performance and needs of the media have led to athletes needing to train all year round and so require money from sport. In the 1980s the Olympics became more open and the rules were altered so that both amateurs and professionals could take part, although the latter will soon dominate as more and more sports become professional.

The development of sport in the UK has not followed a regular pattern. Individuals, groups and clubs have always been free to develop their sport as they liked and the government has never really involved itself directly in the organisation of sport at either local or national level.

Today the *UK Sports Commission* has overall responsibility for British sport, with four national Sports Councils overseeing sport in each of the four Home Countries. However, the administration and affairs of each individual sport are controlled by a governing body; there are well over 200 such bodies in the UK.

These governing bodies are all members of the *Central Council of Physical Recreation* (CCPR), a body set up in 1935 to help coordinate sport. The CCPR was superseded (though not replaced) by the Sports Council. The CCPR now has the duty of telling the sports councils how the governing bodies as a group feel about the development of sport.

The governing bodies of sport, for example the Football Association and the Lawn Tennis Association, represent everyone who takes part in their sport and are members of international governing bodies – in these two cases FIFA and the International Tennis Federation. This membership allows British players to take part in international competition.

A governing body may also be affiliated to the British Olympic Association, allowing participation in the Olympic Games. In the past this affiliation was restricted to amateur sports but now the Olympics have become 'open' and many more sports are receiving Olympic status. In the 1996 Olympics surfing and ballroom dancing will be given trials.

An overview of the structure of sports organisation in the UK is shown in *Figure 21.1.*

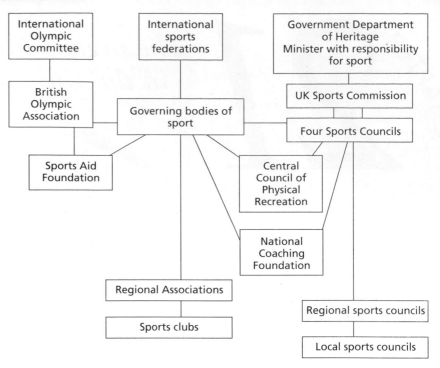

Figure 21.1 The structure of sports organisation in Britain

21.1 History and background

The administrative structure of British sport has changed little, in general terms, since most of our modern sports and physical activities developed in the late nineteenth century.

To control and codify these increasingly popular activities a number of sporting organisations were established, often with strong ties to the upper classes but particularly to the emerging middle class that had begun to dominate industrial Britain. Elements of this social class hierarchy can still be seen in sport today. The upper classes, who had held power before the industrial revolution, jealously guarded their sporting interests by forming clubs and associations to control participation by more lowly members of society.

The Jockey Club and the Marylebone Cricket Club are good examples of these upper-class organisations still evident today. The MCC was set up in 1787 and remains an exclusive gentleman's club. Although its influence is in decline, the MCC is still credited with writing the rules of cricket, selecting England's teams and developing much of the game's traditions. The Jockey Club, set up in 1750, has been the governing body for racing for 240 years.

The industrial revolution led to the rise of the middle class – the factory owners and entrepreneurs. In the same way as they took over the control of commerce and industry, they also took over control of sport. The middle-class approach to sports administration was a little more democratic; however, they introduced the concept of amateurism into sport, which to a large extent still controls the opportunity to take part in sport. Good examples of governing bodies set up during this time are the Football Association (FA) in 1863 and the Amateur Athletics Association (AAA) in 1880. These national governing bodies appeared in response to the increased participation in sport throughout the country. Generally their task was to establish and maintain the rules of the sport and to organise national competitions.

In practice

If you were given the task of reorganising British sport, what areas would you change? What have been the limiting factors in the development of sport in the UK? What have other countries done differently? Try to come up with five major changes, with explanations.

One characteristic of the British system is that sports are very isolated. The clubs that joined these new governing bodies tended to be single-sport clubs and as a consequence so were the organising bodies. The result was a very decentralised organisation, with individual bodies showing little interest in the affairs of other sporting organisations.

In contrast, in the rest of Europe a more centralised approach developed and organised sport developed 15–20 years later than in the UK. Clubs in France and Germany tend to cater for a number of different sports. This approach encouraged the establishment of multisport federations to coordinate the aims of different sports – an example is the UNSS in France, which has responsibility for sport in all schools in France.

It is only relatively recently that an attempt was made to develop a coordinated approach to sport organisation in the UK. This has centred on the evolution of the CCPR and Sports Council and, more recently, the Sports Commission. However, both of these organisations are concerned with encouraging participation and the provision of facilities rather than actually controlling sport.

The individual sports retain their autonomy – this is the key to understanding the organisation of sport in the UK.

ACTIVITY

In 1980 many nations boycotted the Moscow Olympics in protest at the Soviet invasion of Afghanistan but the British government left the decision to compete to the individual governing bodies. How does this reflect the autonomy of British sport?

Key revision box

Sport in the UK does not follow a regular pattern and the British government has little control over sport. The Sports Commission has overall responsibility for sport in the UK – aided by the CCPR. The governing bodies control the affairs of each particular sport – each sport is autonomous. These governing bodies have changed little since their inception 100 years ago.

21.2 The role of government in the administration of sport in the UK

Despite the popularisation of sport and introduction of universal physical education during the early 1900s, sport and physical recreation have never really been accepted as realms of government responsibility. Since the Second World War, the government has increased its involvement in sport, yet it openly accepted the justification of sport in its own right only during the 1960s.

At various times governments have become involved in control of some parts of the organisation of sport, but this has tended to be only in isolated areas and in response to a problem rather than any planning or development. At the beginning of the century the government intervened in sport for a while, in order to get the population fit for war (see Chapter 20 for more information on this). Back in 1541, laws were passed to ban all 'frivolous' sports such as football, golf and bowling to make sure that every man under the age of 60 spent his spare time practising archery – a skill needed to defend the country.

The Taylor Report (1990) into the Hillsborough Football disaster prompted government legislation concerning football stadiums in an attempt to stem football hooliganism. The Taylor Report recommended that all Football League grounds should become all-seaters by August 1999. Part of the money required to carry out this massive undertaking was provided through a levy that the government placed on the Football Pools in 1990, forming the Football Trust – however, most clubs will have to bear most of the cost of refurbishment themselves.

21.2.1 The role of Quangos in sports control

Most of the administration and organisation of sport in the public sector is carried out by Sports Council *Quangos* and local authorities, the latter being the biggest providers of facilities and funders of sport.

21.3 Structure of governmental control

Most of the government's coordination of sport is now undertaken by the *Department of Heritage*. However, sporting concerns do still filter in to other departments, principally the Department for Education and Employment.

21.3.1 The Department of Heritage

Although Britain has had a Minister for Sport since the early 1960s, this role has never really risen in status above that of a junior minister, who was a lower member of the Department of the Environment. The many calls for sport to be given Cabinet status were ignored. The Sports Council initially planned and campaigned for a Department of Sport and Tourism to be set up, but eventually a coalition with the existing Office of Arts and Libraries was seen as the most effective means of gaining a degree of power.

In 1992 The Department of Heritage was set up and now has responsibility for sport and recreation. The new department takes up the responsibilities that were previously shared by six government departments and has an extremely varied portfolio, including: broadcasting, films, the press, national heritage, arts, sport and tourism. It has two ministers, a secretary of state and a deputy. Sport is further served by a sub-department, the *Sport and Recreation Division*.

The major concern of the Department of Heritage after it was set up was the establishment and development of the National Lottery. The National Lottery was established by an Act of Parliament in 1993 and the first draw was made on 14 November 1994. It followed the pattern developed in many other countries as a means of raising funds for worthy causes, including sport. Five areas of 'good causes' benefit from the income generated by the National lottery:

● sport
● art
● heritage
● charities
● The Millennium Fund.

Various bodies send bids for funds to the Sports Council, which scrutinises the bids and distributes the money allocated to sport. The amount of money to be distributed each year is approximately £125 million.

ACTIVITY

Try to find out if any of your local sports bodies have received lottery funding. If any did, how much money did it receive and what was it used for? Information should be available from your local library, council or sports council.

In the summer of 1995 the Prime Minister and the Department of Heritage published a sports policy statement called *Sport – Raising the Game*. This set out the government's proposals for rebuilding the strength of British sport. The main emphasis of these proposals was to recognise the role that schools can play in the development of a sports culture. The publication goes on to outline what the government feels each sector of sport should be undertaking to promote the development of high standards of sport in the country. The other major proposal in the policy statement is that a British Academy of Sport should be set up, similar to the Australian National Institute, which will be a centre of excellence for British sporting talent.

ACTIVITY

Your school, college or local library should have a copy of *Sport – Raising the Game*. Have a look at the proposals and see if they match your ideas on how British sport should be organised.

21.3.2 The Sports Council

This government-funded Quango was established in 1965, receiving its Royal Charter in 1972. It is an autonomous body under the Department of Heritage, with a brief to take overall responsibility for sport in the UK.

The Sports Council has four main aims:

1 To increase participation in sport.
2 To increase the quality and quantity of sports facilities.
3 To raise standards of performance.
4 To provide information for and about sport.

In 1994 it was announced that the Sports Council would be reshaped to create two new bodies: the *UK Sports Commission* and the *English Sports Council*. This brings England in line with the other Home Countries in that it now has its own Sports Council. The UK Sports Commission has a coordinating role ensuring that all councils work in the same direction.

Each council is split further into regional and local sports councils enabling area-specific planning. Funding for the Council comes from the central government in the form of a central grant worth around £49.8m (November 1994). This money is used to run the regional councils, fund campaigns and information services, although most of it is redistributed to sports governing bodies and institutions as grants to be used for increasing sports participation, building new facilities and setting up recreation programmes.

ACTIVITY

Have a look at the sports facilities where you live and look for the Sports Council's emblem. Make an inventory of the facilities the Sports Council has helped to fund in your area.

21.3.3 The Countryside Commission

This Quango is an independent body which investigates matters relating to the conservation and enhancement of the natural environment, and the provision and development of facilities in the countryside for recreation. You have probably come across the *Country Code*, an initiative set up by the Countryside Commission to teach people how to use and respect the countryside. Its link with sport is to help develop access for outdoor sports and also to manage them so that the landscape is not destroyed.

> **Key revision box** ·
>
> *The limited role of central government in sports organisation reinforces the decentralised nature of sport organisation in the UK. Most administration in the public sector is left to Quangos such as the Sports Council or local authorities. The new Department of Heritage has now taken charge of sport – its first major job was to develop the National Lottery to help fund sports and charities. The Sports Council has overall responsibility for sport in the UK.*

21.4 The national sports agencies

21.4.1 An overview

We have already identified that most sports administration in the UK is carried out by individual governing bodies – these will be discussed in detail in the next section. However, a number of *national agencies* coordinate particular areas of sport, once again characterised by their autonomy and diversity.

Some of these agencies have specific tasks, for example the National Coaching Foundation develops coaching expertise and the British Olympic Association coordinates all Olympic matters. Others are more general in their approach, for instance the Sports Aid Foundation is a charitable organisation that helps to fund amateur sports performers, allowing them to compete at international level.

Most of these bodies are funded by the public sector or by voluntary donations – again there is much diversity. In general their role is to advise and provide information rather than administer and organise.

21.4.2 Central Council of Physical Recreation

This independent voluntary body was set up in 1935, and is the 'voice of the governing bodies' in that it represents the governing bodies of sport and after consultation passes on their views to the Sports Council and government.

Its greatest success was in establishing the National Sports Centres, specialist centres where our national teams and performers train. Management of these was transferred to the Sports Council and has now moved toward self-management.

When the Sports Council was developed in the early 1960s it gradually took over many of the roles of the CCPR. The idea was that the Sports Council would replace the CCPR but the governing bodies, fearing too much government intervention, decided to maintain some independence and the CCPR became a charitable trust. The Sports Council still has some control over the CCPR.

The CCPR now acts as a consultative body to the Sports Council, advising it of the views of the more than 240 individual governing bodies. Its other roles include commissioning reports on sports issues and running a number of sports leaders awards. It is funded by a grant from the Sports Council.

21.4.3 The British Olympic Association

This independent organisation is responsible for all Olympic matters in the UK, primarily entering competitors for the Olympic Games. Other functions include raising funds to enable British performers to compete at the games and for the transportation, clothing and other expenses involved in sending a British team (up to £4 million). A more general role is to develop interest in the Olympic movement in Britain. It also helps to coordinate any bids to host the games.

The fund-raising role of the British Olympic Association is unique to the UK. In most other countries, even the USA, central government helps to finance the Olympic team – but the British Olympic Association raises all the money itself. This has traditionally been achieved through school children's sponsored events and donations from the general public and business. Increasingly, more money is being raised through commercial sponsorship, specifically in the use of the Olympic logo (you have probably seen the five-ring logo on Mars Bars and cans of Coca Cola).

21.4.4 The Sports Aid Foundation

The Sports Aid Foundation was formed in 1976 by Dennis Howell, then Minister for Sport. This autonomous fund-raising body is managed by a board of governors and trustees and aims to raise and distribute funds to help the very best amateur sports men and women.

The money issued through grants is used to cover the expenses of training, travelling and attending competitions. If performers are successful they often become self-supportive through sponsorship and prize money and so no longer need the assistance of the Sports Aid Foundation – examples are Torvill and Dean, Daley Thompson, Steve Backley and Nick Gillingham. However, participants in less commercial sports may need funding for their whole career.

The income required is generated through fund raising, voluntary donations, National Lottery contributions and commercial sponsorship. In the past international insurance brokers Minet have provided considerable support, although at the moment the biggest contributor is the Foundation for Sport and the Arts.

The Sports Aid Foundation was established to enable our top amateur competitors to train in the same way as many others throughout the world without worrying about finance. Their slogan reinforces this point: 'Giving Britons a Better Sporting Chance'.

> **Definition**
>
> ## FOUNDATION FOR SPORT AND THE ARTS
>
> *A trust founded in 1991 by the companies organising the football pools. They donate up to £60 million a year, two-thirds of which is passed on to sport. Sport bodies apply for funds and after consultation with other bodies such as the Sports Council the trustees of the foundation issue grants.*

21.4.5 The National Coaching Foundation

Established by the Sports Council in 1983, with its headquarters in Leeds, the NCF is run by a small staff under the control of a director. The Foundation provides a wide range of opportunities for coaches to improve their knowledge and practice of sport. This function is carried out by regional coaching centres based at higher education institutions throughout the UK (eleven in England, two in Wales, two in Scotland and one in Northern Ireland).

The problem that the Foundation faces is the fact that the UK has such a complex sports structure, mainly due to the autonomy of each governing body (and consequently the coaches). Also most coaches work voluntarily and so don't have the time or the funds to obtain qualifications.

237

The NCF has two main aims to overcome these problems:

1. To promote education through its coaching courses and awards
2. To increase knowledge through information centres, its monthly magazine *Supercoach*, videos and its subsidiary (Coachwise Ltd) which provides a service for coaches to purchase books and resources on coaching matters.

21.4.6 The British Sports Association for the Disabled

This was founded in 1961 with the aims of helping to develop sport and recreation for people with disabilities. It is a charitable organisation that raises its money through voluntary fund raising.

> **Key revision box**
>
> *Sports associations in the UK are autonomous. The national sports agencies offer advice and aid, but have no real control over the organisation of sport in this country. The Central Council of Physical Recreation is the voice of the governing bodies, the British Olympic Association looks after the British Olympic team and matters concerning the Olympics, the Sports Aid Foundation raises money to give amateur sportsmen and women a better chance to compete, and the National Coaching Federation aims to develop the education of coaches.*

21.5 The national governing bodies of sport

Most modern sports developed their present form within the last 150 years. As participation in sports began to increase at the end of nineteenth century and many activities became popular recreations, it became necessary for those taking part to agree to a common set of rules or laws. Until this time there had been many regional variations and it was very difficult for teams from different schools or areas to play against each other.

This need for *codification* led directly to the formation of a governing body within each sport. As Houlihan concludes, their 'main concern was to harmonise rules and develop a national pattern of organisation.'

Definition
AUTONOMOUS

A body is self-governing, makes decisions independently without interference from other bodies, including the government.

ACTIVITY

See if you can find out the names of the national governing bodies for the following sports in the UK:

Football, rugby union, athletics, tennis, hockey, badminton.

Try to find out the date each body was formed. Can you suggest why these dates are close together?

It is for this reason that the rules and organisation of each individual sport in the UK lie in the hands of an autonomous national governing body.

21.5.1 Role of the governing bodies

These bodies are responsible for general administration of the sport and the conduct of competitions.

These bodies can be very large organisations – 43 000 football clubs are affiliated to the Football Association – or quite small organisations with the responsibility for minority sports – such as the British Water Ski Federation.

The foundation of the system is that clubs become affiliated to their particular governing body. Clubs pay a fee to become members of these bodies, which gives the club the right to vote on sports issues and to take part in sports competitions.

As participation in sport of all kinds has increased, the duties of the governing bodies have become more demanding and their workload has grown accordingly. Today, a number of governing bodies now require full-time administrators to look after their affairs but there is still an emphasis on voluntary work. This reflects the tradition in British sport – committee work and decision-making still tends to lie in the hands of unpaid volunteers.

At present there are over 300 national governing bodies in the UK. Their major concerns are

1 To establish their own rules and regulations.
2 To organise competitions.
3 To develop coaching/leadership awards.
4 To have direct responsibility for sport at the local and national level, as well as representing the sport in international matters.
5 To select teams and competitors to represent the Home Countries or the UK at international events.

21.5.2 The structure of the governing bodies

Single sports clubs tend to be grouped into regional or member associations such as County Associations, whose representatives have an input to the national governing body. This is outlined in *Figure 21.2*.

Nearly all of the national bodies are members of the international federations for their sport. The international federations decide the rules and regulations of international competition and are responsible for the organisation and administration of major international events and tournaments.

Many bodies in the UK are also linked through membership of the British Olympic Association, which allows a national governing body to enter its members in the Olympic Games.

21.5.3 Funding

The national governing bodies draw their income from a variety of sources.

Affiliation fees – membership fees from clubs, associations and individual members.
Sports Council grants – a number of bodies receive grant aid from the Sports Council.
Development grants – for special events/programmes from the Foundation for Sport and the Arts or the National Lottery fund.
Sponsorship – from commercial companies.
Television rights – TV companies have to pay the governing bodies for the right to televise matches and tournaments.

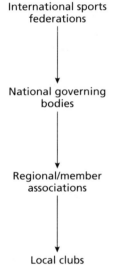

International sports federations

National governing bodies

Regional/member associations

Local clubs

Figure 21.2 Local clubs have an input at national and international level

21.5.3 Future roles

With the many changes affecting sport in the 1990s, the national governing bodies are having to adapt and take on new roles.

Media and commercial interests are essential elements of modern sport and the governing bodies need to become more accountable and efficient in their work. Their structure is likely to become sophisticated and they will probably need to employ more full-time staff. Staff will also need a wider variety of skills – media relations and marketing will be essential roles in all sports governing bodies if they are to survive into the twenty-first century.

The other main issue facing many sports is the gap that is developing between elite performers and amateurs. This may result in the top elite breaking away, forming premier bodies and probably securing most of the funding and resources – this has already occurred in football and rugby league.

21.5.4 An example of the structure and responsibilities of a typical governing body: the Amateur Swimming Association

Affiliated to	International Federation of Amateur Swimming
Headquarters	Freehold offices in Loughborough, Leicestershire
Salaried permanent staff	20
Number of affiliated clubs	1784
Number of members	300 000
Number of registered competitive swimmers	53 000 (each paying an annual fee of £7.50)
Responsible for organisation of	Swimming
	Diving
	Water polo
	Synchronised swimming
Special schemes	ASA education programme for teachers/coaches
	ASA proficiency, life saving, survival awards
	ASA liaison with schools and leisure centres
	ASA contribution to health and safety guidelines
	ASA contribution to medical research
Income	ASA award scheme raises £90 000
	ASA education programme – books, videos, etc.
	ASA Enterprises Ltd – merchandising
	Television fees
	Sponsorship money
	Grant of £632 000 from the Sports Council

21.6 Sport at the local level

The Sports Council estimates that one in three people in the UK regularly participate in sports, mostly at the local level. Local authorities are the main providers of sports and recreational facilities, and are financed by the public sector.

However, most of the actual organisation falls within the voluntary sector, with the base level being small, single sport clubs. The role of some local clubs in British sport is shown in Table 21.1.

Table 21.1 Examples of the role local clubs play in UK sport

Activity/sport	Number of clubs	Total number of members
Athletics	19 000	110 000
Bowls (outdoor)	3 529	161 672
Football	42 000	1 250 000
Hockey	1 850	80 000
Golf	1 700	238 000
Netball	3 300	60 000
Swimming	1 784	300 000
Tennis	2 432	131 800

Sport at the local level consists of many small groups of people taking part quite independently. Clubs are small, the facilities basic and the organisation limited. There is no central organisation at this level to plan and coordinate sport development, again reflecting the autonomy of sport in the UK.

The Sports Council has attempted to tackle this issue by setting up *Local Advisory Sports Councils*. These are independent bodies, made up of local groupings of clubs and other interested bodies. They discuss issues that involve all sports at the local level and pass on their views to the local authorities. However, these bodies are not found in every area and their contribution to the administration of sport is often limited.

ACTIVITY

Sports clubs tend to be administered and organised by small voluntary committees. There are several key positions that all clubs require: Chairman, Secretary, Treasurer, Coach and Captain. Using a sports club you know, try to find out what each of these people actually does. Summarise the roles in a table.

21.6.1 Who provides local facilities?

Sports facilities at the local level are mostly provided by:

- local authorities
- schools
- private sector.

Local authority provision

Local authorities are the greatest providers of facilities. City, Borough and District Councils provide a vast range of sport and recreational facilities – parks, leisure centres and swimming pools, golf courses, community halls, for example. These centres cater for the needs of the local community, although pubic sector facilities can also be quite grand, as in Birmingham's National Indoor Arena and Elland Road, Leeds United stadium which is owned by Leeds City Council.

There are about 1500 swimming pools and 2000 local leisure centres in the UK but the Sports Council states that the UK is under-resourced and has been campaigning to increase the provision of local sports facilities.

In the past much of the money needed to fund these facilities was drawn directly from central government grants and local taxes (Rates, Community Charge, Council Tax). The main objective of these facilities is to maximise participation in sport so prices are often subsidised, allowing lower admission charges and access to all sections of the community – with concessions for students, the unemployed and other low-income groups. However, local authority budgets have become a lot tighter because central government has been steadily reducing its grants. One of the first areas affected has been the sport and recreational facilities. Admission prices have had to rise and costs cut, which has led to the closure of some facilities.

Schools provision

A second major area of facility provision is the education system. Most schools in the UK have a good range of sports halls, pitches and pools. Increasingly these are also being used for public use. The policy of opening up facilities to the public is known as *dual use*. In the main schools allow their facilities to be used after school, clubs and organisations paying to use them.

Opportunities for developing dual use schemes will increase in the future with the recent changes in the financial responsibilities of schools. Local management gives a school's governing body more control over its budget and facilities, which may increase the amount of facilities available.

Private sector provision

This is made up of two main groups: commercial enterprises that provide facilities for the public in return for payment, and companies that provide facilities for their employees.

The role of the first group in providing leisure facilities is growing – the leisure 'boom' of the 1990s has increased demand and many people have seen this as an opportunity to cash in on the leisure trends. These leisure companies tend to cater for specific areas, such as fitness or water sports. Although the facilities provided are usually of a high standard the prices are also correspondingly high. The development of private sector facilities may encourage a move towards elitism, where only those on higher incomes will be able to afford to take part. The main aim of these companies is to make profit, and there is little emphasis on catering for the needs of the community.

Some companies and businesses provide sports facilities for the use of their employees and families. The company pays all the expenses involved in the upkeep of the buildings, pitches, courts and greens. Often a small membership fee is charged, though many companies provide the facilities free of charge. Companies see this as a way of encouraging people to work for them and of fostering the morale of the existing workforce. Recently many companies have put a lot of emphasis on reducing stress levels in their workforce – this can often be achieved through sporting activities.

A commercial fitness centre

KEY TERMS

You should now understand the following terms. If you do not, go back through the chapter and find out.

Affiliation
Autonomy
British Olympic Association
Central Council for Physical
  Recreation
Codification
Decentralisation
Department of Heritage
Dual use
Elitism
Governing body
National Coaching Federation
Open sports
Private sector
Public sector
Quango
Sports Aid Foundation
Sports councils
Voluntary sector

ACTIVITY

Make a list of the sports facilities in a three-mile area near you. Find out where the money comes from to fund them and classify each facility as a public sector, private sector or voluntary sector facility.

Key revision box

Sport at the local level is carried on by small independent groups arranged in voluntary clubs. Three sectors are involved in the administration and funding of sport at the local level: voluntary, private an public. Local authorities provide most local sports facilities but increasingly private enterprises are providing high-quality facilities.

PROGRESS CHECK

1 What problems in the development of sport in the late 1800s led to the formation of national governing bodies?
2 Describe the structure of the CCPR and the role it plays in coordinating sport in the UK.
3 Briefly describe the structure and function of the Sports Commission.
4 Why does a country as small as the UK need regional sports councils?
5 The Sports Council uses the term Target Group. What does this term mean?
6 What does the phrase 'autonomy of governing bodies' refer to in terms of the structure of British sport?
7 How is the National Coaching Federation aiding sport in the UK's general move towards raising standards in performance?
8 How has the Sports Aid Foundation helped Steve Backley to become an international champion?
9 What is the BOA? What specific role does it play in the organisation of elite sports in the UK?
10 Explain why British sports organisations may be unwilling to accept direct funding from the government.
11 How do the aims and objectives of a public sector facility differ from those of a private sector facility?
12 What are the possible disadvantages of a school developing a dual use policy with its sports hall?
13 What benefits may a company hope to develop by providing sports facilities for its employees?
14 'Sport for All' is not yet a reality. What sociocultural constraints have hindered its development in the UK?
15 How might the National Lottery increase the opportunity to take part in sport?
16 The UK's decentralised system of sports administration leads to the limited funds being spread too thinly. What reforms could be introduced to get better value for money?

CHAPTER 22

Sport
in society

Learning objectives:

○ To understand the role of sport in society.

○ To know the way sport reflects the society in which it is played.

○ To understand the concepts of excellence and mass participation in sport.

○ To be able to compare sports in different cultures.

○ To be able to identify discrimination in sport and to understand what causes it.

○ To recognise deviance in sport.

○ To know the role of the media in sport.

Definition
SOCIETY
The structural composition of a community of people.

Definition
CULTURE
The way the society functions and its traditions and beliefs.

Definition
SPORTS SOCIOLOGY
The study of human social behaviour in a sports context.

22.1 Sociological aspects of sport

Sport in the 1990s has become a cultural phenomenon of great magnitude, its influence permeating all aspects of our society. Sport is a compulsory element of our education system, it dominates all forms of media and is increasingly becoming an important section of our economy.

Sport can provide a useful focus for studying different societies. Roberts, Sutton Smith and others have developed the field of *sports sociology*. They foster the view that the games played by a society reflect the values inherent in that society. Sports are also used to teach younger members of the society these values. In other words, sport reflects the society in which it is played.

A particular sport can become an extensive reference for the country or society it is played in. Each game has its own history and pattern of development and this evolution is closely linked to the development, history, geography and values of the country in which it is played.

Take the Gaelic game of hurling as an example. This invasion-type game (see Chapter 20) is only played in Ireland, but is the largest spectator sport in the country. By studying the game we should be able to pick out characteristics of its play and structure that can be linked to the country (Table 22.1). Hurling reflects closely the wider values and traditions in Irish society and remains an important expression of the culture.

Football also makes an interesting study. All countries play the game of Association Football to very similar rules, yet it is amazing how different countries impose their own style on this universal game. This is most evident during the World Cup, when we see the flamboyance of the Brazilians clash with the tactical brilliance of the German team or the exuberance of the Cameroon team.

Sport is a reflection of society and many issues (such as class, gender and race) have an effect on sport. Sport follows the trends of society and a number of patterns can be identified. These are described below.

Table 22.1 Linking the characteristics of sport to society

Characteristics of sport	Societal links
Robust, physical game	Traditional link with hard/rural work, history of violence
Large Pitch	Rural nature of Ireland, allowing traditional large-scale 'mob' games
Few rules – players can hit, kick or throw the ball	Sport that has retained traditional rules, little change – strong traditional culture
Unique to Ireland	Reflecting Ireland's peripheral geographical position on the edge of Europe – not much mixing. Lack of status meant that, unlike England, Ireland imported rather than exported sports

Hurling – Ireland's national sport

ACTIVITY

This type of analysis can be an interesting way of researching the role sport plays in culture. Try to find some video clips of different sports from other countries and see if you can identify aspects of the country it is played in. Perhaps these questions may help: Why is Australian Rules football only played in Australia? How have the West Indies adapted the English Game of cricket to suit their own independent culture? What parallels are there between American Football and American society?

22.1.1 Sociological theories

One recently developed theory is that of *centrality*, which suggests that the dominant roles in sport such as coach, captain, play maker are undertaken by people in the dominant sections of the society in which the sport is played. The sections of the community that are in the minority either numerically or in terms of status, often immigrant or lower-class people, are underrepresented in these roles. For example, in American Football there are very few Afro-Caribbean Quarterbacks and in the UK we have no professional managers in football from ethnic minorities.

Often these anomalies are related to *stereotyping*. This has a great effect in sport on the selection of players and positional decisions. The issue of discrimination in sport will be developed further later in the chapter.

22.1.2 The role of sport in socialisation

Socialisation is the way humans adjust to their culture, the process through which we become participating members of society. During socialisation we acquire our personalities and decide on the roles we will take on in later life.

Sport, especially physical education since it is compulsory, is an important vehicle for transmitting the values of the wider society. Physical education is used at school to develop a range of social skills such as cooperation and communication as well as the practical aspects of fitness and motor skills. Sport allows individuals to express themselves and to experiment with different roles and activities.

Sport may also lead to *social mobility* for certain people. In countries where sport is more liberal than the society at large, underprivileged members of that society can use sport for social recognition and to gain wealth. Sport attracts members of the lower classes because through hard work they can be generously rewarded – and there are many role models to emulate.

22.2 A comparative view of sport

Comparative studies of sport have developed from the sociological base. The emphasis of these studies is on the structure and organisation of sport in other countries and identifying the aspects we should introduce to our own system. This is an important issue for the present British sports organisation since we would appear to be losing our traditional dominance in international sport.

A truly comparative study would view individual countries, but we will confine our study to just four groupings of countries and the ways they develop sport:

- emergent cultures
- the Eastern Bloc cultures
- the New World democratic cultures
- the American model.

22.2.1 Emergent cultures

These are the *developing countries* such as the African nations. In these countries modern sport has often been introduced by previous colonial powers and in the main has replaced the indigenous activities. With their new-found independence, sport has been used as a process of nation building.

The success of countries such as Kenya in athletics, the West Indies in Cricket and Brazil in football has shown that developing countries can take on the developed world and often beat them.

These countries face the problems of limited resources and little infrastructure, but through selection and channelling in only a limited number of sports they area able to compete on the world stage. The model of sports development in these countries is shown in Table 22.2.

Table 22.2 An emergent model of sport

Integration	Sport unites the country by bringing together different races, areas and tribes
Defence	National Service gives a chance for selection. The strict regime is suited to training and development of talent
Shop window	Sporting success puts the country onto the world stage
Selection	Concentrate on limited number of sports, usually the sports suited to the environment or the physique of the people

22.2.2 The Eastern Bloc cultures

Although now only a historical grouping since the communist system disintegrated in the early 1990s this culture, dominated by the Soviet Union, is worth study because of the phenomenal sporting success Eastern Bloc countries achieved in a short time scale.

In countries such as the Soviet Union and German Democratic Republic sport was completely state controlled. Every aspect – from selection to training and diet – was coordinated by the central government. The *shop*

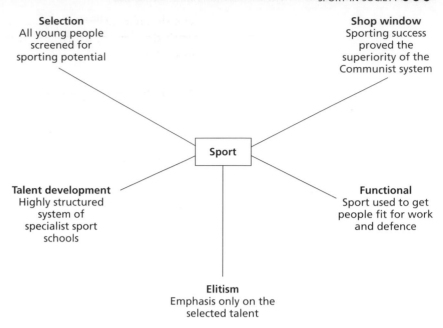

Figure 22.1 The Eastern Bloc model

window was the objective, although in this case it was the political system that was on show (see *Figure 22.1*). As Riordan states 'Every win for the Soviet Union was a win for the Communist system' – and if this win was against an American performer or team, then the political emphasis was maximised.

In all Eastern Bloc countries sport played a very important role. Success came as the result of a carefully structured system that tested the entire population and fed the talented through sports schools and training centres to national teams.

Although much of their success has been put down to the widespread use of drugs, this alone would not account for the level and rate of success. Performers in these countries had the best facilities, coaches and support available. Another important point is that sport in these societies reflected the egalitarian ideology of the system, which fostered the idea that everyone in society was equal in status. Although in practice this was not strictly true, in sport everybody had an equal chance of success. If you were identified as having talent in a sport you were selected, no matter what your race or background. This ensured that the state had the widest possible base to select from.

22.2.3 New World democratic cultures

By this title, we mean societies such as Australia, South Africa and New Zealand. These are cultures with European origins and in the main former British colonies. Most are under 200 years old and, after achieving independence, developed into advanced thriving societies.

In a few sports such as cricket and rugby these countries vie for world honours. Australia in particular is a world leader in an ever-increasing number of sports. South Africa, until recently left out of international sport because of Apartheid, is quickly redeveloping its sporting talent and is again emerging as a powerful force in rugby, cricket and athletics.

What these countries have in common, apart from a shared colonial history, is a culture of 'Bush Ethos'. The environments remain harsh and the people have had to work hard to develop and expand. Being young countries they lack the traditions and history of the Old World and have consequently needed to find new ways of expressing their emotions. Sport has more than filled this role: it is often seen as a substitute for the higher

247

Elitism
Screening to identify
potential talent

State
Importance of
sport reflected in
funding and support
by state

Cultural kickback
'Pom Bashing':
get one over on
the old master

Bush ethos
A natural drive
for success

Sport

New image
Sport used in
forging a
new identity

Religion
Sporting focus for
the whole
population

Colonial history
Most of the games
played were from
colonial power

Figure 22.2   The New World democratic model

forms of culture in Europe. It is no cliché to say that in these societies sport is a religion (*Figure 22.2*).

The other drive is again a form of shop window, although here the focus is different. The ambition of all these new cultures is to beat their old colonial powers – in particular England. Their sportsmen and women seem to have an extra edge to their approach, are driven by the win ethic and do not appear to be restrained by our more traditional values and ethics. To them, *winning* is important, it reflects struggle and hard work – the values that are inherent in their societies.

It is interesting to note that a lot of Australia's success can be linked to a 'Soviet'-style programme of state funding and selection. The Australians have made good use of comparative sports study, adapting many successful methods from around the world but predominantly from the old Eastern Bloc countries.

All young people are now screened for sports talent, the results being fed into a national computer system which then suggests the best sport for the youngster to follow. All talented performers are offered state sponsorship and through the extensive clubs system and chain of national

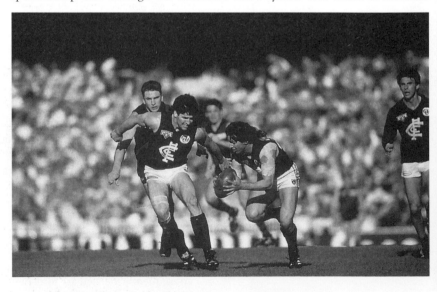

Australian rules football is one of Australia's most popular sports

sports centres are nurtured and groomed for international success. The results have been outstanding and as the programme has expanded into football and other sports, Australia can now rightly claim to be a sports superpower.

Sports testing

The Australian Institute of Sport has recently introduced a system of sport talent-spotting, which they call 'Sports Search'. Sports Search was originally devised as a way of increasing participation in sport but is now an effective means of identifying talent. It is aimed at children in high school of 11–15 years old, and it is hoped the project will visit all of Australia's 3200 high schools. Each child will undertake a series of physical tests which will rate them for size, shape, agility, endurance and explosive power. This information will be fed into a computer and each student will be matched to their ideal sport. The school will follow this up by ensuring that each student has the opportunity to take up the sports he or she is best suited to.

22.2.4 The American model

America (according to the Americans) is now the world's number one nation in all terms, the superpower now without the Soviet Union and with nobody to beat. America's sports are the most technically advanced in the world, its sports stars are the richest in the world, and in a number of sports the Americans are undisputed world champions. What is interesting is that America's major sports are not really played anywhere else in the world – America is so far ahead that it can hold World Championships in American football and baseball, in which only American teams compete!

Like Australia, the USA has colonial links, but these were cut much earlier in the country's development and for many years the USA developed in planned isolation from Europe. During this time its sports developed, adapted from the old European games but modelled and changed to suit America's new image. In fact so American were these new sports of baseball, grid iron and basketball that even with extensive backing they have never really developed elsewhere.

The sports are high scoring and action packed to maximise their entertainment value. They reflect American culture in that the aim is to win – the win ethic is what drives all American people and this fuels the so-called 'American Dream'. (This idea of rags-to-riches success is best personified in the *Rocky* films, where a nobody becomes World Champion overnight.) The American model is outlined in *Figure 22.3*.

But it is the commercial aspect of American sport which makes it so different. Every level, from professional national teams to the local high school football teams, is run as a business. The influence of television is total and most sports in the USA rely totally on the money generated through television deals and advertising revenue. Sports stars in America are millionaires, most professional teams will have a number of players on multi-million dollar annual contracts. Many stars, like Michael Jordan, make even more money through sponsorship deals and endorsements.

There is a flip side to this: sport in the USA is extremely elitist. In athletics, for example, there is not even one amateur club where 'Joe Public' can train. For most Americans sport is something you watch on the television and not something you actually play. The television also dictates the rules – for example, American Football has evolved in to a constant stop–go staccato pattern to allow companies to screen advertisements every five minutes.

Many of these trends are beginning to filter into British sport, and it may be very difficult for us to prevent Americanisation of our sport.

Figure 22.3 The United States model

> **Key revision box**
>
> *Sport plays an important role in modern societies, reflecting the wider values and traditions of the society. Different countries play different sports, and also play the same games differently. Centrality is a sociological theory which states that the dominant roles in sport are taken by the dominant section of society. Emergent cultures select and channel athletes into a limited number of sports to ensure success. In the Eastern Bloc cultures the state controls sport for political gain. The New World democratic cultures use sport as a focus of national identity and to gain status over the Old World. In the USA sport is seen as a commercial commodity and is driven by the win ethic. In all cases, the shop window is the aim.*

22.3 Excellence in sport

Sebastian Coe and his colleagues, in their book *More than a Game*, state that 'Champions are made, not born.' In this section we will discuss how champions are developed and the issues that are related to excellence in sport. Excellence is an important current issue in the UK. Many people have recorded the fall in our sporting standards and in sports such as tennis, where our players were among the elite, we are now slipping down the rankings.

We must first try to define what we mean by 'excellence'. In fact, the word has two meanings, immediately causing a dilemma which we, as sports scientists, need to face. The two meanings can be viewed as two sections of the sports pyramid (shown in *Figure 22.4*).

Elitism

In elitism the emphasis is on a few, the best, performers. The tendency is to look for the most developed and to ignore the rest. We have already seen this approach in the emerging cultures discussed in the previous section.

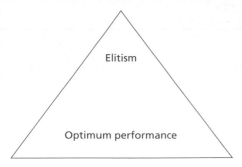

Figure 22.4   The sports pyramid

But the best example of this approach was seen in the German Democratic Republic, a country with a population of only 16 million which managed to be in the top three for sports such as athletics, swimming and boxing. The whole sports system of this communist country was geared up to selecting and developing champion performers, but this was at the expense of the rest of the population.

Optimum performance

In contrast to elitism, the optimum performance model asserts that sporting excellence should be the target of every individual. The society acknowledges that each person has a potential and that the sports system should help everyone fulfil this objective. This model has been used in physical education in the UK, where the aim has been to try to develop in all participants a feeling of achievement. This is reflected by the vast range of activities we undertake in school and the lack of specialisation.

It has been argued that this system has a great disadvantage in that it will not lead to the development of talent on the level required for international success.

Very few societies are concerned with the optimum performance model because it doesn't bring the short-term responses that they crave or because they do not have the finance or resources to allow every member of the population the chance of success.

If we acknowledge that in the main it is the first model that is most relevant in modern sport then let us investigate more closely the issues in the development of excellence.

22.3.1 Development of excellence

Three key stages may be identified in the development of sporting talent:

1   selection of talent
2   development of talent
3   providing support for performance.

The actual methods used differ from country to country, but increasingly a number of policies are being followed by most. A lot of the these have been adapted from the Eastern European model of sports excellence, pioneered by the Soviet Union and the German Democratic Republic from the 1950s onwards.

Selection

Selection is the start of this process, identifying individuals with the potential to become champions. The pyramid theory of sports development suggests that the wider the base then the greater the number at the top of the pyramid. The aim of the selection process is to make the base of the pyramid as wide as possible.

In the old Soviet Union this was achieved by screening every child in the education system for sporting potential. At first this would involve gross motor skills but later more specific skill tests, physiological and psychological tests were used to identify talent and channel it into the appropriate sports. This latter aspect is perhaps a debatable issue – many argue that is wrong for young people to specialise too early because it can lead to problems such as physiological 'burn out'.

Australia has recently implemented a system of screening every child at high school level using sport-related tests. The results are put into a computer which predicts which sport they are most suited to. In most cases this is the sport they will be directed towards. In the UK we have tended to keep away from this approach. Performers tend to specialise later in their development, and the general view is that it is still better to develop skills and experiences in a range of sports.

Andy Cole – a graduate of the FA school of excellence at Lilleshall

Talent development

Stage two is again a crucial aspect. The children selected are coached, instructed and nurtured to become champions. In many countries this process is achieved through the education system, predominantly in sport schools.

Sports schools

Sport schools are found in most European countries and are often controlled by the state. They allow young people to develop their sporting potential while continuing with academic studies. They usually have high-quality facilities and specialised staff, the advantage being that students get more time to practice their skills and the atmosphere of excellence encourages their development.

The Soviet Union was the role model in the field of sports schools. After selection, students were filtered up the sports pyramid through city sports schools, regional boarding schools and (the ultimate aim) the national training centre.

In America a slightly different method of development is followed. Sport is viewed as such an important aspect of the American education system that all schools and colleges have extensive sports facilities and place a lot of emphasis on sports success. Students are offered sports scholarships which pay all their expenses, and are given a lot of time to practice. The aim best college players are selected by the professional teams each year during the annual 'Draft'.

In the UK the number of sports schools is increasing, but these are still few and of little influence. The best known are the FA school at Lilleshall, where the best 22 young footballers board and spend half a day at a local comprehensive school (players such as Andy Cole and Nick Barmby have progressed through the FA school), and the LTA Tennis School at Bisham Abbey.

ACTIVITY

List four advantages and four disadvantages of basing performers in sports schools.

Administration of excellence

The final part of the process is to provide support in terms of administration and funding. If athletes are to be successful they need full support, primarily financial aid to ensure that they don't have to worry about raising the funds to cover their training and competition expenses, which allows them more time to prepare for competition. Again there is wide variation in the method of financial support. In many countries the state funds the top athletes – in Australia, France and the old Soviet Union all top performers are paid grants that allow them to become virtually full-time athletes. In America talented performers are paid scholarships by schools and colleges or athletes under contract to a professional team. We have already discussed how the Sports Aid Foundation in the UK tries to fund up-and-coming athletes – as yet there is little government input to sports in the UK (see Chapter 21 for more on sports funding).

Modern sports performers also require the support of an ever-increasing range of sports specialists: psychologists, dieticians, physiotherapists, as well as video and computer equipment to help improve technique. In the UK such service is now being developed in a number of National Sports Centres, which have been established to enable our international performers to use top-quality facilities for training.

Most other countries have similar national centres for the use of the national squads.

The National Sports Centres in the UK

Bisham Abbey, Bucks. Home of the LTA National Tennis Centre. Also has facilities for football, hockey, squash, golf and weightlifting. England's soccer and rugby teams use Bisham Abbey as a base for training.

Crystal Palace, London. International standard facilities for athletics, swimming, martial arts and up to 40 other sports. Used as a training base for the national athletics and swimming squads.

Holme Pierrepont, Nottingham. The national watersports centre, with international standard facilities for canoeing, rowing and water skiing and provision for many other aquatic sports.

Lilleshall Hall, Shropshire. Home to the FA school of soccer excellence and the National Sports Injuries Clinic. The British Amateur Gymnastics Association has also recently established a national centre here.

Plas Y Brenin, North Wales. This houses the National Centre for Mountain Activities and caters for a wide range of sports and outdoor pursuits.

22.3.2 Constraints on excellence

We should now be able to identify aspects of sporting excellence from other societies that we could take and implement in the British sports system, with the aim of developing our sports potential – aspects such as setting up more sports schools, introducing state or other sponsorship schemes that will allow our sports performers to be able to train harder and concentrate more on their chosen sports.

However, it is not simply a question of transplanting practices from other societies. As we have already suggested, sport and the way it is administered and developed in a country reflects the values and culture of that country. There are several cultural constraints why we in the UK do not actively encourage excellence in sport.

Historical – We invented most modern sports and retain a status in world sport, so it is not important for us to excel.

Geographical – Our population is relatively small, so our pyramid base is much smaller than, say, the USA or China.

Ideological – Most of the world sports powers have a very nationalistic approach, where you are playing for the honour and status of your country, but we are patriotic rather than nationalistic. Similarly, we promote the recreational ethic rather than the win ethic, our heroes are the Eddie Eagles and the Frank Brunos of the world. We also tend to feel that winners are arrogant.

Socioeconomic – Participation in sport in the UK has had the middle-class tradition that taking part counts, not winning, and that sport should not be work.

What should we do to develop a more effective programme of sports excellence? The answer is twofold:

1 A large amount of *money* is required to fund such a programme – high-level facilities and equipment, coaches and the extensive back-up requires a lot of funding. The National Lottery fund could be a possible source of the money needed.

2 Secondly a more coordinated *administration* system is required. At the moment our sports system is too diverse at all levels, we need sports to come together to share aims and objectives for the overall benefit of British sport.

All athletes should have the opportunity to gain from the appliance of science

22.4 Mass participation in sport

Sport is a natural part of life, whether you are one of the elite competing for gold medals or just playing for fun and enjoyment. The opportunity to take part in sporting activity should be a basic human right, however many people suffer constraints that prevent them from taking part.

The aim of mass participation is to break down these constraints, whatever they may be, and so encourage as many people as possible to take up sport.

22.4.1 Why play sport?

After reading the early sections of this book you should now have some firm ideas about why sport is good for us. It promotes mental and physical health, it is a positive use of spare time and is an important emotional release.

ACTIVITY

Write down a list of specific items that a person may benefit from if they regularly play sport. Your list will mainly contain intrinsic benefits, but there may also be extrinsic benefits for the society as a whole if many of its members regularly participate. Try to list some of these benefits.

Everyone should be able to participate in sport

Definition

SPORT FOR ALL CAMPAIGN

This campaign, originally set up in 1972 and still continuing, high-lighted the value of sport and that it was something to which all members of the community should have access. The campaign initially hoped to increase the opportunities for sport and recreation through developing more facilities, but also by informing and educating the public on what was available. More recently the campaign has become more diverse to target groups of community that remain under-represented in sport. Separate campaigns such as '50+ and All to Play For' (aimed at older people) and 'What's your Sport?' (aimed at women) have followed.

Sport for all will also benefit the country as a whole: people will be fitter so there will be less strain on the health system, they will also be able to work harder and more effectively. Another, less positive, aspect is that people will be fit for war if the need arises.

In a sporting context there are also other extrinsic rewards if more people are playing sport the sports pyramid discussed in the last section will have a wider base.

Many countries have set up mass participation schemes, often state sponsored, to encourage more people to take part in physical activity. Even in the decentralised British sports system, the Sports Council's 'Sport for All' campaign has had considerable state involvement, specifically in its funding.

The phrase 'Sport for All' has now become synonymous with the ideals of mass participation. The Soviet Union used the phrase 'massovost', while in France they have 'Sport Pour Tous'.

The whole emphasis in sport for all should be on promoting the intrinsic value of sport – too many people view sport as either something they had to do at school or something they see on the television which is far too advanced for them to try. The real point is that, as we have mentioned many times, sport is an extremely diverse area, involving many different activities and catering for every shape, personality and level of skill. Perhaps we need to use a few more realistic role models to encourage people to take up activities.

Every Sunday morning well over a million people play football in organised leagues. There are 125 000 voluntary sports clubs in Britain catering for six million members, and many more people regularly take part in sport and recreation outside any structural organisation – be it a kick around in the park or joining the 23 per cent of the adult population that walk two miles or more each week. Mass participation, however, is still not a reality in Britain – even the most generous prediction by the Sports Council puts the figure at one in three of the population. The vast majority of people in Britain do not actively participate and, what is more worrying, the activity levels in young people (who were previously the most active group) are also drastically falling.

We now know that the claim by the Soviet Union that everyone undertook physical activity was a propaganda myth and that sport was confined to the elite. In America, a country with the resources to allow the optimum performance form of excellence discussed in the last section, participation levels are low – and falling. If we concentrate on the UK, although we know it is advantageous for us to promote and develop mass participation the success rate of existing programmes or their overall importance is limited. Again we can use our sociocultural analysis to suggest reasons for the failure of mass participation to take off.

22.4.2 Constraints on mass participation

These may be analysed and classified in the same way as we classified the constraints on excellence in the UK.

Historical – In the past sport has been very closely linked to education, and many people's only sporting experience was through compulsory and often harsh physical education lessons. Many are put off sport for life.

Geographical – Many areas of Britain are under-resourced in terms of sports facilities and – equally as important – qualified coaches, teachers and leaders.

Ideological – In our culture, sport has always been seen purely as a non-serious recreation: many other more important issues require attention before you turn to sport. Often at school academically bright students are encouraged to move away from sport so that they can concentrate more time on their studies.

Huge numbers of people take part in events such as the London Marathon every year

Socioeconomic – Amateur/voluntary sport has had a rather middle-class image and the fact is that most of us in the UK must 'pay to play'. We have to pay club subscriptions, fees and facility costs, as well as providing our own kit and equipment.

Consequently, although there have been some successes we are still a long way from achieving sport for all. Marathon running has been one success – a previously minority sport involving serious athletes has over the last few years become a true mass participation event. Events such as the London Marathon or the Great North Run have captured the public's imagination and huge numbers of people have taken up running purely for the intrinsic rewards of finishing the course. At the same time, however, these events have remained high-quality in terms of excellence, with serious runners racing at the front while thousands plod on behind with the only aim of finishing. Other sports could take many pointers from these events in developing the right formula for mass participation.

ACTIVITY

Why has running become such a success in terms of getting people involved in physical activity?

Key revision box

Mass participation means maximising the potential for all sections of a community to take part in physical activity. 'Sport for All' is the campaign set up by the Sports Council to foster mass participation in the UK. Taking part in physical activity has many benefits for both the individual and society. Benefits for the individual are classed as intrinsic. Benefits for society are classed as extrinsic. Mass participation is not yet a reality for most countries. A sociocultural analysis can be used to provide some reasons for this.

Definition
DISCRIMINATION
One section of a community is disadvantaged because of certain sociocultural variables.

22.5 Discrimination in sport

In this section we will see again how closely sport reflects the society in which it takes place. In many societies groups are divided by sociocultural variables which lead to *discrimination*.

In the last section we highlighted the fact that many people do not have equal access to sport, often as a result of discrimination due to a cultural variable.

22.5.1 Cultural factors

Five main cultural factors lead to discrimination in sport:

- gender
- class
- race
- age
- ability.

Unfortunately we do not have the space to investigate fully each of these areas, but to help students gain a sound grasp of each area we suggest

A famous demonstration against discrimination in sport and society took place at the 1968 Mexico Olympics

further and more specific reading at the end of Part 5. In this chapter we will identify the common variables leading to discrimination in sport and briefly outline the areas highlighted above.

Discrimination can be said to affect the following areas in sport:

- provision
- opportunity
- esteem.

Provision

Are the facilities that allow you to participate available to you? We have already suggested that in the UK there is a shortage of facilities and those that do exist are often sited in particular areas. Living in an inner-city would discriminate against you because there is little provision in these areas. Equipment is also required, which is often expensive – those on low incomes may be discriminated against unless equipment is available free or can be hired cheaply.

Opportunity

There may be barriers to an individual's participation in an activity. In the UK most sport takes place in the voluntarily run clubs, which are often elitist organisations. Clubs work on membership systems and membership is controlled either by the ability to pay the fees or, in some cases such as some golf clubs, election to the club membership. This often closes membership to certain members of the community.

Another consideration for the individual is whether they have the time to play. Women in particular are often faced with this problem. The demands of work and family often mean that women have little leisure time, which accounts in some way for the low levels of female participation in sport.

Definition

STEREOTYPE

A group of characteristics that we believe all members of a certain section of society share, usually based on very little actual fact.

SPORTS MYTHS

Stereotypes may lead to myths in sport, and this is where people are discriminated against. Common sports myths are that 'Black people can't swim' and that 'Women will damage themselves internally if they do the hurdles'. Again, myths are based on very little truth, but often become an important aspect in selection and opportunity.

Esteem

This is concerned with the societal view of individuals. In many cultures societal values dictate that women should not take an active part in sport, or if they do it should be confined to 'feminine' sports such as gymnastics and not 'macho' pursuits such as football or rugby. These judgements are based on the traditional roles men and women have taken in the society and may be very difficult to break.

Stereotypes and *sports myths* are also societal variables that lead to discrimination. Often minority groups within a community are labelled as having certain characteristics or traits, and this can lead to them being steered into certain sports or positions and away from others.

One good example in the UK is the current lack of Asian footballers in soccer. Much research has been done into this area and programmes are now being set up to try to address the imbalance but the main problem is that, in our societal view, Asians are not potential footballers.

Stereotypes and myths can become 'self-fulfilling prophecies' – even the people they discriminate against come to believe they are valid and conform to the stereotypes by displaying their appointed characteristics and choosing the sports that fit them. In doing so they are reinforcing society's view. It is only recently that a number of women have broken this system by taking up football and rugby, and it is hoped that the success of the women's England Rugby team will start to change the views of society.

ACTIVITY

The British media are still reluctant to devote a lot of space or time to sports such as women's rugby. What cultural constraints may be causing this?

Let us now look briefly at the groups identified above and suggest key areas that lead to discrimination.

22.5.2 Gender

Each year 33 per cent of all men participate in some form of sporting activity, whereas only 10 per cent of women do. As women make up over 50 per cent of the British population this points to some form of discrimination.

Women's role in society is seen as needing to conform to a set image, referred to as 'femininity', and consequently the amount of and type of sport they play must adhere to this trait guide. There have been many myths about women and sport (see the definition box) and although, thankfully, these have now been largely displaced, many people still hold some faith in them. Other problems concern time – women, due to the demands of work and family, tend to have much less leisure time than men, and even when they do have time they are often physically exhausted.

ACTIVITY

Try to get hold of a variety of newspapers from the same day and go through the sports pages. Make a record of all the sports covered and the gender they are concerned with. What do you conclude? Look through the television listings for the same day and compile an inventory of how much sport is on – and which gender.

22.5.3 Class

This discrimination is related to the history and tradition of sport. The upper classes have traditionally had the most leisure time, which they filled with exclusive sports such as hunting. The middle classes, which grew up during the industrial revolution, rationalised and then controlled sport, imposing their values, specifically amateurism, on our modern sports. The working classes were allowed to participate in sport, but only after they had finished their work – increasingly, spectatorism filled their time.

The main discriminator is money – sport has always cost money and, although many people now have more disposable income, sports such as polo, golf and tennis still require considerable expense.

22.5.4 Race

The UK is a multicultural nation, with a great mixture of races. A major discriminator is still the colour of a person's skin, and this is an area where stereotypes and myths dominate. We discussed in an earlier section the concept of centrality, which affects all minority groups in our culture.

Often there is a double effect, as the minority groups also tend to be in the lower income groups.

22.5.5 Age

In the UK your age is a very important factor in how much sport you play. The General Household Survey found that the age group with the greatest participation in sport was the 16–24 year-olds, with 61 per cent. After this the rate drops dramatically – only 16 per cent of people aged 60 or more take part in any exercise.

In our society sport is definitely the domain of the young, and in many sports you become a veteran at 35! Other societies, such as Japan, encourage participation to continue throughout life, and there are over 70 rugby leagues in Japan. Other programmes, such as masters events and the Golden Olympics, are also attempting to make sport a true 'life-time' recreation.

22.5.6 Ability

This covers two areas: your ability in a particular sport and how generally able you are. People with disabilities have, until recently, had little opportunity to take part in sport. Nearly all the facilities were built solely for the able-bodied. Opportunity for disabled sportsmen and women is now increasing and all new sports facilities provide access for people of all abilities. The media have played an important role in this, and events such as wheelchair basketball, the Paralympics and the London Marathon have done a lot to put forward the case of disabled athletes.

ACTIVITY

Do a quick survey of your school/college and local sports facilities – do they provide access for differing abilities? When were the facilities built? Is there any correlation between when they were built and the facilities they provide?

Disabled people need to participate in sports as much as able-bodied people

Bodies such as the British Paralympic Association and the British Sports Association for the Disabled promote sport for the disabled but they remain a minority and only in a few sports such as bowls can disabled people compete on an equal basis with able-bodied competitors.

The other area mentioned above – that of your ability in a particular sport – can also prove to be a discriminator. Most clubs/teams are elitist in their structure; they only allow the most talented players, often selected through trials, to play. Those who are not particularly talented are left with few alternatives. In some sports, such as football, it may be possible for less able players to join a 'lower' league such as pub football and rugby clubs often run social teams.

Even in schools this causes a dilemma. Who do you pick for the school team – the best players, or do you give all those who want to play or attend practices a chance? For many children a chance to play for their school team will be the pinnacle of their sports career. If, as we discussed in the last section, we should be promoting excellence for all, then we should try to give as any people as possible the chance to enjoy sport.

ACTIVITY

List four advantages and four disadvantages of making your team less elitist and giving as many as possible a chance to take part.

Key revision box

Discrimination in sport arises from sociocultural variables. The five main areas of discrimination are gender, class, race, age and ability. The three elements in sport that are affected by discrimination are provision, opportunity and esteem. Stereotypes have an important influence in sport affecting access and selection. In sport stereotypes often lead to myths and self-fulfilling prophecy.

22.6 Deviance in sport

Deviance in society is where an individual or group breaks away from the expected norms of the society, they drift away from the structural and functional rules. A example is the criminals who disobey the rules of society.

Sport also has its rules and deviance occurs when participants break these rules. We call this *cheating* and this is an important issue in modern sport. The main concern at present is the vast range of cheating – drug abuse, bribing officials and technological cheating in sports such as Formula One motor racing.

Cheating is not a new concept – we know that the ancient Olympians took tonics to try to increase their performances. Some people would argue that cheating is an important element in sport and that without it sport would be dull.

ACTIVITY

Can you write down five ways people can cheat in sport. Why do you think they cheat?

Ben Johnson – banned from competition for taking drugs to enhance his performance

Sport has many written rules but also *unwritten* rules, and these make investigation of deviance more complicated.

UNWRITTEN RULES

Sometimes referred to as 'the spirit of the game', unwritten rules are values and ethics which we expect all sportsmen and women to follow.

22.6.1 The concept of sportsmanship

Sport relies on *sportsmanship*, people conforming to the written and unwritten rules of sport. The idea of *fair play* means that you treat your opponent as an equal and, although you want to beat them, you will do so only by adhering to the rules and a code of conduct that has been developed in the sport through tradition. This includes shaking hands and cheering the other team off at the end of the game.

To cheat not only destroys the game but also detracts from your personal achievement. A win through cheating is a hollow victory as, although you may gain the extrinsic rewards, you will not gain the more fulfilling intrinsic ones.

But is this concept of fair play outdated? It certainly remains an important part of British sport but for many people the overriding factor is to win – at all costs. Governing bodies such as FIFA try to foster sportsmanship by giving out Fair Play awards. It is interesting to note that at the 1990 World Cup England had the honour of winning the Fair Play Award, but only reached the semi-final – which perhaps reinforces the American cliché that 'Nice guys finish last'!

Sport does rely on some form of mutual respect between opponents because often it involves high-speed contact with lethal 'weapons', and to disregard the rules could cause serious injury.

22.6.2 Gamesmanship

The alternative dynamic in sport is known as *gamesmanship*, where you use whatever means you can to overcome your opponent. The only aim here is the win, and for most people it is not a question of breaking the rules – more bending them to your advantage.

Many sports stars of the last few years can be classed as 'gamesmen'. For example, John McEnroe used to disrupt his opponent's concentration by arguing and abusing himself, the umpire and people in the crowd, and Boris Becker was recently disqualified from a tournament for similar gamesmanship.

John McEnroe – a sportsman with a reputation for using gamesmanship as a means of winning

Gamesmanship has now become an acceptable part of modern sport and unfortunately the mood is changing from 'we shall play fairly' to 'if you can't beat them, join them'. The other aspect of gamesmanship is the 'hype' that surrounds the build-up to an event. Primarily for the advantage of the media, this hype is also used by competitors to 'out-psych' or intimidate their opponents.

22.6.3 Drugs in sport

Drug abuse has been one of the main areas of deviance in sport during the last few years. It is not clear whether the actual level of drug taking has gone up or whether we now know more about it because testing systems have improved. It is also very difficult to decide where the line should be drawn between illegal and legal substances – many athletes have tested positive but claim that all they took was a cough mixture or other such product which can be bought over the counter.

Drug taking is the ultimate in gamesmanship – taking something to increase your performance and increase your chances of winning.

The huge increase in the rewards of winning may have meant that the temptation to take drugs became too great for many athletes to bear. For example, Ben Johnson felt the risk was worth while – even though he was stripped of his 1988 Gold medal and banned from competition for several years he continued to make money from his fame.

Most media attention has been focused on the use of *steroids*. These artificial male hormones allow the performer to train harder and longer and have been difficult to trace in the past as they are not actually performance-enhancing drugs. Athletes tend to take them in the closed season when they are building up fitness. A breakthrough in detection of these drugs was the decision to test athletes at any time during the year, meaning illegal activity could be detected even in the closed season.

The very fine line between what is legal and illegal causes many dilemmas for both the performer and authorities. A sprinter can legally take ginseng, although it contains substances that have advantageous effects. An athlete can train at high altitude to try to develop the efficiency of their blood system, but *blood doping* is illegal.

A substance is only illegal if it is on the International Olympic Committee's list of banned substances. It may be possible that athletes with access to highly qualified chemists and physiologists may be able to keep one step ahead by taking substances that have not yet been banned.

Definition

BLOOD DOPING

Removing blood after training at high altitude. The blood is stored and then reinfused shortly before competition in order to improve the aerobic capacity by increasing the number of erythrocytes. Blood doping is very difficult to detect.

ACTIVITY

In the table is a list of drugs commonly used illegally in sport to improve performance. Try to find out what effect each has and give some examples of sports in which they might be used.

Substance	Effects	Sport
Amphetamines		
Caffeine		
Anabolic steroids		
Blood doping		
Beta blockers		

22.6.4 Violence in sport

Violence is also a growing element in modern sport. In some sports the mutual respect that we mentioned above may have disappeared. For example, in rugby we have seen 'stamping', deliberately kicking an opponent on the floor which often means the victim has to leave the field, in American Football the aim of the defence is to 'sack' the quarterback – the more damage you can inflict, the more effective your defence has been – and in football we have the 'professional foul' – an attacker is deliberately knocked down to prevent him scoring a goal.

Violence in sport is another form of sporting deviance

Once again it is usually the result that drives such actions, without a key player the opposition is not going to be as big a threat. A professional foul in football may result in a penalty – but there is a 50 per cent chance of the goalkeeper saving it.

Deviance may be occurring more in modern sport as the rewards become so much greater – the win ethic has definitely begun to dominate high-level sport where the result is often seen to justify any means of achieving it. The problem escalates as amateur sportsmen – and, more importantly, children – are influenced by what they see professionals doing. Could it be that sporting etiquette is dead and that the gamesman has replaced the sportsman?

Key revision box

Deviance is going against the values and ethics of sport, breaking the rules and codes. Rules can be written or unwritten – the letter or spirit of the game. In cheating the drive to win overrides the idea of fair play: the recreational ethic of sportsmanship comes up against the win ethic of gamesmanship. Drug abuse, taking chemicals in order to increase performance, is one form of deviance. Violence, also a form of deviance, can also be used to gain an unfair advantage.

22.7 Sport and the media

'Sport is not a requiem mass. It is entertainment. If you go to a soccer stadium, you see the teams run out and the match. TV gives the viewer a VIP seat . . . Technology enlarges the story you are telling.'
(Dave Hill, Head of BSkyB Sport)

The most important influence on sport in the 1990s is the media. Its impact began in the late nineteenth century with the newspapers and extended into radio coverage in this century. The radio helped to develop major sporting occasions such as the FA Cup and the Derby into essential elements of our culture. In the 1950s television transformed many sports into entertainment packages. Now, in the 1990s, satellite has added another dimension to sport and made it into a truly global commodity.

22.7.1 Media and sports funding

The presence of the media has turned sport into a commodity that can be bought and sold. Television companies pay out huge amounts of money to cover sports and advertisers and sponsors back sport because of the exposure they will get in the media. Individuals train and prepare for sport in the knowledge that the media will give them a stage on which to present their talents – and also gain wealth.

Many sports have either been adapted to suit the needs of television or have changed their structure to attract television coverage. In order to survive a sport needs the media spotlight because without it it will be left behind. In 1994 The Hockey Association paid Sky Television to screen games each week in the hope that it would attract sponsors and other television companies to a sport that has been eclipsed by other games such as rugby and football.

There is a direct link between the funding of sport and the media. Media coverage brings sponsors and advertising to a sport, which are now essential for a sport to remain viable. Companies sponsor sports mainly as a means of cheap advertising, a way of getting into the public's living room. For some companies, like the tobacco firms, sport remains one of the few areas where they can still openly advertise.

The problem for sports such as hockey is that a vicious circle exists – to attract sponsors you need media coverage, but to gain media coverage you often need the funds to pay performers so they can become highly skilful and make your sport more attractive to the media. This is outlined in *Figure 22.5*.

The influence the media, and specifically television, has over sport is epitomised by the Olympics. This great event is controlled by American television companies, who pay well over $400 million for the exclusive

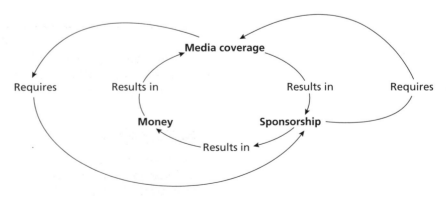

Figure 22.5 The influence of media coverage on sport

rights to screen the Olympic Games. This kind of financial influence gives the companies control over many factors – for example we are now used to having to stay up very late to see key moments such as the 100 m final so that it fits in with the peak viewing time in America.

22.7.2 Does televising sport lead to lower participation?

Actual participation in sport appears to be falling, and it has been suggested that the amount of sport now available on the television may have influenced this – people don't play sport because they're too busy watching it. However, a number of studies (in particular The Wolfenden Report) have found that, although watching television is our most popular pastime (roughly 25 per cent of our leisure time is spent in front of 'the box'), there is little to link television watching and participation in sport. Indeed, television may actually have a positive effect, in that watching sport on the television often stimulates people to take up sports.

This effect is very noticeable when British teams are successful in world events such as the Olympics. During the last few years ice skating, hockey and gymnastics have all witnessed upsurges in popularity when Britons were seen on the television winning medals.

The one negative effect televised sport does appear to have is on spectatorism, where the lure of a 'live' game on the television and the unpredictability of English weather often makes staying home preferable to going to the stadium. Football clubs can now demand very large fees from television companies (in 1995 Sky paid £70 000 per game for Premiership Football), much of which is as compensation for loss of spectators. Cricket and rugby league have also been affected this way.

The media, and the press in particular, have turned sportsmen and women into celebrities, which may be beneficial in terms of potential earnings but which also means that they become 'public figures' and their every move, both on and off the pitch, is scrutinised. There is a general emphasis on sensationalism in the British press where stories (or 'exclusives') are an essential part of the ratings war.

All forms of the media are guilty of concentrating on the critical elements of sport – the action replay questioning an official's decision, or viewing a bad tackle or a violent incident from every possible angle. The use of edited highlights, in which only the goals or action is shown, can also give a rather one-sided view of sports.

Modern technology means that no corner of a sport can remain 'hidden'. We now have cameras in the cricket stumps, in the pockets of a snooker table, on cars, giving the armchair spectator the 'real' view. In some cases this has been very beneficial – many of the deviant practices discussed above are more closely scrutinised and many sports now use video evidence to pick out any foul play the referee missed in the heat of the game.

ACTIVITY

What are the benefits of television technology being made available to sports officials? Are there any disadvantages?

22.7.3 An analysis

The mass media reflects its culture and may also actually shape that culture in fostering values, particularly in establishing and maintaining stereotypes. In general, the mass media will associate itself with the popular view and in sport this will be represented in the most popular sports.

ACTIVITY

Repeat the newspaper analysis you did in Section 22.5.2, but this time make up a table showing the amount of space devoted to different sports. Compare a tabloid newspaper with one of the broadsheet papers.

Even in the quality papers several sports dominate the sports pages – and these will tend to be male-dominated sports often associated with gambling. However, there are some exceptions to this – Channel 4 has successfully introduced a number of ethnic and minority sports to the UK such as sumo wrestling, kabadi, women's football, wheelchair basketball and, most effectively, American football.

Much of the sociocultural elements in sport we discussed earlier will be evident in the media: there tends to an emphasis on the dominant culture and its sport, to the detriment of women and ethnic minorities. Sensationalism often feeds on stereotypes and national prejudice. Headlines such as 'We'll Blitz the Frogs' or 'Venables' Masterplan to Beat Krauts' are blazed across the back pages when our national teams compete. Warlike terminology is often used in reporting sport – you will often see the words 'battle', 'bombarded', 'defence/attack', 'blitzed', 'sniping' in headlines – perhaps reinforcing sport's historical links with war (see Chapter 20).

ACTIVITY

As sports scientists we to take a more analytical view than the media. Here are some areas of study you could develop.

Television – BBC 1, BBC 2, ITV and Franchises, Channel 4, Satellite channels.

● How is sport presented on each of these channels?
● How will the 'ratings war' and increased rivalry between channels affect sport in the future?

The press – Hard, tabloid, daily, local, weekly, national, local.

● How does the emphasis on sport reporting differ in each of these types of paper?
● Which papers lean towards sensationalism?
● Do papers provide a balanced view of sport? If not, identify groups that are discriminated.

The radio – Local, national, BBC, commercial, Radio 5, Radios 1, 2, 3 and 4

● How does the emphasis change in each of these stations?
● How does radio's coverage of sport differ from that of the television?

The arts – Literature, painting/sculpture, music, dance, cinema, theatre

● Can you list any examples of sport represented in these media?
● How is the history of sport linked to the arts?

22.7.4 The future

Sport has become an important cornerstone of the media and each side feels it has the upper hand, although it would appear that the media is slowly beginning to take over power in sport. We have already mentioned that the American networks now own the Olympics, Sky Television has changed football in the UK from a traditional Saturday game into an almost daily event in order to secure maximum viewing potential, and as we write this book rugby league has been bought outright by a media company.

There have been, and there will continue to be, many positive rewards from this 'media-isation' of sport:

- modern technology has transformed sport into a true art form – slow motion and multiangle approaches extol the aesthetics of every sport
- it has generated huge interest in every aspect of sport, leading to the development of sports science, academic qualifications and a whole host of books, magazines videos and films
- our modern sports stars are well known and well paid, receiving much-earned rewards for their effort and dedication and generally providing us with excellent role models.

However, if we look at televised programmes such as *Gladiators* or *WWF Wrestling*, are we seeing the true future of modern sport? Glamour, razzmatazz and the quest for action may kill some sports and ruin others – the wrestlers are very athletic and highly trained performers but they are actors and have lost that essential element that all sportsmen and women posses. In some cases sport may be close to becoming pure entertainment.

Key revision box

The media is a mass communication system made up of the press, television, radio and cinema. The media, and especially television, has been the most influential element in the development of sport over the last century. It plays an important role in the funding of sport by paying to cover sport, by attracting sponsors and advertisers and by making performers into stars who can then attract wealth. Television may stimulate people to take up sport but it may also have a negative effect on spectatorism. The media influences society's views of sport, often fostering and reinforcing stereotypes. It has the power to make or break sports careers. In addition, reports in the media can distort the public's view of sport.

KEY TERMS

You should now understand the following terms. If you do not, go back through the chapter and find out.

American dream
Bush ethos
Centrality
Culture
Deviance
Discrimination
Elitism
Esteem
Emergent culture
Excellence
Extrinsic rewards
Intrinsic rewards
Myths
Opportunity
Optimum performance
Provision
Shop window
Socialisation
Society
Sport for all
Sports pyramid
Sports school
Stereotype

PROGRESS CHECK

1 Why should a society promote sport for all?
2 What social constraints have limited the success of the 'Sport for All' campaign in Britain?
3 How can a sports club be elitist?
4 Why has a country such as Australia placed so much emphasis on developing sports talent?
5 What are the pressures in modern sport that may have increased the incidence of deviance in sport?
6 Cheating in sport means breaking the written and unwritten rules. Explain these two terms.
7 Explain the pyramid system of sports development. How does it make the development of sporting talent more effective?
8 What are the moral arguments against the Eastern European model of early selection and channelling of young children into a particular sport?
9 How can a person's opportunity to participate in sport be affected by sociocultural factors?
10 How is the theory of centrality evident in sport?
11 Gary Lineker was a sportsman, John McEnroe a gamesman. Explain the difference.
12 How can stereotypes and myths affect selection in team games?
13 In what ways has the increased influence of television affected sport in Britain?
14 What role has Channel 4 played in influencing our views of sport?
15 What is the Post school gap and how could we reduce it?
16 What incentives make an athlete turn to drugs as a means of improving performance?

Further reading

L. Allison, editor. *The Politics of Sport*. Manchester University Press, 1986.

D. Anthony. *A Strategy for British Sport*. Hurst, 1980.

J. Armitage. *Man at Play*. Warne, 1977.

D. Birley. *Sport and the Making of Britain*. Manchester University Press, 1993.

D. W. Calhoun. *Sport, Culture and Personality*. Human Kinetics, 1987.

E. Cashmore. *Making Sense of Sport*. Routledge, 1990.

CCPR. *The Organisation of Sport and Recreation in Britain*. Central Council of Physical Recreation, 1991.

S. Coe, D. Teasdale and D. Wickham. *More than a Game*. BBC Books, 1992.

R. Davis, R. Bull, J. Roscoe and D. Roscoe. *PE and the Study of Sport*, 2nd edition. Mosby, 1994.

Department of National Heritage. *Sport – Raising the Game*, 1995

J. Dumazeidier. *Towards a Society of Leisure*. Collier-Macmillan, 1967.

J. Ford. *This Sporting Land*. New English Library, 1977.

P. Gardner. *Nice Guys Finish Last*. Allen Lane, 1974.

R. Holt. *Sport and the British*. Oxford University Press, 1990.

B. Houlihan. *The Government and Politics of Sport*. Routledge, 1991.

J. Huizinga. *Homo ludens, a Study of the Play Element in Culture*. Beacon, 1964.

A. Lumpkin. *PE and Sport – A Contemporary Introduction*. Times Mirror, 1990.

T. Mason. *Sport in Britain*. Oxford University Press, 1988.

P. McIntosh. *Physical Education in England since 1800*. Bell and Hyman, 1979.

C. Mortlock. *The Adventure Alternative*. Cicerone Press, 1984.

H. L. Nixon. *Sport and the American Dream*. Leisure Press, 1984.

S. Parker. *The Sociology of Leisure*. Allen and Unwin, 1976.

J. Riordan, editor. *Sport under Communism*. Hurst, 1981.

G. H. Sage. *Power and Ideology in American Sport*. Human Kinetics, 1990.

W. D. Smith. *Stretching their Bodies*. David and Charles, 1974.

Sports Council. *How to Find out About the Organisation of Sport*. Sports Council Information Services, 1993.

Sports Council. *Into the 90's*. Sports Council Information Services, 1988.

Sports Council. *New Horizons*. Sports Council Information Services, 1994

G. Torkildsen. *Leisure and Recreation Management*. Spon, 1991.

Glossary

A state	Anxiety that is felt in a particular situation
A trait	Anxiety which is experienced by a performer caused by a predisposition towards apprehension
Abduction	Movement away from the midline of the body
Ability	Underlying factors which are largely predetermined genetically
Actin	A protein filament found within the sarcomere
Adduction	Movement towards the midline of the body
Aerobic capacity	The maximum amount of oxygen that can be taken in and used by the body in one minute
Aerobic respiration	The complete breakdown of fats and carbohydrates to carbon dioxide and water. This process requires oxygen
Affiliation	Payment of a membership/subscription to a club which gives the right to perform and take decisions in the administration of the particular sport
Aggression	In sports psychology this means that there is an intention to harm or injure outside the rules of the game or activity
Alactacid component	Part of the recovery process (oxygen debt) where the muscle phosphagen stores are replenished
American Dream	The idea that in the USA anyone can move from rags to riches
Anaerobic respiration	The partial breakdown of carbohydrate to pyruvic acid. This process does not require oxygen
Anaerobic threshold	The point at which the intensity of the exercise leads to a dramatic increase in the anaerobic production of energy
Angular motion	Movement around an axis
Antagonist	A muscle that works in conjunction with a prime mover. As the prime mover contracts, the antagonist relaxes and returns to its original resting length
Anxiety	The negative aspect of experiencing stress. It is the worry that is experienced due to fear of failure
Appendicular skeleton	The part of the skeleton that comprises the upper and lower limbs, the shoulder girdle and the pelvic girdle
Arousal	The energised state, or the readiness for action that motivates a performer to behave in a particular way
Arteries	Blood vessels that always carry blood away from the heart

270

Assertion	When forceful behaviour is controlled and directed within the rules of the game or activity. In sports psychology this is sometimes known as channelled aggression or instrumental aggression
Associationist theories	Theories which connect or bond a stimulus with a particular response
Associative phase of learning	The second phase of learning, which is when practise takes place and feedback is available
Athleticism	A philosophy of physical, moral and challenging activities that fostered the development of character in young men. A term associated with sport developed in the public schools of England in the nineteenth century
ATP	Adenosine triphosphate. A form of chemical energy found in all cells
Atrioventricular node	A specialised node found in the atrioventricular septum that forms part of the conduction system of the heart
Attentional wastage	When a performer's concentration is misdirected to irrelevant cues
Attributional retraining	A process which helps those who have learned helplessness to attribute to more controllable factors
Attributions	The perceived causes of a particular outcome. The reasons that are given for a particular result
Autonomous phase of learning	The final phase of learning, when movements are almost automatic and motor programmes have been completely formed
Autonomy	Self-governing, independent
Axial skeleton	The part of the skeleton that comprises the skull, spine and rib cage
Basal metabolic rate	How much energy we would use to carry out all necessary reactions if we remained at rest
Blood pressure	Blood flow × resistance. The resistance is caused by friction between the blood and the vessel walls
Bohr effect	A drop in pH causes oxygen to dissociate from haemoglobin more readily
Bundle of His	Specialised bundles of nerve fibre found in the septum that form part of the conduction system of the heart
Calorie	The amount of heat energy required to raise the temperature of one gram of water through one degree Celsius
Capillaries	The smallest type of blood vessel. Their walls are only one cell thick. This is where the exchange of gases and nutrients take place
Carbo-loading	Initial depletion of carbohydrate stores, followed by a high carbohydrate diet
Cardiac output	The amount of blood ejected from one ventricle in one minute
Cartilaginous joint	A joint with no joint cavity but with cartilage between the bones of the joint. Examples are the joints between the vertebrae of the spine
Centrality	A sociological theory which states that dominant roles in sport are taken up by the dominant culture in society
Centre of gravity	The point where all the mass of an object is concentrated
Channelled aggression	See Assertion

Chronic response	A long-term physiological adaptation that occurs as a result of training
Circumduction	The lower end of the bone moves in a circle. Circumduction is a combination of flexion, extension, abduction and adduction
Classical conditioning	An unconditioned stimulus is paired with a conditioned stimulus to create a conditioned response
Codification	Creation and maintenance of rules
Coenzyme	A molecule that can carry atoms, transporting them from one reaction to another
Cognitive dissonance	If an individual experiences two or more opposing beliefs which causes disharmony, then the overall attitude will change to regain harmony
Cognitive phase of learning	The first phase of learning. Involves the performer discovering movement strategies
Cohesion	The motivational aspects which attract individual members to a group and the resistance of those members to the group breaking up
Compound	A group of elements combine to form a compound
Concentric	A form of muscular contraction in which the muscle is acting as the prime mover and shortening under tension
Condyle	A large knuckle-shaped articular surface
Connectionist theory	See Associationist theories
Conquest	In a sociocultural sense, where one society takes over another and in doing so imposes its own culture upon it
Cori cycle	The chain of reactions that converts lactic acid back to glycogen
Critical threshold	A training guideline for aerobic work developed by a researcher from Finland called Karvonen. Calculated as resting heart rate + 60 per cent of (maximum heart rate – resting heart rate)
Decentralised	The power of control is spread among many
Dendrite	A process of the motor neurone that carries the nerve impulse from the central nervous system to the cell body
Diastole	The relaxation phase of the cardiac cycle
Distal	Furthest away from the centre of the body
Distributed practice	Practice which includes rest periods between trials
Drive	Directed, motivated or 'energised' behaviour that an individual has towards achieving a certain goal
Drive reduction theory	When performance is perceived to be at its optimum, the performer experiences inhibition which demotivates
Drive theory	The relationship between arousal and performance is linear: as arousal levels increase, so does performance
Dual use	Use of a sport/leisure facility is shared by two sectors of the community
Eccentric	A form of muscular contraction in which the muscle is acting as the antagonist and lengthens under tension
Element	A simple substance that cannot be chemically split any further
Elitism	Activities confined to an exclusive minority
Emergent leader	A leader who arises from within the group
End diastolic volume	The amount of blood in the ventricles just before the contraction phase of the cardiac cycle

Endothermic reaction	A reaction that requires energy to be put into it
Enzyme	A biological catalyst that acts to bring about a specific reaction
Erythrocyte	A biconcave disc containing haemoglobin that helps transport respiratory gases around the body. Also known as a red blood cell
Eustress	A type of positive stress that is actively sought by a performer
Evaluation apprehension	A sense of anxiety caused by the performer perceiving that he or she is being judged by those in the audience
Exothermic reaction	A reaction that releases energy
Expiratory reserve volume	The amount of air that can be forcibly exhaled from the lungs in addition to the tidal volume
Extension	An increase in the angle around a joint
External respiration	The exchange of respiratory gases (oxygen and carbon dioxide) between the lungs and the blood
Extrinsic motivation	External factors which influence behaviour, such as rewards
Fartlek	A form of aerobic training. Fartlek means 'speed play'. An athlete varies the pace and terrain of the run
Fasciculus	A group of individual muscle fibres bound together by connective tissue to form a bundle. Plural is fasciculi
Fibrous joint	A joint with no joint cavity and the bones held together by fibrous connective tissue. An example is the sutures of the skull bones
Field sports	Another term for country pursuits such as hunting, shooting and fishing
Fixator	A muscle which allows the prime mover to work more efficiently by stabilising the bone where the prime mover originates
Flexibility	The range of movement possible around a joint
Flexion	A decrease in the angle around a joint
Foramen	A hole in a bone
Fossa	A depression in a bone
Fulcrum	The fixed point that a lever acts around. In the body the joint acts as the fulcrum
Fusiform	A muscle shape, where the muscle fibres run the length of the muscle
Games cult	A way of thinking about sports which was exported around the world (see also Athleticism)
General adaptation syndrome	A way of explaining how our bodies respond to stress. It involves three stages: alarm reaction, resistance, exhaustion
Gestaltists	A group of German scientists who established principles of perception and insight learning
Glycogen	A complex chain of sugars, made up of a number of glucose molecules. Glycogen is the body's main medium for storing carbohydrate
Haemoglobin	A protein in red blood cells with a high affinity for carbon monoxide, carbon dioxide and oxygen
Health	To be in a state of well-being and be free from disease
Hick's law	The more alternative responses that could be made, the longer the reaction time of the performer
Homeostasis	The maintenance of a stable internal environment
Hyperextension	Continuing to extend a limb beyond 180°

Hypertrophy	Where an increase in cell size leads to an increase in tissue size
Hypoglycaemia	A condition caused by low blood sugar levels
Imagery	A technique of managing stress. Mental pictures are created in order to escape the immediate stressful situation
Inertia	A body or an object is said to be in a state of inertia and needs a force to be applied before any change of velocity can occur
Insertion	The part of a muscle that is attached by connective tissue to a bone that moves
Insight learning	A performer learns through understanding rather than simply connecting a certain stimulus with a particular response
Inspiratory reserve volume	The amount of air that can be forcibly inspired into the lungs in addition to the tidal volume
Interactionist	Linking of traits with environmental factors. Determines behaviour
Internal respiration	The exchange of respiratory gases (oxygen and carbon dioxide) between the blood and the tissues
Interval training	A form of training in which periods of work are interspersed with periods of recovery
Intrinsic motivation	Internal drives such as emotional feelings
Invasion games	Games in which the aim is to invade another team's territory – for example football
Inverted U theory	As arousal levels increase, so does performance, but only to a certain point, usually at moderate arousal levels. Once past moderate arousal level, performance decreases
Isometric	A form of muscular contraction in which the muscle increases in tension but its length does not alter
Joule	The SI unit of energy. One Joule = 4.2 kilocalories
Kinesiology	The study of the science of movement
Lactacid component	Part of the recovery process (oxygen debt) where lactic acid is removed from the muscles
Lean body mass	Fat-free weight
Learned helplessness	The belief that failure is inevitable because of negative previous experiences
Lever	A rigid bar that rotates around a fixed point. In the body bones act as levers
Life-time sports	Sports that can be played throughout life, generally ones that are self-paced or can be adopted
Linear motion	Movement in a straight line
Massed practice	A continuous practice period with very short, or no, rest intervals
Maximum strength	The maximum force that can be generated by a muscle in a single contraction
Metabolism	The sum of all the chemical reactions that take place within our body
Minute ventilation	The amount of air taken into or pushed out of the lungs in one minute. It is calculated by multiplying the number of breaths taken by how much air is inspired or expired in one breath
Mitochondrion	An organelle found in the cell where the process of aerobic respiration takes place. The plural is mitochondria
Molecule	A small group of atoms with at least one atom from each element of the compound

Momentum	The product of velocity × mass
Motor skill	An action or task that has a goal and which requires voluntary movements
Movement time	The time taken from the start of a movement to its completion
Multidimensional model of leadership	Effective leadership is influenced by the qualities of the leader, the situation and the characteristics of the group members
Multipennate	A muscle shape, where the fibres run off either side of small tendons that are attached to the main tendon
Myelin sheath	A fatty sheath that covers the axon of a motor neurone
Myocardium	Cardiac muscle tissue that forms the middle layer of the heart wall
Myoglobin	A protein substance found in the sarcoplasm of the cell. It has a high affinity for oxygen and helps transport oxygen from the capillary to the mitochondria
Myosin	A protein filament found within the sarcomere
Neuromuscular junction	The point where the axon terminal of a motor neurone contacts the sarcolemma of a muscle fibre
Observational learning	A performer learns by watching and imitating others. The extent of imitation depends upon the significance of those that are being watched (see also Significant others)
Operant conditioning	Actions are 'shaped' and then reinforced. The behaviour is manipulated, rather than the stimulus
Origin	The part of a muscle that is attached by connective tissue to a stationary bone
Outcome goals	Goals that are related to the end result or the outcome of competition
Overload	One of the principles of training. A body needs to be made to work harder than normal before any adaptations will take place
Oxygen debt	The amount of oxygen consumed during recovery above that which would have ordinarily been consumed at rest in the same time
Oxygen deficit	When insufficient oxygen is being distributed to the tissues for all the energy production to be met aerobically
Part method of training	A skill is split up into sub-routines for more effective teaching
Partial pressure	The pressure a gas exerts within a mixture of gases
Perception	Interpretation of stimuli as part of information processing
Performance goals	Goals related to performance, which can be judged against other performances
Person-oriented leader	A leader who is concerned primarily with the interpersonal behaviour of the group members
Plyometrics	A form of training used to develop dynamic strength. Plyometric activities involve jumping, hopping or bounding, to make muscle groups work eccentrically
PNF	Proprioceptive neuromuscular facilitation is a form of flexibility training
Popular recreation	Sporting activities before the industrial revolution
Post 16 gap	The 60 per cent drop-off in participation of sport among young people after they leave school

275

Power	The work performed per unit of time
Precapillary sphincters	Found between the arteriole and the capillary. A sphincter is a ring of muscle that surrounds an opening and can effectively open up or close down the capillary
Prescribed leader	A leader who has been appointed from an external source to a particular group or team
Prime mover	The muscle that is directly responsible for creating the movement produced at a joint
Private sector	Ownership of a facility is in the hands of private individuals or companies
Process	A prominent projection of a bone – for example, the spinous process of a vertebra
Progression	One of the principles of training. The workload attempted needs to be closely monitored and increased only after some adaptations have taken place
Progressive relaxation training	Concerned with learning to be aware of the tension in the muscles and then to get rid of this tension by relaxing. Developed by Jacobsen
Proximal	Nearest the centre of the body
Psychological refractory period	The delay caused by the increased information processing time when a second stimulus follows closely after the first
Public sector	A facility in public ownership, usually administered by a local authority
Pulmonary ventilation	The movement of air into and out of the lungs
Purkinje fibres	Specialised nerve fibres found in the ventricles that form part of the conduction system of the heart
Quango	Quasi-autonomous non-governmental organisation
Rationalisation	A term associated with the development of sport that occurred during the industrial revolution, resulting in the codification and organisation of modern sport
Reaction time	The time between presentation of a stimulus and the start of movement
Reinforcement	The process which increases the probability of a behaviour reoccurring. Reinforcement strengthens the S–R bond
Reliability	Research that achieves consistency of results after two or more applications of tests
Repetition	The number of times that an athlete repeats a particular exercise
Response time	The time between presentation of a stimulus and completion of the movement
Reticular activating system	A region of the central core of the brainstem which maintains levels of arousal. It can enhance or inhibit incoming sensory stimuli
Reversibility	Any adaptations that take place as a consequence of training will be reversed when you stop training
Ringelmann effect	When the average individual performance decreases with the increase in group size
Romanticism	An artistic movement in the nineteenth century that encouraged all people to get into 'the great outdoors'
Sarcomere	The smallest contractile unit of a skeletal muscle fibre
Self-efficacy	The degree of self-confidence that is felt in a specific situation

Self-serving bias	A tendency to attribute failure to internal rather than external causes and thus to limit the sense of shame
Shop window	Sport is used to show off a country
Significant others	People who are held in high regard by an individual
Single-channel hypothesis	This states that the brain can only process one stimulus at a time. It is often referred to as the 'bottleneck' theory
Sinuatrial node	A specialised node in the wall of the right atrium, sometimes called the pacemaker, that forms part of the conduction system of the heart
Social facilitation	The influence of the presence of others on performance. These others could be in the audience or performing the same activity (in which case they are called coactors)
Social learning	The influence of others on a person's behaviour, often through observation and imitation
Social loafing	A phenomenon in which some individuals seem to lose motivation in group situations. This may be caused by a lack of personal identity
Socialisation	The process by which humans adapt and grow into their society
Stereotype	A series of characteristics or traits used, often wrongly, to label certain groups in society
Strength endurance	The ability of a muscle to withstand fatigue
Stroke volume	The volume of blood pumped out of the heart by each ventricle during one contraction
Synovial joint	A fluid-filled joint cavity is surrounded by an articular capsule. The articulating surfaces are covered in hyaline cartilage. An example is the hinge joint of the knee
Systole	The contraction phase of the cardiac cycle
Task-oriented leader	A leader who is concerned primarily with completion of a task rather than interpersonal relationships
Thoracic cavity	The area surrounded by the ribs and bordered by the diaphragm. The thoracic cavity is divided into two halves by the mediastinum
Threshold	The point at which the energy system being used is no longer effective in producing energy for ATP synthesis
Tidal volume	The amount of air breathed into or out of the lungs in one breath
Trait	Linked to personality, traits are generalisable behaviours that are enduring and largely innate
Transfer	The influence that the learning and/or performance of one skill has on the learning/performance of another
Triadic model	Attitudes have three important elements: cognitive, affective and behavioural
Validity	Research that has high internal validity is scientific and keeps unwanted variables to a minimum. Research that has high external validity can be generalised to the population as a whole
Variance	One of the principles of training. A training programme needs to include a variety of training methods to help maintain motivation and to avoid overuse injuries

Vascular shunt	The redistribution of the cardiac output during exercise, taking more blood to the working muscles and less blood to other organs such as the kidneys and the liver
Vasoconstriction	A decrease in the size of the lumen of the blood vessel as the smooth muscle of the tunica media contracts
Vasodilatation	An increase in the size of the lumen of the blood vessel as the smooth muscle of the tunica media relaxes
Vasomotor tone	The continual low-frequency impulse received by blood vessels
Veins	Blood vessels that always carry blood towards the heart
Venous return	The flow of blood through the veins back to the heart
Vicarious experiences	What the performer has previously observed (see also Observational learning)
Vital capacity	The maximum amount of air that can be forcibly exhaled after breathing in as much as possible
$\dot{V}O_2(max)$	The maximum amount of oxygen that can be taken into and used by the body in one minute, expressed in millilitres per minute per kilogram of body weight
Voluntary sector	Facilities run and administered by volunteers
Watt	One Watt is the use of one Joule per second
Whole method of training	Teaching skills without breaking them down into sub-routines or parts
Wingate test	A cycle ergometer test that measures an athlete's power output in Watts
Work	Force × distance

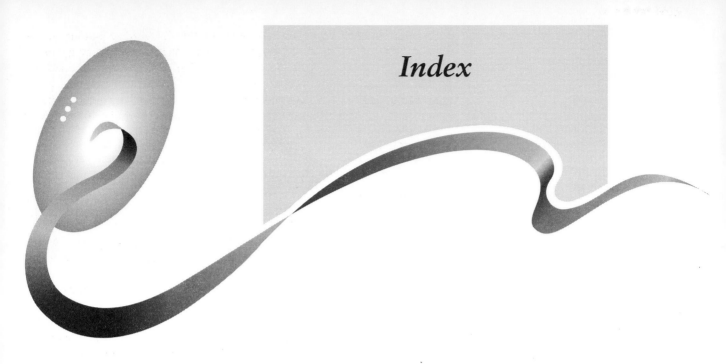

Index

Page references in *italics* indicate figures and/or tables.

A bands (muscles)   22, *22*, 24, *24*
A state   201, *201*
A trait   200, *201*
abduction   6, 7, *12, 13, 14, 16, 17*
abilities   126–7
    see also skills
ability discrimination   260
acceleration, law of   33
acetabulum   16, *16*
acetyl CoA   73
acetylcholine   23
achievement motivation theory   177–8, 180
actin filaments   22, 24, 25
actomyosin   25
adduction   6, 7, *13, 14, 16, 17*
adenosine diphosphate (ADP)   71, 74
adenosine triphosphate *see* ATP
adipose tissue   75, 82
administration of sport   231–4, *252–3, 253*
adrenaline   45, 46, 113
adventure   230
adventure alternative   230
aerobic adaptation   116–18
aerobic capacity *see* VO2 (max)
aerobic exercise   25, 88, 104
    body's response   49, 54, 80, 87, *103*, 112–18
aerobic glycolysis   73, *75*
aerobic respiration   26, 47, 49, 78, 79, *103*, 118
    ATP production   73–5, *75, 76*
    and muscles   25, 46
    and recovery process   85, 86

aerobic thresholds   80–1, *103*
affiliation   231, 239
age   137, 157, 195, 259
agencies, national sports   236–8
aggression   132, 170–3, 186
agility   97
agonists *see* prime movers
alactacid component of the oxygen debt   85–6, *86, 87*
alactic system of energy production   71, *76*
alarm reaction to stress   199
'all or none' law (muscles)   23
altitude training   49, 64
alveoli   58, *57, 58, 59, 61, 63*
Amateur Athletics Association   232
Amateur Swimming Association   240
amateurism   231, 232
America   222, 251, 252, 255, 265
    model of sport   249–50, *250*
American Dream   249
American Football   245, 249
amphiarthrosis   5
anaerobic capacity/power   26, 94
anaerobic exercise   80, 88, 104, 119
anaerobic glycolysis *see* lactic acid energy production system
anaerobic respiration   25, 26, 46, 78, 79, 102
    ATP production   71–3, *72, 76*, 80, 81
anaerobic thresholds   81, 88, 91, *103*
angles of pull   17, 31, *32*
angular motion   33
ankle joints   19

antagonist muscles   26, 27, 95
anticipation   137–8
anticipatory rises   46, 59, *113*
anxiety   200–1, 204
aorta   39, 40, *40*, 42, 45, 51, 52, 53, 65
aortic valves   41
apex of the heart   43
apneustic area   64, *65*
aponeurosis   22
appendicular skeleton   4
aristocracy *see* upper classes
arousal levels   182, 194–5, 196, 200
    and motivation   173, 175–7, *175, 176*
arteries   49, *50*, 53, 118
    and the heart   39, 40, *40*, 41
arterioles   39, 49, 51, 53, 115
articular capsule   5, 6
articular cartilage   3, *3*, 6, *6*
articular discs   6, *6*
articulation   3
Ashbourne Football game   213
assertion   171
Association Football   244
associationist conditioning theories   131–4
associative learning phase   146–7
asthma   57
athleticism   225
atlas vertebrae   15
atmosphere (atm)   60
ATP (adenosine triphosphate)   25, 26, 40, 70, 119
    production   56, 63, 71–6, *76*, 80, 85
    and recovery process   85
ATPase   71

atria 38, 40, *40*, 41, *41*, 42, 43
atrioventicular(AV) nodes *42*, 43
atrioventricular valves 41, 42
attentional wastage 129
attitude objects 165
attitudes 165–70
attribution retraining 179, 181
attributions 179–81, *179*
audiences and performance 193, 194–6
Australia 247, 248–9, 251, 252
  Institute of Sport 235, 249
authoritarian leaders 191
autonomic nervous system 23, 43, 45, 49, 51
autonomous governing bodies 238
autonomous learning phase 147, 153
AV(atrioventicular) nodes *42*, 43
axial skeleton 4
axis vertebrae 15
axon terminal 23
axons 23, *23*

Baggataway 211
balance 34–5, 97
balance boards 97, *97*
ball and socket joints 5, *5*, 13, 16
ballistic stretching 110, *110*
Bandura's research 143, 172, 181, 185
barometric pressure 63, 64
baroreceptors 45, 51, 65
basal metabolic rate (BMR) 81
Basque Games, France 215
behaviour
  attitudes and 166–7
  expected 169–70
  group 186–8, *187*
  observation 164
  social learning 184–6
  see also aggression
bicarbonate ions 64
bicuspid valves 41, *41*
blood 48–9, 56, 65, 75
  and exercise 85, 113, 114, 117
  see also heart; vascular system
blood acidity (pH) 112, 117
  and fatigue 25, 73, 85, 114
  and respiration 64, *64*, 65
blood cells 48, 48–9
blood doping 262
blood flow 49, *49*, 51, 52–4, *53*, 102, 115
blood pooling 51, 54, 102
blood pressure 45, 50, 51, 52–3, *52*, *53*, 54, 102, 114
blood vessels 38, 40, *40*, 48, 49–50, *49*, 53, 102
blood volume 49, 54, 102, 114, 117
BMR (basal metabolic rate) 81
Board of Education 227
body composition 82, 95–6

body fat 82, 95–6
body temperature 46, 64, 65, 95, 113, 115
body weight 82
Boer War (1899–1902) 225
Bohr effect 64, *64*
bones 2–3, *2*, *3*, 9, 10, *11*
  see also joints
boys 169, 224
Boys' Brigade 220
brain 23, 45, 65, 112, 135, 137
breathing *see* respiratory system
Britain *see* UK
British Academy of Sport 235
British Olympic Association 231, 237, 239
British Paralympic Association 259
British Sports Association for the Disabled 238, 259
bronchi 57, *57*, 65
bronchial artery 58
bronchial tree 57
bronchioles 57, *57*, 58, 65
bull baiting 212
bull leaping 211
bundle of His *42*, 43
bursa 6, *6*
'Bush Ethos' culture 247, *248*

caffiene 82
calcium 22, 24, 72
callisthenics 225
calories 70, 81
cancellous bone 3, *3*
capillaries 39, 40, 49–50, 53, 63, 87, 118
  and muscles 25, *26*, 52, 115
carbo-loading 82
carbohydrates 82
  and energy production 25, 72, *72*, 75, 80
  stores 81, 88, 114
carbon 72, 73
carbon dioxide 49, 56, 63, *63*, 64, 65
  and energy production 25, 73, 74, 75, 88
  and response to exercise 112, 113, 114, 115
carbon monoxide 49
carbonic acid 64, 88
cardiac control centre 45, 46, 113
cardiac cycle 42
cardiac muscles 21, 38–40, 41, 42–3, 45–6, 116
  see also heart; muscles
cardiac output (Q) 43–5, *44*, 84
  and exercise 46, 51, 52, 54, 102, 113, 116
cardiovascular system 38, *39*, 96
  the heart 38–47
  vascular system 48–54
carotid arteries 45, 51, 65
cartilage 3, *3*, 4, 57
cartilaginous joints 4, 5, 14

catharsis 172
causality, locus of 179, *180*
CCPR(*Central Council of Physical Recreation*) 231, 233, 236–7
cells *see* blood cells; motor nerves; muscle fibres
cellular respiration 56, 102
  see also aerobic respiration
central nervous system *see* nervous system
centrality sports scoiology theory 245
centre of gravity 33, 34, *34*, 35, 97
chaining teaching method 151
channelled aggression 172
cheating 260
chemical energy 70
chemoreceptors 45, 46, 65
children 185, 223, 224
choice reaction times 136
chordae tendineae 41, *41*
chronic response *see* long-term physiological response
chunking process 139
circuit training 106–7, *106*, *107*
circulation *see* vascular system
circumduction 6, *13*
citric acid cycle 73–4, *74*
class discrimination 259
classical conditioning 131–2
clavicle 11, *12*, *14*
climate and stress 199
closed circulatory network 48
closed loop action control 141, *141*
closed skills 128, 151
clubs, sports 233, 239, 241, *241*, 255, 257, 260
coactors 194
cock fighting 213
codification of sport 213, 214, 232, 238
coenzymes 74, 75
  coenzyme A (CoA) 73
cognitive anxiety 201, 203
cognitive dissonance attitudes theory 168
cognitive evaluation motivation theory 175
cognitive learning phase 144, 146, 154
cognitive learning theories 134
cohesion (group dynamics) 187
collagen 49
command teaching style 157
commercialism in sport 240, 242, 249
communism and sport 246–7, 251
compact bone 3, *3*
comparative sport studies 246–50
competition and stress 199, 200
competitive trait anxiety 200, 201

complete reinforcement 133
complex skills 150, 151
compounds 71, 73
concentration gradient 63
concentric contraction 27, 106
conditioned reflexes 132
conditioning 131–4
conduction system (heart) 42–3, 42
condyle 10, 17
condyloid joints 5, 5
conflict and stress 199
connectionist conditioning theories 131–4
conquest (origins of sport) 210
contingency leadership model 192
continuous running training 104
continuous skills 128
contraction, muscle 21, 24, 25, 26, 27–8, 93, 97, 108
controllability of attributions 179, 180
cool-downs 101–2, 102, 109
coordination 97, 188, 189
Cori cycle 81, 81
coronary artery 40
coronary sinus 40
Cottrell's theory 194–5
Countryside Commission 236
coupled reactions 71, 72
court games 211
creatine kinase 71, 85
credulous group of sports psychologists 164
Crete 211
critical thresholds 103, 104
cross-bridges in muscle fibre 24, 25
cues and cueing 185
culture 244
see also sports sociology
cycling 222

decentralisation of sport 233
decision-making process 136
dehydration 83
democratic leaders 191
dendrites 23, 23
Department for Education and Employment 234
Department of Heritage 234–5
depression (movement) 6, 12
developing countries 246
deviance in sport 260–3
diaphragm 51, 58, 60, 60, 61
diarthrosis 5–6, see also synovial joints
diastole 42, 53, 113
diastolic blood pressure 53, 53, 54, 114
diet and exercise 81–3, 88
diffusion (gaseous exchange) 63, 114, 115, 117
diffusion gradient 63, 117
disabled people 129, 238, 259
discovery teaching style 157

discrete skills 128, 152
discrimination in sport 256–60
distal ends of bones 9
distributed practice methods 152
dominant learned response 175
dorsiflexion 6, 19, 19
douglas bag 92
drill exercises 132, 225–6
drive (motivation) 171, 173
drive reduction theory 134
drive theory 134, 175–6, 175, 194
drugs in sport 247, 262
dual use sports facilities 242
duration of training 101, 103
dynamic balance 97
dynamic flexibility 95
dynamic strength 93, 94, 108
dynamometer 93, 94

Eastern Bloc cultures and sport 246–7, 247, 248, 251
eccentric contraction 27, 106
eccentric force 35
ECG (electrocardiogram) 43, 43
education 217, 224–30, 245, 251
see also public schools; schools
Education and Employment, Department for 234
effector mechanism 135, 136, 141
efferent nerves see motor nerves
effort see force
ego-oriented people 178
elastin fibres 49
elbow joints 9–11, 11
electron transport system 74, 75
Elementary schools 225
elements 71
elevated respiration 87
elevation (movement) 6, 12
elitism 240, 247, 248, 249, 250, 250, 250–1, 257, 260
emergent cultures 246, 246
emergent leaders 189
emotions 166, 174, 202
encoding of information 139
end-disatolic volume 44
endocardium 38, 39
endomysium 21, 22
endothelial cells 49, 49
endothermic reactions 71, 86
endurance strength 82, 93–4, 94, 105, 107
energy 70, 101, 102
and exercise 78–83
production systems 25, 26, 70–6
the recovery process 84–8
stores 47, 115, 118, 119
energy continuum 78, 79
enzymes 81, 85, 118, 119
and energy production 25, 71, 72, 75, 102
epicardium 39, 40
epiglottis 57

epimysium 21, 22
erythrocytes 48, 49, 117
esteem and discrimination 258
eustress 198
evaluation apprehension 194–5
excellence in sport 250–4
executive programme see motor programmes
exercise 69, 84, 96
body's response 112–19
and energy production 70, 73, 74, 78–83, 84
and heart rate 46–7, 46, 73
recovery process 84–8
and respiration 59, 64–5, 73
and vascular system 51, 51–2, 54, 73
exhaustion (stress response) 199
exothermic reactions 71
expectations (behaviour) 169–70
expiration (lungs) 51, 59, 60–1, 60, 65, 88, 113
expiratory reserve volumes 61, 61, 62, 113
extension 6, 7, 9, 11, 13, 14, 15, 16, 17, 17, 18, 19
external respiration 56, 58, 63, 63, 91
externally-paced skills 128
extra-curricular sport 228
extrinsic feedback 135, 136, 142, 143
extrinsic motivation and rewards 174–5, 220, 223
extroverts 156, 176, 195

FA (Football Association) 232
facilities provision 241–3, 257
fair play 223, 261
Fartlek training 78, 104
fasciculi 21, 22
fast glycoltic (FG)(fast twitch) muscle fibres 25, 26, 26, 28, 86, 93, 96, 97, 119
fast oxidative glycolytic (FOG) (fast twitch) muscle fibres 25, 26, 28, 86, 93, 96, 119
fatigue 25, 26, 26, 73, 153
fats 6, 82, 88, 95–6, 118
and energy production 25, 26, 73, 75–6, 80
feedback of information 135, 136, 141, 142–4, 143, 188
femur 2, 16, 16, 17, 17, 18
Festinger's attitude theory 168
fibre in diet 82
fibrous joints 4
fibula 17, 18, 19, 19
Fiedler's leadership model 192
field sports 212, 215
fine skills 128
first-order levers 31, 31
Fishbein's attitudes theory 167
fitness 90–7, 91, 100, 101

Fitts & Posner theory 146
fixators, muscle 28, 105
flexibility 95, 102, 118
    adaptations 119
    improvement 109–10, *110*
flexion 6, 7, 9, *11*, 13, *14*, 15,
    16, 17, *17*, *18*, 19
food 70, 81, 82
football 211, 213, 234, 244,
    245, 258
Football Association (FA) 232
Football Trust 234
foramen 10
force of contraction 46
force (effort) 21, 26, 31, 32–4,
    32, 35, 70, 92–3
forced response 155
fossa 10
Foundation for Sport and the Arts
    237
France 222, 233, 252, 255
free weights 107
frequency of training 100, 104
frontier spirit 222
frustration and stress 199
frustration-aggression hypothesis
    172, *172*
fulcrums 30, 31, *31*, 36
funding of sport 237, 252–3,
    253
    and the media 264–5
fusiform (muscle shape) 93

Game Laws 213
Games Cult 225
gamesmanship 261–2
GAS (general adaptation
    syndrome) 199
gaseous exchange 56, 63, 118
gender 137, 169, 195, 223
    discrimination 257, 258
German Democratic Republic
    246–7, 251
Gestaltist theory 134
girls 169, 223
glenoid fossa 13
gliding joints 5, *5*, 11, 14
glucose 72, *72*, 73, 74, 81, 83,
    114
glycogen
    and energy production 72, *72*,
        73, 80, 81, 85, 119
    stores *26*, *72*, 75, 82, 88,
        118, 119
glycogen phosphorylase 72
glycogen-loading 82, 88
glycolysis 72, 73
    see also lactic acid energy
        production system
goals and goal-setting 143–4,
    143, 204–6
goniometer 95, *95*
governing bodies 232, 238–41
government and sport 233–6
gradation of contraction 28
gradual metamorphosis teaching
    method 151

Grammar schools 228
gravity 51
    centre of 33, 34, *34*, 97
Great Man leadership theory
    189
gross motor abilities 126
gross skills 128, 134
groups 186
    dynamics 186–7, *187*, 192
    performance 187–9
gymnastics 211, 225

H zones (muscles) 22, 24, *24*
haemoglobin 48–9, 88, 117
    and oxygen 63, 64, *64*, 102,
        115
hare and hounds 213
heads of bones 10, *11*
health 90
    related fitness 90, 91–6
heart 38, 52, 102
    and exercise 112, 113,
        116–17
    function 42–7
    structure 38–41, *39*, *40*, *41*
heart murmurs 41
heart rates 43–4, 51, 73, 80, 87
    control 45–7, *46*
    and exercise 103, 113, *113*,
        116–17
heart valves 41
Hering-Breuer reflex 65
Heritage, Department of 234–5
Hick's law 136, 137
Highland Games, Scotland 215
highly organised tasks 150
hinge joints 5, *5*, 9, 17, 19
hip joints 16–17, *16*, *17*
holistic activity 221
homeostasis 112
hormones 45, 46, 113, 262
Hull's drive theory 134, 175–6
humerus *11*, 13, *14*
hunting *11*, *14*, 213
hurling 244
hyaline cartilage 3, *3*, 6, *6*
hydrogen 64, 65, 72, 73, 74
hyperextension 15, *15*, *16*
hypertension 52, 53
hypertrophy 44, 116, 118, 119
hypoglycaemia 81, 83

I bands (muscles) 22, *22*, 24, *24*
identical elements learning theory
    148
Illinois Agility Run 97, *97*
imagery in stress management
    201–2
imitation (social learning) 185
Industrial Revolution 214, 216,
    221, 232
inertia, law of 33
information processing 97,
    135–44, *135*, 148
innate abilities 126
inner drives 173
input *see* information processing

insertions, muscle 9, *11*, *12*, *14*,
    16, *17*, *18*, *19*, 30, 31
insight learning 134
inspiration (lungs) 51, 59, 60,
    60, 65
inspiratory reserve volumes 61,
    61, *62*, 113
instinct aggression theory 171
insulin 76, 81
intangible rewards 174
intensity of training 100, 103,
    104, 105
interactionist approach to person-
    ality 163
intercostal muscles 60, *60*, 61
internal respiration 56, 63
International Olympic Committee
    231, 262
international relations 217
interval training 104–5
intervening variables (learning)
    134
interviews, personality 164
intrinsic control of the heart 45,
    113
intrinsic feedback *135*, 136, 142
intrinsic motivation and rewards
    174, 174–5, 220, 223, 255
introverts 156, 176
invasion games 211, 244
inverted U motivation theory
    176–7, *176*
Iroquios Indians 211
isokinetic contractions 28
isometric contractions 28, 54,
    105–6
isotonic contractions 27

Jacobsen technique 203–4
Japan 259
Jockey Club 232
joints 4–7
    flexibility 95, 109, 119
    and muscles 9–19, 26, 30, 31,
        32
joules 70

Karvonen's principle 103
kilocalories 70, 79, 80, 81
kinaethesis 127, 142, 148, 150
kinesiology 35
kinetic energy 70, 71
knee joints 6, 17–18, *17*, *18*
Kohler's tests 134
Krebs' cycle 73–4, *74*

La Piere's attitudes study 167
lacrosse 211
lactacid component of the oxygen
    debt 86–7, *86*, *87*, 88
lactic acid 25
    energy production system
        72–3, *72*, 76, 78, 80, 81,
        103
    recovery process 86–7, *86*, 88
    response to exercise 46, 85,
        113, 114, 115, 117, 119

laissez-faire leaders 191
larynx 56, 57, *57*
Latane's group studies 188
lateral flexion 6, 15, *16*
leadership 189–93, *190*
lean body mass 82, 95
learned helplessness 180
learning of skills
    information processing
        135–44
    stages in process 146–7
    theories 131–4
    see also teaching of skills
leisure 218–19, 242
leukocytes 49
levers 30–2, *30, 31*
life-time sports 221, 259
ligaments 6, 9, 13, 15, 16, 17,
    19
linear motion 33
lipases 73, 75, 85
lipoproteins 73
liver 81, 115
lobules 57, 58
local advisory councils 241
local authorities 241, 242
local facilities 241–3, *241*
locus of causality 179, *180*
London Marathon 256, 259
long-term goals 205–6
long-term memory stores
    139–40, 151
long-term psychological response
    to exercise 112–13, 116–19
low organisation tasks 150
lower classes *see* working classes
lumens 49, *49*, 50, 51, 53
lung volumes 61, 62, 113, 117
lungs 40, 56, 57–9, *57, 58*
    and exercise 113, 117
    see also respiratory system

manual teaching guidance 154–5
mass 33, 34
mass participation 254–6
massed practice methods 152
massovost (sport for all) 255
maximal exercise 44, 46, 59, *59*,
    79, 113, 116, 117
maximum cardiac output 44,
    116
maximum minute ventilation 117
maximum strength 93, 105
MCC(Marylebone Cricket Club)
    232
mechanical teaching guidance
    154–5
media 215, 217, 240, 264–7,
    264
    see also television
mediastinum 38
medulla 45, 46, 51, 113
memory 136, 138–40, *139*
mental rehearsal/practice 139,
    140, 144, *144*
metabolic fuel 86, 88
metabolism 81

middle classes 220, 221, 232,
    259
military drills 225–7
minerals in the diet 82
Minoans 211
minute ventilation 59, 113, 117
mitochondria 25, 26, *26*, 40, 73,
    74, 87, 118
mob games 211, 212–13
Model Course (1902) 225
models(observational learning)
    184–5
moderation in training 101
molecules 71, 72
momentum 33, 36
Mosston's teaching spectrum 157
motion *see* movement
motion, Newton's laws 33–4, 36
motivation 134, 143, 157,
    173–8, 179, 186, 204
    within groups 187, 188
motor learning phase 146–7
motor nerves (neurons) 23, *23*,
    25, 93
motor neurone pools 23
motor programmes 135, 136,
    140–1, 146–7, 152
motor skills 125
    analysis 35–6, 127–9
    learning 140, 152
    teaching 132, 133, 154–8,
        155–8, *157*
    see also skills
motor units 23, 25, 28, 96
motor-related fitness 96–7
movement 30–6, 70
    see also joints
movement times 136
multi-stage fitness test 92
multipennate muscle shape 93
muscle fibres(cells) 75, *84*, 102
    cardiac 38–40, *40*, 43
    skeletal 21–2, *22*, 23, 24, *24*
    types 25–6, *26*, 28, 80, 93,
        119
muscle phosphagens 85–6, *85*,
    88
muscle receptors 45, 46, 135
muscles *10*, 21, 93, 102
    and exercise 105–6, 115, 117,
        118, 119
    see also cardiac muscles;
        skeletal muscles; smooth
        muscles
muscular Christianity 213, 221,
    225
myelin sheaths 23, *23*, 25, 93
myocardium 38, *39*, 45, 113,
    116
myofibrils 21–2, *22*, *22*
myoglobin 25, 87–8, 115, 118
myosin filaments *22*, *22*, 24, 25
myosin heads 24
myths, sports 258

Nach and Naf personality types
    177–8, 180

narrow band approach to
    personality 162
National Association for Outdoor
    Education 228
National Coaching Foundation
    (NCF) 92, 93, 237–8
National Curriculum 224, 228,
    229
National Lottery 234, 237,
    253
national sports agencies 236–8
National Sports Centres 252–3
National Syllabus in Physical
    Training 225
natural abilities 126
Naturalist movement 221
negative reinforcement 132
negative thoughts 203
negative transfer in skill
    acquisition 147, 149
negative work 27
nerve impulses 64
    and the heart 43, 45
    and muscles 24, 25, 26, 28,
        45, 97, 102
nervous system (neural control)
    23, *23*
    and the cardiovascular system
        43, 45, 49, 51, 113
    and muscles 23, 93, 97
    and the respiration 64–5, *65*
neuromuscular junctions 23
neurones *see* motor nerves
New World democratic cultures
    247–8, *248*
newspapers 217, 264, 265, 266
Newton's laws of motion 33–4,
    36
newton's (N) 32, 33
nodes of Ranvier 23, *23*
nose 56
nutrition 81–3, 88

observations, behaviour 164
obesity 96
observational learning 184–6,
    185
Olympic Games 231, 237, 239,
    264–5
open loop action control 140–1,
    140
open Olympics 231
open skills 128, 150, 151
operant conditioning 132–3, 151
optimum performance model
    251
origins, muscle 9, *11, 12, 14,
    16, 17, 18, 19*
outcome goals 204
outdoor education 228–30
outdoor recreation 220, 221–2
output *see* response
overlearning 140, 152–3
overload training 100–1, 103–4
overweight 95–6
oxaloacetic acid 73, 74
oxidation 74

oxygen 56, 63, *63*, 65
  aerobic capacity 49, 91–2
  debt 85, 85–7, *86*, 87, 88,
    104
  deficit 85, 102
  and energy consumption
    79–81
  and energy production 63, 72,
    73, 74, 75
  and haemoglobin 49, 63, 64,
    64, 102
  response to exercise 45, 46,
    51, 84–5, 113, 114, 115,
    118
  stores 87, 115
oxyhaemoglobin 49, 63
  dissociation curve 64, *64*

pacemakers *42*, 43, 45, 113
pacing skills 128
papillary muscles 41, *41*
paralympics 259
parasympathetic vagus nerve 45
parietal pleura 58, 60
part teaching method 151
partial pressure 63, 64, *64*, 115
partial reinforcement 133
participation 254–6, 265
pascal (Pa) 60
patella 2, 17
Pavlov's experiments 131–2
PC *see* phosphocreatine
peasants 212
  see also working classes
pectoralis minor muscles 60
pelvis 15, *16*, 17, *18*
perceptual skill 125, *135*, 136,
    141
performance 179, 182, 251
  arousal levels and 175–7,
    175, *176*
  feedback 142–3, 143–4, *143*
  and goal-setting *143*, 204–5
  groups 187–9
  and social facilitation 195–6
pericardial cavity 38, *39*
pericardial fluid 38
pericardium 38, *39*, 40
perimysium 21, *22*
peripheral nervous system 23, *23*
peripheral resistance 54
person-oriented leadership 190,
    191, 192
personality 162–5, 176, 189
persuasion and attitudes 167–8
pH *see* blood acidity
pharynx 56
phosphagens 85–6, *85*, 88
phosphates (P) 70, 71, 74, 85
phosphocreatine (PC) 71, 72, 76,
    78, 85–6, 88, 119
phosphofructokinase 72, 73,
    85
physical education 224–8, 245,
    251
physical fitness 90–7, *91*, 100,
    101

physical recreation 220–1
physical restriction 154
physiological response to exercise
    112–19
pivot joints 5, *5*, 15
plantar flexion 6, 19, *19*
plasma 48, 49, 54, 63, 64, 88,
    117
plateau effect 46, 59, 153
platelets 48, 49
play 223–4
Plein Air, Le 222
pleural cavity 58
pleural fluid 58
pleural membrane 58
plyometrics 108–9, *109*
pneumotaxic area 64, *65*
PNF (proprioceptive, neuromus-
    cular facilitation) 110
point of balance *see* centre of
    gravity
popular recreation 212–13
  see also recreation
positive reinforcement 132
positive transfer in skill acquisi-
    tion 147, 148–9
post 16 gap 224
potential energy 70, 71
power (work) 70
practice conditions 149–53
precapillary sphincters 49, 50,
    52, *52*, 115
prejudice 165
prescribed leaders 189
press *see* newspapers
pressure gradient 63
prime mover muscles 9, *11*, 12,
    14, *16*, *17*, *18*, *19*, 26–7
private sector facilities 242–3
proactive transfer in skill learning
    147
process (within groups) 188
process-oriented goals 205
professionalism 215
programmes, motor *see* motor
    programmes
progression training 101
progressive long-term goal
    achievement 205–6
Progressive relaxation training
    (PRT) 203–4
progressive-part teaching method
    151
projective personality tests
    164
pronation 6, 9, *11*, 19
proprioceptive, neuromuscular
    facilitation (PNF) 110
proprioceptors 65, 141
protein filaments 22, *22*
proteins 75, 82
proximal ends of bones 9, 17
psychological refractory period
    137
psychology *see* sports psychology
psychomotor abilities 126
public schools 213, 214, 216,

220, 225
public sector facilities 242
pulleys (in training) 108, *108*
pulmonary arteries *39*, 40, *40*,
    41, 42, 58
pulmonary circulation 39, 41
pulmonary valves 41
pulmonary veins *39*, 40, *40*, 42,
    58
pulmonary ventilation 59
pulse rate *see* heart rate
punishment 132
purkinje fibres *42*, 43
pyramid, sports 250, 251, *251*,
    255
pyruvic acid 25, 26, 72, *72*, 73,
    86

Q *see* cardiac output
Quangos 234, 235, 236
questionnaires, personality 164

racial discrimination 259
radio 264
radioulnar joints 9, *11*
radius 9, *11*
rambling 221–2
reaction, law of 33–4
reaction times 96–7, 102, 136–8
recall schema 141
receptors 45, 46, 65, 114, 135
reciprocal innervation 26
reciprocal teaching style 157
recognition schema 141
recovery process 84–8, 102, 104,
    119
recreation 212–13, 219–22, 234
recruitment (muscles) 28
red blood cells 48, 49, 117
rehearsal, mental 139, 140, 144,
    144
reinforcement learning process
    132, 133, 143, 146
relaxation 203–4, 219
reliability of research 164
religion 220, 248, *248*
repetitions, training 105, 107
research, personality 163–5
reserve volumes 61, *61*, *62*,
    113
residual volume 61, *61*, 62
resistance
  blood pressure 52, 54
  levers 30, 31
  and strength 92, 105, 107,
    108
  stress response 199
respiration *see* respiratory system
respiratory bronchioles 57, *58*
respiratory centre 64–5, *65*, 113
respiratory muscles 58, 60–1, *60*,
    65, 117
respiratory pump 51
respiratory system
  function and control 58–65
  response to exercise 113, *113*
  structure 56–8, *57*

respiratory volumes   61, *61*, 62
response
   and information processing *135*, 136, 149
   and stimuli theories   131–4
response programming   136
response times   96–7, 102, 136
rest intervals   152
results feedback   142, 143
reticular activating system (RAS)   176, 178
retroactive transfer in skill learning   147
reversibility training   101
rewards   133, 174, 220, 223, 255
rhythmicity area   64, *65*
Ringelmann effect   188
ritual games   211, 212
role models   185
Romantic movement   221
rotation   6, 7, *12*, *13*, *14*, 15, 16, *16*, 17, *17*, *18*, 35
rugby   210
rules   213, 214, 260–1
rustic simplicity   222

SA (sinautrial) nodes   *42*, 43, 45, 113
saddle joints   5, *5*
saltatory conduction   23
sarcolemma   21, 22, *22*
sarcomeres   22, *22*, 24, *24*, 25
sarcoplasm   21–2, *22*, 71, 72, 73, 87
sarcoplasmic reticulum   22, 25
scalene muscles   60, *60*
scapula   2, 11, *11*, *12*, 13, *14*
SCAT (Sport competition anxiety test)   200–1
schema theory of action control   141, 149–50, 151, 152
scholarships, sports   252
schools   225, 228, 245, 249, 260
   and local facilities   242
   sports   252
   see also public schools
second-order levers   31, *31*
selection of talent   251–2
selective attention   139
self-confidence   181
self-directed relaxation   203
self-efficacy   181–2, *182*
self-instructions   202–3
self-paced skills   128
self-serving bias   180
self-talk   202–3
semilunar valves   41, *41*, 42
senses, brain input   135, *135*
septum   38, 40, 43
serial skills   128, 150, 151
serous membrane   58
sets, training   105, 107
shop window, sport as   246–7, 248
short-term goals   205–6
short-term memory stores   139

short-term physiological responses to exercise   112, 113–15
short-term sensory stores   139
shoulder girdles   11–12, *12*
shoulder joints   13–14, *12*, *13*, *14*
significant others   172
simple reaction times   136
simple skills   134
single-channel hypothesis   137
sinuatrial (SA) nodes   *42*, 43, 45, 113
sit and reach test   95, *95*
sit-up test   94
skeletal muscle pump   50–1, 102
skeletal muscles   *10*
   function and control   22–8
   and joints   9–19, 30, 31, *32*
   and respiration   58, 60–1, *60*, 65
   structure   21–2, *22*
   and vascular system   50–1, 51–2, *52*, 54, 102
   see also muscles
skeletal system   2–4, *3*, 30
   see also joints
skeptical group of sports psychologists   164
skills   124–5, 176, 224
   analysis   35–6, 127–9
   and information processing   135–44
   learning theories   131–4
   related fitness   90–1, 96–7
   teaching theories   146–57
   training   107, *107*, 108
skin fold calipers   96
Skinner's conditioning tests   132
sliding filament theory   24
slow oxidative (SO)(slow twitch) muscle fibres   25, *26*, 28, 80, 87, 91, 93
smooth muscle   21, 49, 57
social class hierarchy and sport   210, 232
social control and sport   217
social facilitation   193–6, *194*
social learning   163, 184–6
   theory of aggression   172
social loafing   188
social mobility   245–6
social norms   169
social support   188
socialisation   184, 245–6
society   244
   see also sports sociology
somatic anxiety   201, 203
somatic nervous system   23, *23*
South Africa   247
Soviet Union   222, 246, 248, 251, 252, 255
spatial anticipation   138
spatial summation   28
specificity training principle   101

spectacle, sport as a   211, 215
spectatorism   215
speed   33, 96
sphygmomanometer   52, 53
spinal column   *4*, 14–16, *15*, *16*, 23
spinous process   10
spirometer   61, *62*
spongy bone   3, *3*
sponsorship   239, 253, 264
sport
   characteristics of   216–17
   definition   215
   and education   217, 224–30, 245, 251
   history   210–15, 215–16, 223
   importance of   217
   international relations   217
   UK organisation   231–43, *232*
   see also sports psychology; sports sociology
Sport for All campaign   220, 255
Sport competition anxiety test (SCAT)   200–1
Sport Pour Tous   255
Sport-Raising the Game government policy document   235
Sports Aid Foundation   237
sports clubs *see* clubs, sport
Sports Commission, UK   231
Sports Councils   231, 233, 234, 235–6, 236–7, 241, 242, 255
sports myths   258
sports psychology   161
   individuality   162–82
   social influences   184–96
   stress and its management   198–206
sports pyramid   250, 251, *251*, 255
sports schools   252
Sports Search   249
sports sociology   244–67
sports testing   249
sportsmanship   261
Starling's law   46
state anxiety   200, 201
static balance   97
static flexibility   95
static stretching   110, *110*
steady state exercise   46, 59
stereotypes   169–70, 245, 258
sternocleidmastoids   60, *60*
steroids   262
stimuli
   information processing   125, 131, 135, 136, 137, 138, 139
   muscle control   21, 23, 25, 28
   see also nerve impulses
stimulus identification   136
stimulus-response compatibility   137
stimulus-response (S-R) bonds   131–4, 143, 144

strength 92–4
  improvement training 105–9
stress 198–9, *198*, 220
  anxiety 200–1, 204
  management 201–4
stressors 198, 199
stretching 95, 102, 109
stroke volume (SV) 43–4, 46, 50, 51, 102
  and exercise 112, 113, 116
submaximal exercise 74, 82, 102, 103, 117
  and heart rate 46, *46*, 116
  and recovery 86, 88
  and respiration 59, *113*
summation 28
supination 6, 9, *11*, 19
sweat 114, 115
sympathetic cardiac accelerator nerve 45
sympathetic nerves 49, *49*, 51, 113
synarthrosis 4
synchronisation 28
synergist muscles 26–7
synovial fluid 6
synovial joints 4, 5–6, *5*, *6*
  see also joints and muscles
synovial membrane 6, *6*
systemic circulation 39, 41, 53
systole 42, 53
systolic blood pressure 53, *53*, 54, 114

T vesicles (muscles) 22, 25
talent *247*, 248, 251–2
talus 19, *19*
tangible rewards 174
target games 211
tarsal *19*
task-oriented leadership 190, 191, 192
task-oriented people 178
tasks 150
  see also skills
Taylor Report (1990) 234
TCA (tricarboxylic acid) cycle 72–4, *74*, *75*, 76
teaching of skills
  guidance 154–5
  styles 155–8, *157*
  theories 147–57
  see also learning of skills
team games 225, 228
teams 186–9, 260
television 217, 239, 249, 264–5
temperature, body 46, 64, 65, 95, 113, 115
temporal anticipation 138
tendon 21, *22*
terminal bronchioles 57, *58*
third-order levers 31, *31*
thoracic cavity 38, 51, 58, 59, 60, 61, 113

Thorndike's 'laws' 133, 148
thresholds (energy systems) 78, 80–1, 88, 91, 103, *103*
tibia 3, 17, *18*, 19, *19*
tidal volumes (lungs) 59, *61*, *62*, 84, 113, 117
trachea 57, *57*
training 100–10, 225–7
  see also learning of skills
trait anxiety 200
traits, personality 162, 163, 189
transfer in skill acquisition 147–9
transfer-appropriate skill processing 148
translatory mechanism 136
transverse tubules 22, 25
triadic attitudes model 166
trial and error learning 132–3
tricarboxylic acid *see* TCA cycle
tricuspid valves 41, *41*
triglycerides 75–6, 88, 118
Triplett's social study 193–4
tropomyosin 24
troponin 24
tuberosity 10, *11*
tunica externa 49, *49*
tunica interna 49, *49*
tunica media 49, *49*, 51
Type A personalities 162, 195
Type B personalities 162, 195
Type I muscle fibres(SO) 25, *26*, 28, 80, 87, 91, 93
Type IIa muscle fibres(FOG) 25, *26*, 28, 86, 93, 96, 119
Type IIb muscle fibres(FG) 25, 26, *26*, 28, 86, 93, 96, 97, 119

UK
  and excellence in sport 252–3
  mass participation 255–6
  sports organisation 231–42, *232*, 257
UK Sports Commission 231
  see also Sports Councils
ulna 9, *11*
unwritten rules 261
upper classes 211, 212, 213, 215, 225, 232, 259
USA *see* America

validity of research 164
valves
  heart 41, *41*
  veins 50, 51
variable practice 151
variance training principle 101
vascular shunt 51–2, *52*
vascular system 91
  and exercise 51–2, *52*, 73, 114–15, *114*, 118
  structure and function 48–54
  see also heart

vasoconstriction 51, 53, 115
vasodilation 51, 53, 54, 115
vasometer centre 51, 102, 114
vasometer tone 51
veins 39, 40, *40*, 50, 51, 53
velocity 33
  blood flow 51, 53–4, *54*
venea cavae 39, 40, *40*, 42
venous return 45–6, 50, 51, 113
ventilation rates 59, *59*, 65, 73, 87, 102, 113, *113*
  see also respiratory system
ventricles 38, 40, *40*, 41, *41*, 42, 43, 44, 52, 53
venules 39, 50, 53
verbal teaching guidance 154, 155
vertebrae 14, 15
vicarious experiences 182
violence in sport 263
visceral muscle 21, 49, 57
visceral pleura 58, 60
viscosity of blood 54
visual teaching guidance 154
visualisation 202
vital lung capacity 61, *61*, 62
vitamins in diet 82
VO2(max)(aerobic capacity) 79, 80, 81, 91–2, *91*, *92*, 117
  improving 103–5, 116, 118
voice box 57, *57*
voluntary sector 241, 257

wakes 219
war games 210, 211
warm-ups 101–2, 109
water 48, 64, 82, 83
  and energy production 26, 73, 74, 75
watts 70
wave summation 28
weight, body 82
weight training 107–8, *108*
Weiner's classification 179, *180*
white blood cells 49
whole teaching method 150
win ethic 222, 248, *250*, 263
windpipe 57, *57*
Wingate test 94
Wolfenden Report 265
women and sport 257, 258
work 70
working classes 212, 213, 216, 220, 225, 246, 259
working memory 139
wrestling 211

YMCA 220, 221–2

Z lines (muscles) 22, *22*, 24
Zajonc's theory 193, 194, *194*